1986

SHORT HISTORY OF

Anglo-Irish Literature

From its origins to the present day

Ogham Stone, Dunloe, Co. Kerry. Commissioners of Public Works.

SHORT HISTORY OF

Anglo-Irish Literature

From its origins to the present day

ROGER   MAURICE
McHUGH   HARMON

BARNES & NOBLE BOOKS
TOTOWA, NEW JERSEY

© 1982 Roger McHugh & Maurice Harmon
First published in the USA 1982 by
BARNES & NOBLE BOOKS
81 Adams Drive
Totowa, New Jersey, 07512

ISBN 0-389-20316-5

Acknowledgments
The publisher gratefully acknowledges the
assistance of the copyright owners of illustration
material reproduced in this book. The source is
identified in each caption. The index and
illustration selection is copyright Wolfhound Press.

CONTENTS

PART VI: CONTEMPORARY WRITING

Appendix

Notes

Bibliography

Index

LIST OF ILLUSTRATIONS

Preface

The indigenous literature of Ireland in English is generally known as Anglo-Irish Literature. It is the result of the intermixture of two cultures, Irish and English. Part one of this history deals with the old Irish system and its literature, still a strong element in the imaginative resources of the Irish writer. Part two traces the process by which that culture was broken and by which English replaced Irish as the spoken language of Ireland. It also shows how the foundation of modern Irish political thought found expression in English.

The third part discusses the fiction and poetry in English of Ireland in the nineteenth century up to the Irish literary revival in its concluding years, and the means by which the value of a tap-root into Ireland's past was recognised and given literary expression. The literature of this period was subject to the strains and stresses of Irish politics, particularly those concerned with the land system.

The Irish literary revival, which lasted in a concrete form from about 1890 until 1916 and in influence beyond that, is seen as a creative assertion of Irish identity which drew sustenance from Ireland's past and endeavoured to establish artistic standards for the treatment of contemporary realities with truth and insight. As part of the revival, the Irish dramatic movement gave Ireland a national theatre which became world-famous. The writers of this period are discussed in Part Four of this book.

Part five carries this history from the time of the Irish war of independence up to about 1950. This was a period when, despite official restrictions upon both sides of the new political border, the best Irish writers maintained a high standard in fiction and poetry. Where the spirit of the revival had been mainly romantic, the spirit of this period was chiefly realistic, self-critical and socially conscious.

Part Six brings us into contemporary times, when Irish writing is more international, experimental and introspective in temper. There is a parallel between Anglo-Irish literature and American literature. Both are modern literatures in English which, after passing through a colonial phase, acquired a distinctive national quality and at their best achieved those qualities which command international recognition. Where the literature of America displayed many traces of the multiple races that mingled in her peoples, the culture of her aboriginal inhabitants was almost completely destroyed, thought it is interesting to speculate what different paths Americal literature might have taken had a coherent and valuable body of Indian literature developed and survived. The older Irish culture survived to become an important part of the imaginative resources of the modern Irish writer; whether he writes in Irish or in English, it is there to use if he chooses to do so. At the same time he is the inheritor of an international language in which his countrymen have established a worthy tradition. To him as to the American writer it opens a window upon many influences. It may be, as T.S. Eliot suggested, that the future of writing in English lies mainly with their two literatures; but this precarious age contains so many imponderable factors that prophecies about the future of literature must be as tenuous as prophecies about the future of humanity itself. Yet writers are by their nature builders of bridges between the peoples of the world and so their work is an earnest of the flame of hope without which all manifestations of the human spirit, including art, would be meaningless.

The Irish writer of today, whether drawing material from the present or the past and whether writing in English or in modern Irish, is usually aware of a bifurcated literary heritage and of the standards and techniques which it has made available. This book attempts to give the general reader an account of that heritage and of the forces which shaped it.

Roger McHugh and Maurice Harmon

Entrance Stone, Newgrange Tumulus. Commissioners of Public Works.

PART I
The Older Civilisation and its Literature

CHAPTER I
The Poet and the Gaelic System

Ireland's older civilisation was established by a branch of the Celtic peoples of Europe, the Goidels or Gaels, who reached Ireland several centuries B.C. The inhabitants whom they conquered included some of pre-Celtic origin, whose existence is reflected in Gaelic literature and in Bronze Age and Iron Age remains; unlike the Celts they were not of Indo-European origin and we know nothing of their language. It is possible that these early inhabitants had been conquered and absorbed by previous Celtic invaders from Britain and from Gaul some three or four centuries before the Gaels arrived. This would have accelerated the establishment of a stable civilisation by this last wave of Celtic invaders. Stability was helped by the absence of any further invasions of Ireland for a thousand years. The Roman conquest of Britain did not extend there. Before Christianity reached Ireland, Gaelic civilisation had more than a millenium to consolidate itself.

Gaelic civilisation was essentially rural, towns being unknown until Scandinavian invaders established them in the tenth century; it was pastoral, the possession of cattle being the measure of wealth. In structure it was tribal; the basic unit of each tribe was the kin-group of people related to each other in the male line as far as second, sometimes as far as fourth, cousins. The kin-groups held land in common and the term *tuath* was used to designate both the extent of land so held, which was roughly equivalent to that of a barony, and the tribe which held it.

The social order of the Gaels in its early form probably resembled that of the Celts of Gaul as recorded by classical writers; a hierarchical society of priest-kings, warrior-nobles and commoners (*druides, equites* and *plebs*). In its developed form it remained hierarchical but with certain modifications. The tribal king's investiture was associated with various magical and mystical rites. Prominent among them was his symbolic union with the earth-goddess of the land. But the marriage was not necessarily permanent and he was neither a direct hereditary ruler nor an absolute one. Theoretically any of his male relatives, including cousins, could be elected to succeed him if the *oenach* or tribal assembly so decided. The *rí* or king had direct power only over his own tribe, but he could also be an overlord of neighbouring tribes or even a provincial king, ruling Ulster, Munster, Leinster, Connacht or Meath (a separate province until Christian times). The provincial kings received tribute and hostages from the larger under-kings, who were overlords of the tribal kings; these in turn took taxes and rent from their subjects in exchange for some form of protection in time of war. There was no legal high-king, no central monarchy. Yet Gaelic society as a whole was comparatively stable; dynastic wars were rare, fighting largely a matter of expeditions by over-kings to enforce tribute or of local cattle-raids by tribal warriors. The vast slaughter, head-taking and chariot-battles of the tales were carried over from memories of the continental Celts to entertain their Gaelic descendants.

The warrior-class of aristocratic lineage stood next to the king in the tribal system. Its members belonged by right of birth to the *aire* or privileged class, which seems to have included also the wealthier owners or renters of cattle. The warriors protected the person of the king and the frontiers of the tribe and were skilled in fighting in the fields or in the dense forests which covered much of the country, forming a natural protection for the pastures.

On the next step of the hierarchical Gaelic order stood the *aes dána* or men of art. These included judges, doctors, skilled craftsmen and poets. As a class they appear to have been closer in the social scale to the king and to the warriors than to those of lesser rank, the ordinary freemen, farmers and peasants, and finally the servants and slaves, who had no say in the deliberations of the tribal assembly.

The two groups within the *aes dána* who probably contributed most to the relative stability of Irish society were the law-givers and the poets. Each inherited a body of learning which, although not recorded in writing until the sixth or seventh century, had been formulated in pagan times and preserved orally by a professional caste. The original law-givers and poets were the druids; *breitheamh* (judge) and *file* (poet) thus had the sanction of antiquity and an aura of sacredness among the Gaelic tribes. The ancient laws defined the status of each tribal grade, with its duties, obligations and penalties. Disputes within each kin-group were settled privately; disputes between different kin-groups were decided by the judges, who could also arrange agreements with the jurists of other tribes. In general it seems that they helped stability within their own tribes but were less effective in inter-tribal matters, since the isolation of the tribes from each other led to wide variations in legal interpretations.

The power of the poets had not quite the same limitations. The title *file* means 'seer'. Four centuries after Christianity had reached Ireland, we find the poets credited with the power of divination and even in the nineteenth century with the ability to wound or kill enemies by satire. In Gaelic society they were regarded with great reverence for they were also the custodians and reciters of traditional tales, the recorders (often the inventors) of genealogies, the composers of music and the public praisers of kings and nobles under whose special patronage they flourished. The distinction between these various functions is somewhat blurred, the poet being sometimes referred to as a *seanchaidh* or historian, sometimes as a *scéalaighe* or story-teller, sometimes as a *bard* or maker of eulogies before the nobility; doubtless his functions varied from time to time and perhaps from tribe to tribe, although in general it seems clear that the bardic eulogisers were regarded as inferior to the *filí*.

The honour and reverence given to the *filí* transcended tribal or provincial boundaries. They could pass freely from one tribe to another and were given protection by the frontier guards whose duty was to fight all strangers. This practice, which is reflected in some of Ireland's earliest sagas, shows a strong cultural cohesion among the aristocracies of the different tribes, and a common respect for the traditional learning, creative and historical, which strict training enabled the *filí* to memorise, to use for enlightenment and entertainment, and to transmit orally to their successors. They were thus custodians of past, present and future knowledge not yet recorded in writing.

In the fifth century Christianity was brought to Ireland by missionaries from Gaul and from Britain. Its spread was favoured by the hierarchical structure of Irish society; once the kings had been converted this was rapid. By A.D. 600 Ireland was mainly Christian. Her people's thought and behaviour were widely affected but not the structure of her society, for the unit of Christianity in Ireland, the monastic community, fitted into the *tuath,* and the churchmen gradually fitted, not always harmoniously, into the learned caste patronised by the aristocracy. Like the *filí* they were privileged to travel beyond their own frontiers, thus assisting in the cultural cohesion of the tribes.

The effect of Christianity on early Irish literature was wide. Up to this, the Irish tradition of learning, although it had developed through many centuries, was oral; for, although some form of *ogham* writing was known to the Gaels, its use was not developed sufficiently for literary purposes. Now, however, Ireland began for the first time to have a written literature. At first the learning of the monasteries was Latin and manuscripts were made for ecclesiastical purposes; but by A.D. 600 the native Irish were the dominant element in the monasteries and use of the Latin alphabet was being applied to Irish. Gradually the old tales and poems, like the laws, were written down. In many cases they appear to have been recorded exactly as received from the *filí;* in others there were inevitable adaptations by the monks for instructional or devotional purposes.

Christianity also meant the end of Irish cultural isolation from Europe. The early missionaries brought with them a Graeco-Roman culture which spread with the monastic centres and Ireland became a preserver of this culture, since Christianity came comparatively late to her, when it was ebbing in Europe. During the seventh and eighth centuries Ireland zealously sent her Christian missionaries and scholars abroad, establishing monastic centres in France, Switzerland, Germany and Italy; they were largely instrumental in restoring Christianity to Europe and, through this and other traffic with the Continent, Irish literature received further exotic influences. Thus, for example, the principal early Irish prose saga, the *Táin Bó Cuailgne,* in the form in which it has come down to us, seems to consist of a number of the older traditional stories added to and given an exotic framework, probably in an attempt to supply Ireland with its own *Aeneid:* modern Celtic scholars believe that the early eighth-century *Lebor Gabála,* or *Book of Invasions,* was a pseudo-history of Ireland partly modelled on biblical and classical sources. Similarly the *Táin Bó Fraoich,* a beautiful story of the same period, is most probably a continental miracle-story adapted to Irish legendary settings and characters, while many narrative descriptions of royal dwellings and furnishings seem to be based on classical and oriental sources. Not content with such adaptations, the monks began to write poetry for its own sake. Some of the most beautiful nature poetry of the early mediaeval period owed its existence to eremitical asceticism nourished into literary creativity by the solitude of beautiful natural settings.

Another effect of monasticism upon the Gaelic literary scene was that it extended learning outside the ranks of the official literary caste, the *filí.* Recruitment for the monasteries was open to commoner and noble alike.

> If the peasant's son could learn to read and write, to master Latin, let him by all means learn; and thus one who as a layman would scarcely be fit to hold a *file's* horse would become as a cleric a man who might well look down on the *file* as an obsolete purveyor of antiquated superstition and useless knowledge.

Thus Professor Kelleher has summed up the situation, which he sees as contributing to that individualism which stamped Irish missionaries abroad and brought them not infrequently into conflict with the more conservative, more centralized and more disciplined Roman clerics over such matters as the clerical tonsure and the date of Easter.[1]

By the nature of things, the Irish clerics probably stood in an uneasy relationship to the caste of the *filí,* whose association with magic and the supernatural they must have resented. When writing down the traditional laws in the eighth century they were careful to exclude the *druides* from legal status, while retaining them in the sagas.

This antagonism, of course, was not one-sided, for the *filí* undoubtedly resented the intrusion of the monks into their privileged group; it is reflected in such mediaeval tales as *The Vision of Mac Conglinne* in which a wandering 'son of learning' satirises the monks of Cork for their lenten treatment of poets; or in a twelfth-century tale in which a poet-king expresses his dislike of clerics:

> There was a time when I deemed more melodious
> the yelping of the wolves
> than the voice of a cleric within
> a-baaing and a-bleating ...[2]

A happier relationship is seen in Saint Colmcille's defence of the poets at the Convention of Druim Cett in A.D. 575 and in the poem of lament which the *file* Dallán Forgaill wrote upon his death.[3] Indeed, just as the monks learned from the *filí,* the *filí* learned from the monks; the late Latin rhythms and church sequences, adapted by them, influenced the *dán díreach* or strict classical Irish metre, which lasted for more than nine centuries as a poetic form.

Between them, the *filí* and the monks gave to Ireland a literary tradition older than that of any European country except Greece and Rome, and a literature which is the oldest vernacular literature of Western Europe. The development of this literature went on steadily during the middle ages, despite the Scandinavian invasions of the ninth and tenth centuries. The Vikings began with raiding expeditions which wiped out many of the monastic settlements and destroyed many Irish manuscripts written before the mid-ninth century; some of them carried off women and slaves to their Icelandic outpost, thus laying the foundations of a strong Irish element in Icelandic literature and history: it can be seen at its strongest in such epics as Iceland's *Laxdaela Saga.* But even when they settled in Ireland, the influence of the Vikings on Irish society or culture outside Dublin was not comparable to that which they exercised in England; despite some alliance and intermarriage with the Irish, there was no general political or social fusion. On the whole the Norsemen kept to their seaport towns, the first towns that Ireland knew — Cork, Dublin, Limerick, Wexford, Wicklow — and their long-term effect on Irish society and culture was that their towns provided centres from which English influences radiated later. Outside them the old native order persisted and with it the literature preserved by the aristocratic and learned castes. Even the destruction of the monasteries' manuscripts by the Vikings or by warring Irish kings was to some extent remedied during the reign of Brian Boroimhe A.D. 1003-14. He was probably the first actual high-king of Ireland and successfully emulated Charlemagne in restoring learning to his realm; he built or restored monastic schools and churches, sent overseas for manuscripts and encouraged the scribes. Thus he initiated a period of cultural recovery which continued into the twelfth century. The most important great folio vellum manuscripts extant in which the ancient poems and stories are recorded belong to that century. These are the *Book of the Dun Cow* written before 1106 and now in the Royal Irish Academy, the Rawlinson manuscript (compiled in the first quarter of the twelfth century and now at the Bodleian) and the *Book of Leinster,* begun before 1160, completed about thirty years later and now in Trinity College, Dublin. Professor Myles Dillon has described such great books as 'miscellaneous collections of sagas and poems and sacred texts, and history and genealogy too — miniature libraries'.[4] They were the work of monks up to the mid-twelfth century. About that time the reorganisation of the Irish Church along diocesan lines, to free the churches from local and sometimes hereditary control, meant that thenceforth literary matters shifted gradually to the secular literary caste. From the mid-twelfth century on, the *filí* existed as a well-defined hereditary body whose members were trained by a strict discipline of up to fifteen years' duration. They were custodians of place-lore, history, poetry and narrative, skilled in relating them to the kings and aristocracy at assemblies or in the chief households of Ireland. At this point it is necessary to look at the content of their stories.

Overleaf: Interior Chamber, Newgrange Tumulus. Commissioners of Public Works.

CHAPTER II
Mythological Tales

The mythological and pseudo-historical tales of Ireland are largely concerned with explaining the names of places and of people and with the history of Ireland as it was imagined by the *filí* of mediaeval times. Many of them are to be found in the *Dinnshenchas* (History of Places), the *Coir Anmann* (Fitness of Names) and in the *Lebor Gabála* (Book of Invasions), a pseudo-historical account of Ireland from Adam into Christian times. At a later stage, from the twelfth century on, further genealogies were needed to fit new or rising dynasties with respectable pedigrees and so many new legends were invented and earlier ones revised to support them. It is almost impossible to say what original core of belief lay behind the legends or to separate clearly their mythological, pseudo-historical, historical and purely imaginative elements.

For literary purposes of later times, their main attraction lay in their supernatural quality and in the highly imaginative picture which they gave of Ireland's legendary past. Some of them were concerned with pre-Gaelic invaders of Ireland; with Parthalonians, Nemedians, Firbolgs, and especially with the Tuatha Dé Danann (people of the goddess Dana). The last of these were represented as a race skilled in magic, who came to Ireland bringing four great treasures: a Stone of Destiny called the 'Lia Fáil', which was supposed to roar approval when a rightful ruler was crowned upon it; an invincible sword belonging to their god, Lúgh of the Long Arm (obviously a sun-god); a magic spear, and a huge inexhaustible food-cauldron, the property of their supreme god, the Dagda (good god). The legends relate how under their leader, Nuada of the Silver Hand, the Tuatha Dé Danann defeat the previous inhabitants of Ireland, the Fir Bolg, who thenceforward become a servile and inferior race, and later repel the Fomorians, giant pirates from the north, whose mighty king is Balor of the Evil Eye. His huge-lidded eye deals death, but he is killed by the stone-cast of Lúgh of the Long

Arm, who now appears as a human hero, grandson of Balor, prophetically fated to slay him. Although the Tuatha Dé Danann and their predecessors sometimes engage in human activity, they are generally represented as a fairy people, who inhabit burial grounds, seas, rivers, lakes and ancient archaeological sites, from which they sometimes emerge to participate in mortal affairs. The collective name for them is the *Aes side* or fairy people, the word *sid* meaning a mound, their usual location.

Three of the mythological tales in the *Book of Leinster* illustrate their general quality. One is a very short tale which describes how Aengus tricks his father, the Dagda, out of his home near the Boyne river. The Dagda lends it to Aengus 'for a day and a night', but finds that this means forever. In another story Aengus falls sick of love for a fairy maiden whom he sees in a dream. She alternates between a swan-form and a human form, and Aengus, having changed his shape to that of a swan, wins her for his mate. A longer story, 'The Wooing of Etáin', brings in the Dagda and Aengus in its introductory part but is chiefly about the wife whom they secure for Aengus's foster-father, Midir. Her name is Etáin and she is changed into a purple fly by her rival (Fuamnach); after seven years of persecution Etáin falls into the cup of an Ulster woman who swallows her and gives her mortal birth. As a mortal she marries the king of Ireland; but her fairy husband, Midir, seeks her and, by a chess-game, tricks her mortal husband into allowing him to embrace her, whereupon they fly away together in the form of two swans. The king seeks her by digging up the fairy-mounds of Ireland but is tricked again by Midir and carries off instead his own daughter by Etáin. He does not discover this until this daughter in turn has borne him a daughter, whom he casts out and leaves in a kennel. There she is found by a herdsman, who rears her into a beautiful girl. Such variations show the elaborate invention which occurred as the mythological tales were retold through centuries.

With these mythological tales, which are full of supernatural appearances, wonders and magic, may be linked most of the tales which the *filí* classed as Adventure, Voyage and Vision tales *(Echtrae, Immram, Aislinge)*, for in these the same elements are predominant. All three types have in common the idea of a human's visit to a supernatural world, such as that described in 'Cormac's Adventures in the Land of Promise', 'where there is nought save truth, and there is neither age, nor decay, nor gloom, nor sadness, nor envy, nor jealousy, nor hatred, nor haughtiness'.[1] This land is also called the Land of Truth, the Land of the Living, the Land of Youth. Its location is usually somewhere west of Ireland but it is sometimes beneath a fairy mound or on some 'delightful plain' surrounded by a druid mist. Its envoys may be fairy maidens or fairy warriors who entice mortals to their magic land as lovers or as allies against their enemies.

In 'Cormac's Adventures', the king of Tara, Cormac, journeys to that world to seek his wife, son and daughter, who have been carried off by Manannán, the sea-god of the Tuatha Dé Danann. There he sees various marvels: the salmons of wisdom who feed on the hazel-nuts of knowledge; magical food, drink and fuel, which renew themselves each day; a silver house which men are trying to thatch with feathers, only to be worsted repeatedly by the wind, which blows the feathers away. Manannán explains the symbols to Cormac; the thatchers, for example, are the Irish poets who vainly amass riches. A reflection of the antiquity of this story is seen in its chief marvels, a pig which is roasted by a truth told for each quarter, and a beautiful golden cup which is shattered or restored according to whether lies or truths are uttered over it; the idea of the miraculous power of an act of truth is frequently met in Indian as in Irish mythology and is one of several indications of a common antique Indo-European tradition.

Adventure stories sometimes blend into voyage stories, the visit to the other-world involving a tour of various magical islands. A multiplicity of islands figures in the oldest and best of the voyage stories which have been preserved. This is the 'Voyage of Mael Dúin', a very old tale, possibly of the eighth century, and one of the sources of the great tenth-century mediaeval Latin tale, *Navigatio Brendani*. Mael Dúin, its hero, is raised by an Irish queen but discovers that he is the son of a nun and that his father had been murdered. Seeking revenge, he puts to sea with twenty companions. Storms blow them to far-off islands, thirty-one in number, each with its own marvels. One is inhabited by ants as big as foals, another by horse-racing demons, a third by red-hot swine. There is a laughing island and a wailing island, whose inhabitants are black; in each case a scout who lands becomes a laugher or a black wailer and has to be abandoned. The juxtaposition of Christian and pagan tradition in such stories is exemplified by the presence on one island, with a monk and church, of a huge bird tended by eagles, which renews its youth by bathing in a lake into which magical fruit has dropped. Finally Mael Dúin is persuaded by a holy hermit on another island to forego his revenge, in gratitude for the many perils from which God has saved him.

Just as adventure stories merge into voyage stories, so the latter blend into vision *(Aisling)* stories. Later voyage tales contain not only incidents involving Christian monks or hermits but also prophecies and visions of heaven and hell analogous to those of continental early Christian tradition. Mediaeval Irish vision-tales written in Latin, it has been suggested, may have influenced Dante's great work; there are several written in Irish from about the tenth century. One is the Vision of Adamnan, abbot of Iona, whose soul is brought after death by its guardian angel to heaven, where he sees the fiery presence of God surrounded by concentric circles of the blessed; later he visits the Land of Torment and witnesses the various punishments inflicted on the damned. Finally his soul is commanded to return to his body so that he may relate his story.

This account of a return from the other-world, especially in its description of the citadel of heaven, seems to owe much to adventure and voyage tales but is essentially didactic; a holy man is substituted for a pagan hero, wonders are used to point a moral. Christian didacticism, like that of the genealogists and pseudo-historians, fitted in with and sometimes added to the strong supernatural and highly imaginative tradition of Gaelic wonder-tales.

Monastic writing tended to diminish the status of the pagan hero, just as the pseudo-historians tended to reduce the status of the ancient gods of the Tuatha Dé Danann, but this was to some extent counteracted after the coming of the Normans by the increasing emphasis on the entertainment-value of stories and by the influence of mediaeval romance, which between them strengthened wonder and fantasy again in Irish story-telling. This, in turn, had its drawbacks, for rational and dramatic elements were correspondingly neglected; so was a normal ethical motivation. The sense of form also suffered. Many of the tales which have been mentioned are tedious, repetitive, too full of formula-descriptions, unduly ornamentative accretions and additions. Confusion is inevitable when pagan deities, mythical heroes, demi-gods, Christian saints, fairies, historical personages, euhemerised gods and sanctified mortals jostle each other in the *dramatis personae* of literary narration. At the same time the very mixture, with its mystical and magical aura, its flashes of vivid narration, its exciting and arresting symbols and images, was certain to appeal to imaginative writers of a later age, who could impose their own form and interpretation on the material and who could select the most colourful symbols and situations from the inexhaustible cauldron of Gaelic story-telling.

CHAPTER III

The Ulster Cycle

The older of the two best cycles of early Irish narratives is the Ulster or Red Branch cycle, which centres around the king of Ulster, Conor Mac Nessa, his stronghold at Emain Macha near Armagh, and his chief warrior, Cuchulainn. Associated with these are a number of clearly defined personages, including Cathbad the druid, Fergus Mac Roi, who was tricked by Conor's mother out of the Ulster throne, Conall the Victorious, Laoire the Triumphant, and the Thersites of the cycle, Bricriu of the Poison Tongue. All these belong to the Red Branch warriors who defend Ulster, which is represented as standing in rivalry to the rest of Ireland, but especially to Connacht, ruled from Cruachan by the amazonian and amorous Queen Medb (Maeve). Although these characters sometimes take on mythological or magical aspects, or are involved with fairy kings or are influenced by *geasa* or taboos, they are normally represented as humans and their motives and conflicts can be understood, for the most part, in human terms of rivalry, honour, courage, love, hatred and revenge.

Rivalry of one kind or another is the motivating force of most of the principal stories. The central story, the *Táin Bó Cuailgne* or Cattle-raid of Cooley, is in this respect typical. It opens with the pillow-talk of Medb and her husband Ailill, whose argument about their respective possessions leads to a reckoning. The reckoning shows that Ailill's possession of the great White-Horned Bull of Connacht puts him ahead of Medb, and leads to her attempt to seize by force an Ulster bull, the Brown Bull of Cooley. Rivalry in arms now becomes the theme, for the invading Connacht army is opposed on the frontier by Cuchulainn, who takes on its chief warriors in single combat, slaying even his dear friend Ferdia, and so holds up the invasion single-handed through a whole winter until the Ulster warriors recover from an incapacitating curse and put the Connachtmen to flight. Their rivalry is shared by the two bulls; the Ulster bull is captured but slays his rival and bellowing frantically homeward bursts his heart and dies.

Rivalry between the warriors of Ulster is also the theme of the long, rambling tale, 'The Intoxication of the Ulstermen', in which rival drinking-bouts lead to a drunken career to the south, where they barely escape being roasted in an iron house by their enemies. It is used to better artistic purpose in 'Bricriu's Feast'; Bricriu Poison-tongue invites all the Ulster warriors to a feast with the main purpose of setting them at each other's throats. His guests suspect this and part of the fun of the story is due to the elaborate way in which Bricriu prompts the women of the heroes to a competitive scramble for precedence and so puts their menfolk in conflict over the Champion's Portion, the choice part of the meat reserved for the warrior who can establish supremacy over the rest. This is finally decided, after various tests, by the dramatic appearance of a giant warrior with his strange invitation: 'come whosoever of you that may dare, that I may cut off his head tonight, he mine tomorrow night.' The heroes persuade him to reverse the order of this reciprocal decapitation but of the warriors who strike off his head on successive nights only Cuchulainn is brave enough to keep his bond for the honour of Ulster; so he is spared and is awarded the Champion's Portion by the giant, who proves to be a fairy king of Munster in disguise. This latter incident is the established source of part of *Sir Gawain and the Green Knight. The Green Helmet* is Yeats's dramatisation of the Bricriu story.

Competition for the Champion's Portion is an ancient theme, probably based on the practice which Poseidonius attributed to the pre-Christian Celts. It also figures in the Story of Mac Datho's Pig, one of the best examples of the Irish story-teller's art in shorter form. Here Medb and Conor bid against each other for the swift hound of Mac Datho, a Leinster landowner, who knows that refusal to either will mean dire vengeance upon himself. On his wife's suggestion he separately promises to hand the hound over to each of them at a great feast. The chief dish at the feast is Mac Datho's pig: 'Threescore milch cows had been feeding it for seven years', says the tale. 'But on venom that pig had been reared, since on its account a slaughter of the men of Ireland was made.' This slaughter arises through the boasting-competition of the warriors for the Champion's Portion and the fighting that breaks out when the winner, Conall of Ulster, gives only a miserly share to the Connacht men. The plan of Mac Datho's wife indeed works out perfectly, except that the cause of contention, Mac

Datho's hound, 'set to tearing the men of Connacht greatly' and is slain; like the bulls of the *Táin,* the cause of war becomes its victim.

It is worthwhile to look at the method of this story, which is told with great verve; tension is built up by such devices as the dialogue between Mac Datho and his wife and between rival heroes; then the narrative, avoiding digression or repetition, reaches a dramatic climax as Conall, the Ulster challenger, confronts Cet of Connacht in the final round. At first the two warriors greet each other in formal eulogistic verse. Then in realistic prose Cet admits that Conall is the better man. He adds that if his brother Anluan were present, he would give Conall a real contest. Conall's reply is to take Anluan's head from his belt and throw it at Cet, covering his face with blood. This samurai-like blending of courtliness and savagery is a remarkable feature of some of the sagas.

Many of the Ulster tales seem to owe their origin to the popularity of the *Táin* and to have been designed either for insetting into recitals of it or for amplifying its incidents or characters in separate form. Others probably existed in ancient native tradition before the *Táin* was written, and were incorporated into it. Of the latter type is a long digression in which Ailill and Medb of Connacht are told of the boyhood deeds of Cuchulainn; it includes the story of how he got his name, the Hound of Culann, by slaying the giant hound of Culann and replacing him as Culann's sentinel. This is worked artistically into the longer tale through the natural desire of the Connacht rulers to learn all about their chief opponent from Ulster warriors in their service.

Separate amplificatory tales tell of the birth, wooing and death of the *Táin's* principal characters. Of these the birth-tales are the slightest: brief stories, for example, tell how Cathbad, the druid, surprised a warrior queen, Nessa, while she was bathing and fathered Conor Mac Nessa; or how Conor's sister, Dechtire, was visited by Lúgh of the Long Arm and gave birth to Setanta, the boy later called Cuchulainn. The popularity of Cuchulainn battle-tales and of wooing tales probably led to the lengthy narrative, 'The Wooing of Emer', in which Cuchulainn seeks to win Emer:

> While they were thus conversing, Cuchulainn saw the breasts of the maiden over the bosom of her smock. And he

said: 'Fair is this plain, the plain of the noble yoke.'

Then the maiden spoke these words: 'No one comes to this plain who does not slay as many as a hundred on every ford...'

It is to be trained for such prowess that Cuchulainn, having exchanged a vow of chastity with Emer, goes to Scotland, to learn feats of arms from the warrior-queen Scáthach; while there, he becomes the lover of Scáthach's daughter and of her rival in arms, Aoife. Returning to Ireland he carries Emer off by force. The jealousy of Emer is narrated in another long story, 'The Sick-bed of Cuchulainn', in which Cuchulainn is enticed by a fairy maiden, Fand, to the fairy world, where he serves her in love and combat. Unlike Yeats's ending of *The Only Jealousy of Emer,* in this tale it is the mistress and not the wife who finally gives him up.

The death-tales of the Ulster heroes form a coherent group of varying styles and interests. That of Cuchulainn is a blend of heroic and romantic incidents; he dies nobly, tied to a pillar-stone so that he may face his foes to the last, but his death is brought about only after the use of magic against him; the trickery of three hags induces him to break his taboo, that of three satirists to surrender his spears; before the battle his horse weeps tears of blood and Cuchulainn sees the ominous Washer of the Ford; after his death the war-goddesses perch on his shoulder in the form of scald-crows.

Conor Mac Nessa's fate has less of magic about it and is dramatic and well-formed. Cet Mac Matach, the Connacht champion, steals from Conor's jesters a gruesome battle-trophy. This is a brain-ball, a missile made by mixing with lime the brain of a Leinster king, Mesgedra, whom Conor's warriors had unjustly slain. Before dying, Mesgedra had prophesied that he would be revenged after death. Cet prompts the women of Connacht to entice Conor to parade among them so that they may admire him; then with a mighty sling-cast he embeds the trophy in Conor's head. It cannot be removed without causing his death and his doctor cautions him to avoid all strain. This he does for several years, but when a druid's description of the death of Christ causes Conor's battle-fury to come upon him, the missile starts from his head and he dies. His soul is taken to heaven; so a pagan figure is used again to point a Christian moral.

Where in the longer stories the joining of different versions of the same incident or the use of the narrative as a thread on which marvels are strung or as a tapestry into which magic, place-lore and morals are woven, often results in formlessness and confusion, shorter amplificatory tales have often an independent artistic beauty of their own. Thus Cuchulainn's love-making with Aoife in Scotland, a slight incident in 'The Sick-bed of Cuchulainn', leads to the notable story, 'The Tragic Death of Connla', in which Cuchulainn kills his son by Aoife. This story, the more lasting of the death-tales, is remarkable for its directness and its dramatic dialogue, which builds up to Cuchulainn's decision to oppose the boy who has defeated two of his comrades. He does this despite Emer's warning:

> 'Do not go down', she said. 'It is a son of yours that is down there. Do not murder your only son! It is not fair fight nor wise to rise up against your son. Turn to me! Hear my voice! My advice is good. Let Cuchulainn hear it! I know what name he will tell, if the boy down there is Connla, the only son of Aoife.' Then said Cuchulainn : 'Leave off, woman! Even though it were he who is there . . . I would kill him for the honour of Ulster.'

After a severe combat he wounds the boy mortally: 'He took the boy in his arms and carried him until he laid him down before the Ulstermen. 'Here is my son for you, men of Ulster', he said. The boy greets the warriors and dies on Baile's strand.

Equally brief is 'The Weakness of the Ulstermen', which explains how it was that Cuchulainn had to defend the province of Ulster single-handed against the invading Connacht army. This is a good example of the best *dinnshenchas* or place-lore story, for it also tells how Conor's stronghold of Emain Macha got its name. Macha was the beautiful wife of an Ulster cattle-owner named Crunnchú, who boasted unwisely at a chariot-racing contest in which the victorious horses of the king were applauded by the assembly:

> 'My wife runs quicker than these two horses',
>   said Crunnchu.
> 'Seize that man', said the king, 'and hold him until his wife can be brought to the race-contest.'

Macha pleaded that she was pregnant but the king forced her to run against his horses by threatening her husband's execution. She won the contest, gave birth to twins, and laid a curse upon the Ulstermen: 'When a time of oppression falls upon you, each man of you who lives in this province will be overcome with

weakness, as the weakness of a woman in child-birth.'
Cuchulainn, being from Leinster, was exempt from this curse,
and so in the *Táin* story was at first the sole defender of Ulster and
its stronghold, Emain Macha ('The Twins of Macha').

The comparative brevity and austerity of such short tales has
been explained by some Celtic scholars as being due to the fact
that they were really summaries which were expanded by the
story-tellers in their recitals; but their frequent artistry suggests
that the *file* may have had in his repertory tales suitable for long or
short sessions of story-telling.

'The Exile of the Sons of Usnech', the story of Deirdre, the
Irish Helen, is the most famous story of the Ulster cycle, not only
in modern times through its treatment by Yeats, Synge and others
in English, but in Gaelic-speaking Ireland, which produced many
versions. With the Connla story it is among the few Ulster tales
still preserved in the folklore of Ireland and of Scotland. Its
fundamental fascination lies in the rivalry of an old and a young
man for a beautiful woman, in the cycle of revenge which
Deirdre's desertion of Conor for Naoise begins, and in the
manner in which the foretold doom of the lovers is accomplished.
Its relevance to the central *Táin* saga is that Conor's revenge
involves his trickery of Fergus and other Ulster warriors who are
sureties for the safe-conduct of Deirdre and Naoise. When Naoise
is slain in their absence, their honour is affronted and they burn
Emain Macha and lead thousands of their men to take service
under Medb of Connacht; thus these Ulstermen are in the
Connacht army which later invades Ulster.

The best of the Irish versions is probably that published by
A.H. Leahy in *Heroic Romances of Ireland* (1905), reproduced in
Cross and Slover's *Ancient Irish Tales* (1936). It is a comparatively
austere version, particularly effective in the description of
Deirdre's forthright wooing of Naoise and in its ending, in which
the malice of Conor is stressed; for, having kept Deirdre for a year
after Naoise's death, he contemptuously gives her to Naoise's
murderer, Eoghan Mac Durthach. As Deirdre stands in the
chariot with the two men she hates most, Conor taunts her that
she is like a ewe between two rams:

> Now there was a great rock of stone in front of them, and
> Deirdre struck her head upon that stone and she shattered her
> head and so she died. This then is the tale of the exile of the
> sons of Usnech and of the exile of Fergus and of the death of
> Deirdre.

Other versions contain many accretions and embellishments which are preserved in Lady Gregory's conflation of various translations in *Cuchulain of Muirthemne* (1902); this is the version which Yeats and Synge knew, although it is probable that both were familiar with other versions, either literary or in folklore.

Howth, Co. Dublin. Bord Fáilte Photograph.

CHAPTER IV
Tales of the Fianna

The oldest Ulster tales were traditionally believed to refer to the centuries before the birth of Christ, the Fenian cycle of tales to the period about A.D. 300, when Ireland was ruled by a historical or pseudo-historical king, Cormac Mac Art. How far back they first existed in oral form we do not know; some of them appear to date from the seventh century, while from the eleventh century there are literary references to their popularity in folklore. In the later twelfth century they began to displace the Ulster tales in the esteem of Irish audiences and story-tellers.

They resemble the Ulster tales in that they centre around a group of warriors, the Fianna, composed of two clans, the Clann Baiscne and the Clann Morna, who are sometimes united in service to various kings, sometimes divided by rivalry. The Clann Baiscne are led by Finn Mac Cumhaill, the Clann Morna by Goll Mac Morna. Finn is the chief figure of the Fianna and with him are associated a number of comrades: his adopted son, Oisín, the poet; his warrior grandson, Oscar; Caoilte, his steward and narrator of stories; Diarmaid, the irresistible lover, and Bald Conán, the buffoon, all of whom have their prototypes in the Ulster tales.

While the Fenians, like the Ulster warriors, are disciplined by long training in physical feats and in poetry and maxims, they are different in some respects. They are not a warrior-caste of fixed allegiance to a tribe; they are 'kinless men', adventurous mercenaries who move about outside the tribe and prefer a roving life of hunting and fighting to residence at court. The setting for their exploits is mainly in Leinster and Munster, though their duties and pleasures take them further afield. Finn is not tied, like Cuchulainn, to the service of a particular king, but moves freely through the country.

The most notable difference in quality is that the Ulster stories, while blending heroic and supernatural elements, retain a direct human realism; the Fenian tales are dominated by fantastic and magical episodes. They exist, unlike the Ulster tales, largely in a non-social world, an other-world. Their temper is much more romantic than epic. This change may be due in some part to the Normans; the *filí* under their patronage probably became courtly and elaborate entertainers, closer to their counterparts in mediaeval Europe, whose romantic traditions affected their narratives. Christianity also may have favoured this change, since it reduced the hard pagan element and the dignity of the old aristocratic order. But it is also possible that the Fenian tales were closer to popular oral tradition long before they were written down. They are certainly less identified with an aristocracy and with a special location. At any rate they rapidly ousted the Ulster cycle, many of whose tales would not have survived if they had not been written down, while the Fenian tales survived not only in manuscripts but in the oral tradition of Ireland and of Scotland into recent times. They have a close affinity with the mythological tales, with which their characters and episodes often interlace. That is why Lady Gregory joins versions from both cycles in her *Gods and Fighting Men* (1904), supplementing them from contemporary folklore. It seems true that folklore, particularly retentive of the Fenian tales, not only retained but sometimes surpassed written sources; and since the humbler people preferred tales of wonders to heroic tales, they gradually forced the story-tellers to cater for their taste.

The change in literary temper may be illustrated by the principal Fenian love-story, 'The Pursuit of Diarmaid and Gráinne'. Some version of this tale was known in the tenth century but the earliest extant version seems to have been composed some time between the fourteenth and the seventeenth century. It is obviously a variant of the Deirdre story, for its principal ingredients are the same: Gráinne, the daughter of King Cormac, is chosen as a bride for Finn, but elopes with Diarmaid, a younger lover, whose death is contrived, after an apparent reconciliation, by the vengeful Finn. Such is the plot, but the narrative is much longer than the Ulster story and is full of accretions and episodes, some of which seem to be based on earlier mythological and heroic material, others on much later traditional fairy-lore.

Certain features of this expansion are artistically successful. One is the introduction to Gráinne's wooing: Finn is restless without a wife and two of his warriors go to Cormac at Tara to ask

Gráinne's hand for him. Cormac leaves the decision to Gráinne, who accepts. At the betrothal-feast it is gradually unfolded that her acceptance has been a deception, for she drugs her father and Finn and most of the Fianna, then puts Diarmaid under *geasa* to elope with her, after revealing that she has been in love with him since she saw him hurling at Tara some time before. The troubled Diarmaid consults three warriors and is unanimously advised that he must accept the taboo. He takes leave of his companions:

> And not bigger is a smooth crimson whortleberry than was each tear that Diarmaid shed at parting from his people ... and what he said was: 'I believe, O Gráinne, that this is an evil course upon which you are set; for it would be better for you to have Finn for a lover than myself, seeing that I do not know what nook or cranny or remote part of Ireland I can take you to now. Return again home, without Finn's learning what you have done.'
>
> 'It is certain that I will not go back', said Gráinne, 'and that I will not part from you until death parts me from you.'
>
> 'Then go forward, O Gráinne', said Diarmaid.

The body of the tale, which is concerned with the pursuit, shows considerable skill in the manner in which it switches from pursuers to pursued and in the variety and charm of some of its episodes. But it strings too many adventures and marvels together in an elaborate way, and it is only towards the end of the story that the human interest revives.

Here Finn tricks Diarmaid, long after their reconciliation, into hunting the boar that is already predestined to kill him on the slopes of Benbulben; and the subsequent behaviour of Gráinne as compared with that of Deirdre, shows an interesting conception of the character of the *femme fatale*. Having elaborately incited her sons to avenge Diarmaid, Gráinne is wooed by the crafty Finn, who fears their vengeance. She attacks him 'with her keen, sharp-pointed tongue' but, like Richard III in a similar situation, Finn 'plies her with sweet words and with gentle loving speech' and wins her, thereby incurring the scorn of the Fianna who 'gave one shout of derision and mockery at her, so that Gráinne bowed her head from shame; "We hope, Finn, that you will mind Gráinne well from this on", said Oisín.'

'The Pursuit of Diarmaid and Gráinne' is Arthurian in more senses than one, for the story of Tristan and Iseult derived from it[2] and from its earlier Ulster counterpart, and the manner of its telling is that of Arthurian romance. It is notable that Finn is not the hero of it, nor indeed is he sympathetically presented, while Gráinne, more Euripidean than Sophoclean, lacks the nobility of Deirdre and is guileful, fickle and capricious; but such characterisation as the story has is overlaid by its other-world, fantastic material.

So also in the tales of which Finn is the central character, the stern, heroic and direct elements of his earlier prototype, Cuchulainn, are played down, the magical emphasised. Finn, too, is partly of magical origin. His ancestors include Nuada, Balor and Lúgh: he has two names, Denma and Finn; for a time he acquires a fairy wife, Saba, who vanishes from him as Fand did from Cuchulainn. He has, moreover, powers of divination, effective when he bites his thumb; for it was while cooking a druid's Salmon of Knowledge that he burned his thumb and so tasted wisdom. This is related in 'The Boyhood Deeds of Finn' which, for the most part, follows the earlier narrative concerning Cuchulainn. His opponents are usually hags, goblins and fairy warriors, and there is a lack of human motivation about his adventures which do not differ notably from those of his comrades.

One of these, Conán the Bald, is the main source of comedy; in one tale he loses the skin of his posterior when torn by his friends from an enchanted chair; they clap on the skin of a black sheep, which grows there ever after. This fantastic element is strong in all the comic Fenian tales, such as 'The Chase of the Tough Servant' or 'The Enchanted Cave of Cesh Corran'. The substitution of Conán, the buffoon, for Bricriu of the older cycle is in its way typical of the reduction of the grimmer and more realistic heroic spirit.

The longest Fenian narrative, the longest in Irish literature next to the *Táin,* is 'The Colloquy of the Old Men', a framework-story of the early thirteenth century in which the last leaders of the Fianna, Caoilte and Oisín, meet Saint Patrick and the king of Tara, whom they entertain with stories of pagan Ireland; some of these are *dinnshenchas* or place-lore stories, others concern the Fenian heroes and their adventures in the fairy world.

The saint is represented as at first expressing a more or less formal resistance to the magic of the stories: 'Were it not for us an impairing of the devout life, an occasion of neglecting prayer, and of deserting converse with God,' he remarks on one occasion, 'as we talk with you, we would feel the time pass quickly, warrior.' But after consulting his guardian angels, who tell him to write down the stories on poets' tablets for the entertainment of future companies, he blesses Caoilte and his lore. Relations between the giant pagans and the saint are cordial in the Colloquy; Patrick shares his food with Caoilte, requests from him a lake of clear water for baptismal purposes and Caoilte obliges, using Patrick's staff to create the lake. Then Caoilte is baptised with his companions and gives to the saint 'a ridgy mass of gold in which there were three times fifty ounces', which Patrick uses to equip himself with bells, psalters and missals for the conversion of Ireland. Caoilte conducts him on a tour of the legended hills, strands and lakes of Ireland, regaling him with stories and songs: Patrick in turn praises minstrelsy and promises salvation for the Fianna. At the king's court at Tara they meet Oisín and further stories are told.

The narrative is unfinished but the anonymous author who compiled the Colloquy certainly produced a fine variety of stories based on older sources. He was obviously a man of considerable artistry who preserved the dignity of the chief personages of the framework-story as a counterbalance to the fantasy and verse of the tales and who counterpointed the generally cheerful and good-humoured atmosphere of the telling with the occasional pathos of Caoilte's nostalgia for the Fenian days and his consciousness of the loneliness of old age. Although, as in the *Táin,* there is some artificial narration, there are many arresting passages of description and of dialogue; when Patrick asks Caoilte about Finn's character. Caoilte replies:

> 'If the brown leaf the tree sheds from it was gold, if the white waves were silver, Finn would have given it all away.' 'Who or what was it that sustained you so in your life?' asks Patrick: and Caoilte answers, 'Truth that was in our hearts and strength in our arms and fulfillment in our tongues.'

Some of the Fenian tales are mere anecdotes. Longer stories include the story of Oisín in the Land of Youth, which is clearly based on the mythological voyage tales and influenced by 'The Colloquy of the Ancients'. The version which Yeats chiefly used was written in Irish in the eighteenth and translated in the nineteenth century.

CHAPTER V

Other Tales

The mythological or pseudo-historical, heroic and Fenian tales comprise the bulk of Irish written mediaeval literature. Further categories include king tales and romantic tales; but these often overlap with the others, or stand apart for special reasons. 'The Vision of Mac Conglinne', written before A.D. 1200, is unusual in being a long satirical story about a wandering scholar and poet, who cured a Munster king of a hunger-demon; it is highly sophisticated, satirising kings and monks, the recital of visions, of learned disputations and genealogies and even its own conventional method of narration. Its ironic straight-faced recital of absurdities, its disquisitions upon the pedigrees and qualities of a variety of food and drink, its gusty fantasy, all anticipate Rabelais. Probably it was written by a scholar trained as a schoolman, impatient with conventions.

Again, *Buile Suibhne* ('The Frenzy of Sweeney') is very different from most king tales; Sweeney, an Irish king, is cursed by a saint whom he has insulted and is made the victim of levitation; his fate is to flit naked through the tree-tops, living on cresses and water, torn by briars and branches, pursued by apparitions, and unable to consort with humans; until at last he is befriended by a kindlier saint who records his tale and shrives him when in accordance with his doom he is slain by a spear-thrust. The prose narrative is skilful but the bulk of the tale is in verse and one of its attractions lies in the verse-passages in which the mad king laments his lot and celebrates the beauty of the trees and of the scenery of Ireland. Both of these tales have been treated in English by modern Irish writers.

During the twelfth century, tales of Greece, Troy and Rome were translated from Latin into Irish: Norman cultural influence was strong from the mid-fifteenth to the mid-sixteenth century, encouraging some Arthurian tales and many *romans d'aventure* were adapted from French and Italian stories of knightly tasks and wooings; these affected native Irish stories in which foreign monarchs of real or imagined eastern lands participate or in which Irish warriors accomplish wonders in far-off places. Such influences combined to make the sixteenth and seventeenth centuries the heyday of the romantic tale in Ireland; her story-tellers already had many mythological and Fenian tales of a highly imaginative kind and now set about recasting even the sterner Ulster cycle into romantic form. Hence this form, episodic and fantastic, often over-decorated, prevailed in manuscript as well as in folklore until the Gaelic order was broken in the seventeenth century.

It is difficult to say how far the artistic weakness of most Irish tales, a lack of disciplined form, is due to mediaeval romanticism. Even the _Táin_ is straggling in parts and is largely held together by its central conflict for the Ulster bull and by the principal figure, Cuchulainn. Some of its episodes, such as the Deirdre story, have an independent artistic form; but its later romantic version is comparatively artificial. Yet the long tale of how King Conaire broke his taboos and incurred his death in 'The Destruction of Da Derga's Hostel', written down before A.D. 1100, seems partly romantic in temper. So are the two stories which with the Deirdre story make up 'The Three Sorrows of Story-telling'. These are 'The Fate of the Children of Tuireann', in which three sons, guilty of the murder of Cian, accept an enigmatic fine which turns out to be a series of superhuman tasks; its last demand for 'three shouts on a hill' is met by their three death-cries. The third story, 'The Fate of the Children of Lir', is a long tale of four children changed into swans by their stepmother and fated to wander the waters of Ireland, musically lamenting their lot in human voices. Both of these stories, which seem to belong to the fourteenth century, have controlled passages of beauty and of pathos but are often episodic and prolix. While this is the handicap of most European mediaeval romances, these characteristics seem to belong partly to earlier Irish tradition and were not disciplined by the Renaissance as they were in continental Europe.

In his book _Early Irish Literature_ Professor Myles Dillon summed up its qualities:

If there is nothing in Irish literature of the epic stature of Homer or the grandeur of Virgil, there are qualities that some Irishmen at least will hold equally precious — an incandescent vision, a wildness of imagination, sensibility to sound and colour and form, sometimes perhaps perceived as signs of an ideal beauty; and human passion, love, sorrow or anger, often expressed with a sincerity and directness that can still persuade us.

Its extraordinary variety of interest is still a challenge and an inspiration to the creative writer, to whom it is an additional resource to be drawn upon at will.

Oisin Kelly's 'The Children of Lir', Garden of Remembrance, Dublin, Courtesy of The Irish Times.

CHAPTER VI

Irish Poetry

The bulk of extant Irish material is in verse, since verse was the mnemonic medium used for pseudo-history, genealogies and legal tracts; essentially aural, its musical style was often weighed down by embellishment and unnecessary tags. For enduring poetry we have to turn to various groups of poems whose quality is purer.

Among these are a number of early Irish anonymous nature poems, dating from the eighth century on. These celebrate the seasons and the places of Ireland. Here is one such lyric translated by Kuno Meyer:

Summer is gone
My tidings for you: the stag bells,
Winter snows, summer is gone.

Wind high and cold, low the sun,
Slow his course, sea running high.

Deep-red the bracken, its shape all gone —
The wild-goose has raised his wonted cry.

Cold has caught the wings of birds;
Season of ice — these are my tidings.[1]

This is fairly close to the syllabic couplets of the original and gives some idea of its deft impressionism and its objective tone. Homely detail often anchors such poems in reality, as this extract from Meyer's translation of a poem about summer shows:

Bees with puny strength carry
A goodly burden, the harvest of blossoms;
Up the mountain-side kine take with them mud,
The ant makes a rich meal ...

A flock of birds settles
In the midst of meadows,
The green field rustles
Wherein is a brawling white stream.

This direct, concrete quality, with its use of simple primary colours, is particularly striking.

With these nature-poems is linked another group of early poems, associated with saints and hermits; for these often praise nature or the sights and sounds of particular places. The scribe copying the gospels rejoices in the bird-song around him or in the flicker of sunlight upon the page; or praise of Ireland is put into the mouth of Saint Colmcille by a poet writing centuries later:

> Delightful to be on the Hill of Howth
> Before going over the white-haired sea:
> The dashing of the wave against its face,
> The bareness of its shores and of its border ...

> There is a grey eye
> That will look back upon Erin:
> I shall never see again
> The men or Erin nor her women ...

Other interesting early lyric poems are interspersed through some of the older prose sagas and are usually spoken by the principal characters; by Deirdre lamenting Naoise or Cuchulainn his friend, Ferdia; by Fand as she surrenders Cuchulainn to Emer or by Midir as he pleads with Etáin. Here are the concluding stanzas of Ferguson's version of Deirdre's lament:

> Woe to Eman, roof and wall!
> Woe to Red Branch, hearth and hall!
> Tenfold woe and black dishonour
> To the false and foul Clan Conor!

> Dig the grave both wide and deep;
> Sick I am and fain would sleep!
> Dig the grave and make it ready;
> Lay me on my true Love's body.[2]

The purpose of such interspersed lyrics seems to have been to heighten emotion, at least in the earlier sagas, which like the Indian sagas are in prose and use poetry sparingly. In some later sagas, such as 'The Frenzy of Sweeney', the reverse is true; and the bulk of the Fenian tales are written in verse. But it should be noted that the dramatic lyric is frequent, whether inside or outside the tales, in early and mediaeval Irish poetry; in this respect many modern Irish poets are traditional. Probably the use of this mode was originally due to intimacy with the dramatic lyrics of the heroic sagas; it seems to have had a particular attraction for the Irish temperament ever since.

Most of the poetry written between the ninth and the seventeenth century is known as Irish classical or bardic poetry. The former is perhaps the better term, since the latter begs the difficult question of the exact distinction between *file* and bard. For our purposes it is sufficient to know that almost all the surviving poetry of this long period was written by professional poets organised in a hereditary corporation of great power and privilege and, by the thirteenth century, rigidly traditional. The court poetry which they wrote included eulogistic and elegiac poetry.

The continuity in the tradition of this poetry can be seen in the fact that one of its greatest protagonists of the early thirteenth century was Muireadhach Albanach O Dálaigh or Murrough O'Daly the Scot, so called because in refuge from a chief whose tax-gatherer he had killed, he was forced to fly from Ireland to Scotland; five centuries later a descendant of his, Niall Mór MacVurich, who was hereditary bard to the MacDonalds of Scotland, wrote one of the best of these bardic poems in Scotland, where the tradition lasted longer than in Ireland. In Ireland itself the great disasters of the seventeenth century were the subject of bardic verse up to the middle of that century.

The technique of Irish poetry seems to have consisted at first of simple alliterative groupings of uneven length. Gradually rhyme, rhythm and stanza form were acquired; one determinant of these was possibly the catalectic trochaic tetrameter of Latin poetry which probably came into the Irish consciousness through church hymns. Meyer calls this measure the original type from which the great variety of Irish metres has sprung. A hymn which he quotes begins:

> Ymnum dicat turba fratrum,   ymnum cantus personet,
> Christo regi concinentes   laudem demus debitam

If the half-lines are arranged in the form of a quatrain, they give a clue as to the nature of the basic Irish stanza; but it may have been shaped independently of the Latin form.

The classical stanza of four lines was constant. Its rhythm and music could vary but not in any major way. In one form *(séadna)* the four lines are alternately eight-syllabled and seven-syllabled: the former end in an unstressed, the latter in a stressed syllable, and the rhyme is alternate. Another type *(rannaigheacht mhór)* also has alternate rhyme but all four lines are seven-syllabled and end on a stressed syllable. In the most usual metre of early Irish poetry *(deibhidhe)* the quatrain of seven-syllabled lines is made up of two couplets which rhyme unrhythmically. In the *dán díreach,* the prevailing classical metre in which court poetry was written, the determinant of rhythm was the syllabic count; that is, the number of syllables in the line and the regularity of the syllabic count of the word ending the line.

The complexity of the quatrain's music was even greater. Possibly as a reminiscence of the older alliterative poetry, the developed bardic or classical Irish poem was expected to have at least one alliteration in the line. Rhyme was more complicated than in English verse, where it depends upon the agreement both of vowel-sounds and of the following consonantal sounds. The Irish poets divided their consonants into classes (p, t, c: b, d, g, etc.) and also into palatal and non-palatal categories. Irish rhyme occurred only when agreeing vowel sounds were followed by consonants of the same group and category. Thus the English equivalent of Irish rhyme could be rhyme, near-rhyme, half-rhyme or assonance. Another Irish ornament was consonance, the chiming of different vowels of the same quantity followed by consonants agreeing in class and category. Rhyme or assonance could occur at the end of lines, within the lines or (by a special embellishment called *aicill)* the end sound of one line might chime with some sound within the next line. The vowel-sounds within a line might chime successively and in exact order with those of the corresponding words in the next line or through all the lines of the quatrain. Thus harmony might have a complexity of horizontal, diagonal and vertical patterns.

The technique of Irish classical poetry was acquired by the professional poets in the bardic schools, where their long training ensured that they were also skilled in learned reference and allusion to history or to what passed in genealogy and in place-lore for history. The result was a whole complex of learning which resulted in highly figurative language, stock metaphors and symbols for Ireland and her chiefs, often in stereotyped panegyric. Most 'bardic poetry', as Irish classical poetry is loosely called, does not survive the weight of this learning. On the other hand, as Eleanor Knott points out in *Irish Classical Poetry,* its skilful word-music was integral and presented a challenging aesthetic mode to a good poet.

This is certainly borne out by poetry of the *amour courtois* type which probably came in through Norman-French influence and which was written from the fourteenth to the sixteenth century by professional poets and by Norman and Irish nobles; at its best it combines a courtly style and a formal music with passionate or ironic love-poetry, the first considerable body of such poetry written in Irish. The strength of French influence on Irish poetry may be seen also in the *pastourelles, chansons de la mal mariée* and versions of the mediaeval court of love to be found as late as the eighteenth century. By that time the classical tradition had gone with the caste that preserved it; its dominance for centuries laid a shadow over the less disciplined popular measures that had coexisted with it and which then began to come into their own under different circumstances.

For those seeking a closer knowledge of Irish poetry many studies are available; Kuno Meyer's *Ancient Irish Poetry,* Gerard Murphy's *Early Irish Lyrics,* Myles Dillon's chapter on Irish Poetry in *Early Irish Literature* and Eleanor Knott's *Irish Classical Poetry* are among these. Notable examples are to be found in Robin Flower's *Poems and Translations,* Sean O'Faolain's *The Silver Branch,* Kenneth Jackson's *A Celtic Miscellany* and Frank O'Connor's *Kings, Lords and Commons. An Duanaire* (Ó Tuama and Kinsella) gives an excellent idea of the poems of the dispossessed Irish, 1600 – 1900. From such books it is possible to get a fair idea of the variety of Irish poetry between the eighth century and the eighteenth, when freer measures prevailed.

'The Marriage of Strongbow and Aoife' by Daniel Maclise. Courtesy of the National Gallery of Ireland.

PART II
Cultural Conflict and Transition

CHAPTER VII

Invasions: Scandinavian, Anglo-Norman, Elizabethan, Cromwellian and Williamite

In James Joyce's *Finnegans Wake* Ireland is sometimes seen as a beautiful temptress, who attracts and is ravished by various invaders but finally absorbs their strength and assimilates them into her family. The Norse and Danish invaders of the ninth and tenth centuries followed this pattern. The Irish system survived the ravages of the monastic centres and their cultural treasures by these invaders or by their occasional allies, the disunited Irish tribal leaders. Brian Boru's victory at Clontarf in A.D. 1014 not only broke the power of the Scandinavians and their Leinster allies but made possible the flowering of a cultural renaissance. Since Brian himself had a Danish wife, Gormlaith, the process of absorption seemed almost complete when in 1040 Sitric, the Danish ruler of Dublin, founded two centuries before by the Norse, married Brian's daughter and founded the cathedral of Christ Church. From about that time on those Ostmen who stayed in Ireland operated mainly as traders from Dublin and the other seaport towns which their ancestors had founded.

The Anglo-Norman invasion was more effective. A century after 1169, when Dermot MacMurrough brought them in, these new invaders ruled about half of Ireland, establishing their system of law and of land-tenure in perhaps a dozen Irish counties, and centralising their administration in Dublin, where in 1297 they set up their own parliament. Where their system prevailed it naturally ousted the Irish system of law and of collective land-holding. Culturally, the Normans at first were the ruthless enforcers of a rigid cleavage between the Irish and themselves. But their system could not be maintained without a sufficient flow of emigrants from England and this was not forthcoming. By the fourteenth century they were facing cultural absorption. Such enactments as the Statutes of Kilkenny (1366) laid down rigid penalties, including the death-penalty, for intermarriage with the Irish or for adopting their language or customs, but these could not be enforced in the greater part of Ireland. The Normans continued to be absorbed, the process incurring the hostility of the English administrators and of the English settlers in the towns, who held their privileges by royal charter.

Between assimilation by the Irish and Norman baronial feuds the effective area of English rule by the mid-fifteenth century was reduced to the Pale and the towns. Outside these many Norman and Irish lords showed a political ambivalence to the English monarch, nominally acknowledging him as 'lord of Ireland' but really concerned with the maintenance of their own power. In culture they were indistinguishable, although the native poets might side politically with either, depending upon whether their patrons were Irish or Anglo-Norman. 'In poetry for the English, we promise that the Gael will be banished from Ireland', wrote Godfrey O Dálaigh in a fifteenth-century poem to the Earl of Desmond; 'in poems for the Irish we promise that the English shall be scattered across the sea.'

> I ndán na nGall gealltar linn
> Gaoidhil d'ionnarba a hÉirinn;
> Goill do shraoineadh tar sál sair
> i ndán na nGaoidheal gealltair.[1]

In the previous century another Earl of Desmond, Gearoid Iarla, had been a noted Irish poet and patron of Irish poets; and he was an English official, chief justice of Ireland in 1367.

This cultural absorption of the Anglo-Normans probably accounts for the dearth of good poetry written in English in Ireland during the mediaeval period. Almost the only examples extant are from a manuscript written in the early fourteenth century at the Franciscan monastery in Kildare. The name of the author of one of its religious poems is known, because he gives it as 'Frere Michel Kildare', Friar Michael of Kildare, who could strike an effectively simple note in his didactic verse (here slightly modernised):

Poor was thine incoming
So shall be thine outgoing,
Thou shalt not from all thy thing
A penny bear to mould.[2]

The other religious poems have not the same merit but there is a long poem, 'The Land of Cokaygne' (Cookery), which is a lively, well-written satire. Like many mediaeval poems it describes a land in which meat and drink are plentiful. It is preferable to paradise, where men have to quench their thirst with water; here water is used only for boiling or washing, and there are rivers of milk, honey, oil and wine. The main beneficiaries of this plenty are the white friars and grey friars of an abbey made of food, who dine well on the geese, already roasted, which fly there crying 'Geese, all hot!' Nearby is a large nunnery, with whose nuns the young monks disport themselves in a most unascetic way. The poem concludes with a warning:

Whoso will that land come to,
Full great penance he must do;
Seven years in dirt of swine
He must wade, although he pine,
All anon up to the chin
So he to that land shall win.[3]

The location of Cokaygne is mentioned as 'Far at sea and west of Spain', which may indicate Ireland, and the allusions to white and grey monks near a nunnery may point to Kildare as the scene. The author is unknown: if the contemporary injunction against native Irishmen belonging to religious orders in the Pale was observed in Kildare, he may have been English or Anglo-Norman; the linguistic evidence points to that conclusion. It is interesting to notice that there are similarities of spirit and of subject-matter between 'The Land of Cokaygne' and the earlier Irish prose satire, 'The Vision of Mac Conglinne', but there are closer French counterparts.

Another anonymous 'Kildare poem' cited by Alspach is known

as 'A Satire on the People of Kildare', in which various orders of
clerics and tradesmen are laughingly chided for their failings:

> Hail be ye merchants with your great packs
> Of drapery, avoirdupois, and your wool-sacks,
> Gold, silver, stones, rich marks and eke pounds!
> Little give ye thereof to the wretched poor.
>   Sly he was, and full of wit,
>   That this lore put in writ.[4]

Apart from these poems there is little of interest, except for an
anonymous fourteenth-century stanza written in a dialect of
southern England:

> Ich am of Irlaunde
> Ant of the holy londe of irlande
> Gode sir pray ich ye
> for of saynte charite,
> Come ant daunce wyt me
> In irlaunde.[5]

It has a grace of its own, recaptured in Yeats's poem 'I am of
Ireland', but its provenance is uncertain. This is a general
problem with all this fourteenth-century literature, in which some
scholars discern the fragmentary beginnings of Anglo-Irish
literature.

The next century has nothing similar to offer. Towards its end
the accession of the Tudors in 1485 marks the beginning of a
policy which ultimately brought down the prevailing culture
shared by Irish and Anglo-Normans. It was the centralised
despotism of the Tudors which made the Anglo-Norman
parliament in Dublin completely subservient to Westminster by
Poyning's Law (1494) and which broke the power of the
Fitzgeralds of Kildare in 1537. Four years later Henry VIII
substituted the title 'King of Ireland' for that of 'Lord of Ireland',
which had lasted for four centuries, and set about securing the
allegiance of the Irish chiefs in return for English titles. By the
time that Elizabeth I ascended the English throne, the principal
ecclesiastical and legal officials in the Pale and the towns were
English, Protestantism had been proclaimed the official religion of
Ireland and the Catholic religious foundations had been dissolved
and sacked. Even Elizabeth's predecessor Mary I, a Catholic but
a Tudor, had initiated the policy of plantation in two Irish

counties, and her Catholic archbishop of Armagh had suggested that the elimination of the native Irish and their replacement by English colonists might settle the whole Irish question.

Under Elizabeth these policies, sharpened by English fears of effective military help reaching Ireland from the Catholic powers of Europe, were intensified. Wherever Irish or Anglo-Norman leaders rose in opposition, the process of devastation of their lands, indiscriminate slaughter of their people and plantation went on. Spenser reflects it in his *View of the Present State of Ireland*, written in 1596. He had come to Ireland in 1580, as secretary to Elizabeth's Lord Deputy, Grey de Wilton, whose task was to crush the Desmond Geraldines. By 1583 Munster had been laid waste and the Desmond leaders executed. Spenser described the conditions of the people:

> Out of every corner of the woods and glens they came creeping forth upon their hands, for their legs could not bear them. They looked anatomies of death, they spake like ghosts crying out of their graves, they did eat of the dead carrions, happy were they could find them, yea and one another soon after in so much as the very carcasses they spared not to scrape out of their graves, and if they found a plot of water cress or shamrocks, there they flocked as to a feast. . .[6]

Spenser in 1586 became one of the planters or 'undertakers' who undertook to settle the lands of the dispossessed. He lived at Kilcolman castle, a former Desmond stronghold, where he wrote much of the *Faerie Queene*, and was interested enough in Irish poems to have some translated to him:

> . . . and surely they savoured of sweet wit and good invention, but skilled not of the goodly ornaments of poetry. Yet were they sprinkled with some pretty flowers of their own natural devise, which gave good grace and comeliness unto them, which it is the great pity to see so abused to the gracing of wickedness and vice . . .[7]

The abuse of which Spenser complained was probably the support of Irish traditions. Other Elizabethans, including Shakespeare, Ben Jonson and Sir Philip Sidney, refer to the reputed power of the Irish poets to rhyme humans to death or into another shape by satire. Elizabeth's officials were conscious of the importance of the poets in the traditional Irish system. As Professor David Greene has shown, an English agent, Thomas

Smyth, reported at length upon their activities, which he linked with prophecy and witchcraft.[8] There was also the interesting case of Aongus Ó Dálaigh, an Irish poet commissioned by the Elizabethan leaders to write satires in Irish upon Irish tribal chiefs, stressing their unforgiveable meanness, in order to diminish their standing among their own people.

Spenser wrote charmingly of the Irish rivers in *The Faerie Queene* but his attitude to the native Irish, the models for his Satyrs, is reflected in the same poem, and he seems to have favoured their extermination as a race. The hostility was mutual; two years after he wrote his *View,* another Munster rising, sparked by that of O'Neill and O'Donnell in Ulster, caused the burning of Kilcolman castle and hastened Spenser's death in London a few months later. He did not live to see the Irish and Spanish forces defeated at Kinsale, or the flight of the last great Irish earls from Ulster and the plantation of that province by Scots and English settlers, events of which he would have approved.

The tragedy of Ireland, as Yeats called it, continued all through the seventeenth century. Munster and Ulster plantations were followed by Cromwellian plantations during its middle years and by Williamite plantations after 1691. By 1700 six-sevenths of arable Irish land was owned by one-fifth of the inhabitants, differing from the majority in language, religion and culture. This majority had survived largely through the failure of planters to secure cheap labour from England but its people were almost entirely reduced to the condition of serfs. Their leaders were gone, their native system of law and of land-holding abolished and tolerance of their religion denied. Toleration had been promised by the Treaty of Limerick, before Sarsfield and the 'Wild Geese' departed, but was immediately cancelled by the Protestant parliament in Dublin. It proceeded to initiate the Penal Laws, which Edmund Burke described as:

> a machine of wise and elaborate contrivance, as well fitted for the oppression, impoverishment and degradation of a people, and the debasement in them of human nature itself, as ever proceeded from the perverted ingenuity of men.

The aim, as Lecky put it, was 'not the persecution of a sect, but the degradation of a nation'. The psychology which guided it was not new, nor was it fundamentally Protestant; it can be seen as far back as Giraldus Cambrensis's twelfth-century defence of the

Norman conquest of Ireland on the grounds that 'this nation is the foulest, the most sunk in vice, the most uninstructed in the rudiments of faith of all nations upon earth'. In Elizabethan times the Protestant Spenser and the Catholic Edmund Campion had adopted the same line; the Irish were barbarous, lawless and licentious; 'for the most part infidels, wild and furious', wrote Campion. What the Williamite parliament ·did was to institutionalise this cast of thought by a form of sectarian apartheid which shut out the Catholic majority from political, legal and professional power.

The history of Ireland in the seventeenth century might be seen largely in terms of the significance of three flights; the flight of the last Irish earls, at its beginning; the flight of the landed Irish beyond the Shannon under Cromwell; the flight of the Wild Geese at its end. The result was that Ireland, by the early eighteenth century, had become a colony.

Bone trial piece (11th/12th century) with designs similar to those executed in bronze on the Clogán Óir bell shrine from Scattery Island, Co. Clare. Found in High Street excavation, Dublin. Courtesy of the National Museum of Ireland.

60
161·2

Eorge Martin fitz
Walter Mayor

Peares Martin
fitz Walter and
Domicke Lynch fitz
Peares shirriffes

Marcus Martin Recorder the
Nine and twentieth of September
1632 the Councell

Sr Thomas Rotherhame Knight

Henri Lynch knight Barronett
Vallentyne Blake knight and Baronett
Richard Blake knight
Marcus Martines Recorder
Nicholas Lynch fitz George Alderman
Geffrey Martin mayor of the staple
James oge Darsey Alderman
Androw Lynch fitz John Alderman
Patricke Martin Alderman
Robert Blake Alderman
Nicholas Lynch fitz Gomckno Alderman
Oliver Martin Alderman
Thomas Blake fitz vallentyne Esqr
Stephen Lynch Esqr
Patricke Darsey Esqr
Thomas Lynch Esqr
Richard Martin Esqr
Dommicke Browne Esqr
James Reogh Darsey Esqr

21 John Blake Esqr
    Androwe Kiruan Esqr
22 Nicholas more Lynch Burges
23 Martin Darsey Esqr
24 Patricke ffrench fitz George
25 Nicholas Martin Burges
26 Anthony Lynch fitz James B
27 Edmound Boskine Burges
28 Thomas ffrench fitz Anthony
29 John ffrench fitz Anderson
30 Androwe Browne fitz Dr
31 John Boskine fitz Peter
32 Peares Martin fitz walter

Council Book of Galway, 1632. Courtesy of the National Library of Ireland.

Chapter VIII

The Struggle of Two Cultures

Thus during the later seventeenth century and the first half of the eighteenth, a great cultural divide existed between the minority rulers and the dispossessed majority. The latter were forbidden to send their children abroad for education or to keep schools of their own or to enter the one university, Trinity College, Dublin. Outside the law there sprang up a rough system of popular education in the 'hedge-schools', which lasted into the nineteenth century. These might have spread English more rapidly among the people but the language of instruction was often Irish, Latin or Greek, especially in Munster, where the prospects of advancement abroad were knit to vocational, educational, military or trade contacts with France, Spain, Italy or Austria.

The advancement in Europe's professional schools of Irish Catholics who had received their preliminary training in the hedge-schools indicates that the quality of teaching in some of them, especially in classics and in mathematics, was sometimes high. But the difficulties under which they laboured and the lack of a regular supply of trained teachers must imply a low general standard. In trade with the Continent there were also openings for Catholics, since trade was regarded by the ascendancy as a low occupation; these must have created a demand for some training in mathematics and in languages. Several Irish families sent their sons abroad to learn continental languages and such contacts were undoubtedly a factor in the gradual rise through the eighteenth century of a Catholic middle class. In the hedge-schools the teaching of English must have varied in proportion to the strength of Irish in particular areas and to the students' prospects of escape abroad. Several of the remaining Irish poets taught in them and as many of these were scribes, they were among those who circulated Irish manuscripts, thus passing on their traditional lore in written as well as in oral form.

Such poets show a fragmentary continuity with the bardic

schools, which had steadily declined during the seventeenth
century, as the great hereditary families of poets and genealogists
followed the earls and the Wild Geese abroad. The poets who
remained were poor men, schoolmasters or day-labourers; but
they thought of themselves as inheritors of the old aristocratic
order and could fashion in Irish classical measures a poem of
praise for a benefactor, a lament for a lost horse, or a satire on
some unpopular local bailiff. In Munster, where the old learning
died hardest, they periodically held 'Courts of Poetry', perhaps in
some of the few Irish homes of substance left in isolated areas, in
the houses of Protestant landowners who had changed their
religion to retain their lands, and increasingly, as times grew
worse, in a labourer's cottage or a tavern. Some lines of Austin
Clarke sum up the contrast between seventeenth-century Irish
learning at home and abroad:

> All Belgium shone on Gothic column
>   Through leaded pane.
> Monks laboured at printing press, selected
> Type for a Gaelic or Latin text.
> Our poets stumbled to the next
>   Mud cabin through rain.[1]

These courts had a special ritual of being summoned by a
'sheriff' by 'warrant' and at them the poets recited new poems,
recalled the lineage of poets from earlier times, tested each other's
skill in extempore verses and copied and exchanged manuscripts.
There is a continuity of these poets from Dáithí Ó Bruadair, who
wrote in the later seventeenth century, to Seán Ó Coileán who
died in 1817; the greater poets — O'Carolan, Ó Rathaille,
Eoghan Ruadh Ó Suilleabháin — come in between. These last
inheritors of the bardic tradition were to some extent voices
singing out of exhausted wells. Much of their elaborate poetry,
formally perfect, lacks any spirit save that of nostalgia for the
glorious past or hope for the return of the Stuarts, a hope which is
often cast in the *aisling* form. Their common theme is lament;
lament for past greatness, for their own neglect by the boors
around them, whether Irish or Cromwellian, who care nothing
for real poetry. When by circumstances they are forced to write in
the stressed, not syllabic, measures of the popular folk-songs of
the eighteenth century, they grumble in verse about debasing
their art. Yet manuscript copies of their poems were often

circulated and it may have been partly through their art that the popular songs 'became inwrought with delicate cadences, with finely modulated assonances, with bewildering alliterative music'.

This is the view of Professor Corkery in *The Hidden Ireland* (1925), a study of the Munster poets. Unfortunately we do not know the history of the popular songs which passed from mouth to mouth among the ordinary people for centuries before writers of the nineteenth century began to write them down. But the richness of Irish oral tradition both at the time when it attracted the attention of Lady Gregory, Yeats, Synge and other writers of the revival and into this century, when it was more fully recorded, shows that despite all the disasters and chaos of the seventeenth and eighteenth centuries the Irish cultural tradition survived among the farmers and fishermen of the Gaelic-speaking areas.

The possibilities of what might have happened if Irish and English culture had met on equal terms are glimpsed in the work of Michael Comyn (1688-1760), who wrote an excellent poetic version of the 'Lay of Oisin in the Land of Youth', which had to await a translator until 1859 when Brian Ó Luanaigh published it in the *Transactions of the Ossianic Society* (Vol. IV) and a worthy poetic adaptor until W.B. Yeats turned it into 'The Wanderings of Oisin' (1889).

They can be seen also in Brian Merriman's 'Cúirt an Mheadhon Oidhche' ('The Midnight Court'), one of the best poems written in modern Irish. Merriman was a Clare teacher of mathematics, occasionally a farmer, who seems to have had a good classical training and some conversance with English and perhaps with French literature. His long poem, written in 1780, is a satirical attack on men who need the bait of a dowry to marry, on the wilfulness of women and on clerical celibacy. The argument is dramatically conducted by a young woman as plaintiff and an old man, whose son was born on his marriage night, as defendant. His praise of bastards is surprising but logical enough; for they are born without the expense of marriage. The woman-plaintiff counter-attacks by ridiculing the impotence of old men and suggests that the abolition of clerical celibacy would do away with clerical indiscretions and female frustration. Finally the queen declares her judgement; a number of unmarried men are to be made an example; as the revengeful women advance on their first victim, the poet himeself, he awakes.

The real theme of the poem is the claims of nature against those of convention and of greed; but what makes it so interesting is its spirit and style. It is joyous, irreverent and bawdy, and thus in the line of mediaeval satire, yet in its rational satirical temper and its appeal to nature it is of contemporary Europe. Its music is intricately assonantal yet the couplets in which it is written have a kind of barbed precision, like those of Swift or Pope; and parody — here of the *aisling* and of the mediaeval court of love — is another Augustan feature. But the language used, in a complete departure from conventional Irish practice, is the contemporary Irish speech of Clare, and the daily life and settings of the people are described realistically. In this Merriman is in line with the romantic temper of his time. There is some slight evidence that he was influenced by the English poet, Richard Savage, and it is possible that he knew something of Swift, whose verses were used in English and in Irish translations in some of the hedge-schools. He remains a fine, if enigmatic poet, who in more tolerant times might have had a greater fame and literary influence; as it was his poem was copied widely and also transmitted orally in Ireland a century after it was written. Dr P. W. Joyce met a Clareman who knew it by heart. Merriman died in Limerick in 1805, unknown to the English-speaking world. The first full translation of his poem was published in German by Christian Stern in 1905. Recent translations into English have made it familiar to many readers. Yeats thought it of European status, but such recognition was impossible during Merriman's time.

Despite the complete dominance of the ascendancy from 1691, English was at first slow to spread; the social and cultural divide between the wealthy and the poor was too great. Since Elizabethan times there had existed a certain body of Protestant opinion which favoured the use of an Irish translation of the New Testament, made in 1603, and the fostering of Irish among divinity students in Trinity College, for proselytising purposes. This never got very far; Swift's contemporary, Archbishop Synge, an ancestor of J.M. Synge, lamented that: 'there are too many of us who would rather keep the Papists as they are, in an almost slavish subjection, than have them made Protestants and thereby entitled to the same privileges as the rest of their fellow-subjects.'

Swift thought that any such encouragement of Irish would 'prevent the Irish from being tamed' and that its abolition would be an easy, practical matter, and would 'reduce great numbers to the national religion' (and adds, characteristically, 'whatever kind may then happen to be established'). But he could see the dilemma of the smaller farmers or 'squireens', largely of Cromwellian planter stock, although he regarded them (as did the bardic poets) mainly as boors. Learning Irish might be useful to them in dealing with their tenants, he admitted, but if they spoke it they should keep out of England, 'for I do not remember to have heard of any one man that spoke Irish, who had not the accent upon his tongue easily discernible to any English ear'. He explained that, while other accents were tolerated in London, the possessor of an Irish brogue would be expected to produce bulls and blunders and would be ridiculed and despised: 'Neither does it avail whether the censure be reasonable or not, since the fact is always so.'

Among Swift's papers is one, 'A Dialogue in Hibernian Style', which hits-off the effect of Irish speech on English by framing a mock-dialogue between two squires who use many Irish loanwords: buddogh *(bodach,* churl), garrawns *(garan,* horse), spawlpeen *(spailpin,* labourer), coshers (exercises the right to hospitality, *coisire).* He included some idioms: 'a good warrant you have' (you have a right to), 'it is kind father for you' (you are your father's son in this), which are still current in Irish-English.[2] Swift was derisory about the matter, but he was recording a linguistic reality which outlasted him. Some thirty years after his death Arthur Young noted that in his Irish travels he found only in Dublin and Wexford 'the speaking of the Saxon tongue without any mixture of the Irish'. By that time English was probably the prevailing language in more than half Ireland. Although we find Grattan favouring the preservation of Irish and Flood leaving a bequest to Trinity College for its encouragement, in their time whatever interest existed among the gentry was chiefly antiquarian. The dominance of English must have spread among the people about that time, for the new Catholic colleges, allowed legal existence after 1782, chose it as the medium of instruction. Maynooth followed suit in 1795, so that English was the language of all higher education for Catholics in Ireland before the end of the eighteenth century.

The writing of poetry in English in Ireland reflects the cultural and linguistic divide. From the sixteenth and seventeenth centuries comes almost nothing of any real literary merit. James

Farewell's *The Irish Hudibras,* published in London in 1689, refers to some Irish legends:

> And here was that prodigious Tool
> That monstrous geant, Finn Mac-Heuyle,
> Whose Carcass bury'd in the Meadows,
> Took up nine Acres of Pottados . . .[3]

His satire, however, is crude and the poem is interesting mainly because it contains some dialectical characteristics of the Pale district. There is more poetic value in Luke Wadding's *A Small Garland of pious and godly songs* (1684)[4]. Wadding came of an old Anglo-Norman family, took his doctorate at the Sorbonne and returned to Wexford, where he acted as Catholic titular bishop of Ferns and was sheltered from persecution by Catholic and Protestant friends. He was well-read in English classical poetry and the influence of the English metaphysical poets can be seen in his poem about the infant Christ:

> Heaven's great treasures are now but small,
> Immensity no extent at all,
> Eternity's but one day old,
> The Almighty feeleth the winter cold.

Wadding's carols are still sung in Wexford. It is significant that his book was published in Ghent, for the press in Ireland, first set up in 1550, was banned to Catholic printers for about two centuries; such poems as were printed there were undistinguished occasional poems, usually of welcome, eulogy or elegy concerning English royalty or its representatives.

These gleanings indicate that it would be idle to search for the beginning of Anglo-Irish poetry of much distinction during this period. In discussing the work of poets living in Ireland and writing in English during the eighteenth century, Professor Alspach notes their general mediocrity: 'they were for the most part utterly unoriginal in form or diction, aping slavishly the English poets', he writes. But as their writers regarded themselves as English, the situation could scarcely have been otherwise; it is paralleled in American colonial verse of the same period. What one gets in Ireland is some good minor English verse, of which Swift's is probably the best example. His verses, largely *jeux d'esprit,* sometimes touch upon the Irish scene; they contain some street-ballads, proclaiming, for example, the merits of Dublin Bay herrings, or the villainy of Sergeant-at-law Bettesworth:

Jolly boys of St. Kevan's, St. Patrick's, Donore
And Smithfield, I'll tell you, if not told before,
How Beetesworth, that booby and Scoundrel in grain,
Hath insulted us all by insulting the Dean.
  Knock him down, down, down, knock him down ...[5]

From this ballad, 'The Yahoo's Overthrow', Yeats adapted the refrain for one of his own political ballads.

Swift also Englished 'Pléaracha na Ruarcach', a roistering Irish poem written by his contemporary, Hugh MacGowran, about a gargantuan feast held by O'Rourke of Breffni in the sixteenth century. The author, who was one of a circle of poor Gaelic scholars living in Dublin, may have provided Swift with a literal translation. 'O'Rourke's Noble Feast' breaks up in disorder with a recital of pedigrees counterpointing an exchange of blows:

What Stabs and what Cuts,
What clatt'ring of Sticks,
What Strokes on the Guts,
What Bastings and Kicks!

It is not poetry of a very high order, though the fact that it is a fair translation perhaps suggests that there may have been earnest as well as jest in the accusation of his friend, Delany, who wrote to Swift at Quilca in 1722 that he was hob-nobbing with Irish labourers:

Conforming to the tatter'd rabble,
He learns their Irish tongue to gabble ...

Certainly Swift enjoyed talking to the English-speaking, poor Irish cottagers, whom he praised for their 'good-sense, humour and raillery', but it is unlikely that he had more than a nodding acquaintance with Irish.

Assertions that there are links between *Gulliver's Travels* and Gaelic literature are similarily tentative. There are parallels between Gulliver's voyages to a succession of islands and Celtic *immram* wonder-tales of islands inhabited by a variety of people and of beasts, including horses. There are also Celtic stories of giants and of pygmies, including one in which the tiny poet, Eisirt, like Gulliver in Brobdingnag, is nearly drowned in a drinking-vessel and cannot stand the reek of human breath. Remains of such wonder-tales must have passed into the oral tradition of the people of Swift's Ireland and may have reached him. Professor Mercier in *The Irish Comic Tradition* has pointed out most of the possibilities. But Swift's literary perspective is that of the classics and of English and French literature, where similar parallels are discernible and sometimes acknowledged.

What is more evident in Swift's verses written in Ireland is the critical eye they turn on the Irish establishment of his time, which he viewed as essentially fraudulent, in the sense that it preserved the legal fiction that Ireland was a separate kingdom, while really exploiting it as a dependancy through the manipulations of English officials, higher ecclesiastical placemen, and peers —

... Fools of Rank, a mungril Breed,
Who fain would pass for Lords indeed;
Where Titles give no Right or Power,
And Peerage is a wither'd Flower ...

These *Verses on the Death of Dr. Swift* are skilfully satirical but also reflect seriously the political views expressed in his Irish prose-writings.

Swift thought William Dunkin the best contemporary poet in Ireland. The judgement is questionable. Dunkin had some ability in burlesque poetry, first displayed in *The Murphaeid,* a long mock-heroic poem about a porter who kept the main gate of Trinity College, Dublin:

From great O'Murphy's thickest blood he springs
August descendant of Hibernian kings . . .
Mark well his figure and imagine then
You see dread Polyphemus in his den.

But this sort of verse wears thin in a long poem, like Dunkin's better-known *The Parson's Revels* (1750) which seems to be based on 'O'Rourke's Noble Feast', to which it alludes. It is about a Leitrim landlord who roasts an ox whole and invites the local notables to attend. They include parson, Presbyterian minister, a Quaker and even the parish priest — the Penal Laws were relaxing by that time — who are entertained by a blind Irish harper's song about Ireland:

He sounds in more majestic strains
How brave Milesians with their skanes
Had butcher'd all the bloody Danes
                         Like wethers.

> While Brian Borough with a yell
> Flat on the bed of honour fell
> When he might sleep at home as well
> > On feathers.

The harper also sings about the Desmonds, O'Neill and other great earls; then 'though much against his heart' about William's victory at the Boyne, after which the proceedings culminate in riotous drinking. Although Dunkin's wit has a jagged edge for the non-establishment guests, there is some interest in the clash of character of local types whose differences are dissolved in whiskey. Burlesque, of course, was the usual contemporary method of writing about popular life; one sees it in Gay and Swift as well as in Dunkin, but Dunkin does not reach any real intimacy with his subject; the very mode of burlesque hinders it.

A minor poet who got closer was Laurence Whyte, a Dublin schoolmaster, whose *Original Poems on Various Subjects, Serious and Diverting* were published in Dublin about 1740. It contains some good sketches of Irish types, including Tom Ryan, a Dublin publican, who was something of a scholar, knew Latin well and had vivid recollections of the Williamite wars, in which he soldiered on the Jacobite side:

> When he was in the humour to be merry
> He could relate the siege of Londonderry.
> Of all the sieges he omitted none,
> Including Limerick, anno ninety-one.
> He told the battles fought by horse and foot,
> How many slain, how many hacked and cut;
> The numbers taken and who ran away ...

Whyte was from Westmeath and his best sketches are those of a Westmeath farming-family in 'The Parting Cup or the Humours of Deochadorus'. Deochadorus, whose name denotes the hospitable 'parting drink', is a strong farmer whose grandfather and father lost their estates in the Cromwellian and Williamite confiscations; but his own industry has built up a comfortable, plentiful farm. His sons are trained to help him but also read Irish and speak Latin. The daughters are taught well by their mother:

> She often made them labour hard
> To brew and bake, to spin and card,
> To dress a dish or two of meat
> Fit for the squire himself to eat;

> To use their needle, read and write
> And dance the Irish Trot at night ...
> Though never bred in town or city
> With repartee or pun could fit ye;
> And as their heels denote them dancers
> Their heads were turned for witty answers.
> And when at work could sweetly chime
> Their Irish songs in tune and time.

The measure of this poem is Swift's four-stress couplet, which Whyte admired for its speed and strength. He also emulated Swift in his attack upon absentee landlords

> Who live in Luxury and Pleasure
> And throw away their Time and Treasure,
> Cause Poverty and Devastation
> And sink the Credit of the Nation ...

and condemned the rack-renting which drove so many people from the land to the emigrant ship.

During the second half of the eighteenth century the story was much the same. Samuel Whyte who like his namesake was a Dublin teacher, published *The Shamrock; or Hibernian Cresses* in Dublin (1772), but its contents are of little worth and the title is misleading, except perhaps as a gesture to the growing feeling of 'Irishness' among the Anglo-Irish of Grattan's time. Whyte is better remembered because the pupils of his academy in Grafton Street included Richard Brinsley Sheridan and Thomas Moore, although his work must have had some attraction in his own day, for it was pirated in a London edition of 1774. Another minor poet with some contemporary reputation was Thomas Dermody, a Clareman of precocious talent, a kind of Irish Chatterton, who emigrated to London, where he died in 1802, aged twenty-seven. His poems were collected and published there posthumously under the title *The Harp of Erin*. It contains some verses that are felicitous and graceful but in general is undistinguished and full of the false poetic diction which Wordsworth was attempting to overthrow.

Goldsmith, the one great poet of Irish birth in the eighteenth century, is rightly ranked in the tradition of the great English Augustans in form and language but repays some investigation in his Irish context. He is not quite with the Augustans in temperament, as readers of Boswell will have noticed, for his playful wit and his straight-faced adoption of absurdities often made him a butt for satire in the Club and his 'Retaliation' shows that he could hit its members off wittily and perceptively. Like other Irish literary invaders of London, Goldsmith had a double allegiance. He had at first found England 'a country where being born an Irishman was sufficient to keep me unemployed', while Ireland, to which he was tied by memories of friends and of places, gave little opportunity to wit or learning:

> There has been more money spent in the encouragement of the Padareen mare there is one season, than given in rewards to learned men since the time of Usher. All their productions in learning amount to perhaps a translation, or a few tracts in divinity; and all their productions in wit, to just nothing at all.

So he wrote to his friend Hodson in 1757. The memory of Lissoy, of his Irish friends and their songs, the letter confessed, soured his pleasures in London. Yet a few years later some of London's greatest men were his friends. Both Irish and English experience of the inhuman system of land-clearance entered into *The Deserted Village:* 'I remember it in my own country', he said, perhaps referring to General Napier's clearances in his home-area, 'and I have seen it in this.' But this poem may also owe something to his experience of feudal decay in France. Goldsmith, admirer of Voltaire, seems to have been much less conservative than his friends; a playful, somewhat rueful irony, a sympathy with the underdog, are part of his individual charm.

His one essay upon a figure of the native Irish world, Turlough O'Carolan (1670-1738), is of some interest. The blind Carolan was the last of the great Irish harper-composers; he travelled Ireland for some fifty years, playing in the houses of his many patrons, in whose honour he composed most of his pieces. He knew Swift and Delany and composed the music for the original poem 'O'Rourke's Noble Feast'. In Dublin he became familiar with the work of Corelli, Geminiani and Vivaldi, who influenced his style. He certainly composed a wedding-tune for the marriage of Goldsmith's first cousin, Elizabeth Goldsmith of Roscommon, and died not far from Goldsmith's neighbourhood when Goldsmith was a boy of ten. Goldsmith's essay pays tribute to Carolan's skill and reputation:

> the original natives never mention his name without rapture; both his poetry and music they have by heart; and even some of

the English themselves who have been transplanted there, find his music extremely pleasing.[6]

Goldsmith himself was related to both groups but is typically Augustan in his attitude: 'There can be perhaps no greater entertainment', he remarks in the same essay, 'than to compare the rude Celtic simplicity with modern refinement.' Carolan's music in fact shows how sophisticated he was in both Irish traditional and contemporary Italian music, which in places he combined with remarkable skill.

Carolan also wrote the music for a ballad, now lost, called 'Squire Wood's Lamentation for the Refusal of his Halfpence', which indicates an aspect of the contacts between the two cultures through music and song. One finds slight evidence of this in the work of minor poets of the eighteenth century included in nineteenth century anthologies of 'Irish literature' on the basis of their Irish birth and an occasional use of Irish themes; George Ogle's 'Molly Asthore', Edward Lysaght's 'Kitty of Coleraine' or John Philpot Curran's 'The Deserter's Meditation', a version of the Irish poem 'Preab san Ól' by Richard Barrett.

Closer contacts are found in the popular ballads. Thousands of popular songs in Irish existed during the seventeenth and eighteenth centuries, for the Irish 'used worse than negroes by their lords and masters', as Chesterfield said, had the black slaves' tenacity of song. The verses of many such songs were written down from the eighteenth century on, but their airs were rarely recorded; we know, however, that while they retained some of the devices of formal Gaelic poems, they modified them considerably by a looser rhythm and a simple diction. When rendered into conventional English metrics and diction, the merit of the best of them was obscured. It was otherwise with the English or Scottish folk-songs preserved by the settlers or brought home by migrant labourers, songs like 'Barbara Allen' which Goldsmith remembered hearing sung in Longford, mainly Irish-speaking in his day.

As spoken Irish declined, the people made songs in English to Irish airs. 'When the Irish language was fading', wrote Colm Ó Lochlainn in the Preface to *Irish Street Ballads* (1939), 'the Irish street-ballad in English was the half-way house between the Irish culture and the new English way.' In Swift's time political ballads, squibs and verses on public events circulated chiefly in broadsheets in the cities. Later in the eighteenth century the ballad-singer began to spread new ballads in English throughout the country. He carried news about politics, foreign and domestic; he sang about exciting events; evictions, abductions, races, robberies and shipwrecks; he celebrated local beauties, boxing-matches, tragic accidents:

> It might happen to anyone
> As it happened to me
> For to shoot your own true love
> In under a tree.

Political ballads like 'The Boyne Water' survived from the Williamite wars. Others were written during the period of Grattan's parliament, some, like 'Harry Hood's election song', blending Irish and English speech in 'macaronic' verse. With the 1798 rising came a new crop, 'The Boys of Wexford', 'Roddy McCorley', 'The Shan Van Vocht'.

Later came ballads in which political hope was replaced by macabre mixtures of gaiety and lament for crippled Irish soldiers returning from British service in the Peninsular wars — 'Johnny I hardly knew you' and 'Mrs McGrath' are good examples — and others in which the visionary woman of the *aisling* poem appears, not as a symbol of Ireland but simply as a local beauty. The directly political ballad tradition has continued into our own time, often fraught with the old symbolism.

These ballads of the turn of the eighteenth century are interesting technically. Their sound-pattern often preserved the assonantal music of Gaelic verse or replaced it by internal rhyme. Their English has an interesting variety of range. Some of them seem to have been composed by hedge-schoolmasters who searched for a dignified poetic diction combined with classical references. A pretty young girl might be described as 'a fair juvenile female' or as 'a darling phoenix' who deserves the attention of great heroes:

> If Jason famous had known young Katie,
> With her he'd sail to the Persian shore,
> And bold Ulysses for to release her
> The briny regions he would search o'er ...

Again, polysyllabic Latinate words might be forced into a laboured form of internal rhyme:

To end my lamentations I am in consternation
No one can roam for recreation until the day do dawn;
Without a hesitation, we're charged with combination
And sent for transportation with the Boys of Mullabaun.

On the other hand the language of these ballads often has a refreshing simplicity:

'Twas early, early in the Spring
The birds did whistle and sweetly sing,
Changing their notes from tree to tree
And the song they sang was old Ireland free ...

The assonantal pattern of others hints at its possibilities in less transient poetry:

I am a bold rake and this nation I travelled all round
In search of a fair one her equal was never yet found,
She was neat in each limb and her skin far whiter than snow —
And if I don't gain her quite crazy to Bedlam I'll go.

Thanks to a line of collectors from P.W. Joyce to Colm Ó Lochlainn, who printed both words and music together, we can see clearly that the quarter-tones of Irish music favoured the wavering rhythm which was discernible, although less explicable, when the folk-songs and ballads were simply printed without music. That sense of song persists in Anglo-Irish poetry through the nineteenth century into contemporary times. In general the ballads are an important strand in the intertwining of two cultures.

CHAPTER IX

Scholarship in a Submerged Culture

By the time that such ballads were made at a popular level, a greater knowledge of Irish history and antiquities had spread slowly among the educated classes.

The attitude of Elizabethan historians had been one of hostility to the cultural side of a system they wished to destroy. Campion, in his hastily written *History of Ireland,* gave Fenian tales, such as the meeting of Caoilte Mac Ronan with Saint Patrick, short shrift as 'blinde legends'. The change was due to two causes: the adoption of a more scholarly approach by English or Anglo-Irish writers and the work of Irishmen at home and abroad. The first may be seen in the work of Sir James Ware, son of the Recorder of Dublin, who published in 1633 a *Chronicle of Ireland* compiled by the English divine, Meredith Hanmer, who recounted several Fenian tales taken from the sixteenth-century *Book of Howth.* Ware was an indefatigable collector of Irish manuscripts and also encouraged and co-operated with the last of the Irish hereditary historians, Dubhaltach Mac Firbhisigh, whose *Book of Genealogies* is still extant. A similar co-operation existed later in the seventeenth century between William Molyneux who, besides being the author of *The Case of Ireland Stated* (1698), collected from Roderic O'Flaherty and other Irish historians material for a projected Description of Ireland; he also founded in 1683 the Dublin Philosophical Society, which concerned itself chiefly with antiquarian studies and was the precursor of the Royal Irish Academy, founded a century later.

The seventeenth century also saw the advancement of Irish studies through the Franciscans at Louvain, who encouraged Michael O'Clery to return to Ireland to collect Irish manuscripts. In his native Donegal between 1632 and 1636 he and his colleagues compiled *The Annals of the Four Masters,* which cover the period from the Anglo-Norman invasion to A.D. 1616. The *Annals* include some pseudo-history, mingle fact and legend, but preserve many records of the disintegrating Gaelic order and some remarkably vivid accounts of such figures as O'Neill and O'Donnell.

But the greatest Irish historical work of the seventeenth century was that of Geoffrey Keating. Tipperary-born and trained at Bordeaux, Keating was priest, poet and scholar. As an active priest and as a refugee in the Galtee mountains he worked on ancient books and manuscripts from which he compiled his *History of Ireland,* which was written in Irish and entitled *Foras Feasa ar Eirinn* ('base of knowledge about Ireland'). It was completed about 1625 and covers the period from the earliest times to the victory of the Anglo-Normans in the twelfth century.

Keating himself came of Anglo-Norman stock and distinguished carefully between the 'Old English' and the 'new foreigners' of Elizabethan and Jacobean times. Part of his aim was to expose the misrepresentations of foreign writers from Cambrensis on; they are like dung-beetles, he says, who pass by flowers to roll in filth, and he examines the inaccuracies of Stanihurst and others. Keating set down all he could discover about the old system: the pseudo-history and history of its tribes, invaders and places. He also set down many stories and poems, giving most prominence to the Ulster cycle, whose tales he recounted with restrained artistic skill. Unlike the Annalists he did not bowdlerise and narrated without comment King Conor's incest or how a noted lecher got his nickname 'crop-ear' from a victim's bite. Although he was accused by some later antiquarians of confusing legend with history, Keating made it quite clear that he was setting down myths or fables because they were part of the records of Ireland and indeed were to be found in the primitive records of most countries even after they had become Christian.

His work was of the greatest importance both in preserving this material, since many of his original sources were destroyed during the Cromwellian wars, and in providing a model of modern Irish prose. Irish scribes, both in Ireland and in Irish centres abroad, continued to copy and to circulate it for over two centuries. English translations in manuscript seem to have been made from the later years of the seventeenth century but we have little knowledge of their provenance or of their fate. Keating's history became known to readers of English in the eighteenth century through a published translation by Dermot O'Connor in 1723. This work contained many inaccuracies of translation but ran through six editions by the mid-nineteenth century.

The growing interest in Irish literature and antiquities during the eighteenth century was quickened by the publication of James Macpherson's *Ossian* (1760-63). This rhetorical fabrication was erected on fragmentary remains of a body of Scots-Gaelic folklore which preserved some of the tradition shared by Scotland with Ireland until the collapse of the bardic schools. Macpherson's blending of legend, pseudo-history, folklore and invention, presented in a vigorous baroque style, influenced the beginnings of the romantic movement in Europe; even the reactions of Johnson, Lessing and Voltaire against it helped to focus attention on the possibility that, underlying its rhetoric, there were some genuine remains of Celtic literature. Consequently the collection of Gaelic manuscripts and folklore received an incentive and such bodies as the Irish Ossianic Society and the Scottish Highland Society were formed. In Ireland Charles O'Conor of Belanagare, a noted antiquarian, attacked Macpherson's inaccuracies in the second edition of his *Dissertations on the History of Ireland* (1766) and was encouraged in his work by Dr Johnson, perhaps as an *amende honorable* for his former declaration that Gaelic possessed no written literature and no manuscripts.[1] O'Conor also did some valuable work in the *Collectanea de Rebus Hibernicis* (1770-1804), to which contributed Joseph Cooper Walker, Sylvester O'Halloran and Charles Vallancey. The last of these was an unreliable scholar but an indefatigable collector, who purchased the *Leabhar Breac* (the Speckled Book) for the Royal Irish Academy. O'Halloran published a *History of Ireland* (1778) which used the material of Keating and other historians in a fairly competent but dully-written manner. He made a point that 'the very names of territories, rivers, lakes and mountains and even the surnames of families, allude to different periods of our history'; a point well-taken a century later by Standish James O'Grady, the 'father of the Irish literary revival'.

The soundest work produced by any of these eighteenth century antiquarians was Walker's *Historical Memories of the Irish Bards* (1786). It gave details of the *fili*, their training and dress, and some examples of their poetry and of Irish music. The same year the foundation of the Royal Irish Academy provided a stable centre in Dublin for the developing interest in Irish literature and antiquities. Walker was active in it, as was his friend Theophilus O'Flanagan, Irish scholar and teacher, upon whom Walker

'*Portrait of Harper*' *by James Barry. Courtesy of the National Gallery of Ireland.*

depended, for his own knowledge of Irish was slight.

The recognition of the literary value of Irish remains had been hampered by two things. One was the disputation as to what was legend and what was history; we find both Macpherson and Charles O'Conor attacking Keating for confusing the fabulous with the historical. The second was the lack of an exact knowledge of Irish among the antiquarians; Vallancey, for example, knew no Irish but relied upon an Irish scribe, Maurice Gorman, yet both he and O'Halloran made absurd statements about its linguistic origins. Hence the value of Charlotte Brooke's *Reliques of Irish Poetry* (1789), for this Cavan lady knew Irish and had an excellent education which made her realise the literary value of the material and the possibilities of its treatment in English. Her father, Henry Brooke, was a considerable literary figure, remembered in English literary history for his novel *The Fool of Quality* (1760). On his Cavan estate Irish was largely spoken and Charlotte, who was attracted by the workers' interest in poetry, music and dancing, was vividly impressed by hearing a poor labourer reading to his companions tales of Cuchulainn, Fionn and Oisín from two bound collections of Irish manuscripts. When she read Macpherson's work she recognised the outlines of some of these tales and determined upon her book. Her father, who was himself interested in Irish antiquities, put her in touch with leading antiquarians. Walker was a friend of her family and had included two of her translations in his book. O'Flanagan also helped her, while her notes drew upon sources from Keating to O'Conor.

The full title of her book is *Reliques of Irish Poetry: consisting of Heroic Poems, Odes, Elegies and Songs, translated into English verse: with Notes Explanatory and Historical; and the Originals in the Irish Character. To Which is Subjoined an Irish Tale.* The poems cover a wide range, from the Red Branch and Fenian cycles, through 'rapparee' (Irish *rapaire,* rapier or short pike) or outlaw poems of the seventeenth century, to Carolan's poems and even songs taken down from living singers. Since the originals were printed in Irish script and her scholarly notes were used to authenticate them and to light up their background, the *Reliques* provided convincing proof of the strength of the Irish literary tradition, its association with music and its continuity, despite the destruction of the older Irish order, into her own time. The quality of her translations was only moderate:

He call'd his fleet and faithful hounds
The doe's light steps to trace;
Sgeolan and Bran obey'd the sounds
And sprung upon the chase.

In general her prose translations (especially from Carolan) are better. In her verse translations the diction is stilted, and form conventional; but both appealed to current English literary taste. Her accounts of legendary heroes, of a shrouded history and a neglected folklore also coincided with the stirrings of romanticism and with the concomitant spread of interest in antiquities stimulated not only by *Ossian* but by Percy's *Reliques of Ancient English Poetry: consisting of old Heroic Songs and other pieces of our Earlier Poetry; together with Some Few of Later Date* (1765). The title of Charlotte Brook's *Reliques* may have had that of Percy in mind, and she certainly emulated him in prefixing to her collection an excellent preface. This discussed intelligently the qualities of the Irish language, whose great variety and distinctive beauty, she considered, made translation into English comparatively flat:

> It is really astonishing of what various and comprehensive powers this neglected language is possessed. In the pathetic it breathes the most beautiful and affecting simplicity; and in the bolder species of composition, it is distinguished by a force of expression, a sublime dignity, and rapid energy, which it is scarcely possible for any translation fully to convey; as it sometimes fills the mind with ideas altogether new, and which, perhaps, no modern language is entirely prepared to express.

Emphasising the complexity and the refinement which Irish writing had achieved 'at a period when the rest of Europe was nearly sunk in barbarism', she elaborated one difficulty of translation which continues to our own time:

> One compound epithet must often be translated by two lines of English verse, and, on such occasions, much of the beauty is necessarily lost; the force and effect of the thought being weakened by too slow an introduction on the mind; just as that light which dazzles, when striking swiftly on the eye, will be gazed at with indifference, if let in by degrees.

This is also interesting because it seems to indicate a temperament which impels some Irish writers towards a certain kind of condensed lyrical impressionism; it may also have a remote bearing upon James Joyce's eventual creation of an almost bardic and hieratic prose style, condensed, complex and evocative.

Miss Brooke is discerning about the suitability of Irish for lyric poetry; its assonantal music, she points out, is assisted by the aspiration of consonantal sounds. This naturally raised the problem of translation into a non-aspirated language such as English. She herself, while conscious of the loss, did not attempt to carry over the assonantal or the rhythmic pattern of Irish poetry, a process already at work in the popular ballads of the eighteenth century. The Irish tale to which the sub-title of her book refers is the story of Maon, which had been related by Keating, O'Halloran and others. Lowry Maon (Lowry the Mute), the central figure of this story (and of Padraic Colum's version in 1937), is saved in childhood by a shepherd from his royal father's murderers and returns in manhood to avenge him. Charlotte Brooke's verse rendering is well-developed structurally but her diction is too conventional to sustain characterisation. It is an interesting anticipation of Ferguson's versions of Irish epic material over a century later.

Lesser known is the work of her contemporary, Charles Wilson, whose *Poems Translated from the Irish language into English* (undated, probably published about 1782) contains the Irish text of 'O'Rourke's Noble Feast', with a fuller and better English version than Swift's. His other translations of Irish poems are of little merit but he has one or two good prose renderings from the Fenian tales. He, too, probably found readers among the supporters of Grattan's parliament.

Berkeley, Bishop of Cloyne and his family by John Smibert.

Grattan addressing the House of Commons. Photograph courtesy of the National Gallery of Ireland.

CHAPTER X

The Prose of Politics from Swift to Wolfe Tone

Seventeenth-century prose of Irish interest had been chiefly polemical, much of it written in Latin by church dignitaries, and all of it bound up with the religious and political controversy of the time. Among the Latinists may be mentioned John Lynch, a Galway priest and schoolmaster who fled to France when Galway was surrounded by Cromwellian forces in 1652 and published his *Cambrensis Eversus* in St Malo in 1662, dedicated to Charles II. His refutation of Giraldus Cambrensis, which is pedantic and prolix, need not concern us here, but part of his argument lights up one theme of the best eighteenth-century prose in Ireland. Lynch was of Anglo-Norman or old English settler stock and held that it is not the country of a man's ancestors but the place of his own birth that is man's true country; the old English settlers were therefore Irish. They spoke Irish (which, Lynch says, comes near Spanish in gravity, Italian in courtesy, French in conciliatory love, German in impressing terror), but its use was perfectly consistent with allegiance to the English Crown, whose sway was established in 1171. The difficulty, argued Lynch, was that the laws of Ireland had passed into the hands of English officials. Before that, laws passed by the English legislature never had force in Ireland unless they were adopted by the Irish legislature; for never, since the memory of man, did the foreigners or sojourners in any state constitute its council.

It is this part of Lynch's reasoning which found an interesting parallel in a purely Protestant context only eight years after the Battle of the Boyne put a stop to the Catholic cause. In 1698 William Molyneux, born in Dublin in 1656, Master of the High Court of Chancery, published a pamphlet, *The Case of Ireland's being bound by Acts of Parliament in England, Stated.* Dedicated to King William, it argued that Ireland was a separate kingdom, united under the same crown as England since the twelfth century, but that it was

against natural equity and reason that a kingdom regulated

within itself and having its own parliament should be bound
without their consent by the parliament of another kingdom ...
which may make the lords and people of Ireland think that they
are not well used and may drive them into discontent.

The influence of his friend, John Locke, can be seen in
Molyneux's contention 'that Ireland should be bound by Acts of
Parliament made in England is against Reason and Common
Rights of Man'. This pamphlet marks the beginning of a trend of
thought among the Protestants of Ireland which was to develop
with remarkable results during the eighteenth century, enlisting
in turn the services of Ireland's greatest writer, her greatest orator
and her most revolutionary thinker.

Molyneux's pamphlet was condemned by the English House of
Commons to be burned by the common hangman. This gave
point to his prefatory remark: 'We are in a miserable condition,
indeed, if we may not be allowed to complain when we think we
are hurt.' It also indicated to many Irish Protestants that England
was determined to reduce the Irish Protestant parliament,
through the control of English officials and placemen, to a mere
rubber-stamp for English mercantilist legislation which, by the
Navigation Act of 1663 and subsequent measures, damaged Irish
interests as much as those of the American colonists.

In this context Swift's Irish writings are particularly important.
The best known of them, the *Drapier's Letters* (1724), develop
Molyneux's central idea with a particular force:

Tis true indeed that within the memory of man the Parliaments
of England have sometimes assumed the power of binding this
kingdom by laws enacted there, wherein they were at first
openly opposed by Mr. Molyneux ... but the love and torrent
of power prevailed. Indeed the arguments on both sides were
invincible: For in reason, all government without the consent
of the governed is the very definition of slavery: But in fact,
eleven men well armed will certainly subdue one single man in
his shirt. But I have done. For those who have used power to
cramp liberty have gone so far as to resent even the liberty of
complaining, although a man on the rack was never known to
be refused the liberty of roaring as loud as he thought fit ...

The fourth Drapier letter, in which this passage appears, was
entitled *A Letter to the Whole People of Ireland,* by which Swift meant
the Protestant minority; but Primate Boulter reported in alarm

that in Dublin the *Drapier Letters* were having 'a most unhappy influence in bringing on intimacies between Papists and Jacobites and the Whigs'; so the claim that the defeat of 'Wood's halfpence' made Swift a national hero is partly true.

Two of his early political pamphlets, *The Story of the Injured Lady* and *An Answer to the Injured Lady,* both written about 1707, show the same attitute to Ireland's constitutional position. They were cast in allegorical form and have not the incisive clarity of his Irish writings published between 1720 and 1729. First of these was *A Proposal for the Universal Use of Irish Manufacture,* (1720) whose cause was the plight of the Protestant weavers of Swift's congregation, severly hit by English mercantilist policy. Swift urged the retaliatory measure of 'utterly rejecting and renouncing everything wearable that comes from England', and attacked absentee landlords 'who by unmeasurable screwing and racking their tenants all over the kingdom, have already reduced the miserable people to a worse condition than the peasants in France, or the vassals in Germany and Poland ...'. This pamphlet went beyond parochial grievance to advocate national self-sufficiency.

In 1724, the year of the *Drapier Letters,* appeared *Maxims Controlled in Ireland,* which contradicted prevalent government maxims about Ireland's prosperity by testing them against the actual condition of the country. For example, Swift acknowledged the truth of the maxim 'That people are the riches of a nation', but pointed out that in Ireland 'five children in six who are born, lie a dead weight upon us, for want of employment ... Trade is the only incitement to labour; where that fails, the poorer native must either beg, steal, or starve, or be forced to quit his country.' He mentions country parishes and villages 'where the wretches are forced to pay for a filthy cabin, and two ridges of potatoes, treble the worth; brought up to steal or beg, for want of work; to whom death would be the best thing to be wished for, on account both of themselves and the public.'

This widening of Swift's social perspective is seen again in his *A Short View of the State of Ireland* (1728), which set out in a very logical form the causes of a nation's prosperity and demonstrated Ireland's frustrations in relation to them; the positive measures suggested are legislative autonomy, national self-sufficiency, the development of a sense of responsibility in both landlords and tenants, and the curbing of factions in the public interest. A year later Swift apparently realised that there was no hope of his measures being adopted and wrote his famous pamphlet, *A Modest Proposal for preventing the Children of Poor People from being a Burden to their Parents or Country, and for making them Beneficial to the Public*. The mask of monstrous benevolence which Swift assumed to suggest that annually 100,000 poor Irish children 'may at a year old be offered in sale to the *Persons* of *Quality* and *Fortune*' as food, was perfectly chosen for his most ironic thrusts:

> I grant this Food will be somewhat dear, and therefore very *proper for Landlords;* who, as they have already devoured most of the Parents, seem to have the best title to the Children ... we can incur no Danger in *disobliging* ENGLAND; For this Kind of Commodity will not bear Exportation; the Flesh being too tender a Consistence to admit a long Continuance in Salt; *although, perhaps I could name a Country, which would be glad to eat up our whole Nation without it.*

The savagery of Swift's attack had a close connection with the immediate situation. One of Ireland's recurrent famines was then in progress and poor people were dying in large numbers. The proposal mentioned this in an apparently casual digression:

> Some Persons of a desponding Spirit are in great Concern about the vast Number of poor People, who are Aged, Diseased, or Maimed; and I have been desired to employ my Thoughts what Course may be taken to ease the Nation of so grievous an Encumbrance. But I am not in the least Pain upon that Matter; because it is very well known that they are every Day *dying*, and *rotting*, by *Cold* and *Famine* and *Filth*, and *Vermin*, as fast as can be reasonably expected. And as to the younger Labourers, they are now in almost as hopeful a Condition: They cannot get Work, and consequently pine away for Want of Nourishment, to a Degree, that if at any Time they are accidentally hired to common Labour, they have not Strength to perform it; and thus the Country, and themselves are in a far Way of being soon delivered from Evils to come.
>
> I have too long digressed ...

The irony is beautifully sustained; the proposal is elaborated with painstaking concern for everybody's welfare; it will lessen the number of papists and potential rebels; the poor people will have something valuable of their own, the rich a luxury food; it will increase goods of Irish manufacture and wonderfully encourage matrimony. Finally we are assured fo the altruism of the proposer.

The general force of the pamphlet is due to the tension it sets up between the shocking inhumanity of the proposal and the benevolent common sense manner of the argument. It is also deepened by the way in which, under the pretence of dismissing 'other expedients' Swift proceeds to state the positive remedies which he had proposed in the *Short View* and other writings for 'this one individual Kingdom of Ireland, and for no other that ever was, is, or, I think, ever can be upon earth'.

Burke thought that Swift's tracts did honour to his heart as well as to his head. Certainly *A Modest Proposal* seems a *cri de coeur,* a last effort to shock people into attention to an immediate evil. His best Irish writings have that sense of immediacy which springs from real and immediate situations. They may have some slight connection with Swift's greatest work, *Gulliver's Travels* (1726), most of which was written 1721-5 in Dublin. Its narrator is not, as originally intended, the learned Martin Scriblerus but the homely, plain-spoken Lemuel Gulliver, a Drapier type. Gulliver's benevolent defence of mass-slaughter in Brobdingnag is curiously like the proposal to butcher infants in Ireland and his attack on the method of planting and governing colonies seems to reflect many aspects of Swift's experience of the one colony he knew.

While it would be impossible and undesirable to confine Swift to his Irish context, it would be unwise to neglect that it was in Ireland Swift was born, spent most of his life, had his most enduring political influence, wrote his greatest book, played out his intimate role with Stella and Vanessa and died, leaving his money to found a great mental hospital in Dublin.

> He gave the little Wealth he had,
> To build a House for Fools and Mad:
> And shew'd by one satyric Touch,
> No Nation wanted it so much.

So he wrote in his anticipatory *Verses on the Death of Dr. Swift* (1739). He could not have foreseen the satiric touch by which his Irish writings would cause his identification with conceptions of Irish liberty and nationhood to which he would have been thoroughly hostile. He wrote from the viewpoint of a reforming English colonist of the Irish Protestant nation, a view which was well expressed in George Berkeley's writings in *The Querist* and Patrick Sheridan's in *The Intelligencer;* but it was Swift who expressed it most forcibly in lasting literary form.

Mention of George Berkeley (1685 - 1753), Bishop of Cloyne, may remind us that his philosophical writings had some influence on Anglo-Irish literature in modern times. He was an idealist who opposed the prevailing mechanistic and materialistic view of the universe; 'we Irish do not hold this view', he wrote, arguing that material things could not be judged without God-implanted reason: 'to be is to be perceived'. To Yeats this line of thought (which in fact can be found as early as Duns Scotus Eriugena, the fourteenth-century philosopher) represented the birth of the modern Irish intellect; the natural cast of his own mind favoured the idea that spiritual, aesthetic and moral values transcend material appearances and Berkeley became one of the referent images of the poetry and thought of his middle period. Berkeley also was to influence the ideas of Samuel Beckett, and, incidentally, of some modern physicists who believe that behind the physical world is a mental or spiritual world.

Before he died Swift had come to believe that to write upon Irish affairs was only to prescribe a dose for the dead but his ideas continued in the next generation of Irish Protestants and were expressed most notably in the oratory of Henry Grattan (1746 -1820). Grattan's ancestors were Swift's friends and at seventeen he broke with his father, the Recorder of Dublin, through supporting a Dr Lucas, editor of the Dublin *Citizen's Journal,* whose ideas of reform were derived from Swift. Grattan entered the Irish parliament in 1775, the year in which the American colonists rose and in which, influenced by the ideas of Molyneux and Swift, they issued a manifesto to the Irish, pointing out their common political and economic grievances. With the formation of the Irish Volunteers in 1778, ostensibly to protect an Ireland drained of English troops, Grattan became the chief spokesman of the Irish Protestant demand for free trade and for legislative independence. Concessions in trade were granted and Grattan, after due meditation 'along the banks of the Liffey and amid the groves and bowers of Swift and Vanessa', decided to move his Declaration of Irish Rights, which he did with great eloquence in 1780. It was defeated, but Grattan's closing words were prophetic:

I do see the time is at hand, the spirit is gone forth, the declaration is planted; and though great men should apostatize, yet the cause will live; and though the public speaker should die, yet the immortal fire shall outlast the organ which conveyed it, and the breath of liberty, like the word of the holy man, will not die with the prophet, but survive him.

Two years later he spoke with confidence in the success of his measure for Irish legislative independence:

I am now to address a free people: ages have passed away and this is the first moment in which you can be distinguished by that appellation ... Spirit of Swift! Spirit of Molyneux! Your genius has prevailed; Ireland is now a nation. In that new character I hail her; and bowing to her august presence I say, *Esto perpetua!*

His conception of the Irish nation was wider than Swift's. 'The question is now', he said in 1782, 'whether we shall be a Protestant settlement or an Irish nation?' He visualised a limited form of Catholic emancipation. But the Volunteers, the real source of Grattan's power, split over the Catholic question and disbanded without securing parliamentary reform. Pitt, the English premier, who had decided that an independent Irish parliament might become 'too subservient', in his view, 'to the prejudices or opinions of the Irish nation to acquiesce in an English government', soon set about securing the self-extinction of the Irish parliament. Grattan spoke strongly against the Act of Union and the open bribery used to force it through in 1800. His last words before parliament voted itself out of existence were eloquent:

Yet I do not give up the country: I see her in a swoon, but she is not dead: though in her tomb she lies helpless and motionless, still there is on her lips a spirit of life, and on her cheek a glow of beauty —

'Thou art not conquered; beauty's ensign yet
Is crimson on thy lips and on thy cheeks,
And death's pale flag is not advanced there.'

Grattan's oratory gave voice to the best currents in Irish Protestant nationalism of the eighteenth century. The integrity and moral earnestness of his character caused him to survive in the consciousness of succeeding Irish generations in a way which

Burke, who was peripheral to the Irish situation, did not. His speeches had an impassioned eloquence at times and also a biting invective frequently exercised against corruption. His style was mannered, full of forced antithesis, of figures which are fanciful rather than imaginative. He lacked Burke's wider sweep and variety but he could be forceful within a more limited range. His epigram on Burke, 'that he was so fond of arbitrary power that he could not sleep on his pillow unless he thought the king had a right to take it from under him', shows his occasional wit and he could sometimes hit off a general situation in memorable words, as in his description of the frustration of all patriotic endeavour in Ireland as the curse of Swift — 'to have been born an Irishman, to have possessed a genius, and to have used his talents for the good of his country'.

His oratory and that of a number of his fellow-members — Henry Flood, John Philpot Curran and Hussey Burgh included — gave 'Grattan's Parliament' a reputation for oratory which was remembered in Parnell's time and even in James Joyce's early days. Sir Jonah Barrington's *Personal Sketches* (1827) and *The Rise and Fall of the Irish Nation,* (1833), although superficial, are among the most readable contemporary accounts of the period and of its duelling parliamentarians, its bucks and blades, its hectic colour of decay. When Barrington concluded his description of the fall of the Irish Protestant parliament with the words, 'Ireland as a Nation was EXTINGUISHED', he was speaking with the sentimentality which Grattan sometimes displayed about 'the middle Irish nation' and the 'revolution' of 1782. The real development of Irish political thought in the later eighteenth century and some of its best prose are to be found in the writings of the man who described that revolution as 'the most bungling, imperfect business that ever threw ridicule on a lofty epithet by answering it unworthily'.

This was Theobald Wolfe Tone (1763-98), the Dublin barrister, whose first pamphlet on Irish affairs, *A Review of the Conduct of the Administration* (1790), was written from the standpoint of a moderate reformer offended by the administration's corruption of Grattan's parliament by open bribery. 'The people of Ireland', he wrote, echoing Swift, 'are not that blatant beast that will bear any burden, provided their long ears be scratched and they are indulged in the liberty of braying'. Quoting Grattan's argument that such prostitution would sabotage parliamentary authority, he concentrated on the infringements of civil rights involved. In a pamphlet of the same year on an expected English war with Spain, he applied the Molyneux – Swift – Grattan line of argument to trade, pointing out that Ireland, which had a beneficial trade with Spain, had nothing to gain by a war in the interests of a British trading monopoly.

His power of clear exposition is perhaps best exemplified in his *Argument on Behalf of the Catholics of Ireland* (1791), which was addressed particularly to Tone's fellow-Protestants. Significantly it opened with an account of Ireland's potential and neglected resources, derived from Swift's *Short View of the State of Ireland,* and passed to the cause of frustration, English misgovernment. The Irish Volunteers, by breaking up when their demands for parliamentary reform were rejected, 'in one moment demolished the glory which five years of virtuous success had flattered them would be immortal'. Parliamentary reform was essential and must include the representation of Irishmen of all denominations:

> But it will be said that the Catholics are ignorant and therefore incapable of liberty; and I have heard men of more imagination than judgement make a flourishing declamation on the danger of blinding them, by suddenly pouring a flood of light on their eyes, which for a century have been buried in darkness. To the poetry of this I make no objection, but what is the common sense or justice of the argument? We plunge them by law, and continue them by statute, in gross ignorance, and then we make the incapacity we have created an argument for their exclusion from the common rights of man! We plead our crime in justification of itself.

In the course of his argument Tone referred to the examples of America and of France in abolishing religious tests for parliament. He thus developed the ideas of Swift and Grattan by adding to them the positive egalitarian ideas of the American and French revolutions. Where Swift had little concern for disabilities inflicted upon Catholics or Presbyterians, Tone was concerned with abolishing the divisions between Protestants, Catholics and Presbyterians. Swift had disliked the last as potential promoters of Protestant disunity; Tone thought them a potential force towards national unity since they were, he wrote, 'devoted to liberty and, throughout all its changes, enthusiastically attached to the French revolution.'

In 1792 he acted as assistant secretary of the Catholic Committee, which represented a substantial body of opinion among Catholics who had risen through trade and commerce and were in a position to protest, as John Lynch had done in early Restoration days, against the subordination of the Irish legislature by 'foreigners and sojourners', and the denial of civil and religious liberty. He had already founded in Belfast the Society of United Irishmen, strongly supported by the Presbyterians, 'for the promotion of constitutional knowledge, the abolition of bigotry in religion and politics and the equal distribution of the rights of man through all sects and denominations of Irishmen'. In 1792 and 1793 he wrote pamphlets signed 'A Liberty Boy' and 'A Liberty Weaver', thus identifying himself again with Swift; but by that time he was a convinced republican and separatist who escaped arrest in 1794 by going to America.

Tone's journals and autobiographical writings, although not published until 1826, provide a fascinating record of events in Ireland from 1790-93; they tell of his life in America from where, on the verge of becoming a New Jersey farmer, he responded to his Irish associates' requests and sailed for France to seek military aid for Ireland, and give a close account of the Bantry Bay and Texel expeditions of 1796 and 1797. They also describe his military service in the French army and the events leading up to the third French expedition which resulted in his capture and death.

Tone's mercurial temperament and resolute character are shown engagingly in his mixture of accurate description, reflections on political and military events, witty sketches of characters and situations. His style is without affectation. His journal was written chiefly for his wife; he describes it jokingly to her as 'a thousand times wittier than Swift's, as in justice it ought; for it is written for one a thousand times more amiable than Stella'. His pages contain, besides intimate sketches of his Irish associates, some unforgettable pictures of Carnot, Grouchy, Hoche and, most strikingly, of Buonaparte:

> General Desaix brought Lewines and me this morning and introduced us to Buonaparte, at his house in the Rue Chantereine. He lives in the greatest simplicity; his house is small, but neat, and all the furniture and ornaments in the most classical taste. He is about five feet six inches high,

slender and well made, but stoops considerably; he looks at least ten years older than he is, owing to the great fatigues he underwent in his immortal campaign of Italy. His face is that of a profound thinker, but bears no marks of that great enthusiasm and unceasing activity by which he has been so much distinguished. It is rather to my mind, the countenance of a mathematician than of a general. He has a fine eye, and a great firmness about his mouth; he speaks low and hollow. So much for his manner and figure ... I then observed that I did not pretend to be of the smallest use to him whilst we were in France, but that I hoped to be serviceable to him on the other side of the water; that I did not give myself to him at all for a military man, having neither the knowledge nor the experience that would justify me in charging myself with any function. *'Mais vous étes brave'* said he, interrupting me. I replied that, when the occasion presented itself, that would appear; *'Eh bien'*, said he, *'cela suffit.'* We then took our leave.

Tone's political thought, a logical development of Swift's and Grattan's, made him the founder of modern Irish republicanism. The quality of his autobiographical and political writings ranks them with the best that came out of Ireland in the eighteenth century.

Portrait of Dean Swift by Isaac Whood.
Courtesy of the National Gallery of Ireland.

Maria Edgeworth. After Chappel. Courtesy of the National Gallery of Ireland.

PART III
The Nineteenth Century
to the Revival

CHAPTER XI

Fiction

In nineteenth century Ireland a tradition of Irish writing in English struggled into existence through the first half of the century. Its main strength was in fiction, its main readers the English public, who wished to understand the troubled country to the west, theoretically united with them, yet continually in agitation. In Ireland agitation was inevitable; the land question and the Catholic question were still unsettled, the Union a mere pretence. Through the Catholic Association, founded in 1823, Daniel O'Connell called into existence a huge Catholic democratic movement, which enforced a limited form of Catholic Emancipation in 1829; it did not abolish tithes or absenteeism; widespread land-agitation continued. In 1840 O'Connell founded the Repeal Association and rallied huge mass-meetings behind it, only to see his power collapse when he called off a vast culminating meeting at Clontarf in 1843, in compliance with a government ban. His lack of an agrarian policy had already caused a rift with the Young Ireland movement led by Thomas Davis.

The fiction written by Irish writers during this period was rarely of first calibre. They presented in varying degrees of power and fidelity a picture of the Ireland they knew or imagined. But it was not 'written down in fiery shorthand' as Yeats romantically remarked. It was in fact too involved with explanation, didacticism or defence, for it was bedevilled at every hand's turn by political considerations in addition to current conventions. Yet it was a tradition on which one could build in times more favourable to creative writing and it proved of some value to subsequent writers.

The Famine struck in 1845, halving Ireland's population by death and emigration over the next decade. It also hastened the decline of Irish by striking the Gaelic-speaking areas of the west more severely. The Young Ireland rising of 1848 and the Fenian rising of 1867 were both abortive protests in arms against misgovernment and the refusal of reform. Hope had risen with the progress of the Tenant Right movement of the fifties only to be dashed by the defection of Sadleir and Keogh in 1852. It revived in 1879 with the foundation of the Land League by Michael Davitt (1846 - 1907) and the rise of Parnell (1846-91) as leader of the Home Rule movement. Their junction, the conversion of Gladstone to Home Rule, and some improving land acts made the eighteen-eighties a time of some promise. Then in 1890 came the fall and in 1891 the death of Parnell. A period of Irish frustration ended the century.

Irish regional fiction in English began during the first half of the nineteenth century. It was initiated by the publication in 1800 of *Castle Rackrent* by Maria Edgeworth (1767 - 1849). This short novel is an account by Thady Quirk, an old steward of the Rackrent estate, of its decline and fall under the mismanagement and neglect of four successive squires.

The first, Sir Patrick Rackrent, is good-natured but shiftless, extravagant, and drunken; 'A monument of old Irish hospitality', according to his tombstone. Next comes Sir Murtagh, skinflint and miser, a grinding master whose tenants are shackled by unjust leases, which compel them to give him much free labour, and by fear, which exacts from them 'presents' of all their best produce, so that they gradually break and disappear. Sir Murtagh's grim determination to teach them the law of landlord and tenant thus recoils on his own estate, part of which has to be sold to pay for his litigation. 'But he was a very learned man in the law', adds Thady, apologetically, with an unconscious irony which runs through all his history of the Rackrents.

The grasping and litigious Sir Murtagh is succeeded by the spendthrift Sir Kit, who leaves everything in the hands of his agent, Jason Quirk, the son of Thady, while he himself becomes an absentee landlord and lives, says Thady, 'to the honour of his country abroad, which I was proud to hear of'. His return, with a rich Jewish wife, whom he imprisons at Castle Rackrent, is merely the prelude to lavish spending, further debts and finally his own death in a duel and the departure of his wife for England. The Rackrent cycle of disaster is completed by Sir Condy Rackrent, profligate and drunken, a throwback to Sir Patrick. His last illness is brought on, appropriately enough, by his efforts to emulate Sir Patrick's drinking-feats; and so the Rackrent estate, which has been hastening to its end 'just as you see the ducks in the chicken-yard, just after their heads are cut off by the cook, running round and round faster than when alive', passes from the Rackrents to the crafty agent, Jason Quirk, who for years has been exploiting his own knowledge of the law and his masters' weaknesses to this end.

The device of telling this story through a narrator who 'has a great regard for the family' gives it a sustained irony of tone, while the cycle of ruin from Sir Patrick to Sir Condy gives it effective form. It is told in a racy, idiomatic prose which is easy to follow and yet has the stamp of strangeness. The narrator himself, old Thady, with his muddle-headed apologies for four successive irresponsibles, his loyal determination to 'follow the fortunes of them that have none left', his familiarity with the intricacies of Irish land law and popular customs, is more authentic, more clearly defined as an individual than any of his masters or their unhappy wives. Maria Edgeworth knew such a man when she came from England to her father's County Longford estate in 1782 at the age of fifteen and grew so familiar with his dialect and character that when 'for mere amusement, without any idea of publishing, I began to write a family history as Thady would tell it, he seemed to stand beside me and dictate; and I wrote as fast as my pen would go'. The spontaneity of the narrative and the authenticity of Thady and of the family anecdotes on which his history is based are thus explicable.

It is clear that Maria Edgeworth was writing about the landlords of her own time. Yet her preface says that 'the race of the Rackrents has long since been extinct in Ireland'. These words were written by Maria's father, Richard Lovell Edgeworth, to avoid giving offence to the government. He himself was a good landlord but so cautious that he would not allow classical history to be taught in his school because it conveyed ideas of democracy and liberty. His influence on his daughter and her own disposition favoured the inculcation of right and prudent conduct: her Irish novels, they agreed, should not encourage 'agitators' but should point out to her readers, mainly English, the necessity of reforming Irish landlords, particularly the absentees.

This was the theme of her next two novels with an Irish setting, *Ennui* (1809) and *The Absentee* (1812). Both were similar in plot: in *Ennui* young Lord Glenthorn, bored with fashionable life in England, arrives as a last resort at his own Irish estate and becomes a conscientious improving landlord, only to discover that the proper legal heir to the estate is a humble tenant, his foster-brother, Christy O'Donohue. Despite Christy's plea to 'say nothing to nobody but just keep asy on, even as we are', the noble Glenthorn assembles the tenantry, calls on them to witness that 'I voluntarily give up the fortune I enjoyed, the moment I discovered it was not justly mine', and returns to England. There his success as a barrister is counterpointed by the failure of the incompetent Christy, who accidentally burns down the Big House, mismanages the estate and implores Glenthorn to return to rule over a grateful peasantry.

The Absentee has a similar hero, young Lord Colambre, whose parents, the Clonbronys, are in many ways typical of the Anglo-Irish who after the Union left their estates in their agents' hands and lived in London, where they endeavoured to climb in a society which ate their dinners but really despised them. Lord Colambre, as an Irishman, is perplexed by the problem of belonging to a nation supposed to have lost its separate identity by the Union. The problem brings him to Ireland. He finds in Dublin a process of transition at work by which the rising Catholic middle classes are stepping into the absentees' shoes and are inheriting also their social pretenses. Travelling incognito to the family estate, he suddenly sees the effects of absentee neglect and squandering in the squalor of his own town, with its wretched cabins and its ragged children. This is the cost of his parents' social climbing; like Sir Kit Rackrent, they have 'left all to the agent', and the agent Garraghty, like Jason Quirk, is a rack-renter who plays off master and tenant against each other. He is about to gain control of the estate when Colambre reveals his identity, foils the villain and persuades his own family to return to the estate whose tenants, rid of the wicked agent, greet it with a blind harper and tears of joy.

The Absentee, which was first planned as a play, was rejected by Sheridan on the grounds that the Lord Chamberlain would never license it for production owing to the disturbed state of Ireland; but its original form probably accounts for its structural superiority to *Ennui.* It also goes somewhat deeper into the Irish scene: although its peasants are a cardboard lot, Maria Edgeworth, in her pictures of native Irish gentry and of the antiquarian, Count O'Halloran, a descendant of the Gaelic aristocracy who had left Ireland with the Wild Geese and had returned hastily from a revolutionary Europe, seems to be trying to come to somewhat uneasy terms with the older civilisation which they represent; her hero, Colambre, eventually marries a girl of old Irish stock, once it is clear that she is not, as alleged, illegitimate, 'an object which his prudence told him ought to be insurmountable'.

Her last Irish novel, *Ormond* (1817), carries this attempt still further. Harry Ormond, an orphan, has been raised by foster-parents in an Irish cottage and has to choose between the worlds of his two uncles; Sir Ulick O'Shane, the polished, affable intriguer in the political milieu of the ascendancy in its hey-day in Dublin about 1770, and Cornelius O'Shane, jovial and generous, choleric and obstinate, who lives among his own tenantry on the Black Isles off the west coast of Ireland. Both are of Gaelic stock, but the former has discarded his traditional loyalties for the sake of the power offered by Dublin Castle to venal placemen, while 'King Corny' prefers the mixture of tribal rule and outlawry of the older Gaelic system. He dispenses rough justice to his tenants, keeps a Catholic chaplain, and leads a free and easy, hard-drinking life of feudal but decaying glory. After both his uncles die, Ormond, who has inherited a fortune, marries the daughter of a righteous and improving Anglo-Irish landlord, acquires the Black Isles and returns there to rule over a grateful tenantry for whom, we may readily imagine, the free and easy life was thenceforward changed, changed utterly by this young man whose salvation, we are told, began when his future mother-in-law countered the evil effects of his reading *Tom Jones* by placing in his hands Richardson's story of an impossibly virtuous male, *Sir Charles Grandison.*

Although *Ormond* moves outside the Anglo-Irish axis of London and an Irish estate, its real theme is that of all these Irish novels, the responsibility of the Anglo-Irish landed class, and its literary fault is that of all her novels, English or Irish, a didactic and utilitarian purpose. Yet, *en route,* she had enough of the novelist's art to write with an authenticity, unusual at that time, about the Irish scene. Her work encouraged Walter Scott to develop the Scottish regional novel.

It also interested a wider circle of English readers in a society about which they had been badly informed. Maria was no Jane Austen but the comparative instability of Irish society did not breed the latter's kind of objectivity. Edgeworthstown had been briefly threatened by the '98 insurgents; following the Union the rise of O'Connell seemed to threaten the whole system. Hence, after *Ormond,* she wrote no more novels about Ireland; 'realities are too strong, party passions too violent, to bear to see, or to care to look at their faces in the looking-glass', she wrote to her brother in 1820, before Catholic Emancipation had been conceded. Repeal and the land question then became the dominant issues.

Meanwhile her friend, Mary Leadbeater, wrote directly and vividly about village life. Her *Annals of Ballitore,* a chronicle of events from 1766 to 1824, including the rising of 1798, were published as *The Leadbeater Papers* in 1862.

While the Irish novels of Maria Edgeworth form only a small part of her large literary output, which is properly classed with the minor English novels of that time, all the work of William Carleton was concerned with Ireland. He was the first home-based Irish writer of fiction to support himself for the greater part of his life, however precariously, by his pen; which indicates the growth of interest in Irish regional fiction for which Edgeworth had set a fashion. Where her life was sheltered, Carleton was exposed to many harsh winds of circumstance from an early age. He came from the other side of the social divide, from the hidden Ireland which she but dimly understood.

He was born in 1794 of Gaelic-speaking Irish stock whose ancestors had been dispossessed in the seventeenth century by the Ulster plantations; his father had settled in County Tyrone in a district where the Catholic tenant-farmers tilled hungry holdings and looked with envy at the broader and richer acres of the Scots-Irish planters. The older culture lived on in his parents, from whom he heard Gaelic poems, stories, songs and folklore. He acquired fluent Latin and English from hedge-schoolmasters and classical masters and at nineteen, destined by his parents for the priesthood, his wanderings as a 'poor scholar' took him around the neighbouring counties and eventually, both vocation and religion discarded, to Dublin.

Carleton's story up to this point is told in his autobiography, which he began in his last years and never completed. It was first published in D.J. O'Donoghue's *Life of William Carleton* in 1896 but is perhaps an indispensable preliminary to reading his fiction; for it shows his background and tells of his life as athlete, pilgrim, wandering scholar, 'spoiled priest', temporary Ribbonman, itinerant schoolmaster, and of his experiences of a wide variety of Irish people and events. He was potentially an Irish Gorki, whose university was 'the book of the people', for he possessed remarkable creative talent. But he first discovered this talent by chance, when Caesar Otway, a leading proselytiser, recruited him as a writer for *The Christian Examiner,* to which he contributed a number of stories designed to illustrate the superstitions of the Catholic Irish. They were sectarian in tone but contained some remarkable characters and scenes. Later, some sympathetic studies of Catholics caused a break with Otway in 1831 and during the next decade Carleton wrote for new periodicals which in the eighteen-thirties published articles and stories. Many of them were short-lived; Ireland lacked a substantial English-reading public and English periodicals competed for those who were well-to-do. The most lasting were the *Dublin University Magazine* (1833-77), founded in the Protestant interest by a T.C.D. group, which expanded its literary content under the editorship of Isaac Butt in 1834 and of Charles Lever (1842-45); and the *Dublin Review* (1836-69). The latter was published in London and attracted the interest of those Catholics in England and Ireland who were better-off and conservatively nationalistic. Both journals offered scope to Carleton. By 1833 two volumes of his *Traits and Stories of the Irish Peasantry* had been published. A German translation appeared in Leipzig in 1837, by which time he had gained a reputation in England and America.

Traits and Stories is the work by which Carleton is best remembered. Planned originally as a series of tales told around the fire, it developed into a number of long, rambling stories independent of each other and each loosely knit around some character or situation. The central character of 'Denis O'Shaughnessy going to Maynooth' is a young farming lad, forward in learning and disputation, who is ambitious for the priesthood, not because of any real vocation but in order to obtain status and culinary comfort; the lengthy intrigues of his father with the local clergy secure admission to Maynooth, but at the first opportunity Denis returns home and gets married. The story is slanted and the ending abrupt, but the character of Denis, a comic Milton church-outed by his fondness for the girls, delighting in the effect produced by his bog-Latin and his chop-logic, and cheered on by his proud father at every turn of his ostentatious disputations, has a crude comic vitality. So has Mat Kavanagh, the philomath of 'The Hedge School', who rules over his ragged pupils with slapdash authority and learning, and who is in addition the local scribe and head Ribbonman of his area. The plot is little more than the incident of Matt's arrest tacked on to a broadly comic account of this rambunctious character and his school. Behind its comedy is a serious record of the circumstances of the hedge-schools, the people's earnest desire for learning, the mediaeval survival of public disputation in the battles of the philomaths against challenging scholars, the co-operative support which supplied them with sod-houses and sustenance, reverence and authority; and it is the accumulation of authentic background detail, together with lively and authentic, if somewhat heightened dialogue, which gives Mat Kavanagh such vitality and force.

The basis of Carleton's literary power was intimacy with his subject. He had lived in the cabins which Maria Edgeworth had seen from the outside or had dutifully visited; he knew at first hand the land-hunger of landless men and the violence which could flower suddenly in a land tilled by labourers without hope. Some of his best stories convey that violence well; 'Wildgoose Lodge' shows it starkly in its local agrarian form, 'The Party-Fight and Funeral' in its sectarian form, 'The Battle of the Factions' in its inter-family form. Land-hunger underlies all three conflicts, whether expressed in Ribbonmen's attacks on landlords and consequent hangings, in the murderous party-fight of Orangemen with Whiteboy Catholics or in the dispute between the O'Hallaghans and the O'Callaghans which, beginning over a stream which 'changed its mind' and altered a disputed boundary between farms, ends in a bloody faction-fight in which the well-intentioned and peaceable John O'Callaghan is slain by the scythe-wielding brother of his betrothed; she in turn kills her brother and the shock causes her madness.

Carleton's power of narration is perhaps seen best in the last two of these stories, for 'The Party-Fight and Funeral', which centres around Denis Kelly, a mettlesome but quarrelsome young man full of 'blackthorn ambition', is told from the outside by a detached, slightly disapproving observer who records with great fidelity the process of eviction, land-grabbing, raiding and revenge which underlies the eventual meeting in single-combat between Kelly and the Orangeman, Grimes; while 'The Battle of the Factions' is told by hedge-school master Frayne in the jocular, racy style of a partisan connoisseur of faction fighting. In the first story the power comes from the slow cumulative effect of a deliberate style which conveys the single combat with an epic strength. The second has something of the 'gaiety and horror' of the ballad 'Johnny I hardly knew you', for the tragedy of its star-crossed lovers, whose marriage would have reconciled the warring factions which eventually destroy them both, is counterpointed by the jocularity of the narrator who speaks with approval of the deadly instrument of faction-fighting, the lead-filled cudgel with its 'widow-and-orphan-making quality, a child-bereaving touch, altogether very desirable', and is full of casual euphemisms about conflicts in which a man can 'get his jaw very dacently divided into three halves' or can be left 'lying in a state of imperception'. The terrible climax is reached via a graveyard battle and a merry shower of skulls and bones, 'so that it might truly be said, the bones of contention were numerous'. The narrator concludes with a lament for the poor madwoman, 'a fair ruin, but silent, melancholy and beautiful as the moon in the summer heaven', and typically adds that his own grandfather, a judge of pretty fighting, 'condemns the scythe and every other weapon except the cudgels', which, to a connoisseur, are the only instruments of 'nate fighting'.

Some of Carleton's stories are little more than anecdotes given depth by detail; others follow the method of one of his fictitious narrators who announces that he 'will commence a small sub-narration, which will afterwards emerge into the parent stream of the story', and it sometimes happens that several narrators manage to divert the mainstream from its course. Although he often tells his story in the guise of an educated observer — 'a gintleman on a horse, wid boots and spurs on him, that's looking in at us', as one of his peasants says — he is perhaps at his best, as a narrator, when speaking in the voice of one of the people. In the former role, that of 'one well acquainted with the Irish peasant', he is often a faithful recorder but strikes many false notes and is full of moral strictures; in the latter there is a truer ring but often an air of derision or of forced whimsicality and drollery when dealing with the people. Both roles are revealing about the conditions of Irish fiction-writing; one either had to be on the side of the governing class or to convey the impression that the people were interesting, droll but irresponsible, and that, as Carleton put it, 'when no political or religious feeling influences the heart and principles of an Irish peasant, he is singularly sincere and faithful in his attachments'. The marvel is that, despite all these limit-ations, the abundant life of the people crams his stories with vitality. What comes over, along with the wit and whimsicality of the Irish peasantry, is their mercurial temperament, close to the changes of nature, their deep sense of religion and of learning, the ingrained wiliness and duplicity, humanity and savagery, of a submerged, downtrodden and land-hungry people just beginning to emerge from a mediaeval and feudal past into a modern world.

Between 1839, when his reputation as a writer at home and abroad had been established by *Traits and Stories,* and 1862, Carleton wrote some dozen novels which won him the title of 'the peasant novelist'. The first of these, *Fardorougha, the Miser* (1839), is perhaps the best, for the miser himself, torn between greed for money and affection for his son, is well-drawn and the circumstances by which greed dominates him and helps to bring disaster upon the young man are convincingly related. Of all Carleton's novels, this is freest from moralistic strictures. Then in 1845 appeared *Valentine M'Clutchy, the Irish Agent,* which marked a different approach to the Irish scene, prefaced by Carleton's statement that 'Within the last few years a more enlarged knowledge of life and a more matured intercourse with society have enabled me to overcome many absurd prejudices with which I was imbued.' Where his previous works were written for periodicals with an ascendancy policy, he wrote this novel for *The Nation,* to catch the rising tide of popular feeling, but Thomas Davis, whose personal influence had helped this change in Carleton, thought that this spasmodically powerful novel would have more influence if published separately. Although melodramatic and sentimental, it manipulated stock characters like Phineas Lucre and Solomon M'Slime to attack rack-renting and evictions with vigour.

Its popularity launched Carleton on a series of somewhat wearisome didactic 'Tales for the People': *Art Maguire or the Broken Pledge* in support of Father Mathew's temperance crusade, *Parra Sashta or the History of Paddy-go-Easy,* to inculcate industry in the peasantry, *Rody the Rover or the Ribbonman* to warn the people against secret societies, which were frequently riddled with *agents provocateurs* like Rody himself. These works, more tracts than tales, added little to his literary reputation but showed that he could indict misgovernment as well as revolution, landlord cruelty as well as peasant shiftlessness and intemperance; so that by 1846, alternately applauded, derided, wooed and denounced by different interests, he was still the centre of Irish literary attention.

In 1846, when the Great Famine was a year old, Carleton wrote the *Black Prophet* for the *Dublin University Magazine.* This novel, which used his experiences of famines in 1817 and 1822, was prophetic about the magnitude of the contemporary disaster, appearing during its worst year, Black '47. It is a strange story, which is still arresting and tragic, not because of its involved plot, but because of the authenticity of its background of famine. Across its horizons wander gaunt multitudes of starving people. 'There was in the eyes of all a dull and languid motion, as if they turned in their sockets by an effort.' The roads are black with funerals; waiting near soup kitchens and relief works are 'wild crowds ragged, sickly and wasted away to skin and bone struggling for the dole of charity'. Long lines of provision-carts, full of grain *en route* to the ports, pass by naked corpses and starving mobs. They are attacked sometimes and the surviving attackers stagger away under huge loads, while old men and women may be seen hirpling homewards . . . a kind of dim exulting joy feebly blazing in their heavy eyes and a wild sense of unexpected good fortune working in unnatural play upon the muscles of their wrinkled and miserable faces.
The children are living skeletons, wan and yellow; any surviving dogs are mere ribs and skin, their hungry howls blending at night with the death-wails of the people.

Against this background moves the central figure, a tall,

sinister, crooked-nosed 'prophecy man', Black Donnel. Such men could be met with long after Carleton's day; they were wanderers who recited their set prophecies, compounded of revelation and imagination, in a high monotone. Even this fantastic character is credible as he chants the doom that the rotting crops, the unhealthy air and the rain foretell:

> Doesn't the sky without a sun, the heavy clouds, an' the angry fire of the West foretell it? Isn't the airth a page of prophecy and the sky a page of prophecy, where every man may read of famine, pestilence and death? The airth is softened for the grave, an' in the black clouds of heaven you may see the death-hearse movin' slowly along — funeral after funeral — funeral after funeral — an' nothin' to folly them but lamentation an' woe, by the widow and orphan — the fatherless, the motherless and the childless — woe an' lamentation — lamentation an' woe.

He was indeed, as Carleton may have felt, a symbol of the passing of his Ireland, for the Famine, which wiped out whole communities, drove survivors to the towns or to the coffin-ships, and reduced multitudes of human beings to hungry animals, also meant the loss of much communal feeling, hospitality, custom, observance and tradition. It was the death-blow to the Gaelic world of his parents, for it hit the Gaelic-speaking areas worst: and it left a deep scar on the self-respect and independence of his people, a despair and resentment out of which nothing could arouse them collectively except the prospect of a successful struggle for land.

Only one or two novels of these middle years recaptured anything of Carleton's old power. *The Emigrants of Ahadarra* (1848) is really a study of the effect of evictions and emigration on his own Clogher valley of County Tyrone. Its plot is contrived and artificial but Carleton, centring it in the townland of Ahadarra, weaves into it a real theme handled with understanding and insight: the pull of emigration set against the desire to cling to the land, despite its hardships, because to leave it is to tear up one's roots of affection, association and memory. The simple words of Tom McMahon sum it up:

> For many a long year have our names been — but no matter — the time has come at last and the McMahons of Carriglass and Ahadarra will be known no more. It wasn't our fault; we were willing to live.

Famine was only the immediate cause of Ireland's trouble, Carleton stated in his preface; the real cause was the land-system. Although he was careful to balance this view by warning the people against insurrection, the book caused tremors among the more conservative of his friends, who had joined with nationalists in a move to secure him a government pension. A friend of Maria Edgeworth wrote her in 1848 to tell her how he had impressed upon the Viceroy, Clarendon, the importance of detaching a writer, who had such influence with the middle classes, from dangerous purposes. Carleton got his pension and was immediately attacked in the Dublin press as a venal writer. *The Tithe Proctor,* written in 1847 and published in 1849, showed little evidence of this. It was a novel of occasional power, polemical in its indictment of tithes, landlords, and revolutionaries. Its preface attacked nationalists who wanted only the favourable side of Irish life depicted in novels and, less reasonably, the vicious nature of all Repealers.

Carleton's later novels have little interest as literature today and are more likely to interest the social historian; they record many traditional folk-tales, customs and types, but are weak in creative power and show the strain of hackwork. He was always too ready to satisfy his readers' wish for intricate plots, lurid melodrama and moral exhortations. Yet he could make a scene come alive by just the right touch of detail: the urbane ritual of mockery preceding a faction fight; the young women carrying their boots to the chapel, then donning them before entering; the little girl so lost in admiration of a priest's boots that she forgets to baste a goose. This intimacy, born of exact recollection, is a continual source of strength in his work, particularly in his depiction of country people. In general he failed to depict the landed class; he lacked intimacy with it, as he confessed, 'except for a peep into a squire's house or an outside glance at a courtly gathering'. Thus he is a good counterpart to Maria Edgeworth.

His novels' merits are usually submerged by prolixity; less hampered, although often threatened by it, are his short stories. Even in his best work his 'messages', although intermittent, often weaken the effect of some scene of power; but he was continually bedevilled by his own need to survive. Some of his enduring strength comes from the authenticity of speech of his rural characters. Even where it is heightened for comedy, it usually has a ring of truth. 'Quicken yourself with the hydraulics', calls Mat

Kavanagh to his wife, who is at the pump getting water to cure his hangover, 'or the best school master in Ireland is gone to the abode of Euclid and Pythagoras, that first invented the multiplication-table.' Mat, Carleton said, was drawn from life; and his unfinished autobiography sketches many stranger types. It also shows how powerfully he could write when simply setting down his own experiences without any literary market in mind. There are unforgettable descriptions of the roadside gibbets with the putrefying corpses of Ribbonmen that he saw at every cross-road on his way from Louth in 1818 and of Dublin down-and-outs who were his companions when he reached the city.

Before his death in 1869 Carleton was honoured there by some seven thousand people, including many foreigners, who thus gave public assent to his claim that he had risen up from a humble cottage and described a whole nation. The claim is true enough. He was the first and perhaps the only Irish writer of the nineteenth century to depict the mass of the Irish people before the Famine with anything approaching real literary power. At his best he was a first-rate writer.

Among his contemporaries was Charles Lever (1806-72), probably the most popular Irish novelist of the time. Born in Dublin, he was the son of a prosperous builder from Lancashire. He had a gay, carefree life of it at Trinity College, Dublin, studied medicine in Dublin and Germany, and travelled to American and Canada before working as a dispensary doctor in various provincial towns in Ireland. In this capacity he met the sporting parson and writer, William Hamilton Maxwell, who lived at Balla, 'where game was abundant and parishioners scarce', and whose readable book *Wild Sports of the West* was a popular success. Maxwell seems to have suggested a literary career to Lever, who had written only a few humorous sketches for various papers. A few years later, when he was practising in Brussels, he began to contribute *The Confessions of Harry Lorrequer* (1839) to the *Dublin University Magazine*. Lorrequer, his author said, was invented 'to give what consistency I might to a mass of incongruous adventure', and the story was 'little other than a notebook of absurd and laughable incidents'. Anecdotes, escapades, practical jokes, wagers, duels, drinking-bouts and mistakes of identity, were assembled around the dashing and absurd dragoon, a young man of phenomenal capacity for strong drink, horse-play, hoaxes, fighting and story-telling. The magazine's circulation rose steadily and when Lorrequer's rollicking career was finally guillotined — with the words 'The next day I got married. The End.' — Lever replaced him by *Charles O'Malley, The Irish Dragoon,* a slightly more serious hero who, after a riotous period at Trinity, fights in the Peninsular wars and returns to Ireland to live as a reforming landlord on his western estate. The serious military events are counterpointed by O'Malley's comic manservant, Mickey Free, with his inevitable fund of droll adventures, anecdotes and songs.

The success of these two books brought Lever back from Brussels to edit the *Dublin University Magazine* from 1842 to 1845. This involved him directly with politics. The magazine, he wrote editorially, was 'the steady defender of the Protestantism of these realms', and its policy reflected the hostile attitude of the establishment to O'Connell, repeal and the growing power of the Catholic clergy. During these three years verbal clashes with Carleton and O'Connell, attacks by diehard Tory papers who thought him too liberal, and two controversies which all but reached duelling-point, were among his troubles. He still managed to publish four more novels: *Jack Hinton, Tom Burke of Ours, Arthur O'Leary* — more or less in the *Charles O'Malley* line — and *The O'Donoghue,* a poor attempt at an historical novel. But in 1845 ill-health and the feeling that he was writing himself out caused him to leave Ireland. The rest of his life was spent chiefly in Florence, where he settled down to steady writing in Spezzia, where he was British vice-consul, and in Trieste, as consul.

Lever wrote over thirty novels. The earlier ones are superficial: the heroine, for example, is usually brought briefly on-stage whenever the hero runs out of anecdotes or requires, through some lover's quarrel, an excuse to return to campaigning. But some of the anecdotes are entertaining and most of the battle-scenes well done. From the highly coloured panorama of minor characters — hard-drinking squires, hard-riding Galway horsewomen, drunken dragoons, convivial priests, droll servants, crafty lawyers and intriguing politicians — a few, like the unaffected Baby Blake or the purple-faced Major Monsoon, attain a life usually missing from the principal characters; villains and heroes are usually stereotypes; situations are repeated with little variation. Lever's nickname, Doctor Quicksilver, hits off his mercurial temperament. He was convivial, extravagantly hospitable and impressed Thackeray, Trollope and others by his genial, witty conversation, full of anecdotes and sparkling take-offs. The anecdote was his natural forte. Hence the ease and verve of his early work.

He had begun to take the novelist's art seriously before he left Dublin, where he had written but not yet published *St. Patrick's Eve* and *The Knight of Gwynne*. The former, based on his experience as a doctor in cholera-striken areas, made a serious attempt to show how famine and rack-renting could drive tenants to attack landlords. Although short and rather slight, it caused Tory attacks on Lever as a repealer. *The Knight of Gwynne* was a more solid work about the downfall of Grattan's parliament but its serious characters are insipid, there is no real sense of the conflicts which the Union aroused, although the intrigues of Castlereagh and his henchman, Con Heffernan, and the occasional adventures of Bagenal Daly, the duellist, and Freney, the outlaw, give some life to the novel.

In *The Martins of Cro' Martin* Lever carried this closer scrutiny of the Irish land system into the period after Catholic Emancipation. The older generation of Martins are either indifferent or hostile to their tenants; young Mary Martin busies herself, like Maria Edgeworth, in organising their methods of farming, draining and afforestation. Her good intentions are frustrated by the division between landlords and people, who are played off against each other by the English parties and their agents. A strong character in the story is the ironical old barrister, Repton, who can remember Grattan's time and who warns Mary that she has come too late: 'The old social compact between Proprietor and Peasant is repealed', he tells her:

> Now, if your grandfather had pursued the path that you are doing today, this crisis might never have arrived; but he did not, young lady. He lived like a real gentleman; he hunted, and drank, and feasted, and rack-rented, and horse-whipped all around him; and what with duelling of a morning and drinking overnight, he taught the people a code of morals that has assumed all the compactness of a system.

The Martin estate drifts into the Encumbered Estates Court, the logical development of the process seen in *Castle Rackrent* written half a century before. By his time Lever could look at it more objectively; on the Continent he realised that it was merely one aspect of a widespread European decay of landed power.

Although he returned repeatedly to the Irish scene in his later novels, it was only incidental to his study of the blunders and affectations of English and of Irish families abroad, the glittering follies of continental society and the parasitic swindlers who preyed on it. This kind of mixture was the staple formula of his later novels, whose occasional sparkle in minor characters and dialogue was usually spoiled by weak construction. The success of his slapdash novels, the pressure of initial publication in serial form, financial strain and his own temperament combined to prevent his development; and, like many of his English counterparts, he was prepared, as his letters show, to add or to subtract characters and incidents in accordance with popular demand. For all that, it is impossible to see him only in the terms of Thackeray's satirical novel, *Harry Rollicker*.

The work of Edgeworth, Carleton and Lever indicates the growing taste for Irish fiction among English readers in the period between the Union and the Famine. After the Union they wished to know more about Ireland but were handicapped by many prejudices or misunderstandings and by the official reports and commissions on Irish crime, disaffection and disregard of English law. The whole situation was bedevilled by the fact that the Union, in Byron's phrase, had been 'the union of a shark with its prey' and had left the religious and social situation still controlled by ascendancy and English power. Where the English novel had reached a degree of sophistication and objectivity in the realistic depiction of English society, the Irish presentation of Ireland was only beginning and, if it did not take an escapist form, was faced with the necessity of explanation, of didacticism, or in more venal writers, of pandering to existing prejudices.

The Irish novels of Lady Morgan (1783-1859) clearly belong to escapist writing. Born in Dublin, Sydney Owenson was the daughter of an Irish actor named originally MacEoin, anglicised to Owenson, who specialised in stage-Irish parts. Her novel, *The Wild Irish Girl* (1806), set in Connacht, centres around Innismore, a dispossessed noble of the old Irish order who lives in his ruined castle by the sea, where a young Anglo-Irish landlord meets the wild Irish girl, Glorvina, the harp-playing, romantic heroine. Their romance is conducted amid moonlit historic ruins, poor but loyal peasants, and Atlantic tempests, interspersed with lengthy information about Irish customs and antiquities, presented with a nostalgic sentimentality. It is a kind of Gothic fantasy blended with impassioned appeals about Ireland's ancient glories and it had an extraordinary success. Sydney Owenson became the centre of a Glorvina cult and after her marriage to Charles Morgan, an English physician of liberal sympathies, wrote *O'Donnel* (1814), whose hero, a Catholic nobleman, returns from service in the Austrian army and eventually, through a series of incredible happenings, regains his Irish estates. *Florence Mac Carthy* (1818) follows the same recipe, but is interesting because it adds to the study of the native Irish noble an examination of a corresponding pride of ancestry among those Anglo-Irish who had opposed the Union and who later became committed to the Irish cause. This theme also appears in *The O'Briens and the O'Flahertys* (1827), where Lord Arranmore, an adherent of Grattan's party, is pushed by the denial of reform into the United Irishmen, has to flee to France and ends up as one of Napoleon's generals. Her novels suffer from sentimentality, distortions of history and cardboard characters. On the other hand their popularity and even their polemics had some effect in winning sympathy, however sentimental, for the Catholic Irish at a time when Catholic Emancipation was in train; but she was a determined Whig; O'Connell and his repeal mobs were a reality she could not face. An escapist, in her Dublin salon as in her novels, which never really face up to genuine issues, she left Ireland in 1837.

Among the visitors to her salon were two Dubliners who added slightly to the Irish fiction of the day. Charles Maturin (1782-1824) had published *The Fatal Revenge or the Family of Montorio,* a Gothic romance, in 1807. In 1808 he tried to emulate Lady Morgan by bringing out *The Wild Irish Boy* and in 1812 *The Milesian Chief.* Justifiably dissatisfied with these experiments, Maturin returned to the field of Gothic horror, in which his most noted production, *Melmoth the Wanderer* (1820), won him a wide if ephemeral European reputation.

The other Dubliner was Samuel Lover (1797-1868), journalist, dramatist, popular entertainer, best known as a song-writer in London and Dublin. Lady Morgan is said to have urged him to present the genuine Irish character in song; the result was a number of sentimental ditties, full of synthetic charm, roguery and drollery. Lover's best known novel has similar ingredients; *Handy Andy* (1842) is simply an account of the blunders of a comic but faithful servant; usually described at the time as 'irresistibly droll', it may still be found amusing in places. Of Lover's other writings only *Legends and Stories of Ireland* (1831) need be mentioned. They were written to cater for a demand which Thomas Crofton Croker had initiated by publishing *Fairy Legends and Traditions of the South of Ireland* in 1825. Croker described his own method as 'hunting-up and bagging all the "grey superstitions" I could fall in with'. His work, although displaying contempt for his informants, still has some slight value for the folklorist and some of his tales are still readable; but neither in these nor in Lover's does one find much literary quality. Yeats was to write of Lover and Croker that they 'imagined the country as a humorist's Arcadia' and helped to create the stage Irishman. While this is true enough it is also true that such stories aroused a serious interest in Irish folk-tales in Grimm and other European folklorists, and also created a market which a later generation of Irish writers, including Yeats himself, was to supply.

The possibilities of this market had been suggested to Croker by a fellow Corkman, William Maginn (1793-1842), contributor to and editor of several London magazines. He and Francis Sylvester Mahony (1804-66) were at the centre of London journalism in their day; both were Tory partisans and had reputations as linguists and as erudite satirical writers. Mahony, whose pseudonym was 'Father Prout', was a master of the erudite 'spoof' who, having translated Moore's *Melodies* into Greek and Latin, maintained that Moore was a plagiarist of classical poetry. Today Father Prout's *Reliques* or Maginn's *Miscellanies* make heavy reading, even for the erudite. But Maginn did a good deal to encourage Irish writers to write about the Ireland they knew.

Among these were John Banim and Gerald Griffin. Both had tried their luck in London with classical verse-tragedies before turning to Irish material, and both developed the common aim of presenting a faithful picture of Irish society to the English public, with the intention of helping to reconcile the two peoples. This was no easy task at a time when memories of 1798 and of the Union were still alive, when 'agrarian disturbances' and Coercion Acts in Ireland were frequent and when the rise of O'Connell renewed many of the old bitternesses: Protestant fears of dispossession, Catholic hopes to bring down the ascendancy.

The best work of John Banim (1798-1842) of Kilkenny was written in collaboration with his brother Michael (1796-1874). *Tales by the O'Hara Family* (1825-29) consists of a number of stories of peasant life in Ireland during the late eighteenth and early nineteenth centuries, dealing usually with the conflicts of Whiteboys and other agrarian groups, Orangemen, priests and proselytisers, landlords, tithe-proctors and tenants, military and rebels. The incidents are usually lurid and melodramatic, the serious explanatory characters mere prototypes; and the attempt to give some perspective to the violence without offending anybody vitiates the occasional reality of peasant character and dialogue. 'I'll give you a curse on my two bended knees if you touch a hair of his head!' cries a priest to a violent man in *Peep o' Day;* 'And then you'll see how you'll look, going about on a short leg, and your elbow scratching your ear, and your shins making war on each other, while all the world is at peace.' But such graphic passages are swamped by the confused melodrama of the story. In *Crohoore of the Billhook,* a tale of eighteenth-century Ireland, the horror of the slicing-off of a tithe-proctor's ears, a frequent occurrence, is heightened by a jocular discourse upon his art by the man who performs it and by the learned rhetoric of the Ribbonman hedge-schoolmaster who defends it; the power of such incidents dissipates in a medley of sensational and violent events which have much contrivance but little coherence outside a general demonstration of disregard for the law both by ascendancy and peasant types. While this fitted in with the aim of the Banims, it did not make good fiction.

In their historical novels, mainly written by John Banim, there is a genuine attempt to discover and to reveal the Irish identity by serious examination of the Williamite and penal law periods and by demonstrating the values which the older Gaelic civilisation, liberal Protestantism and the Catholic majority could contribute, through recognition of a common country. The best of them was the first, *The Boyne Water* (1826), which deals with a key-period in Irish history, from the accession of James II to the passing of the Penal Laws. There are two heroes, McDonnell on the Irish side, Evelyn in the Williamite army. Both have noble aspirations, defeated by the propaganda of the fanatic Protestant Walker and the fanatic Dominican O'Haggerty; both take part in the campaign and are conveniently captured by the other side; and both end unhappily, Evelyn in the sectarian parliament in Dublin, McDonnell, one of the Wild Geese, in the army of France, awaiting his chance to return. The merit of the book is that it presents the struggle not only as a dynastic one for the

English throne, which in its Irish perspective meant the renewal of a conflict at least a century old, but as a vital one for Europe where it meant the blocking of Louis XIV's sway by the forces of Protestant Europe and the clearing of the way for world-expansion of the British Empire. Banim's historical sense was not matched by his literary power; he was content to borrow much of his plot from Scott's *Waverley* and to transpose Scott's contrasting prototypes to an Irish setting which they did not quite fit. The result was a set-piece which never took on much creative life, except in an occasional character like Rory na Chopple, the jovial killer who preys on both sides.

The Croppy (1828), a novel about the Wexford rising of 1798, had some genuine human interest; Banim took many of its prototypes and scenes from life; but he wrote the novel at a time when fears of a Catholic rising led by O'Connell were aroused by O'Connell's victory in the Clare election of 1828, and so presented a rising entirely due to 'agitators' — Orange, Catholic or United Irish emissaries — which became almost as unreal as the artificial romance with which it was woven. The limitations which Banim imposed upon himself can be seen from his preface to two novels about the penal times published together in 1830; they have been revised, he says, so that they cannot give offence to Catholic or Protestant. *The Last Baron of Crana* and *The Conformists* have no offence; they retain little interest for the reader.

The historical novels of the Banims were pioneer work; but their well-intentioned purpose was defeated by a time when, as Maria Edgeworth observed, realities were too strong and party passions too violent. They could write well enough of rural types, catching appearance, setting and speech; they knew the middle-class Catholic well and could present convincingly the divided mind of the apostate priest in that didactic novel about proselytising, *The Nowlans;* but they were not familiar with the governing landlord class and lacked dimension as well as creative freedom. They were not alone in this dilemma.

Their friend and colleague Gerald Griffin (1803-40) of Limerick began his Irish tales with *Holland-Tide* (1827) and *Tales of the Munster Festivals* (1827), containing a medley of stories about fairies and ghosts, murderers and highwaymen, smugglers, coiners and fortune-tellers. Some of them hardly rise above the level of Crofton Croker's stories; several resemble those of the

Banims in vivid sketches of hedge-scholars, rapparees and farmers, and also in their tendency to dissipate into melodrama. Yet Griffin's expressed aim was to write 'short stories of manners and events precisely as they are now in the south of Ireland'. 'Reality is all the rage now', he continues in a letter of 1826; 'Scott's novels have done away with the old sentimental romances.' Yet stories like 'The Aylmers of Ballyaylmer', about the smuggling families of Kerry, or 'Suil Dhuv, the Coiner', have little more than a certain crude melodramatic reality.

In *The Collegians* (1829), the work by which he is best known, Griffin almost succeeded in writing a good novel. The plot, which centres around the murder of Eily O'Connor by Danny Mann, the servant of a dashing but dissipated young squire, Hardress Cregan, was based upon a contemporary murder in County Limerick. Placing it in the late eighteenth century, Griffin concentrated on creating a wider setting and motivation than this crime, the murder of a young girl for gain by the servant of her seducer, provided. Cregan is secretly married to Eily, feels he has married beneath him and determines to marry Anne Chute, a young lady of quality, who is admired by his friend, Kyrle Daly. Daly is middle-class, Catholic and virtuous, Cregan an ascendancy type, reckless and self-indulgent but admired by his peasantry for his wasteful generosity. Griffin carefully builds up the setting of Irish provincial life with its contrasting classes and types, from ascendancy bucks to Lowry Looby and Miles na Coppaleen, the garrulous servant and the dashing Kerry horse-trader, who represents the Gaelic world in contrasting ways.

It is in his presentation of these characters, and of communal gatherings, trials, wakes and hunts that Griffin excels, and he has a knack of lighting up the history of the area, not by laboured descriptions but by casual anecdotes. The two Collegians (both Kyrle Daly and Hardress Cregan are Trinity men) serve as foils for each other with reasonable success, although the sincere but rigid principles of Daly make him less interesting than the open-handed Cregan, whose casual code of honour conceals an essential selfishness. One of the novel's weaknesses is that, perhaps deliberately, Griffin blurs Cregan's degree of guilt in inciting or acquiescing in Danny Mann's murder of Eily. Mann, on the other hand, acts from a defined mixture of devoted loyalty and a subconscious wish to see his master destroyed. Griffin maintained his curiously equivocal attitude towards Cregan to the end. Perhaps because he realised that his villain was far more popular than his hero, he could not bring himself to hang him, as he had originally intended, but ended with his transportation for life, adding that before he reached the land of exile 'Hardress had rendered up the life which the law forbade to take'. Having tidied up everything else by hanging Danny Mann, marrying Kyrle and Anne, and providing Lowry Looby with a cottage and a pension, Griffin ended the novel with the hope that his readers might learn improvement from the ruin of Hardress Cregan.

The Collegians, which Boucicault was later to adapt for the stage as *The Colleen Bawn,* was Griffin's most successful work. He wrote other novels; *The Rivals* (1830), a confused story of agrarian and sectarian conflict; *The Invasion* (1832), a dull tale of a Scandinavian invasion of Ireland in mediaeval times; *The Duke of Monmouth* (1836), based on Monmouth's revolt against Charles II. None of these has much merit. *Tracy's Ambition* (1830) is better; Tracy is a well-meaning Protestant squire who marries a Catholic girl of old Gaelic aristocratic stock; his decision to advance himself by taking the ascendancy side in a local land-war is disastrous; it turns wife and tenants against him, involves him with the violent Whiteboy Shanahans and leads to the death of innocent people. There is a plethora of melodrama in this novel but it does not quite destroy its power.

Griffin's other stories belonging to the thirties, *Tales of my Neighbourhood, Tales of The Jury Room* and *Adventures of an Irish Giant,* add little to his reputation. *The Christian Physiologist* (1830) is a didactic devotional work indicative of the strong religious feeling which impelled him in 1838, after burning most of his manuscripts, to enter the newly established order of the Christian Brothers. He died of famine fever in their North Monastery in Cork in 1840. A deeply religious man, he seems in his literary life to have been torn between his moralistic conciliatory aim — his desire to present past and contemporary realities of his people, his horror of all lawless and violent realities which had to be explained without offence to his readers — and the deadening conventions of the popular fiction of his time.

During the period before the Great Famine to which these writers chiefly belonged, English had been spreading rapidly as a spoken tongue. The new elementary school system, from its inception in 1831, forbade the teaching of Irish history or of the Irish language. O'Connell's view that since English was the language of power it should be learned well by the people, induced strong co-operation between parent and primary school-teacher in ensuring that Irish was not spoken without penalty. By 1840 the majority of Irish people read and spoke English but could learn little of their own history or traditions.

Largely because of these circumstances the success of *The Nation* newspaper was rapid. It was established as a sixpenny Saturday weekly in 1842 by the Young Ireland leaders, Thomas Davis, John Blake Dillon and Charles Gavan Duffy and was something completely new in Irish journalism. Before that Irish newspapers at first had been entirely polemical. Later a number of journals, notably the *Dublin Penny Journal* (1832-36), the *Irish Penny Magazine* (1833-34) which was edited by Samuel Lover, and the *Irish Penny Journal* (1840), published articles and stories of Irish interest. All were ephemeral, partly because they had no national policy. *The Nation* was definitely committed to the policy of the Young Ireland movement, to repeal the Union and to reform the landholding system, two of the primary issues in Irish politics. 'Educate that you may be free' was the burden of Davis's spirited prose, which aimed at educating the people in their history and their potential resources. He and his colleagues wrote for the Irish people as a whole, not for any particular creed or class, and sought also to interest the Irish abroad.

The sale of *The Nation* throughout the country was phenomenal. It did much to counteract the effect of the 1831 Education Act in making people aware and proud of their own country's history and scenic beauty. Its verses, although lacking any originality of style, had plenty of spirit. Many survive because they were written to known Irish tunes; others, through association with Irish places or historical events. A later age would reject the vapid emotion and exclamatory rhetoric of the bulk of them but there can be no doubt that they served their purpose at the time in developing a sense of national consciousness. The prose of *The Nation* was mainly polemical and rhetorical; two notable exceptions were the writings of Davis, which, although suffering from an enthusiastic didacticism, were spirited and were given strength by his familiarity with Irish history, general and local, and the letters of James Fintan Lalor (1807-49). Lalor represented the extreme wing of the Young Ireland party. Disgusted by O'Connell's lack of agrarian policy, he favoured the expropriation of the landlords and the

'The Senachie' by Phiz. Illustration for a Carleton story.

Reading The Nation *by Henry McManus. Courtesy of the National Gallery of Ireland.*

nationalisation of land. He saw this as a universal question on which Ireland could lead Europe, if she separated from England:

> Mankind will yet be masters of the earth. The right of the people to make the laws — this produced the first great modern earthquake, whose latest shocks, even now are heaving in the heart of the world. The right of the people to own the land — this will produce the next.

In 1845 Thomas Davis died and the Great Famine began. The experience of the Famine caused Lalor to found *The Irish Felon,* in which he preached open revolt. He was imprisoned and died shortly after his release. His incisive writings influenced the American socialist, Henry George, who in turn influenced Michael Davitt. A collection of his writings edited by John O'Leary was published in 1895.

In his own time Lalor influenced John Mitchel (1815-75), the Banbridge solicitor, who edited *The Nation* after Davis's death; the experience of the Famine then caused him to found the *United Irishman,* which openly advocated separation by force. Although Mitchel wrote other books about Ireland — including a *Life of Hugh O'Neill* (1846) and *The Last Conquest of Ireland (perhaps)* (1860) — it is his *Jail Journal* (1854) which ranks him among the considerable literary figures of the time. This autobiography begins with his transportation for the newly-invented crime of 'treason-felony' and ends some six years later with his escape from Van Diemen's Land and his arrival in the United States. Its chief purpose, Mitchel wrote, was to 'preserve the continuity of my thoughts, or *personal identity',* menaced by the prospect of fourteen years enforced exile, and the book is a full expression of himself, his experience of people and places, his probings of his own philosophy, his hatred of imperialism, his continual remembrance of Ireland. It is a receptacle of his own *saeva indignatio,* even, as he acknowledges, of his tirades, but is also an exciting personal story.

Mitchel was well versed in the classics and in the bible, and was widely read in contemporary literature. His literary style has an unusual diversity of analogy, rhetorical power with the strength and some of the weaknesses of his friend, Thomas Carlyle, and exactness of observation which gives particular vividness to a variety of scenes, ranging from the Boer settlers' boycott which defeated attempts to establish a British penal settlement in South

Africa, to kangaroo-hunting in a wild Tasmanian setting. His gallery of characters includes other Young Irelanders, ship's captains and doctors, settlers and convicts. Here is Garrett, a transported swindler of a British railway company:

'Forty thousand pounds, sir: — left it behind me, sir, with Mrs. Garrett: she is living in England in very handsome style. I have been here now two years, and like it very well — devilish fine brown girls here, sir; — I am very highly thought of — created a great sensation when I came. In fact until *you* came, I was reckoned the first man in the colony. Forty thousand pounds, sir — not a farthing less. But now *you* have cut me out.' I rose and bowed to this sublime rascal. The overwhelming idea, that I should supersede a swindler of forty-thousand-pound-power, was too much for me. So I said, graciously bowing, 'Oh, sir, you do me too much honour: I am sure you are more worthy of the post of distinction. For me, I never saw so much money in all my life as forty thousand pounds'. 'My dear sir', said my friend, bowing back again, 'My dear *sir!* but then you are a prisoner of state, patriotic martyr, and all that. Indeed, for my part, my little affair was made a concern of State too. Lord John Russell, since I came out here, had a private application made to me, offering to remit my whole sentence if I would disclose my method — the way I had done it, you know: they want to guard against similar things in other lines, you understand. . . .'

Mitchel could be ironic even about his own dignity. His Swiftian irony was directed against imperialism and his prayer, 'Give us war in our time, O Lord!' reflected his belief that only a widespread rising of subject-peoples could destroy it; 'the revolutionary leveller,' he wrote 'is your only architect.'

In fiction little work of note appeared between the Great Famine and the literary revival. Two novels by Charles Kickham (1828-82), *Sally Cavanagh* (1869) and *Knocknagow* (1879), were popular for their sympathetic presentation of Irish rural people but had little literary merit. More widely known is the work of Joseph Sheridan le Fanu (1814-73) — the grandnephew of Sheridan the dramatist — who is remembered chiefly for his novels and short stories of mystery and the supernatural. *The House by the Churchyard* (1863), a mystery novel set in Chapelizod, has some interesting characters but a very diffuse plot. *Uncle Silas* and *Wylder's Hand* (1864) showed le Fanu to be at least of the calibre of Wilkie Collins and lasted best of his longer works; but his finest writing went into his short stories of the supernatural, which have appeared in numerous collections since his time. Le Fanu was a student of Swedenborg and of the occult, and developed his own theories of the supernatural. His ghosts are not mere external terrors but seem to emerge from the subconscious depths of their witnesses or victims. Their gradual dominance is often associated with decaying manors and past guilt, perhaps an Anglo-Irish undertone. Even though *Uncle Silas* is ostensibly about England, it has this undertone; it was set in Ireland in its original version in the *Dublin University Magazine*.

As editor of this magazine from 1861-69, le Fanu encouraged the work of folklorist Patrick Kennedy (1801-73) who published several collections of folk-tales, notably *Legends of Mount Leinster* (1855), *Legendary Fictions of the Irish Celt* (1866), *Banks of the Boro* (1867) and *Evenings in the Duffrey* (1867).

Thomas Moore by E. Hayes. Courtesy of the National Gallery of Ireland.

CHAPTER XII
Poetry

During the first half of the nineteenth century Irish poetry in English began to take on an occasional distinction either in theme, reference or allusion. Thomas Moore (1779-1852) was the dominant Irish-born poet of this time. After graduating at Trinity College, where he was friendly with Robert Emmet, he left Dublin for London in 1799: there his translation of Anacreon's Odes had a great success, repeated later with his long 'Persian' poem, *Lallah Rookh;* the latter had a tremendous vogue in Europe, where it was widely translated. He also wrote satires, occasionally barbed with an incisive wit, as in his attack on political bigots:

> Who, arm'd at once with prayer-books and with whips,
> Blood on their hands, and Scripture on their lips,
> Tyrants by creed, and torturers by text,
> Make this life hell, in honour of the next ...

but all this work as a whole is rather thin and superficial, however popular at the time. More lasting were Moore's *Irish Melodies* which were published sporadically from 1808 to 1834. These were based on John Bunting's *General Collection of Ancient Irish Music* (1795), which Moore adapted for polite society. He was a very tuneful song-writer but the diction is commonplace and belongs rather to the previous age than to the new romantic age of simpler poetic speech which Wordsworth and Coleridge had initiated. Although the restrictions of Moore's conventions diminished the beauty of the songs, they hit society's taste and many of them lasted. The accusation that he had turned the harp of Erin into a musical snuff-box had some truth but the *Melodies* have held his countrymen's affection into this century. Many of them deal with Irish themes — the daughters of Lir, the death of Emmet, the glories and sorrows of Irish history — and their basic music is traditional. Moore sometimes captured a hint of their wavering rhythm:

Through grief and through danger thy smile hath cheer'd my
    way,
Till hope seem'd to bud from each thorn that round me lay ...

but for the most part they are clad in a regular and sentimental
garb.

Moore's two contemporaries, Jeremiah Joseph ꞏCallanan
(1795-1829) and Edward Walsh (1805-50), illustrate the same
difficulty of diction. Walsh's *Reliques of Irish Jacobite Poetry* was
published in 1844, Callanan's *Poems* in 1847. Unlike Moore they
were familiar with the verbal music of Irish ballad poetry and
recaptured something of it in their translations:

Five guineas would price every tress of her golden hair,
Then think what a treasure her pillow at night to share!
These tresses thick-clust'ring and curling around her brow —
O Ringlet of Fairness, I'll drink to thy beauty now!

So Walsh, whose assonances give a delicate music to his verse.
Here is Callanan in the same manner:

'Tis down by the lake where the wild tree fringes its sides,
The maid of my heart, my fair one of Heaven resides;
I think, as at eve she wanders its mazes along,
The birds go to sleep by the sweet wild twist of her song.

Both of these poets are interesting examples of the difficulty of
writing half-in and half-out of the English literary tradition. In his
conventional verse Walsh is poor, his language often as
uninspiring as Moore's, while Callanan renders the simple, stark
line

Mo thruagh mar atáid Gaodhal
(My pity how the Irish are)

as:

'How dimm'd is the glory that circled the Gael!'

Here, as with Moore, convention is the trap of the writer; also the
sentiment blurs the vision, takes the edge off poetry. One might
instance another contemporary, George Darley (1795-1846), in
this connection. Darley, a Wicklow friend of Tennyson, wrote
some good minor verse in Caroline style:

It is not beauty I demand,
A crystal brow, the moon's despair,

Nor the snow's daughter, a white hand,
Nor mermaid's yellow pride of hair.

But when he turned to Irish themes he became merely declamatory:

Clan Tir-oen! Clan Tir-conel!
Atha's royal sept of Conacht!
Desmond red! and dark O'Donel!
Fierce O'More! and stout McDonacht!

These four minor writers illustrate in various degrees the growing consciousness of the older culture which spread among Irish writers of English verse during the early nineteenth century. Some of them were content to select occasional themes from Irish history or places and to write of them in conventional English metrics. This was true of Sir Aubrey de Vere (1788-1846), Byron's contemporary at Harrow, whose sonnets were greatly praised by Wordsworth and who wrote good poems on Gougane Barra, the Rock of Cashel, and sundry Irish historical and legendary themes. His son Aubrey T. de Vere (1814-1902) followed suit and, as collections of his poems appeared well into the 1890s, his Irish poems were known to the writers of the Irish literary revival, who respected the measured classical manner of 'The March to Kinsale' or the symbolism of 'The Dirge of Rory O'Moore' but found his diction too stilted to have any sustained poetic impact. A more original quality was to be found in the poems of William Allingham (1824-89) and William Larminie (1849-1900). Allingham wrote some good lyrics about his birthplace, Ballyshannon, and a long poem, *Laurence Bloomfield in Ireland* (1864) about evictions. Larminie's assonantal verse in *Fand and other Poems* (1892) had a quality overlooked by the revival writers, but influencing Austin Clarke later.

Of all Irish poets of this period James Clarence Mangan (1803-49) had most of the seeds of genius, although the wretched circumstances of his life — his poverty, his hackwriting, his addictions, his eccentricity — seemed set against its flowering. He first came under the influence of the German romantic poets and wrote many versions and translations of their work, in the course of which he developed a very skilful use of the refrain but rarely rose above mediocrity. These poets had set the fashion for Eastern themes and Mangan then published many 'Oriental poems', although badly equipped for the task; some of these were

James Clarence Mangan by F. W. Burton. Courtesy of the National Gallery of Ireland.

downright fakes, paraded with a great show of learning; others
were vitiated by the faults of late-romanticism: luxuriant diction,
strained fancies, melodramatic rhetoric; but there were some
poems marked by a genuine lyricism, by daring experiments in
rhyme, and above all by haunting refrains:

> All passed like snow, long, long ago
> With the time of the Barmecides;
> All passed like snow, long, long ago
> With the time of the Barmecides!

Mangan's personal and miscellaneous poems show the same
uneven level. His autobiographical poem, 'The Nameless One',
has a sustained poetic power, the pulse of its feeling driven home
by the short concluding line at the stanza's end:

> And he fell far through that pit abysmal,
> The gulf and grave of Maginn and Burns,
> And pawned his soul for the devil's dismal
>   Stock of returns.

Too often the power is buried under false literary diction although
it is apt to improve in intensity, as Yeats and Joyce both noted,
whenever the thought turns on the darkness of man's path, the
remote prospect of salvation or on his own heavy burden of guilt
and doom, as if these were the real concerns of a poet whose work
was often exhibitionist and trivial. One must read through many
dull verses before coming on a poem like 'A Vision of Connaught
in the Thirteenth Century', with its lyrical, tranquil atmosphere
abruptly changed to grim reality, a change reinforced
magnificently by the tolling recurrence of its refrain.

During the last years of his life Mangan produced some of his
best poems; translations or versions of Irish poems. He himself
knew little Irish but learned something about Gaelic poetry from
the translations by Ferguson in the *Dublin University Magazine* or
from personal contact with scholars like John O'Donovan or
Eugene O'Curry, who supplied him with literal translations. His
method was not to keep too close to the form of the originals but to
follow their general drift, to borrow graphic images and phrases
from them and to express their feeling in his own form of romantic
lyricism. There were some gains, some inevitable losses. What
Mangan sometimes missed was the hard directness of the

original. Ferguson, for example, renders one verse of Dark Rosaleen as follows:

If I had a plough, I would plough against the hills;
And I would make the Gospel in the middle of the Mass for my
    black rosebud;
I would give a kiss to the young girl that would give her youth
    to me,
And I would make delights behind the fort with my Rosaleen
    Dubh ...

Mangan, more romantic in manner, avoids the direct, half-joking touch:

I could scale the blue air
    I could plough the high hills,
O, I could kneel all night in prayer
    To heal your many ills;
And one beamy smile from you
    Would float like light between
My toils and me, my own, my true,
    My dark Rosaleen!

Yet the lyrical sweep of his version and the thrust of his refrain established the value of his poem in its own right. This is true of his best Irish versions; 'O'Hussey's Ode to the Maguire', 'A Farewell to Patrick Sarsfield' and 'O Woman of Three Cows'. He seems to have been moving towards a more natural, direct form of speech when he died, aged forty-six, of famine fever in the Meath Hospital, Dublin. Interest in his work was slight until the revival at the end of the century called attention to its antecedents. D. J. O'Donoghue brought out a book on his life and writings in 1897, and the fullest edition of his poems to date in 1903.

. Sir Samuel Ferguson (1810-86), antiquarian and scholar was probably a greater seminal force in the revival, through his *Lays of the Western Gael* (1865), *Congal* (1872) and *Poems* (1880). His dominating idea was, he said, 'to raise the native element of Irish history to a dignified level', and in his epic poetry, whose style was consciously modelled upon that of Homer, he proceeded to treat Irish heroic themes in a mode of dignity and power. For the first time the stories of how Conor tricked Fergus out of the throne of Ulster, of the fate of Deirdre, of the destruction of Da Derga's hostel, of the poet's search for the lost *Táin*, were handled in English with the high seriousness and the imaginative sweep of formal

epic verse. Ferguson was hampered by two difficulties, arising
inevitably out of the changed linguistic and literary circumstances
of Ireland. This sometimes led him into a jarring kind of pseudo-
Elizabethan language:

> Whence then that haughty knitting of thy brow
> And turning of thine eye away from mine?

but he had often a dignified force in parts of his retelling of these
ancient tales. Here, for example, is a striking passage from his
epic poem *Congal*. It describes Congal's encounter with that grim
apparition of Irish epic, the Washer at the Ford, omen of the
death of heroes:

> Then Congal from the foremost rank a spear-cast forward
> strode
> And said, 'Who art thou, hideous one; and from what curst
> abode
> Comest thou thus in open day the hearts of men to freeze;
> And whose lopp'd heads and severed limbs and bloody vests
> are these?'
> 'I am the Washer of the Ford', she answered; 'and my race
> Is of the Tuath de Danaan line of Magi; and my place
> For toil is in the running streams of Erin; and my cave
> For sleep is in the middle of the shell-heaped Cairn of
> Maev,
> High up on haunted Knocknarea; and this fine carnage-heap
> Before me, and these silken vests and mantles which I steep
> Thus in the running waters, are the severed heads and hands
> And spear-torn scarfs and tunics of these gay-dressed, gallant
> bands
> Whom thou, O Congal, leadest to death. And this', the Fury
> said,
> Uplifting by the clotted locks what seemed a dead man's head,
> 'Is thine own head, O Congal.'
> Therewith she rose in air
> And vanished from the warrior's view, leaving the river bare
> Of all but running water ...

Ferguson's second difficulty was the obscurity which at that stage
shrouded Irish literature and antiquities from the consciousness of
his readers. He tried to surmount this partly by prefatory notes,
explanatory of the matter of his verse and sometimes full of odd

information; 'As late as the beginning of the 13th century the chess-men of the O'Neills of Tyrone', he tells us, for example, 'were formed of the polished *tibiae* of the men of Leinster.' But the prefatory notes can contain only a certain amount of explanatory detail and the burden of making things clear by genealogical and archaeological reference in the lines themselves or in footnotes often drags down his epic muse. Ferguson was sometimes more a scholar-antiquarian writing epic verse than a poet, and his serious purpose and natural solemnity often gave his narrative style the effect of pomposity.

While his epic poems are best read in extract today, his shorter narrative poems, like 'The Táin Quest', where he is not so weighted by these handicaps, display better his narrative force. He was also a good ballad-writer who, though lacking Mangan's lyrical fire, had greater ability to tell a story and a similar, if less striking, power of varied metre and forceful refrain:

So the Barrets with sewing-needles sharp and smooth
Let the light out of the eyes of every youth
And of every bearded man
Of the broken Lynott clan;
Then their darken'd faces wan
    Turning south
    To the river —
Sing the vengeance of the Welshmen of Tirawley ...

But the poems which seem to stand out in his work with the most lasting freshness are his translations from the Irish. These have a vital distinction of style resulting from Ferguson's exact knowledge of the metrics and the verbal music of his originals:

My purse holds no red gold, no coin of the silver white
No herds are mine to drive through the lone twilight;
But the pretty girl that would take me, all bare though I be and
    lone,
Oh, I'd take her with me kindly to the County Tyrone ...

In retrospect Ferguson's importance for the later course of Irish writing in English is seen to lie in the breadth of his vision and in the pioneering quality of his work. Although he wrote at a time when the audience for his kind of poetry was small and when Irish popular interest was attracted mainly by political writing, he was confident that his time would come. Yeats's words, written in the year of Ferguson's death, show that in 1886 his time of influence was already at hand; for the young poet, who compared him to 'some aged sea-king, sitting among the inland wheat and poppies, the savour of the sea about him and its strength', confidently prophesied that a great national literature would find its morning in his work; which was in fact what Ferguson himself had intended.

John O'Leary by J. B. Yeats. Courtesy of the National Gallery of Ireland.

CHAPTER XIII

Scholarship

The greatest cultural achievement in Ireland in the period between the Famine and the Irish literary revival was in the field of Irish history and archaeology. Eugene O'Curry (1796-1862) became the first professor of Irish History and Archaeology in the Catholic University of Ireland, of which John Henry Newman was Rector. O'Curry, who came of Clare farming-stock, had worked in the topographical and historical section of the Ordnance Survey and had earned his living copying and arranging manuscripts for the Royal Irish Academy, Trinity College, Dublin, and other bodies. He had also examined the Irish manuscripts in the British Museum and the Bodleian. His lectures gave a full account of the principal Irish mediaeval manuscripts and their contents and were published in 1861 and 1873. His preface to *Lectures on the Manuscript Materials of Ancient Irish History* is revealing. 'As to the work itself, its literary defects apart,' he wrote, 'I may claim for it at least the poor merit of being the first effort ever made to bring within the view of the student of Irish History and Archaeology an honest, if not a complete analysis of all the materials of that yet unwritten story which lies accessible, indeed, in our native language, but the great body of which, the flesh and blood of all the true history of Ireland, remains to this day unexamined and unknown to the world'. His brother-in-law, John O'Donovan (1809-61), was of County Kilkenny farming-stock and worked in the same department of the Ordnance Survey, for which he researched the topography and history of many places of Ireland. He wrote several articles on these subjects for such papers as the *Dublin Penny Journal* and the *Irish Penny Journal*. His greatest works were *The Annals of the Four Masters,* 7 vols, (1848-51) and *A Grammar of the Irish Language* (1845). The work of these two men added immeasurably to the sum of knowledge about the ancient Irish system, its history, legends and place-associations. With them is associated the work of George Petrie (1789-1866), their colleague in the Ordnance Survey, who published much on the ecclesiastical architecture of Ireland before the Norman invasion. A vast fund of knowledge about Irish antiquities was thus built up during this bleak time.

Before the end of the nineteenth century the work of Eleanor Hull, William Hennessy, Whitley Stokes and other Irish scholars; of Kuno Meyer, de Jubainville, Ernst Windisch and other scholars of continental Europe showed that the continuity of Celtic studies was assured. Later would come the establishment of university chairs and in Ireland a research institute for advanced studies. These developments owed a great deal to the scholars of the nineteenth century.

Although exact scholarship in Irish literature advanced greatly through O'Curry, O'Donovan, Petrie and their successors in the nineteenth century, the most direct influence on the writers of the Irish revival was exercised by Standish James O'Grady (1846-1928), whose early works were published 1887-91. After graduating as a classical scholar at Trinity College, Dublin in 1868, a chance reading of O'Halloran's *History of Ireland* (1778) interested him in the Celtic world and in the work of O'Curry and other scholars. His *History of Ireland: Heroic Period* (1878) and *History of Ireland: Cuchulain and his Contemporaries* (1880) were the seminal books of the revival a decade later. They were written with great zest and enthusiasm, in prose which, though rhetorical and romantic, had a strong imaginative force. Here is how he wrote of his particular concern, the world of Celtic legend:

But all around, in surging, tumultuous motion, come and go the gorgeous, unearthly beings that long ago emanated from bardic minds, a most weird and mocking world. Faces rush out of the darkness, and as swiftly retreat again. Heroes expand into giants, and dwindle into goblins, or fling aside the heroic form and gambol as buffoons; gorgeous palaces are blown asunder like a smoke-wreath; kings, with wand of silver and ard-roth of gold, move with all their state from century to century; puissant heroes, whose fame reverberates through and sheds a glory over epochs, approach and coalesce; battles are shifted from place to place and century to century; buried monarchs reappear, and run a new career of glory. The explorer visits an enchanted land where he is mocked and deluded. Everything seems blown loose from its fastenings. All that should be most stable is whirled round and borne away like foam or dead leaves in a storm.[1]

O'Grady depicted Cuchulainn in heroic epic proportions. His concentration upon the Cuchulainn cycle influenced Yeats strongly. So did his stressing of the importance of archaeology because of the extant remains and places all over Ireland which were visible links with the past. The literature and culture connected with them, he held strongly, could attract and nourish the artistic minds of the future: 'the craftsmen of the future', he wrote prophetically, 'will find therein and in unfailing abundance the material of persons and sentiments fit for the highest purposes and sentiments of epic and dramatic literature and of art, pictorial and sculptural.'

When the revival came a decade later, its leaders acknowledged him as its father. Subsequent opinion was to find O'Grady's rhetoric tedious, his scholarship inexact, but there was little question of the power and influence of his early work. Later he turned to the writing of historical romances; *The Bog of Stars* and *The Flight of the Eagle* are still readable but most of them were spoiled by an increasingly didactic and explanatory style. As editor of *The Kilkenny Moderator* and *The All Ireland Review,* and as a political journalist who at first vainly tried to persuade the gentry to lead the people in an enlightened reform movement and ended by advocating guild socialism, he continued to have some influence well into this century. Like Ferguson and O'Curry, he anticipated vital change and contributed to it.

Others who affected the future direction of Irish life were the historians W.E.H. Lecky (1838-1903) and Alice Stopford Green (1847-1929). Lecky's *A History of England in the Eighteenth Century* (1892), of which more than half is devoted to Ireland, was written 'to refute the calumnies of Froude against the Irish people' and is still the most authoritative work on the period. His *Leaders of Public Opinion in Ireland* (1912) contains valuable biographies of Flood and Grattan and shows his formidable learning. Green was a nationalist historian with strong anti-imperialist views. *The Making of Ireland and its Undoing* (1908) was vigorously attacked by English reviewers, but it was her *Irish Nationality* (1911) that was most popular in Ireland and that most affected the views of the emergent generation.

PART IV
The Irish Literary Revival

CHAPTER XIV

The Course of the Revival to 1916

... even a superficial consideration will show us that the Irish nation's insistence on developing its own culture by itself is not so much the demand of a young nation that wants to make good in the European concert as the demand of a very old nation to renew under new forms the glories of a past civilisation.

James Joyce

In the 1880s Ireland's sense of national identity was growing stronger. Politically and socially it expressed itself in the Home Rule movement and the Land League, led respectively by Parnell and Davitt. It could be seen also in the foundation in 1884 of the Gaelic Athletic Association, which spread rapidly throughout the country and carried both the sanction of past tradition and the drive of nationalism with it. In 1887 the G.A.A. started a little paper, *The Gael,* which carried a literary section, edited by the old Fenian, John O'Leary, who persuaded his friends to write for it. Among them was W.B. Yeats. The contact was slight for *The Gael* vanished after a year, bearing Yeats's contributions along with it, but it is indicative of the change which O'Leary had begun in the young poet.

They had met in 1886, the year in which *Mosada* appeared, and O'Leary had lent him poems by Thomas Davis and other patriotic writers. Both attended the Contemporary Club started by Professor Charles Oldham of Trinity College, Dublin, editor of the recently founded *Dublin University Review,* and the debates of a Young Ireland Society of which O'Leary was President. 'From these debates, from O'Leary's conversation, and from the Irish books he lent or gave me,' Yeats recalled, 'has come all I have set my hand to since.'[1] In those early days he dreamed of an opportunity to create a new image of Ireland which would appeal across sectarian divisions and he thought then that a theatre might attract a people who read little but were fond of oratory.

Some years were to pass before the opportunity came but the existence of writers who would avail of it was seen in 1888 with the publication of *Poems and Ballads of Young Ireland,* which was planned by a group of poets, including Yeats and his friends, Katharine Tynan and Douglas Hyde, all in their twenties, with the co-operation of older men, such as T.W. Rolleston, George Sigerson and John Todhunter. The last three were all scholars. Sigerson, scientist and historian, was a direct link with the older Irish tradition, having published (with John O'Daly) *Poets and Poetry of Munster* in 1860; Rolleston was schooled in Greek, Irish and German literature, had completed a life of Lessing and was about to introduce Whitman's *Leaves of Grass* to German readers; Todhunter, formerly a doctor and a professor of literature in Dublin, had settled in London and under the influence of Standish J. O'Grady had turned to Irish themes in his book *The Banshee and other Poems* (1888), planned after the manner of Aubrey de Vere's *Innisfail.* Of the younger group, Hyde also was a scholar but a scholar with the immediate aim of saving the Irish language from extinction. Like Yeats he was awaiting his chance to lead a cultural movement. Finally, Katharine Tynan, who had won some reputation as a poet with *Louise de la Vallière,* written in the pre-Raphaelite tradition, handled Irish legend and landscape in her second book, *Shamrocks* (1887), written under Yeats's influence.

Poems and Ballads of Young Ireland thus appears as the focus of many interests; scholarship and translation, Irish legend, history, language and landscape. It was the work of a group of writers whose work came out of their own environment rather than out of opinions about it. Differing in religion and in political views, they wrote out of a wider sense of national identity. The book, which was dedicated to John O'Leary and to the Young Ireland Societies, had on its title-page a quotation from William Allingham:

We're one at heart if you be Ireland's friend,
Though leagues asunder our opinions tend;
There are but two great parties in the end.

This newer wave of Young Ireland poets, it was clear, was different from that of Davis and his friends in that artistic standards rode its crest. The general quality of the book, despite the inclusion of some weak poems, won a critical success in Ireland and in England, partly because it lacked the vigorous political rhetoric of the *Nation* writers but also because its impact was that of a fresh force expanding in new directions.

The event which really placed Yeats at the centre was the publication in 1889 of *The Wanderings of Oisin.* Here by the best standards was the work of a good, perhaps a potentially great, poet. Yeats now commanded increasing attention in literary circles and the demand for his work was growing in England and America, while Irish poets paid him more heed. Yeats's letters to Katharine Tynan and the memoirs of both establish what he was trying to do. He was trying to persuade Irish writers not to accept as inevitable the prevailing canons of taste of English publishers and writers. The overwhelming prestige of English literature and the set attitude of English publishers to what was expected from Irish writers — the titles of *The Banshee* and *Shamrocks* perhaps reflect it — often caused them to produce verse which was stilted, imitative and insipid, or written in the rollicking tradition exemplified by Alfred Percival Graves, whose *Father O'Flynn and other Irish Lyrics* also appeared in 1889. The bitter remark of Stephen Dedalus about Malachi Mulligan's shaving-mirror — 'It is a symbol of Irish art. The cracked looking glass of a servant' — reflects a truth of which Yeats was aware. His repeated insistence that Irish writers who stray from Irish themes and feelings usually make only alms for oblivion might appear chauvinistic in any other context. But Yeats also knew that political or religious argumentation might engulf an Irish writer. The lawyer and writer, J.F. Taylor, whom he had met through O'Leary, seemed to him to typify the potential Irish creative writer who is misled into rhetoric: 'He saw himself pleading for his country before an invisible jury, perhaps of the great dead, against traitors at home and enemies abroad.' Taylor, whose oratorical force later received a double-edged tribute in *Ulysses,* was an able advocate but carried his advocacy into literary criticism.

Yeats was convinced that rhetorical writers inevitably created false trappings of a nation's individuality, 'Kilts and bagpipes and newspapers and guide-books', leaving the best minds unsatisfied and therefore easy victims to English taste. 'Ireland was placidly accepting for poetry what was merely propagandism or heartless exercises in unsimple simplicity', wrote Katharine Tynan:

> These were the things we young ones were reproducing with great satisfaction up to the time when W.B. Yeats brought a new soul into Irish poetry . . . he established or at least re-established the artistic conscience and the artistic ideal in Irish poetry.[2]

As the potential leader of an artistic movement Yeats, during the period 1887 to 1891, had the tactical advantage of living in London and visiting Ireland when possible. He thus became familiar with such institutions as the Southwark Literary Club (established 1883) and the Pan-Celtic Society in Dublin (founded 1888), both of which were attended by most of the foregoing writers. They were thus potential centres for the spread of the new movement now taking shape. In 1887 Yeats wrote to Katharine Tynan of the growth of his feeling that a school of Irish poetry founded on Irish myth and history was coming; in 1890 he stated in the introduction to *Representative Irish Tales* that a true literary consciousness, 'national to the centre', was forming and that an Irish literary movement would show itself in the first lull in politics.

That lull, preceded by the storm of the Parnell split in the same year, came with the death of Parnell in 1891. On December 28, Yeats, Rolleston, Todhunter, D.J. O'Donoghue (the biographer of Mangan and Carleton) and a few other members of the Southwark Club met at Yeats's house and decided to transform the club into the London Irish Literary Society, with an active policy of fostering Irish literature by lectures, discussions and publications. This decision was put into effect in 1892; in addition the Irish National Literary Society replaced the Pan-Celtic Society in Dublin during the same year. Thus the Irish literary movement was formally launched. To either or both of its centres gravitated the poets already named; also men like Sir Charles Gavan Duffy, a direct link with Davis and the earlier Young Ireland movement, Standish O'Grady and Stopford Brooke. The inaugural lectures stressed the value of Ireland's older literature, the necessity of making it available to the public in ordered form with the collections of Irish folk-tales and of Irish writers in English. This emphasis on the past was not alien to Yeats and the younger writers but the New Irish Library, published under the editorship of Gavan Duffy, the first President of the Irish Literary Society, put so much emphasis on political ideas and inferior writers of the past that the series had little relation to the present and failed. Yeats and his group could rely upon the societies over the next decade or two to provide them with a popular forum and to spread interest in their work, once it had won attention, the type of qualified assistance displayed by Chesterfield to Johnson. But the progress of the movement, if it was to develop into a renaissance, now depended upon the activities of the poets themselves, and of Yeats in particular.

For the rest of the nineties most of the propulsion of the movement was supplied by Yeats himself; partly through his growing reputation as poet *(Poems,* 1895; *The Wind Among the Reeds,* 1899), as an editor of various volumes of fairy and folk-tales *(Irish Fairy Tales,* 1892; *The Celtic Twilight,* 1893) and as a writer of stories. To *John Sherman* and *Dhoya* (1891) were added the stories of *The Secret Rose* (1897) and *The Tables of the Law* (1897). In England his editing of Blake commanded critical attention, and his contributions to the publications of the Rhymers' Club, of which he, Rolleston and Ernest Rhys were the guiding spirits, showed that he was no insular and encapsuled poet. His London contacts with William Morris and the pre-Raphaelite group, with Arthur Symons, who introduced him to the work of the French symbolists, and with editors and publishers such as W.E. Henley and Edward Garnett, also assisted in spreading interest in his own work and in that of other Irish writers, whom he was indefatigable in urging to write out of their own environment and to improve their craftsmanship; Katharine Tynan, Eva Gore-Booth, Dora Sigerson and A.E. were among these, only the last displaying any strong resistance to Yeats's advice. Even necessity, the mother of journalism, was turned to good account; new poets such as Nora Hopper, J.H. Cousins, and Althea Gyles found themselves mentioned (more kindly than critically) in Yeats's articles in various Irish, English and American papers. He also availed of every chance to show that Ireland had already a respectable tradition of prose and poetry in English. In 1895, for example, he published *A Book of Irish Verse* from which, for the most part, he omitted political poems, and published in Ireland and in England his selected lists of the best Irish books of mythology, folklore, fiction, poetry and history.

Although Yeats was the pivotal artistic figure of the movement during these years, a number of people and of events helped it in various ways. Douglas Hyde's publication of *Beside the Fire* (1890) and of *The Love Songs of Connacht* (1893) proved to be two of the most seminal books affecting Irish literature in English. The former was a translation of some of the stories in his *Leabhar Sgeuluigheachta* (1889) for a publisher who had been attracted by his translations of folk-tales in works edited by Yeats. *Beside the Fire* was an excellent collection of folk-tales gathered by Hyde from Irish-speaking peasants and game-keepers in the West or taken down by other collectors such as William Larminie or Patrick Kennedy. It was dedicated to the memory of the poet-scribes and hedge-schoolmasters of the eighteenth and early nineteenth centuries who had tried to preserve such native lore; vainly, as Hyde then thought, since the policy of the British government, of the Catholic Church and of O'Connell had since turned the Irish people away from their language and had given the middle classes 'an itch after greatness and nothingness'. The book gave the Irish text of the stories, faced by Hyde's translations into an Irish-English which was simple, racy and idiomatic, not stilted by a false literary approach nor heightened for the sake of comicality. It had a certain literary trueness which Yeats at once greeted as perfect and hoped would help to develop a distinctive Irish literary style in English suitable for the retelling of old Irish tales.

The Love Songs of Connacht added to the effect of this book by demonstrating the quality and music of the popular Irish folk-songs which Hyde wrote down from the farmers and fishermen of his native province or translated from old manuscripts. He recaptured their qualities of simplicity, intensity and concreteness by using the same kind of Irish-English speech, fresh and idiomatic, although he occasionally used conventional English diction; and he retained something of their music by following, not usually to an obtrusive extent, the rhythms and assonances of the originals. Thus he helped to open up a whole imaginative vista of Irish popular tradition in poetry as well as in prose. Yeats, Synge and Lady Gregory owed much to his work, which was continued with *The Religious Songs of Connacht* (1906) and other translations. But Hyde's real purpose, which he pursued with the single-mindedness of Yeats, was to save the Irish language from extinction and his translations as well as his histories of Irish literature were part of that work.

In 1892 Hyde delivered to the Irish National Literary Society in Dublin his presidential address on 'The Necessity for De-Anglicising Ireland'. He pleaded strongly for all Irishmen, Unionist as well as Nationalist, not to cast aside 'the mantle of its own past' and the continuity of its own civilisation. Ireland, he said, once

> one of the most reading and literary peoples has become one of the *least* studious and most *un*-literary and ... the present art-products of one of the quickest, most sensitive and most artistic races on earth are now only distinguished for their hideousness.[3]

His audience was not responsive and Hyde later found discussion of the matter ruled out of order at the Contemporary Club on the ground of its lack of substance. Yeats went with him a certain distance on the theme of de-Anglicisation but differed in believing that a cultural revival could take place without a revival of Irish.

The following year Hyde formed the Gaelic League, dedicated to his purpose. Its rapid spread throughout the urban areas — it never took root in the areas where Irish was the mother-tongue of all or most of the inhabitants — had some curiously contrasting effects. As long as Hyde succeeded in keeping it non-political it really cut across divisions of creed, but by 1915 the triumph of its nationalist wing caused his resignation as the leader and that cement was gone. Its cultural affinity with some aspects of the Irish literary movement and the participation of men like Rolleston in both must have been mutually advantageous; yet from about 1906 a certain 'linguistic sectarianism' developed, doubtless assisted by English and ascendancy reactions to the League, which resulted in hostility to the idea that a national literature in English was possible and desirable.

Yeats, who remained friendly with Hyde, regretted the loss of

> Hyde before he had beaten into prose
> The noble blade the Muse had buckled on

and perhaps missed the propagandist as much as the poet. But there were other allies to hand. One of them was Lionel Johnson, a member of the Rhymers' Club. He was an Oxford graduate who had been tutored by Walter Pater and who had won a literary reputation in London circles. A recent convert to Catholicism and with some Sligo ancestry, he readily became an enthusiastic supporter of the new literary movement and was active in helping the Irish Literary Society in London and in addressing the National Literary Society in Dublin. His address to the latter on 'Poetry and Patriotism' in 1894 (reprinted in the Cuala series in 1908) showed general agreement with Yeats on the importance of craftsmanship in poetry, which he saw as a traditional Celtic characteristic, and on the value of Irish materials. He agreed with Hyde on de-Anglicisation, if that meant a refusal to be bound by current English standards of literary taste, and with Yeats on the possibilities of a distinctive Irish literature in English, provided that this did not exclude the adaptation of the themes and methods of foreign artists. 'Our race is not lost by spreading itself over the world', he said, 'and our literature would not lose its Irish accent by expeditions into all lands and times.⁴ While his enthusiasm sometimes misled him into questionable generalisations about the 'Celtic passion for perfection', Johnson's central attitudes displayed individuality and commonsense. He supported Hyde's language movement as valuable in itself and recognised the claims of the patriotic verses of *The Nation* writers on the affections of the people; but he saw that there was no necessary antagonism between Hyde's aims and Yeats's and there was a place for rhetoric in poetry provided that it did not dominate the poet's art. Thus he seems to have anticipated Yeats's use of controlled rhetoric in his middle and later years. Johnson's untimely death in 1902 robbed Yeats of a valuable ally whose sense of literary perspective was wide, whose arguments had a prevision which Yeats's sometimes lacked and whose support of the movement carried considerable weight in England. With Katharine Tynan, who also wrote frequently on Catholic themes, Johnson enabled Yeats to show that, like Hyde's, the literary movement ignored sectarian differences.

Before Johnson died the movement had been strengthened by the association of George William Russell (A.E.) with it. Russell and Yeats had been at school together in Dublin and were old friends but Russell was almost unknown as a poet until about 1892, when he was editing *The Irish Theosophist* and publishing many poems. Collections of these appeared in *Homeward: Songs by the Way* (1894) and *The Earth Breath* (1897), which established his reputation as a mystical poet whose themes were not Ireland but the Universal Self, and not nationalism but 'the politics of eternity'. Russell was one of the central figures of the Theosophical movement which established a Dublin Lodge in 1886, absorbing the Hermetic Society which Yeats had formed the previous year after reading A.P. Sinnett's *Esoteric Buddhism* and *The Occult World.* The Lodge became a centre of philosophical discussion for such contrasting people as Sigerson, O'Leary, Rolleston, John Eglinton, Yeats and A.E., and assisted in publishing the first books of A.E. and of Eglinton. Thus its activities complemented and in many ways assisted those writers who were principally concerned with the literary movement.

Yeats, who had been quick to claim Russell as a specifically Celtic mystic (a description which the latter was slow to accept) was glad when his friend overcame his distrust of the National Literary Society, whose Young Ireland wing he thought too restrictive, and joined it in 1895. About this time, under the influence of Standish O'Grady's *History of Ireland,* Russell began to write on Irish subjects and so became more closely identified with the movement. His association with it necessitates more subtle qualifications than in Hyde's case. Russell was essentially engaged in a search for spiritual perfection which took mystical, transcendental and theosophical forms. 'I was pagan in my childhood', he wrote to Dowden in 1894, 'and have grown naturally into Indian methods of thought and so I must continue until I can see the True without a veil.'[5] What he called 'the mystical adventure' provided his central drive and this, in a special sense, made him indifferent to causes. His work for co-operative, agricultural and other causes, including literature, was of peripheral importance to his meditative quest. Ireland was important to him chiefly as a centre of potential spiritual regeneration. He could write enthusiastically to Yeats of the gods returning to the sacred mountains of Ireland and that 'the universal heart of the people will return to the old druidic beliefs', or of how he had seen and heard in the Dublin hills a harper of the De Danann playing, and yet could insist that he was not a Celt and that it would be futile for him to try to be consciously Celtic; a necessary warning to Yeats who was claiming him as a typical writer of the Celtic twilight. To A.E. the Celtic world was but one manifestation of the Twilight of the Gods.

Although Russell was of importance to the literary movement

as a poet, he was even more important as a discoverer and sponsor of young writers. In 1904 he published *New Songs,* which included the work of Padraic Colum, Thomas Keohler, Alice Milligan, Susan Mitchell, Seumas O'Sullivan, George Roberts and Ella Young; all of them owed something to Russell's intellectual influence and several were adherents of the theosophical movement. Five years later he had discovered and had found a publisher for James Stephens, whose *Insurrections* (1909), dedicated to A.E., marked the beginning of a creative effort which, like that of Colum and O'Sullivan, lasted far into this century. Russell regarded this new wave of poets as expressing a new mood, subjective, spiritual and intellectual rather than patriotic or consciously Celtic or Irish. In his standards of literary taste Russell obviously went a certain distance with Yeats, especially in believing in the necessity of spiritual vision in the poet and of keeping opinions out of poetry. On the other hand Russell would not agree with him that beauty was the sole end of poetry and preferred to think of art as the avenue to spiritual vision. 'If I held your ideas', he wrote to Yeats in 1900, 'I could never write another line', so far apart were their mystical and fundamental ideas. Thus he did not emphasise the importance of craftsmanship to the same extent as Yeats, who in turn sometimes regarded Russell's 'genius of the religious teacher' as producing bad craftsmanship among the poets he encouraged. Yeats's poem 'The Choice' seems to sum up the central difference between the two poets; for Yeats perfection of the work came first; for Russell, perfection of the life. Where Yeats's artistic influence greatly influenced the standards of the literary movement as it developed, Russell's unique personality, kindly, patient and tolerant, was at least as formative a force among the younger writers.

It is possible to make a rough distinction between the group of poets who preceded the appearance of *New Songs* and those who contributed to it or who emerged about that time. Most of the first group were anthologised by Stopford A. Brooke, then President of the Irish Literary Society, and T.W. Rolleston in *A Treasury of Irish Poetry* (1900). Besides representing Yeats, Russell, Lionel Johnston and Katharine Tynan, it contained the work of translators (Sigerson, Todhunter, Hyde, Larminie, Rolleston, Whitley Stokes), of older figures (de Vere, Allingham, Standish James O'Grady), of popular Irish songsters (Alfred Perceval

Graves, F.A. Fahy and P.J. McCall) and of numerous women writers, who made up in numbers what they lacked in strength. The most substantial of them in literary production proved to be Moira O'Neill (*Songs of the Glens of Antrim,* 1902), Nora Hopper (*Ballads in Prose,* 1894) and Dora Sigerson (*Collected Poems,* 1907), all of whom wrote with occasional felicity and with a real sense of song; but today their connection with the literary movement or their use of Irish themes or of Irish-English dialect does not seem enough to sustain their reputation as poets of real quality. A process of merit by association is eventually one of erosion. They had moderate talent and it played its part at the time. Yeats assisted them to play it and in later years might not have written that arrogant line 'But was there ever dog that praised his fleas?' if he had recalled his own introduction in this book (*Treasury,* pp 471-73) to that shameless borrower of his themes and phrases, Nora Hopper. Katharine Tynan had a much more genuine talent, and a greater control of craftsmanship, as the selection of her poems which Yeats made for the Dun Emer Press in 1907 demonstrates. He considered her an Irish Christina Rossetti, which is a qualified but just judgement. Unfortunately the necessity of ceaseless literary hackwork prevented her further development as a poet, but her anthologies, *Irish Love Songs* (1892) and *The Wild Harp* (1913), were helpful to the revival at its start and near its end.

The general effect of this group was to spread among Irish poets writing in English a tradition of writing on Irish themes, of using older Irish literature and tradition, contemporary Irish speech, folklore and folk-song in their work, and of linking the Irish landscape with its older associations. Stopford Brooke judged the distinctive elements of the Irish tradition to be nationality, tempered by defeat and suffering, a religious spirit, whether Catholic or mystical, rebellion against the denial of freedom, and a melancholy born of oppression, famine and exile, occasionally lightened by hope and resilient laughter. He saw the work of Yeats and his contemporaries as fitting into and renewing this tradition, chiefly by strengthening its national quality through recapturing the Celtic past or expressing Irish spirituality of different forms, as Yeats, Russell and Lionel Johnson were doing, and especially by providing those standards of artistic perfection which could prepare Irish writing for its full maturity. The inclusion of much inferior and some very bad poetry in the

Treasury does not prevent this assessment from validly applying to
its better poets.

Between them they created what was known at the turn of the
century by such titles as 'the Celtic school', 'the Celtic
renaissance' and 'the Celtic twilight', rather than the Irish
literary movement. The term 'Celtic' was popular with English
critics who had been conditioned by Matthew Arnold's work *On
the Study of Celtic Literature* (1867), and, on the whole, were
favourably disposed to Irish work which they considered to fit its
formula: readiness 'to react against the despotism of fact',
liveliness of personality, sensitivity, a magical quality close to
nature, elaborate poetic techniques; these qualities being
hampered and vitiated by sentiment, sensuousness, lack of
balance, of reason, of sanity and of the architectonic quality
necessary for great literature. Arnold's sympathetic and well-
meaning assessment was hampered by a complete lack of first-
hand knowledge of Celtic literature and by an imperfect
interpretation of secondary sources, but it gave the English critics
a touchstone for judging the new movement, whose writers were
invariably searched for 'Celtic effects'. Yet Ernest Boyd's
description of this convention as an invention of English
journalists is misleading. The movement clearly involved the
Celtic past, although it was not confined to it, and the term Celtic
was repeatedly used and often misapplied by its leading figures.
Yeats applied it to a variety of subjects from Irish folklore to
Carleton's eyes, and spoke of his fellow poets as 'tongues of fire
uttering the evangel of the Celtic peoples'; Johnson, although he
recognised the difficulty of exactly defining Celtic or Irish
qualities, urged the writers of his day to raid foreign literatures
and 'triumphantly Celticise' the spoils, while Stopford Brooke
accepted the term 'Celtic revival' as applying to the movement as
a whole although Hyde referred in the same book to the 'so-
called' Celtic revival.

Such difficulty of terminology was of course inevitable at that
time; the Gaelic Athletic Association had chosen its title to
distinguish itself from the Irish Athletic Association, which was
concerned with English games, and might well have chosen the
Celtic Athletic Association if no other convenient title had been
available. Further, many of the writers of the movement were
unfamiliar with the Celtic or with Gaelic literature; its second-
raters cheerfully accepted the Arnold formula, sentimentality and

W. B. Yeats. Courtesy of Bord Fáilte.

all, and went on writing to it long after Yeats and other writers of calibre had discarded it.

It is notable also that a distinctive mode in poetic technique modelled upon that of Irish poetry made little headway during the first phase of the movement. George Sigerson's *Bards of the Gael and Gall: Done into English after the Modes and Metres of the Gael* (1897) was unfortunately done into stilted English which spoiled some good attempts at syllabic verse after the Irish manner; Todhunter made a few better but sporadic attempts, and William Larminie's more fruitful experiments in assonantal verse in *Fand* (1892), although praised by A.E. in the *Treasury,* were neglected until after the revival. Hyde was almost alone in affecting poetic technique at the centre.

The confusion caused by the term Celtic was increased by the addition of the word 'twilight'. Yeats used it in *The Celtic Twilight* (1893) to describe the vestigial remains of older tradition in the stories and anecdotes, mainly concerned with Sligo ghosts and fairies, which the book contained. He treated them with a mixture of scepticism and of belief in their imaginative truth. In 1902 he republished them under the same title but included in the book some of the stories first published in *The Secret Rose* (1897). Now 'twilight' acquired a different connotation, for these stories were not folk-tales but sophisticated stories written in a style of cultivated simplicity, blending Celtic mythology, occultism and folk-tradition, esoteric in their use of an obscure symbolism drawn from Indian, Rosicrucian, theosophical and French symbolist thought. The dedication of *The Secret Rose* was to A.E., who probably was the model for 'The Visionary' in *The Celtic Twilight,* and pays tribute to him as the leader of the Irish mystics, adding that 'so far as this book is visionary it is Irish'.

The Celtic twilight element in the literary movement was really the creation of Yeats, Russell and their imitators. As it was thought of during the first decade of this century it was a shadowy world of subdued speech and nuance, full of world-weariness and idealistic longings, of remote, dim, mythological figures and occult lore. 'Soon all that is vague, wistful and dreamful was assumed to be characteristic of the Celtic race here and elsewhere', wrote Austin Clarke, who correctly linked its vogue with that of the *fin de siècle* movement and regarded it as a diversion which at least left a residue of beautiful verse.[6]

Dissatisfaction with this predominant poetic atmosphere was

expressed in 1889 by John Eglinton,[7] who contended that a national literature should spring from a native interest in life and its problems rather than from interest in legendary material and that poetry should be philosophical in the Wordsworthian sense and should illuminate life. Yeats, he thought, was too much the aristocratic craftsman concerned with the material of the past. Yeats, nettled by this, denounced the philosophical approach as productive of commonplace popular verse, 'which mixes up anecdotes and opinions and moral maxims for their own sake — the things dull temperaments can understand', and stated that the test of real poetry was the volume and intensity of its passion for beauty and the perfection of its workmanship.

This involved him in a defence of the poetic power of symbolism and of the aesthetes. Eglinton and Larminie attacked him on both points. They regarded the French symbolists as having pushed the valid idea of the suggestive magic of words to an absurd limit at which the cult of the private symbol had led to mere obscurity and the effort to approximate poetry to music had induced mere musical inanity. Larminie thought that aestheticism as represented by Morris, Swinburne and Rossetti was a form of escape from the great animating ideas of true poets and from the natural sunlight of great poetry, while Eglinton described the doctrine of art for art's sake as 'the declaration of a beauty past her prime that she will have nothing more to do with men'. This controversy, which began in the *Daily Express* and was published in separate form in *Literary Ideals in Ireland* (1899), led to a certain agreement among the participants about the validity of legendary material and the worthlessness of a purely material view of life; all of them, like Russell, who played a brief role in it, were transcendentalists. It also helped Yeats to define his attitude to poetry and is of some value in indicating the change in poetic direction.

The younger poets of *New Songs* helped to turn the tide of poetry into less esoteric and dreamy channels. Although they were in one way or another disciples of A.E., his influence helped the development of their very different personalities. The slighter poets, Ella Young and Thomas Keohler, went on writing in his manner; Susan Mitchell published the theosophical poems of *The Living Chalice* (1908) in the same year as her satirical verses of *Aids to the Immortality of Certain Persons in Ireland*, which had some popularity for its portraits of the leaders of the literary movement but was too topical to have much appeal today. Eva Gore-Booth wrote more in the manner of Ethna Carbery, Alice Milligan expressed national sentiments in an uneven but sometimes finished and more enduring style. In general all these poets, like the minor writers of the earlier group, survive only in anthologies, through a few good poems or because of some local associations. The same fate has befallen James H. Cousins who went on writing mystical, heroic Celtic twilight verse in a succession of slim and dreary volumes long after he had left Ireland in 1913 to teach theosophy in India.

The real change of mood expressed with proper poetic style is to be seen in the work of Padraic Colum whose individual talent, rooted in his experience of rural Ireland, was nourished by the craftsmanship of Yeats, the humanity of A.E. and the influence of Hyde's translations. The publication of *Wild Earth* (1907) confirmed A.E.'s confident prophecy of 1902 that Colum would be a poetic force. Dedicated 'To A.E. who fostered me', it showed a tempered strength in its handling of people and places of the Irish countryside and in its use of ballad forms, as well as of a freer verse-form owing something to Whitman. Yeats, who had written of Colum's 'peasant realism' in 1904, had already captured Colum for the Irish theatre, and it was not until 1916 that his second volume of poems appeared. About the same time the work of the Ulster poet, Joseph Campbell, especially in *The Mountainy Singer* (1909) and *Irishry* (1913), was showing that a talent not unlike Colum's could flourish independently of the Dublin group.

Meanwhile James Stephens, whose *Insurrections* was also dedicated to A.E., was further justifying his mentor with *The Hill of Vision* (1912), *Songs from the Clay* (1915) and *The Adventures of Seumas Beg* (1915). Although described by A.E. as 'a disciple of the system', which he and Yeats were planning for the regeneration of the Irish spirit through contact with the Celtic gods and the Earth Breath, Stephens rapidly developed a highly original approach to deities, earth, its inhabitants, rural and urban, and to universals, which he wrote about seriously, comically, whimsically, fantastically and starkly in a variety of lyrical forms and rhythms, thereby causing considerable anxiety to the critics searching Stephens' poetry or the series of novels, which began with *The Charwoman's Daughter* (1912), for 'Celtic effects'.

A.E. himself was most appreciative of the change and some of his essays (collected in *Imaginations and Reveries,* 1915) provide its best index. In 1902 he felt that Yeats was still more interested in the shadows of life than in life itself and had not yet reached his true worth; also that he had been followed into the twilight by too many poets. In 1909, while praising the delicate poetic craft of Seumas O'Sullivan, he warned him that the twilight world was too narrow a world and that 'he should adventure out into new worlds in the old quest'. Three years later, in a review of James Stephens' poetry, he summed up the changes that had occurred since the 1880s. First, the rhetoric of nationalist poets had been succeeded by light and dreamy twilight poetry. Yeats, although a great poet at his best, had led an eclectic movement followed by many imitators who standarised his attitudes and his symbols:

> in their writings one wandered about, gasping for fresh air and sunlight, for the Celtic soul seemed bound for ever by the pale lights of fairyland on the north and by the darkness of forbidden passion on the south, and on the east by the shadowiness of all things human, and on the west by everything that was infinite, without form, and void.

Acknowledging that he himself had contributed to this dimness, Russell greeted with relief the sturdy voice of Stephens, 'blaspheming against all the formulae and violating the tenuous atmosphere', and concluded:

> With writers like Synge and Stephens the Celtic imagination is leaving its Tirnanoges ... and is coming down to earth intent on vigorous life and individual humanity ... and I watch the doings of the new-comers with sympathy, all the while feeling I am somewhat remote from their world, for I belong to an earlier day, and listen to those robust songs somewhat as a ghost who hears the cock crow, and knows his hours are over, and he and his tribe must disappear into tradition.[8]

The poetry of the period from 1904 to 1916 has a less uniform appearance and seems to issue from new poets of individual talent, aware of the value of Yeats and Russell but not obtrusively influenced by them and not thinking of poetry as needing a movement, formulae or labels, When one considers the dates of the first publications and the diverse poetic talents of Stephens and Campbell, Thomas MacDonagh *(Songs of Myself,* 1910), James Joyce *(Chamber Music,* 1907), Joseph Plunkett *(The Circle and the Sword,* 1911) and Francis Ledwidge *(Songs of the Fields,* 1914), this impression is strengthened. One also notes that the poets of the movement were lyrical and that, apart from *The Wanderings of Oisin* and Herbert Trench's *Deirdre Wedded* (1901), no notable epic poem had appeared. Also from 1904 Yeats was increasingly busy with the theatre and in any case must have felt that his propulsion of a movement in poetry was no longer necessary and that the place for concerted action was in the Abbey Theatre.

Lady Gregory at Coole House, Co. Galway. Bord Fáilte photograph.

CHAPTER XV

The Irish Dramatic Movement

I

The late development of an indigenous drama in Ireland was due to a number of causes. The Gaelic world had no dramatic tradition. During the middle ages such miracle or morality plays as were performed by the churches or by the town guilds were English in type. Later, Elizabethan companies of players visited Dublin and other towns such as Cork and Kinsale; but the first theatre in Dublin, the Werburgh Street Theatre, did not open until 1637 and was closed by the Cromwellian wars. After the Restoration came the theatre of Smock Alley, while the eighteenth century added new Dublin theatres at Crow Street and at Fishamble Street.

These theatres had chequered careers, being sometimes closed by financial difficulty, by riots or by mob destruction. On the whole they performed the function of provincial theatres, offering the same fare as English theatres or providing premises for visiting English companies which, increasingly in the eighteenth century, toured the Irish provincial towns. Such theatres attracted the talents of some English writers and of several who were of Irish birth, but their contributions were of little artistic worth. The better writers naturally sought their careers in England, Congreve, Farquhar and Goldsmith among them; or, like Richard Brinsley Sheridan, went to London at an early age. These playwrights set their mark on Restoration and on eighteenth-century English comedy. They also initiated a tradition of the literary invasion of the English theatre by Irish writers which was continued in the nineteenth century by Wilde and Shaw. It is not accidental that all these writers were satirists, for their half-way position between two cultures made them, in general, less committed to and more objective about English values, or conventions in the theatre.

Nothing which could be called indigenous Irish drama emerged during these centuries. Ireland was occasionally the setting for stock adventures or romances but the most consistent 'Irish' feature of such plays was the conventional stage Irishman. The Elizabethan playwrights, including Shakespeare, Jonson, Dekker and Beaumont and Fletcher, had portrayed a number of Irish types, usually soldiers or servants, whose peculiar dress, speech, habits and addictions were treated with a mixture of realism and of comic exaggeration. From the Restoration on such types hardened into stock characters. These were usually dashing and amorous military officers in English service, their faithful and comic servants, absentee landlords (inveterate fortune-hunters), peasants engaged in seasonal labour, occasionally priests or doctors. Their dialogue became stereotyped, restricted to a few standard mispronunciations of the 'faix and begorra' type, and their stock line of comedy consisted of bulls in speech, blunders in action. This was chiefly a commercial formula: in the later eighteenth century the actors Moody and Johnstone, who drew audiences to Covent Garden as Irish character-actors, had such parts repeatedly written for them, while in the eighteen-thirties Tyrone Power specialised in Irish parts, many of which were provided for him by Samuel Lover. Power popularised the image of the 'lovable Irish blunderer' who, though garrulous, combative and drunken, was presented as a clever and vivacious rogue, and as a good singer.

This type was capitalised upon by the facile writer of melodrama, Dion Boucicault. Born in Dublin about 1820 he ran away from school in England to become an actor and scored his first success with *London Assurance* (1841). In 1860, after writing successful plays in London and New York, he turned to Irish themes, drawing on Gerald Griffin's novel *The Collegians* and Lover's *Rory O'Moore* for *The Colleen Bawn* (1860) and *Arrah-na-Pogue* (1865), both sentimental melodramas built mainly around the lovable Irish rogue-type character in which the author excelled. *The Shaughraun* (1874), a huge financial success in New York, followed the same recipe. Synge commented on how beneath Boucicault's absurd plots and sentiment lay some good acting comedy, while O'Casey, who played Father Dolan in *The Shaughraun* in 1895, learned something of the successful blending of serious and comic incident from Boucicault's craft.

Boucicault, however, did not essentially affect the situation of the nineteenth-century Irish theatre any more than did the choice of Irish settings by a number of minor writers of his time; these were invariably chosen in order to introduce Irish songs, dances, drinking, races and faction-fights. The deletion of the song 'The Wearing of the Green' from *Arrah-na-Pogue* by government edict because of some added reference to Fenianism, showed also that Irish plays were under political scrutiny by the censors. Under such circumstances it seemed impossible that a genuine Irish theatre could ever take shape. Ironically the two leading dramatists of the English theatre at the end of the century were two Dublin-born Irishmen.

The plays of Oscar Wilde (1854-1900) and of George Bernard Shaw (1856-1950) properly belong to English theatrical history. Both men left Dublin for London in their twenties. By 1899 Wilde had achieved a remarkable success with four plays: *Lady Windermere's Fan* (1892), *A Woman of No Importance* (1892), *An Ideal Husband* (1895) and *The Importance of Being Earnest* (1895), his masterpiece of satirical comedy. Wilde exploited with brilliance the conventional form of contemporary London society-drama. His earlier plays, notably *Salome* (1893-4), suggest certain affinities with Yeats's poetic plays. He died the year after the Irish Literary Theatre began. Shaw had a harder struggle to win recognition, mainly because of the radical ideas for which he used the vehicle of conventional dramatic form. He was nearing international fame by 1904 and had achieved it by 1910. He had sporadic contacts with the Irish theatre, notably over *John Bull's Other Island* (1905) and *The Shewing-up of Blanco Posnet* (1909). The preface to the former should be read if one is to understand Shaw's perception of his own individual Irish quality.[1] His prose owes a good deal to Swift, his drama to Ibsen's use of the argument in exposition.

II

In the late nineties when Yeats, Edward Martyn and Lady Gregory began to discuss the possibilities of an Irish theatre, they were united in their dislike of the commercial theatre and in their wish to provide Ireland with a better means of dramatic expression. Yeats had been interested in this idea for almost a decade. In Dublin in the later eighties he had realised that theatrical expression might suit the Irish nature; in 1889, when living in London, Maud Gonne had discussed with him the seemingly remote possibility of having his *Countess Cathleen* staged by amateurs in Dublin, and about the same time his experience of a little theatre in Bedford Park, with which his friend John Todhunter was associated, had shown him what gifted amateurs could achieve in the production of verse-plays with simple artistic settings.

In 1894, through the backing of Miss A.E.F. Horniman, daughter of a wealthy English tea-merchant, who was altruistically interested in the artistic development of the English theatre, Yeats's play *The Land of Heart's Desire* had been produced in London as a curtain-raiser to Shaw's *Arms and the Man* and a play by Todhunter. About that time Yeats had met George Moore. Since Moore was an old friend of Martyn, had travelled with a touring company to obtain 'copy' for his novel, *A Mummer's Wife,* and had written his first play about 1876, it was natural that he should be asked to help in the work of the Irish Literary Theatre. Its appeal for the production of some Irish plays in Dublin each year which would help to build up an Irish school of dramatic literature and so 'bring upon the stage the deeper thought and emotions of Ireland' met with considerable response and the Irish Literary Theatre, whose expenses were underwritten by Martyn, began its productions in 1899.

If one considers 'the three A's of the theatre', authors, actors and audiences, the obstacles to success were many. Yeats had one produced and one published play to his credit; Martyn was in process of writing a play; Lady Gregory had not as yet even thought of playwriting. Moore had some reputation as a dramatist but was much better known as the author of the realistic novel *Esther Waters.* As far as the group knew, there were no home-based Irish actors of the requisite professional training and no competent Irish directors who could train them. Irish audiences could be found for Shakespeare, for imported commercial plays or for the melodramas of Boucicault or Whitbread, but seemed even less likely to support intellectual or poetic drama than their English counterparts.

On the other hand Europe recently had provided examples of what could be done by intelligent and determined theatrical groups prompted by the works of Ibsen, Strindberg, Chekhov and Maeterlinck. To produce such dramatists there had sprung up in turn Antoine's Théâtre Libre in Paris (1887), Stanislavsky's Society of Literature and Art (1888), Germany's Freie Buhne Theatre (1889) and J.T. Grein's Independent Theatre in London

(1891). The Irish Literary Theatre could look further back, to Ole Bull's National Theatre in Norway, which in 1850 had switched dramatic activity from Danish to Norwegian hands, or to the more recent establishment by Stanislavsky and Nemirovitch-Danchenko in 1898 of the Moscow Arts Theatre, whose productions of Chekhov were soon to make it famous.

A notable difference between these continental theatres and the Irish Literary Theatre is that, except in the case of Norway, the nations concerned had centuries of native drama behind them and were trying to reform by artistic innovation, while Yeats and his friends were facing the more formidable task of creating an Irish dramatic tradition where none existed. This involved two kinds of innovation; the authentic artistic use of Irish material — which *inter alia* would dispose summarily of the Boucicault tradition and what Yeats called that 'comic scarecrow, the stage Irishman' — and, within the wider orbit of the English-speaking theatre, the restoration of poetic and imaginative drama to the stage, from which it had almost completely disappeared.

The links between European drama and the Irish movement in its early stages were Moore and Martyn. Moore had been associated with the Independent Theatre almost from its inception; he had written one play for it, *The Strike at Arlingford,* and had helped to direct several others. He was more interested in making Ireland an artistic centre where the best dramatic literature of all countries, including Ireland, could flourish than in concentrating on the creation of a specifically Irish tradition. The latter, to which he was not antagonistic, might well come through the revival of Irish, for which he was temporarily enthusiastic; but he thought that contemporary Irish drama in English should be developed by contact with such writers as Ibsen and Maeterlinck. Martyn, in whom the influence of Ibsen and Strindberg was hampered by a decidedly conservative Catholicism (continually at odds with Moore's anti-Catholicism), had a similar aim. Yeats and Lady Gregory, on the whole, had other ideas. The initial statement, which they composed together in 1898 to announce the formation of the Irish Literary Theatre, referred to the projected production of 'Celtic and Irish plays' and 'a Celtic and Irish school of dramatic literature'. Lady Gregory later had doubts about their casual use of the term 'Celtic', but when in January 1899 Yeats spoke to the Irish National Literary Society about the forthcoming production of *The Countess Cathleen* and Martyn's Ibsenish play *The Heather Field*, he described them as 'a mediaeval Celtic drama in verse and a modern Celtic drama in prose'. The terminology is not important except in indicating that Yeats and Lady Gregory were then thinking primarily in terms of Irish literary and traditional sources.

These different views did not prevent the co-operation of the founders of the Irish Literary Theatre in finding English players, including Florence Farr, May Whitty and the Bensons, for the productions of their three seasons. The principal authors were Martyn *(The Heather Field,* 1899; *Maeve,* 1900) and Moore *(The Bending of the Bough,* 1900, a social play adapted from Martyn), who wrote *Diarmuid and Grania* (1901) in collaboration with Yeats, whose *Countess Cathleen* (1899) was performed with a prologue written by Lionel Johnson. The other authors were Alice Milligan *(The Last Feast of the Fianna,* 1900) and Douglas Hyde, who played in his own play *Casadh an tSugáin* ('The Twisting of the Rope', 1901), which was acted in Irish by members of the Gaelic Amateur Dramatic Society. Of these seven plays only *The Countess Cathleen* has stood the test of time, but it is one of the weakest of Yeats's plays. Some of the others are of slight interest; Martyn at least made a bid to write modern psychological and symbolic plays, Moore a play of social conflict after the manner of Ibsen, while Hyde's little one-act play certainly helped to influence both Synge and Lady Gregory about the possibilities of the 'peasant play' and stirred many Irish language supporters to attempt plays in the following years. Artistically the plays could be faulted in many respects, Martyn's on the grounds of vagueness and lack of dramatic power, Moore's because of intolerably long speeches which read like public addresses, Hyde's as a simplistic trifle, while Alice Milligan's legendary play needed the saving grace of good verse. Further, English players, for the most part, sounded oddly in Irish plays, while the Irish audiences who attended them were uncritical, both in praise and in blame, often judging the plays on nationalistic, religious or linguistic grounds.

They received little critical guidance from the popular press or from the few current literary reviews. The *Freeman's Journal* attack on *The Countess Cathleen* (later published as the pamphlet *Souls for Gold)* was echoed in the *New Ireland Review* by George O'Neill, S.J., although its editor, Thomas Finlay, S.J., had privately approved of the play. Yeats's defence in *Beltaine* unfortunately used the argument that the play belonged to the world of the folk-tale and had no definite connection with Ireland, whereupon O'Neill quoted Yeats's preface to the published version of 1892 in which the contrary was stated. O'Neill's praise for the idealism of Martyn's *The Heather Field* in 1899 contrasted oddly with the review's attack on all three productions of 1900 as either abnormal, pagan or trivial, since almost the only thing the plays had in common was that they were idealistic. While this kind of criticism was the product of the conservative Catholic policy of the *New Ireland Review*, what could one make of Standish James O'Grady's dismissal in his *All Ireland Review* in the same year of the whole principle of the dramatic treatment of heroic material as writing for tourists and the mob? O'Grady followed this up in 1901 by denouncing *Diarmuid and Grania* as immoral because Finn was represented as a man of vengeance: 'the hero and prophet is sullied and his character aspersed'. Apparently O'Grady was trying to have it both ways; he was convinced that the sagas could be used to form the moral character of youth, but had suppressed from his *History of Ireland: Heroic Period* such incidents as Cuchulainn's love-affair with Aoife, part of the legend treated by Yeats in *On Baile's Strand*. While the 'father of the Irish literary revival' was thus attacking his own literary children on moral principles, Joyce was soon attacking them on artistic principles. His pamphlet *The Day of the Rabblement* (1901) accused the Irish Literary Theatre's leaders of 'surrendering to the trolls' by concentrating on Irish plays and ignoring the production of continental masterpieces, the proper models for Irish dramatists.

And yet, for all that was done and said, the three seasons of the Irish Literary Theatre accomplished much. They had begun a dramatic movement which was taken seriously. They had proved their own sincerity of purpose; this was acknowledged even by some hostile critics. For all their defects their plays had shown that the poetic-legendary, the socio-political and the psychological play could be written by Irish authors, and that audiences could be found for these and for plays in Irish. Incidentally Yeats had discovered that *The Heather Field* and *The Bending of the Bough* were more popular than his own verse-drama. He announced before the last season's performances in October 1901 that they would end the experiment of the Irish Literary Theatre and that a new movement of a different type was projected.

Thus the second phase of the Irish dramatic movement was heralded. By this time the cleavage of aims between Martyn and

Moore, Yeats and Lady Gregory was more definite. Martyn was tired of having his own plays adapted or rewritten by Yeats and Moore; Moore's collaboration with Yeats had proved an uneasy alliance of mutually antagonistic personalities. Both Moore and Martyn wanted a more modern type of Irish play. Yeats, as he clearly explained in *Samhain* (1901), was hoping 'to get our Heroic Age into verse and to solve some problems of the speaking of verse to musical notes'; both he and Lady Gregory wanted 'peasant plays' in English.

At this stage, Edward Martyn had refused to back any more productions but soon other possibilities offered, for the brothers William and Frank Fay appeared on the scene. The former had produced Hyde's play and had decided that what Irish drama needed at that point was a native Irish company with competent training in the arts of the theatre rather than a theatre whose bias was literary. The brothers formed such a group from members of their own small Ormonde Dramatic Society and of Maud Gonne's Inghínídhe na h-Éireann ('Daughters of Ireland') who were then active in producing patriotic pageants; they called it the Irish National Dramatic Company. Yeats saw the company's production of an historical play by Alice Milligan and gave it his *Cathleen ni Houlihan* to be played with A.E.'s *Deirdre* in April 1902. The latter is a vague and static treatment of the legend, but it was well received, while the appearance of Maud Gonne as Cathleen increased the audience's enthusiasm for Yeats's play; 'the first play where dialect was not used with an exclusively comic intention', he wrote later. Lady Gregory had helped with the dialogue and so was herself one step further towards play-writing.

The success of the first venture of 1902, which was financed by Inghínídhe na hÉireann, was somewhat diminished through the Fays' determination to have their own theatre-workshop; this led them to choose a small hall in Camden Street, Dublin, where the cramped conditions handicapped their October production. The plays (to judge by those that survive in printed form) were inferior to those of their previous bill; *The Pot of Broth* by Yeats (owing a great deal to Lady Gregory), two plays by J.H. Cousins, an Ibsenish play by F.W. Ryan and a play in Irish by P.T. MacGinley. Meanwhile the Fays had decided to form the Irish National Theatre Society and this decision was put into effect in February 1903, Yeats being elected as president, with Maud Gonne, A.E. and Hyde as vice-presidents, and W.G. Fay as stage manager.

Yeats was now the figure-head of a society whose company included the Fays, Dudley Digges, Máire nic Shiubhlaigh, Maire Quinn and Sara Allgood, but he had no real authority. The company had two principles: to remain unpaid and to make their decisions, including their choice of plays, co-operatively. It had a workshop which served for rehearsals and other preparatory activities and soon became a focus of literary attention. A.E. was at its centre, writers like Colum and Seumas O'Sullivan were among its players, and others — Martyn, Moore, Joyce, Gogarty — were frequent visitors. The playwrights of the Society's 1903 seasons were those who really determined the future course of events; first in March came Yeats's *The Hour-Glass* and Lady Gregory's *Twenty-five;* then in October Synge's *In the Shadow of the Glen* followed Yeats's *The King's Threshold;* and finally the December production was Padraic Colum's *Broken Soil* (later rewritten as *The Fiddler's House*). Thus the verse-play and the heroic play, represented by Yeats, and the 'peasant play', represented by the others, set the mould of the future.

Joyce's attack, natural enough from that fervent disciple of Ibsen and translator of Hauptmann, now seemed unjustified in one respect: except for Lady Gregory's trifle, *Twenty-five,* these plays were of considerable artistic merit and represented no surrender to popularity. But, in fact, Colum's conception of drama had been completely changed by reading Ibsen, and *Broken Soil* was the result. The struggle of Con Hourican, the old fiddler, between a secure life on the land and the practice of his art in the wandering life of the roads was 'realistic' in its characters and in its subdued but quietly poetic rural dialogue; yet it was symbolic and universal in its counterpointed values. This transformation in Colum lends strength to Joyce's central argument that Ireland needed good productions of foreign masterpieces as models for her playwrights.

On this matter Yeats's attitude seems ambiguous. He sometimes praised Ibsen as the great modern dramatist, singling out the poetic folk-play *Peer Gynt* and the heroic play, *The Warriors of Helgeland,* for special mention. Yet both he and Synge seem to have shared a fundamental distrust of Ibsen's influence. About this time Yeats warned Padraic Colum of the danger of becoming 'obsessed with the translation', by which he appears to have meant that translations of Ibsen and other continental masters might damage the personal language of the playwright. It is also possible that William Archer's pallid translations of Ibsen's plays of social realism and the mediocre quality of Martyn's and Moore's emulations increased this feeling. In *Samhain* and elsewhere, Yeats's advice to learn, construction from such masters and dialogue from ourselves was sound enough. Yet in his dismissal of 'the modish interest in psychology' he was much too casual about one current of contemporary thought which had helped both Ibsen and Strindberg to achieve greatness in an area other than that of construction, the dramatic probing of human personality, a form of psychological realism.

These considerations did not immediately affect the progress of the Irish National Theatre Society during 1903. The great literary event had been the arrival of Synge as one of its dramatists; the artistic quality of *In the Shadow of the Glen* had impressed discerning critics and even the controversy which it aroused had helped to create interest in the company. Such is the way of controversies. They are inevitable in any progressive theatre, as the examples of Ole Bull, of Ibsen, of Antoine or of J.T. Grein prove, and they are of more sociological than literary interest after a decade or two, by which time the offending works have been accepted as classics. Today the attack of the *Independent* newspaper which condemned the departure of Nora with the poetic tramp as highly immoral and ignored the fact that her old husband had thrown her out, with the pious hope that she would end 'like a dead sheep with the frost on her', seems as absurd as Arthur Griffith's argument that the play was derived from a foreign pagan source; it was in fact a dramatisation of old Pat Dirrane's folk-tale told to Synge on Aran. The morale of the company, already strengthened by success outside Dublin, in Loughrea, and later under the auspices of the Irish Literary Society in London, was raised further by Miss Horniman's response to Yeats's appeal after *The King's Threshold*. She would give him a theatre.

A good deal of Yeats's writing in *Samhain* (1903) had been devoted to a defence of Synge but his article on the reform of the theatre, which helped to influence Miss Horniman, stated clearly what he wanted: plays of intellectual excitement, where language was supreme; simple, restrained acting, scenery and costume. In 1904, while the old Dublin morgue and Mechanic's Institute were being reconstructed for the new theatre,[2] his *Samhain* articles were expanding his views on such matters as the necessity for proper voice-production, the dramatic possibilities of using choruses and interspersed lyrics, as in the Greek and Elizabethan theatres, and the effect of speaking dramatic verse on a planned series of musical notes. The last point remained somewhat obscure; Yeats's exposition of it in 1902 had not been particularly clear and Florence Farr's demonstration to the psaltery had seemed to prove that intoning or chanting words in a stage play could make them monotonous and insufficiently articulated. Shaw wrote impatiently to her that chanting involved no new art ('Yeats thinks so only because he does not go to church') and that the chief business of the player was to convey the meaning and feeling of the author. Although in 1904 Yeats seemed to be restricting his argument to established practice, his reference to new efforts 'to find out some way of setting serious poetry which will enable us to hear it' indicates that he probably had in mind the choruses of his new play *On Baile's Strand,* with which the new theatre was to open late that year.

These essays were written with new confidence and hope. The patent for the theatre, although opposed by the commercial theatres, had been granted

> to produce plays written in Irish or English by Irish writers or on Irish subjects, or such dramatic works of foreign authors as would tend to educate and interest the public in the higher aspects of dramatic art.

Since the laws governing theatrical performances had been passed by the old Anglo-Irish Protestant parliament, the Lord Chamberlain of Britain had no rights of censorship over the new theatre. Yeats emphasised this point, although it seemed insignificant enough at the time. He also hoped that the new theatre would assist the spread of amateur societies throughout Ireland and would become a link with them and with the various Irish language productions which writers like Father Peter O'Leary and Father Dineen were fostering in the Gaelic League. Yeats was obviously gaining power as a positive tactician as well as a controversialist; his attacks on propagandist art and on prejudicial criticism, launched with a well-tempered rhetoric, reinforced those idealistic passages which explored the nature of art or appealed to the 'vivid sensitiveness as to the reality of things' of his potential audiences.

His belief in the native dramatic potentialities inherent in his countrymen's fondness for conversation, for vivid gesture and self-dramatisation was supported by the artistic success of the I.N.T.S. in Synge's *Riders to the Sea* (February 1904), and by the London tour (March 1904), which more than compensated for the comparative failure of Yeats's poetic but dramatically vague play, *The Shadowy Waters,* in January of the same year. Yeats was now qualifying further his admiration of Ibsen's art and of Antoine's production-methods, while Frank Fay was writing to Joseph Holloway to say that playwrights should study Ibsen, as one of the theatre's principal difficulties would be to get strong modern plays: 'When it is not Shakespeare who is hurled at our heads, it is Boucicault, who was a master of commonplace stagecraft with nothing to say.' As if to justify Yeats's qualifications, Edward Martyn's play *The Enchanted Sea,* probably based on Ibsen's *The Lady from the Sea,* was performed shortly after by the short-lived Players' Club which he had founded, and failed dismally. W.G. Fay had turned it down after two rehearsals.

Meanwhile Moore, not long before the Abbey Theatre opened its doors, was trying to resume friendship with Yeats, who wrote to Frank Fay that Moore's return to the Irish theatre was out of the question: 'he represents a rival tradition of the stage and would upset your brother's plans at every turn.' Ibsen's drama was now identified by him with the naturalistic play — a narrow conception when one considers Ibsen's note on *Ghosts* ('like a picture of life ... but only an appearance — everything is ghosts') — and his *Samhain* articles were soon publicly dismissing Shaw, Wilde and Moore as writers who 'never keep their heads for long out of the flood of opinion'. His concurrent praise for the maxim of the writers of the Norwegian national movement, 'To understand the saga by the peasant and the peasant by the saga', was due to his own preoccupation with the dramatisation of Irish heroic legend for which Lady Gregory's *Cuchulain of Muirthemne* (1902) had provided a source-book, and in this direction as well as in that of the folk-play he intended the Irish playwrights to go.

The two plays which with *Cathleen ni Hoolihan* made up the opening programme of the Abbey Theatre on 27 December, 1904, were Yeats's *On Baile's Strand* and Lady Gregory's *Spreading the News;* the first a verse play on the heroic theme of the death of Cuchulainn's only son, the second a folk-comedy in which local gossip inflates a bubble of trivialities into an imagined murder before the 'corpse' punctures it by stepping from the grave untimely forth. The quality of the three plays, the acting of the

J. M. Synge

from a drawing by John B. Yeats R.H.A.

J. M. Synge. Courtesy of Bord Fáilte.

Fays, of Máire nic Shiubhlaigh and Sara Allgood, and the simple but colourful settings all contributed to an electrifying sense of a great beginning.

The next five years saw the first phase of the history of the Abbey Theatre. Artistically this was its most successful phase. Synge's first full-length play *The Well of the Saints* (1905), although the most static of his plays, was full of poetic tragi-comedy, *The Playboy of the Western World* (1907) a masterpiece, while the posthumously produced *Deirdre of the Sorrows* (January 1910) showed that a heroic theme and folk-idiom could be combined in a work of tragic beauty. Yeats's *Deirdre* (1906), *The Unicorn from the Stars* (1907) written in collaboration with Lady Gregory, and *The Golden Helmet* (1908) were produced during the same period. So were the more lasting of Lady Gregory's plays, *Hyacinth Halvey* (1906), *The Rising of the Moon* (1907) and *The Workhouse Ward* (1908), all short comedies. They are only a small part of her dramatic output between March 1905 and November 1909, for she also tried her hand at tragedy and at the 'folk history' play, producing in all eleven plays as well as three translations from Molière *(The Doctor in Spite of Himself,* 1906; *The Rogueries of Scapin,* 1908, and *The Miser,* 1909). New playwrights also began to appear: George Fitzmaurice turned from the naturalistic peasant play *(The Country Dressmaker,* 1907) to the folk fantasy *(The Pie-Dish,* 1908); Lord Dunsany started his series of fantasies with *The Glittering Gate* (1909); realistic playwrights included William Boyle *(The Building Fund,* 1905; *The Eloquent Dempsey* and *The Mineral Workers,* 1906), W.F. Casey *(The Man who missed the Tide* and *The Suburban Groove,* 1908) and Lennox Robinson *(The Clancy Name,* 1908, and *The Cross Roads,* 1909).

In 1905, Bernard Shaw, always a good friend, offered the Abbey *John Bull's Other Island* on patriotic grounds. It seemed an ideal offering, for it got good comedy out of satirising many English misconceptions about Ireland, and in fact had been written at Yeats's request. The directors refused it on the ostensible grounds that the company had no Broadbent, but the anti-romantic nature of the play and Yeats's opinion of Shaw must have had some influence on their decision; Yeats's remark to Florence Farr in 1907 is significant: 'Ah if he had but style, distinction, and was not such a barbarian of the barricades.' However, when *The Shewing-up of Blanco Posnet* (which Shaw subtitled 'A Sermon in Crude Melodrama') was banned in

England by the Lord Chamberlain, it was successfully produced at the Abbey in 1909. As the theatre had already stood firmly against Irish faction-censorship of *The Playboy of the Western World,* its stand against Dublin Castle on this occasion increased the directors' reputation for artistic integrity both at home and abroad.

This period of artistic success was marked by fluctuations of fortune in the theatre's affairs. Audiences were unpredictable; controversy over the *Playboy* caused a temporary boycott while *Blanco Posnet* played to packed houses, largely because the theatre was defying the government. The *Well of the Saints* and Lady Gregory's serious plays usually kept them out, as did Yeats's. Audiences preferred Lady Gregory's comedies, the more naturalistic kind of play written by Colum *(The Land,* 1905) and W.F. Casey, and the 'rollicking comedies' written by Boyle. From what details are available it appears that performances (irrespective of audience numbers) of plays by Gregory, Yeats and Synge during the period 1904 to 1912 account for roughly half the theatre's productions, and of this amount more than half were by Lady Gregory.

The company ran into trouble when in 1905 it decided to form itself into a limited company, with Yeats, Lady Gregory and Synge as directors holding the bulk of the shares. This was followed by a decision, passed by a share-holding majority but numerical minority, to accept Miss Horniman's generous offer to provide a sum which would put the company on a completely professional basis. While this made complete sense, the majority of the members appears to have felt that the new employer-employee relationship and professonalism conflicted with their original co-operative aims. A.E., Padraic Colum, Maire nic Shiubhlaigh and the bulk of the members resigned in 1906, to form the nucleus of the 'Theatre of Ireland', which Edward Martyn financed. The Fays remained, as did most of the best players, and the Abbey Theatre weathered that particular storm. A worse one was already blowing up.

It began with a number of personality and policy clashes in which Yeats, Lady Gregory, Miss Horniman and the Fays, in varying combinations, were involved. Sometimes the matters concerned were administrative, as when Miss Horniman wanted a stricter discipline over the players, whose English tours she financed and whose faults she attributed to the Fays. Sometimes they were technical; differences of opinion about acting or elocution or casting between Yeats and the Fays. At other times they were tinged with politics; neither the Fays nor Miss Horniman were without bias on this score. And sometimes they were downright personal. It is difficult to imagine the ethereal lady of John Butler Yeats's portrait writing to Yeats that Lady Gregory and Synge 'grovel at Fay's feet' and that he himself was

> ceaselessly victimised by Lady Gregory on the score of your gratitude for her kindness: You are being made a slave, your genius is put under a net in that precious 'garden' and you are only let out when you are wanted to get something out of *me*.[3]

If one glances at Mancini's ebullient portrait of Lady Gregory, which also hangs in the Abbey foyer, one perhaps glimpses some truth in the bitter words.

Yet all of them had good intentions: Miss Horniman thought primarily of drama, Yeats and Gregory of a national drama, and the Fays, who thought of both aims, were the best available means to achieve them. Certainly William Fay's recollection of the brothers' aims in 1907 refers specifically to that of a real art theatre, as visualised by Miss Horniman, with a company capable of playing any type of play. To get this, he told the directors, would take ten years' hard training and he would need the usual power of a manager and producer; otherwise they would have to continue with peasant plays, 'which would mean first stagnation and ultimately, when we found no more pots to boil and no more news to spread, death'.[4]

The phrasing is clearly aimed at Yeats and Lady Gregory; but Fay was depressed by the failure of Lady Gregory's *Dervorgilla* and of *The Unicorn from the Stars*. Also he felt that he had worked hard but at thirty-five was getting nowhere; and about this time Frohman, the American producer, was taking an interest in him. When the directors turned down his request for full authority, he and his brother resigned and soon departed for America. Later, polite meaningless words were followed by public recriminations from which nobody emerged with credit. In effect, the Fays were lost to the Abbey Theatre.

Shortly afterwards so was Miss Horniman. In 1910 she was at odds with the directors who had not closed the theatre on the occasion of the death of King Edward VII of England. Yeats in France left the decision to Lady Gregory at Coole and her telegram arrived too late to prevent the new manager, Lennox Robinson, from opening. Miss Horniman demanded his dismissal, which was refused. This helped to bring to a head her determination to withdraw from the affairs of the Abbey Theatre. She was generous to the last and in effect transferred the theatre to the Irish National Theatre Society Ltd at a purely nominal cost. She and Lady Gregory, Maud Gonne discerned, should have been allies but, as she put it, 'both like Willie too well'.

Meanwhile the Abbey Theatre suffered its biggest artistic loss with the death of Synge in March 1909. His plays by that time were receiving continental productions. The posthumous production of *Deirdre of the Sorrows* in January 1910, even in its unrevised form, showed his essential power in treating a heroic theme and he had planned to write a play set in the Dublin area of Swift's cathedral. He was the greatest original dramatic genius of the movement at that point and many hopeful prospects were suddenly blocked by his untimely death at the age of thirty-eight. Yeats thought that it marked a phase, the end of the Celtic phase and the beginning of the Irish phase of the dramatic movement. What he seems to have meant is that the day of the heroic play and of the imaginative 'peasant play' was over and that plays of a naturalistic kind would triumph.

This is precisely where the Abbey Theatre was vulnerable from an artistic point of view. The position is clearly stated in a memorandum which Yeats prepared for the directors about the end of 1907: the company was excellent in peasant comedy and in nothing else and its popularity depended chiefly on two writers, Boyle and Gregory; there was little demand for verse plays. More writers might appear if the players widened their range by acting in foreign masterpieces. The theatre should ultimately become, like the independent European theatres, capable of performing all great drama, and at the same time it should be unique in some special aspect of drama.

This review of the situation, which seems to have incorporated the views of the Fays, was sensible. The continental theatres had not set out to become folk-theatres but the Abbey Theatre in effect had become one. The company had its special excellence but lacked range. One of its aims, as stated in the patent, had been the production of foreign masterpieces, but up to 1907 it had produced only Lady Gregory's translation of *A Doctor in Spite of Himself* and a one-act play by Maeterlinck (*Interior*, 1907). The models which Joyce had demanded had not appeared and the help which Moore, Shaw, Miss Horniman and the Fays might have given had not been properly developed. From the practical point of view the loss of Miss Horniman's subsidy later meant that the theatre had to depend more than ever upon audiences. It was a vicious circle, for the audience for foreign masterpieces had not been created and the players were in no position to create it.

It is easy to understand why the seven years after the death of Synge were comparatively lean years. Yeats contributed only one new play, *The Green Helmet* (1910), a poetic revision of his prose play *The Golden Helmet*. Lady Gregory had some eight new plays produced; none of them, except perhaps *Shanwalla* (1915), had any lasting quality. Plays which might be called roughly 'realistic' were in fashion. Colum continued in this tradition with *Thomas Muskerry* (1910), perhaps his best play. Then there were the 'three Cork realists', Lennox Robinson, T.C. Murray and R.J. Ray. Ray's plays were of slight merit, being crudely-written melodramas. Murray's *Birthright* (1910) and *Maurice Harte* (1912) were somewhat melodramatic but had genuine power of character and speech, the former dealing with fratricide over disinheritance, the second with the 'spoiled priest' in a small farming family. Of these three playwrights Lennox Robinson was the most competent and the most prolific. His appointment as manager and producer in 1909 had begun a close association with the theatre which was to last almost half a century, and the five plays which followed *The Clancy Name,* 1908 (*The Cross Roads,* 1909; *Harvest,* 1910; *Patriots,* 1912; *The Dreamers,* 1915 and *The Whiteheaded Boy,* 1916) showed remarkable professional competence, the last of them being a comic masterpiece. Robinson like Colum had begun to explore the dramatic potentialities of Irish middle-class life. So had W.F. Casey and William Boyle, cruder writers of melodrama and comedy, whose work was immensely popular at the time but appears much too 'dated' today. Another of the realists, a better dramatist than either of this pair, was St John Ervine. Like Robinson he owed something of his skill to a study of English repertory methods; his most lasting plays of this period are probably *Mixed Marriage* (1911) and *John Ferguson* (1915), a strong melodrama about Ulster middle-class life. Ervine was manager of the Abbey Theatre for a few years but his eyes were too much on English repertory fare, which he sometimes plagiarised (*The Magnanimous Lover,* 1912), and his unpopularity with the players led to his early departure in 1916.

The period after the death of Synge was therefore marked by the triumph, in one form or another, of realism in the Abbey Theatre. It was also a period of professionalism. The theatre alrady had a good professoinal company. Only from 1910, it should be remembered, did its authors receive royalties; and the authors, whether they thought primarily of royalties or not, wrote the kind of play which they knew the actors could do best, while the directors, whatever their principles, had to take cognisance of what audiences liked, for their theatre was no longer subsidised. The rise of professional playwrights, good or bad, in fact helped the players' professional competence, though within a restricted range, kept the theatre afloat and partly preserved its reputation, if on a less artistic level.

It was thought that an American tour might bring in funds and raise this reputation, as tours in England had done, and in 1911 part of the company travelled to America , bringing *The Playboy, In the Shadow of the Glen, Birthright* and *Hyacinth Halvey*. The tour lasted six months and successfully fought again the old battles whose storm-centre was *The Playboy;* the company was legally vindicated of the charge of performing 'immoral and indecent plays' at Philadelphia and returned home after an artistic and financial victory. Subsequent tours in 1913 and 1914 were not so profitable but met only slight opposition; all three certainly helped the theatre's artistic reputation abroad and also had some effect on the American 'little theatre' movement and the formation of such groups as the Provincetown Players, which included Eugene O'Neill.

In Dublin the 'Theatre of Ireland' had first seemed likely to offer serious and healthy competition to the Abbey Theatre. Its authors included Martyn, Padraic Colum and J.H. Cousins, and it had considerable support from literary figures such as A.E. and James Stephens, from young nationalists such as Padraig Pearse and Thomas Kettle, and from the Gaelic League. In 1906 its opening programme included Act IV of Ibsen's *Brand,* as well as revivals of plays by Cousins and by Hyde. From that until 1912 it had a large following which it failed to keep through incompetent acting and production and through lack of permanent venue. However, it did bring to the notice of the public one reasonably good new playwright, Seamus O'Kelly. His play, *The Shuiler's*

Child (1909), which dramatised a wandering woman's surrender of her child to a couple who could provide for it, had considerable tragic power. Like Máire nic Shiubhlaigh who played the 'shuiler' in 1909, this play found its way eventually to the Abbey. This actress recalled O'Kelly telling her that the play was conceived when he saw the *Brand* performance. The Theatre of Ireland might have provided an international counterpart to the national theatre but its collapse in 1912 meant that Dublin had to wait until 1928 for that kind of theatre.

The Irish dramatic movement also played some part in stimulating drama in Belfast, first through contact between the Fays' Irish National Dramatic Company and the Belfast Protestant National Society which led to the formation of a Belfast branch of the movement in 1902. Under its auspices some of the Dublin company's plays were performed in Belfast in 1902 and 1903. The following year the Ulster Literary Theatre was founded, opening its first season with plays by Lewis Purcell and Bulmer Hobson, and a little quarterly journal *Uladh* was published in which Hobson explained its aims. These were similar to those of the Dublin movement, but concentration was to be on the Ulster theatre, whose talent, Hobson thought, would be more satiric than poetic, and on the publication of Ulster plays. The Ulster movement unfortunately lacked cohesion and had no base like the Abbey Theatre. *Uladh* lasted only a year, the plays of almost all the playwrights remained unpublished, and although the group played in Dublin, London and America as well as in Belfast during the decade after its foundation, it failed to maintain the promise of its early individuality. The work of its best playwright, 'Rutherford Mayne' (Sam Waddell), indicates where that promise lay: *The Turn of the Road* (1906), *The Drone* (1908) and *The Troth* (1909), show a good grasp of Ulster character and of distinctive Ulster speech. Ernest Boyd, who considered that those plays faithfully reflect 'Irish conditions modified by prosperity and Protestanitism', perceptively pointed out that 'a cottage scene in an Ulster play evokes circumstances absolutely different from those suggested by the same setting for a play by Synge or Colum', and that the unity of a Catholic and Protestant tenant in destroying their rapacious landlord (in *The Troth*) reveals the real sense of values underlying their religious differences. Mayne wrote a one-act play, *Red Turf*, for production by the Abbey Theatre in 1912. His best full-length play,

Bridgehead, was produced there many years later, in 1934. He was almost the only dramatist of the Ulster Literary Theatre whose plays found publication and perhaps the only one whose literary qualities deserved it.

The period after the death of Synge had been difficult enough; the Rising of 1916 and its aftermath brought new dislocations. The events of Easter week closed the theatre in April 1916; the following months Yeats and Lady Gregory decided to let the Abbey Theatre for business premises about the same time that the players, who were playing in Limerick, rebelled against Ervine's policy and politics, and refused to play under his direction. By September the directors were rid of Ervine and a new producer (J.A. Keogh) had begun a series of Shaw plays. Then from 1919 to 1921, during the guerilla war of independence, curfew and ambushes in the city streets caused the theatres to close; this hit the Abbey particularly hard. By the end of the Civil War Yeats and Lady Gregory were facing the probable bankruptcy of the theatre. It was still full of vitality; it had a considerable repertory, new popular dramatists, including Sean O'Casey, were writing for it and Lennox Robinson was proving a successful producer; but the financial situation forced Yeats and Lady Gregory to offer the theatre, which they had built up for the Irish nation, to the new Irish government as a state theatre. The offer was not accepted but led to the grant of a state subsidy, the first given to any theatre in the English-speaking world. So, after a quarter of a century, with the Abbey Theatre coming of age in 1925, the Irish dramatic movement had issued in a national theatre established on a permanent basis.

Interior and exterior of the old Abbey Theatre. Photograph G. A. Duncan.

CHAPTER XVI

Critical Assessment of the Dramatists

I

Perhaps the most striking thing about that period of 1899 to 1925 was the artistic quality of the movement's best dramatic works. All of Synge's plays and most of the best plays of Yeats, Lady Gregory, Padraic Colum and Sean O'Casey belong to it. It is upon them that the 'Abbey tradition' was founded and little of a comparable quality has been added to it since. Twenty-five years is a small span in a country's history of dramatic literature and it is extraordinary that a movement within that period of time, starting from scratch, could produce a body of work which became acted and studied as a contribution to the world's classics of the theatre.

When Yeats received the Nobel Prize for Literature in 1923 he visualised Synge and Lady Gregory standing by his side, linked to him by the common cause of serving their country. Synge was certainly the greatest dramatist of the movement. Up to 1902, his thirty-first year, only beginnings and potentialities can be seen. His trained naturalist's eye, his interest in music, his first choice of a career, then his study of Racine and of Molière, as his aim changed towards literary criticism, were to prove of importance later; so was his interest in Irish, which probably became active in his teens, when, as he tells in his *Autobiography,* he abandoned his inherited evangelical Protestantism and political loyalty for a temperate nationalism. This made him 'the black sheep of the family' (a discarded title for the *Playboy*) and deepened the isolation which this enigmatic artist had to cope with. Yet his poetry showed only a moderate talent. Then in 1896 came Yeats's advice to go to Aran and the shock of discovery which was to transform his art, a sudden reaching out of temperament to a primitive way of life and a chiefly oral tradition which sparked-off elements within himself. While *The Aran Islands* and his writings about Wicklow and West Kerry are excellent records of what he observed as possible material, Hyde's translations of *The Love Songs of Connacht* published in the eighteen-nineties and in *Beside the Fire* (1890) seem to have helped towards a belief in the validity of Anglo-Irish dialect as a literary medium. In 1901 Hyde's one-act play, *Casadh an tSugáin* (The Twisting of the Rope), called his attention to a new idea, the possibilities of the folk-play. Although a slight enough play, some of the passages spoken by Hanrahan the poet, as translated by Lady Gregory, seem to anticipate Synge:

> . . . three-quarters of my heart is burned and scorched and consumed, struggling with the world, and the world struggling with me . . . you have not knowledge of the life of a poor bard, without house or home or havings, but he going and ever going a-drifting through the wide world, without a person with him but himself . . . There is nothing standing to me but the gift I got from God, my share of songs . . .

Here are touches of the concreteness, the rhetorical enlargement, the antiphonal cadence which are sometimes thought to be Synge's invention.

In 1902 the stirrings came to life. Synge turned from his first attempt at a symbolist prose-play and from his efforts at blank verse to write two plays, *Riders to the Sea* and *In the Shadow of the Glen,* and the first draft of *The Tinker's Wedding* — three of the six plays by which in some six years he became a dramatist of international reputation. The form of the dramatic dialogue which he chose seemed at once to combine the austere impressionistic quality of Irish nature poetry with the high imaginative flights of Irish story-telling at its best. In *Riders* the latter is held in check but the quiet although vivid quality of the speeches suits the ritualistic procedure of the action, which is concerned with the last stage of an inevitable doom, so that telescoping of time in its events is unnoticed and the essential quality of the human tragedy is conveyed through Maurya. 'Profound insight finds the inner and essential mood of the things it treats of', wrote Synge in his notebooks, 'and hence gives us an art that is absolutely distinct and inimitable.'[1] But this does not explain the extraordinary harmony of the play, its blend of atmosphere, primitive feeling and religious ritual, its ordering of simple things so that, like Maurya herself, they have overtones which are archetypal, in a pattern which gives the play its organic unity.

Synge had learned much from his study of Molière and Racine.

The debt to Molière is probably greater in *In the Shadow of the Glen* where the essence of a rough folk-tale is adapted into dramatic form by being centred around the shared secret that old Dan Burke is really 'letting on to be dead'. The action moves to and from that discovery. The dialogue, while sketching the characters adequately, Dan Burke and Michael Dara static in their meanness, Nora and the Tramp developing through their imaginations, is richer and skilfully weaves references to loneliness, fear and madness with the foggy and desolate images of the glen. While Nora's decision to go with the tramp seems to some to be unconvincing, the injustice of her husband's rejection makes it appear inevitable enough and it is appropriate to this ironic tragi-comedy that the curtain falls upon the old fogey and the young fogey drinking whiskey to each other's squalid security, the older really despising the younger man for his lack of courage: 'I was thinking to strike you, Michael Dara, but you're a quiet man, God help you, and I don't mind you at all.' Yeats's interpretation of Nora, that she is 'intoxicated by a dream which is hardly understood by herself', was romantic in view of her final speech, which accepts the hazards as well as the pleasanter prospects of a wandering life which the tramp has presented so poetically.

The Tinker's Wedding has led to more division between the scholars than its comparatively slight, farcical quality would seem to justify. Synge himself thought it somewhat unsatisfactory. 'What merits it has', he wrote to a friend, 'lie in a humorous dialogue that would have to be very richly and confidently spoken.' There is little point in discussing it as being about the clash between Christianity and paganism, although that had something to do with fears about public attitudes which explain its delayed production in Ireland and perhaps lie behind Synge's slightly defensive preface of December 1907. It is essentially a farcical play of conflicting pretences between young Sarah Casey, who has a sudden whim to get married, Michael Byrne her unenthusiastic companion, her mother, an unrepentant tinker who (like Michael James Flaherty in the *Playboy*) is against anything that interferes with drinking, and a venal priest who distrusts all tinkers, although he has a certain affinity with them. Built on a slight anecdote, it is reminiscent in manner of the old French farces on which Molière based plays like *Le Docteur Amoureux*. While there is power in the character of old Mary Byrne and some shrewd stage contrivance centred around a tin can, the farcical horseplay of the second act does not fulfil the development of deeper comedy implied in the first.

It is also interesting as a step in Synge's passage to a full-length play. His first three-act play, *The Well of the Saints,* was completed in 1904 and produced in 1905. This tragi-comedy of the aging, blind beggar couple who, given back their sight by a wandering friar, are so repelled by the harsh realities which assault the romantic pictures they have of the world and of each other that they choose blindness again, is deeply poetic. The action moves from their situation in which 'darkness' is lit by inner visions to their cure and their first bitter reaction to each other; to the full impact of the harsh realities of the naked and open daylight of the second act; and to the double reversal of the third act in which renewed blindness is accepted, then rejected as they prepare for their permanent cure, then chosen finally and emphatically as Martin dashes the can of healing water from the hands of the friar; 'I'm thinking it's a good right ourselves have to be sitting blind, hearing a soft wind turning round the little leaves of the spring and feeling the sun, and we not tormenting our souls with the sight of the grey days, and the holy men, and the dirty feet is trampling the world.' The language of this play is orchestrated with natural images, whether expressed by the visionary saint or by the imaginative beggars. It is perhaps, like Shakespeare's *Richard II,* more a poet's than a dramatist's play; for the construction makes it somewhat too static — the second act elaborates rather than develops the first — but Synge's probing of the problem which obsessed Pirandello, the contrast between illusion and reality, is sensitive. Frank O'Connor thought that *The Tinker's Wedding* failed because it had no Synge in it, *The Well of the Saints* because it had too much. Both, on the other hand, may be seen as having virtues as well as faults from which Synge learned on the way to his second masterpiece, *The Playboy of the Western World.*

The incidental source of this play was an anecdote heard on Aran, the deeper origin lay in the psychological reality behind the exuberant imagination of the folk-tales of the islanders. Christy Mahon's gallows story makes him welcome in a wild coastal village. It progresses into mythical proportions — he let fall the loy on the ridge of his father's skull — he halved his skull — he split him to the knob of his gullet — he divided him to the breeches belt. The construction is organised around the creation, the inflation and deflation of the myth and the survival of Christy's new self-confidence after his 'dirty deed' has turned the villagers against him. This plot is strengthened by the complications of Christy's involvement with Pegeen Mike and the widow Quin and by the shared secret, midway through the play, that old Mahon is still very much alive. Its tension is increased by the deferment of the confrontation between father and son and by the unexpected result of it, for it unites them in a changed relationship of mastery and leaves Pegeen lamenting her loss. This is merely an indication of the development of Synge's dramatic skill, which can be seen also in his grasp of the verbal implications of visual action and in the appropriateness of language to dramatic turns of emotion or of events. Although the spirit of the play is that of extravagant comedy rooted in graphic language, the tender love scenes between Christy and Pegeen are deeply lyrical and convey the developing maturity of both. The lesser characters are not mere stereotypes; Old Mahon's imagination matches his son's; Widow Quin's gaudy opportunism, Michael James Flaherty's obsession with the necessity of organising life around the opportunities for comfortable drinking, even Shaun Keogh's timidity are sufficiently individual to provide strong acting parts; and, as the opening of Act III shows, all the characters are potential myth-makers, who collectively are dismayed only when as a community they become involved in the underlying realities of the central myth. There is a wider interplay of character than Synge had attempted previously; the combined mockery of Shaun Keogh in Act 1, the interplay of the girls before Christy's boots, the communal hero-worship of Christy before his communal rejection, give depth and extension to the whole comedy, which has an organic unity and yet is full of surprising turns of plot and of mood.

'I am half inclined to try a play on "Deirdre" — but I am a little afraid that the "Saga" people might lessen my grip on reality', wrote Synge before undertaking *Deirdre of the Sorrows,* which he wrote in 1907-08 and was revising when he died. This fear seems to have been obviated by his approach to Deirdre as the kind of woman the islanders would have understood in terms of their own lives and of their own doom and his. Like Yeats in dealing with this well-known legend, Synge could work with 'a sense of the final chord' and furthermore with a sense of his own approaching death. The theme which Naisi speaks in distress in the first act — 'we've a short space only to be triumphant and brave' — is spoken grotesquely by Owen and decisively by Deirdre in determining on the return to Ireland from Alba; and it culminates in Deirdre's triumphant lyrical speeches before her suicide. Synge, who had worked with de Jubainville in Paris, knew more versions of the legend than Lady Gregory's and may have intended to make Owen the executioner of the sons of Usna in the last act. This probably would have strengthened the construction of a play which is still a near-masterpiece of the theatre and an adequate swan-song of a great artist.

Synge was not given to theorising and, although he affirmed his general agreement with Yeats's principles in *Samhain,* believed that 'all theorising is bad for the artist because it makes him live in the intelligence instead of the half subconscious faculties by which all real creation is performed'. We learn something about his views on art from his brief prefaces; something more from his notebooks of the deeper processes of his thought, of the contemplative cast of mind which made him enigmatic, with the habit of quietly watching, of soaking-in a thing, a scene, a person, so as to catch its mood and essence. 'The profound is always inimitable', he wrote in his notebooks. 'Things have always a character and characters have always a mood. . . . The individual mood is often trivial, perverse, fleeting but the national mood is broad, serious, provisionally permanent.' His art owed a great deal to the intimacy which came of close observation and deep contemplation; the essence of tragedy is seized as truly in *Riders* as that of comedy is in *Playboy;* in each a depth of treatment lifts the local into the universal. Synge argued that a writer needs the national mood as well as intellectual temper and that place, period and personal distinction, inspired by this mood, result in art.

His own personal distinction rests chiefly on his lyrical prose style, which is seen also in his best prose translations from Villon and other poets. It is realistic only in the sense that its basis is the vocabulary, idiom, syntax, rhythm and cadence of Irish-English; but it is a selective distillation of these elements which gives it a personal stamp, whether used austerely in *Riders,* richly in the *Playboy* or in the intermediate style of the other plays.[2] Synge had once noted, when hearing an old man reciting Gaelic verse which he did not then fully understand, that the rhythm and cadence brought tears to his eyes. His own preferred cadences can be detected, especially at the ends of sentences, but they may be found in less concentration in Hyde and in Lady Gregory, for they are largely cadences of folk-speech. But there is a wider kind of cadence which this dramatist possesses and which consists in the harmonic balance of character — the friar's celebration of nature balances that of the blind beggar's, Old Mahon sketches his son's picture in language recalling Christy's vivid portrait of himself. Synge may have owed something to Racine in this respect; his art frequently reminds us of music. From Molière he learned, as well as the technique of construction, a healthy respect for the sanity of real humour which he defended against the less healthy tendencies he associated with the 'Decadents' of his time. Although he had some misconception of Ibsen's work, he would have understood the Norwegian's description of poetry as 'doom session upon the soul' and also the famous address to the students in which Ibsen spoke of the necessary affinity of the poetic dramatist with the mood and experiences of his countrymen.

II

Yeats contributed some twenty-five plays to the Irish dramatic movement and in many cases made revisions and new versions of them over a long period. Hence his work varies enough in type and quality to support varied estimates of his power as a dramatist. His plays fall into certain fairly well-defined groups which reveal his dominant themes, modes and techniques. *The Land of Heart's Desire, The Countess Cathleen, Cathleen ni Hoolihan* and *The Shadowy Waters,* all produced between 1894 and 1904, are allegorical, poetic fantasies, full of shadow and the lure of the ideal or of the supernatural world. *The Shadowy Waters* stands at one poetic extreme; it is weighed down by its dreamy, lyrical verse, although it has much enchanting music:-

O flower of the branch, O bird among the leaves,
O silver fish that my two hands have taken
Out of the running stream . . .

and it was originally included in the 1933 edition of his *Collected Poems*. The *Countess Cathleen* is more a pageant than a play and the arguments of the poet Aleel, oddly world-weary in a mediaeval setting, do not provide any tension as the events move towards a kind of *deus ex machina* solution. *The Land of Heart's Desire*, for all its fairy theme, shows better dramatic power; as F. R. Higgins pointed out, it uses a genuine conflict to knit its structure, 'the conflict between Christianity and the emanations of a life one mentioned just under the breath, a conflict still felt beneath the surface of Irish rural life'.[3] *Cathleen ni Hoolihan* handles a more open conflict, that of patriotism against comfort and security, with a clearer line and a surer touch, in a form of poetic prose, a few symbols with ancient associations being used simply with a fine dramatic effect:

> Did you see an old woman going down the path?
> I did not; but I saw a young girl, and she had the walk of a queen.

The temperament revealed in these subjective plays is reminiscent of Joyce's description of the romantic temper which 'sees no fit abode here for its ideals and chooses therefore to behold them under insensible figures'; it tends towards fantasy, type characters, the morality play. Louis MacNeice's statement that 'Yeats always wrote morality plays' may not be completely accurate but it is true of these early plays; the poet is too concerned that his eternal verities are going to prevail.

With this group *The Unicorn from the Stars* and *The Hour-Glass* seem of a piece; the underlying idea is the same: that spiritual reality is more real than what the world means by reality. In the former play (written in 1902 as 'Where there is nothing') the visionary who embodies it treats it as such a privately mystical idea that the struggle against the established order which kills him has little significance for the audience. *The Hour-Glass*, which is sub-titled 'a morality', is more genuinely dramatic, since the wise man's search for some pupil to refute his own teaching is given dramatic sharpness by a clear situation and a visible focal point, the hour-glass itself.

The four plays which resulted from Yeats's determination to get the heroic legends into verse were produced between 1903 and 1910. Those were *The King's Threshold, On Baile's Strand, Deirdre* and the *Green Helmet*. Yeats, now brought into the heart of 'theatre business, management of men', may have regretted the loss of time from lyric poetry but he was learning that in the theatre you cannot turn back the page and that the impact of dramatic verse must be sharper, more immediate. The dialogue of Cuchulain and Conchubar in *On Baile's Strand* shows a new flexibility, a closer accommodation to action. In *The King's Threshold,* while the fixity of the poet's determination to die on hunger-strike rather than abandon his poetic rights is a retarding element in the development of the plot, it is compensated by the magnificently dramatic ending when the poet's pupils, threatened with execution, urge their master to die and thus proclaim the rights of the poets. This is one of the plays which Yeats changed drastically over the years; after the death of Terence MacSwiney on hunger-strike he abandoned the original happy ending for the grimmer treatment of moral victory through self-sacrifice. The rewriting of the prose play *The Golden Helmet* (1908) into *The Green Helmet* (1910) was less satisfactory. Yeats was attempting a difficult task, the splicing of the Green Knight theme to that of Bricriu's Feast, which is not particularly consonant with it. The play opens well with the swinging hexameters in which Cuchulain is told by the apprehensive heroes of the Red Man's strange challenge to a game:

> And when we had asked what game, he answered,
> 'Why, whip off my head!
> Then one of you two stoop down, and I'll whip off his', he said.
> 'A head for a head' he said, 'that is the game that I play.'

But this mood and pace dissipate as the women of the heroes enter. The comedy suddenly becomes clumsy; Yeats's attempts at comedy were rarely successful.

Deirdre is probably the best of these plays. The one-act form imposed a tighter discipline, seen for example in the First Musician's summation of Deirdre's story to that point, or in the skilful way in which omens of doom are woven into the action. Yeats preserved this clear line of dramatic progression, sketching Fergus as an optimistic Polonius and Naisi merely in outline, so that he might concentrate on Deirdre (who was to be played by Mrs Patrick Campbell, to whom the changes of Deirdre's transitions gave an excellent chance). Yeats used the three musicians sparingly, as narrators, chorus, singers and participants, thus achieving a Greek unity, partly at the expense of all but the central character.

In an appendix to his *Collected Works* (1908) Yeats commented that this form of dramatic structure 'continually forces one by the rigour of logic away from one's capacities, experiences and desires'. It was perhaps this restriction that made him want to develop a similarly spare form which would be less personally limiting. This may explain his later preoccupation with the form of play which he invented from the Noh drama about 1916 and which directly or indirectly accounts for most of the dozen plays he wrote before his death. This form is only very roughly based on the Noh sequences of plays, which aimed at a perfect union of the arts of narrative, lyric, acting, movement and music, inducing meditation by perfection of form. Noh plays were usually concerned with an encounter at a legended place and their climax was usually a dance. Since their chief aim was to train the warriors of the samurai caste in the ritual, religion, literature and folklore of Japan, it is not surprising to find that, like the mediaeval morality play, they used stylised characters, costume, masks, movement, music and speech. In the plays which Yeats modelled on them, the focus shifts from human motive and character to the implications of human existence, speculations on the involvement of types of character in significant events, the patterns of human behaviour over long cycles of time. This kind of drama is essentially abstract, is in line with the symbolist drama of Maeterlinck, and, further, demands not only trained artists but a trained audience, quick to catch nuance and suggestion. Yeats aimed at this kind of perfection.

The three Cuchulain plays *(At the Hawk's Well, The Only Jealousy of Emer, The Death of Cuchulain)* which he wrote in this form are concerned with the quest for immortality by old and young, the relationship between wife, hero and mistress, the fate of the heroic type. Only the second of these carries a clear line of conflict, centred on Emer; the others depend too much on literary associations of the Cuchulain figure with the poet's other works and an excess of critical energy has been expended on such relationships or on their connections with Yeats's life. *The Dreaming of the Bones, The Cat and the Moon,* and perhaps *A Full Moon in March* and *Calvary,* where the conflicts are more dramatically braced, would seem to represent Yeats's best achievement in this kind of play. *Resurrection, Purgatory* and *The Herne's Egg,* while not in the same form, have been affected by the Noh technique. *Purgatory* applies to a family the idea of cyclic involvement treated in *The Dreaming of the Bones,* but its fine, pared style and colloquial speech do not quite save it from the idiosyncratic convictions which Yeats put into it. *The Resurrection* is treated speculatively and has a curious resemblance to the straight prose play, *The Words upon the Window-Pane*. In both plays different explanations of superhuman phenomena are given and we are led to a climax in which the irrational is preferred. Here again, perhaps, is Yeats's old thesis; but there are few more dramatically successful endings in his plays than the cry of the Greek in *The Resurrection;* 'O Athens, Alexandria, Rome, something has come to destroy you! The heart of the phantom is beating', or that of the old medium in the other play, speaking in Swift's voice: 'Perish the day on which I was born!' This tragic sense predominates in his best work. Apart from *The Cat and the Moon,* he comes nearer the spirit of comedy in *The Player Queen. The Herne's Egg,* based on Ferguson's *Congal,* set out to be a bawdy, farcical comedy, but somehow became enmeshed in the theme of the death of the hero, the serious topic of *The Death of Cuchulain,* another of his last plays.

His great achievement was to restore poetry to the English-speaking theatre. All his verse-plays carry the attraction of excellent lyric poetry and, although many were written for a bare stage or a drawing-room, have proved stimulating when adapted to modern techniques by good modern directors working with actors who acquire (as they do too seldom) the necessary discipline of speech, movement and stillness. In fact they can fulfil, by their demands on designers, choreographers and composers, that fundamental union of the arts which Yeats aimed at in the theatre; a difficult but a challenging and not impossible task.

III

Lady Gregory was a practical mainstay of the Irish dramatic movement from the time she met Yeats in 1896 to her death in 1932. She was an initiator, a director who was resolute in defending its leading figures. She was fifty when she wrote her first play and seventy-six when she retired from the theatre, after she had written over thirty plays. Those which proved most lasting are her comedies, *Spreading the News, The Workhouse Ward, Hyacinth Halvey* and *The Rising of the Moon,* simple and clear in craft and setting, with characters and speech based upon those of her own Clare-Galway area. Later she wrote legendary plays *(Grania, Dervorgilla);* folk-history plays based on noble, ill-starred characters, Brian Boru *(Kincora)*, Sarsfield *(The White Cockade)*, Parnell *(The Image, The Deliverer)*, miracle plays *(The Story brought by Brigit)*, and plays of wonder for children *(The Golden Apple, The Jester)*. She was essentially a moralist writer, simplistic and somewhat sentimental in approach, always hoping to show her comparatively unsophisticated audience how the 'innocents' of this life — tramp, fool, ballad-singer or beggar, could hold better values than and sometimes could defeat the worldly-wise with their 'roast and boiled and all the comforts of the day'. Influenced by Hyde, she learned Gaelic and perceived the essential poetry of her people's speech. Her dialogue ('Kiltartanese') is local, flatter than Synge's but often delighting in what she called 'music — the balanced delight of sentences — of words', and her work is full of phrases which she culled from the folklore of her district ('as straight and clean as a green rush on the brink of a bog') and epithets like 'a speckled skin' which Yeats admired and captured. Her dialogue is an interesting contrast at one extreme with that of Padraic Colum (*Three Plays*, 1916), who dramatises the problems of rural Ireland in naturalistic speech with its quiet touches of poetry and at the other with that of George Fitzmaurice (*Five Plays*, 1914), whose racy Kerry idiom dominated the situations and characters of his fantasies.

Besides supplying plays to the movement, Lady Gregory collaborated with Hyde and sought advice from Synge. Yeats owed much to her; *The Pot of Broth*, *The Unicorn from the Stars* and *Cathleen ni Hoolihan* were almost as much her work as his and many of his plays benefited from her advice, especially on matters of speech. She also translated Molière for the early Abbey Theatre, wrote an indispensable account of its history to 1913 in *Our Irish Theatre* and gave the movement two notable source-books of Irish legend, *Cuchulain of Muirthemne* (1902) and *Gods and Fighting Men* (1904). She was a most courageous defender of the theatre's integrity — even defending *The Playboy*, which she hated — being, as she recorded towards the end of her days, a rebel 'with the nationalists all through — more than they know or my nearest realised'. Without her the Irish dramatic movement might not have existed and certainly would not have taken the exact course it did.

IV

'I did feel proud and satisfied — a theatre of our own, Irish plays, such a fine one by our countryman — company playing it so splendidly, all our own — something to have lived to see!' So Lady Gregory recorded in her journal in 1927. By that time Sean O'Casey had written the three Dublin plays, *The Shadow of a Gunman* (1923), *Juno and the Paycock* (1924) and *The Plough and the Stars* (1926), which with a few slight one-acters had helped to save the Abbey Theatre. O'Casey was born in 1880 of middle-class parents who had fallen on hard times, so that, after his evangelistic father's death, he experienced the real poverty of the working-class as office-boy, messenger, casual labourer, navvy and hod-carrier. The family background contained strands of Protestant, Catholic, loyalist and nationalist opinion, and his development brought him in touch with most of the vital currents of his time: the Gaelic League, the Gaelic Athletic Association, the I.R.B., the Irish Citizen Army and the Irish dramatic movement. As a young man he was at first very nationalistic, using the Gaelic League to recruit members for the I.R.B. His experience as a worker made him also a socialist. What swung him more towards socialism than republicanism was the refusal of the I.R.B. to support the workers against employers and police in the 1913 strike. Shortly after came James Larkin's announcement of the formation of the Irish Citizen Army of which O'Casey became Secretary. He drew up a constitution for it in March 1914, and openly expressed his hostility to the Irish Volunteers as a middle-class body, eventually resigning from the I.C.A. after an ill-advised attempt to expel Constance Markievicz from its ranks. Isolation from the Republicans and from the active socialists gave O'Casey a detachment which with his background and experience made him ideally equipped to write plays of this period.

'It is only the catastrophes of life that give substance and power to the tragedy and humour which are the two poles of art', wrote Synge. O'Casey might have taken this as his text for the blend of tragedy and comedy in his trilogy. All of his Dublin plays are entitled tragedies. True, they all end unhappily; the masquerade of the escapist Davoren as the gunman leads to the death of an innocent unselfish girl; in *Juno* the hopes built by the Boyle family upon a shaky legacy and the betrayal by their son of a former comrade in the Civil War result in ruin and death; in *The Plough*

Marie O'Neill as 'Pegeen Mike'. Courtesy of the National Library of Ireland.

A scene from The Plough and The Stars. *1966. Photograph G. A. Duncan.*

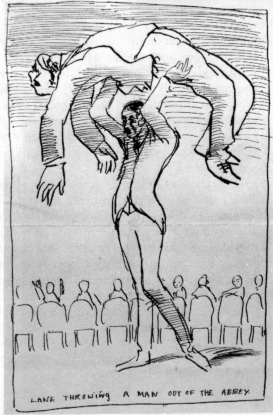

LANE THROWING A MAN OUT OF THE ABBEY.

'Lane throwing a man out of the Abbey' by W. Orpen. Courtesy of the National Gallery of Ireland.

and the Stars the romantically awaited Rising brings death and madness to the Clitheroes, ruin to their city. Yet comedy occurs at every turn of the game, deepening the sadness in all but the first, in which it predominates. O'Casey had learned the technique of tragi-comedy partly from Shakespeare, partly from Boucicault, in both of whose plays he had acted as a young man in the Mechanic's Institute in Dublin. If his absence from the vital struggles of 1916-22 may have reinforced the anti-heroic stance of his socialism, it also put him into a more detached position where he could mock the romantic poet, the extreme nationalist, the dogmatic socialist — the roles of his own life, in Davoren or Uncle Peter or the Covey — with equal comic validity. His transitions from comedy to tragedy are sometimes slowly developed, as in the passages before and after Johnny's vision of the dead Tancred in Act II of *Juno,* sometimes rapidly, as at the end of *Juno* or all through the *Gunman,* but always with great skill.

The Shadow of a Gunman* is the slightest of these plays; O'Casey's power to create comic types and to satirise them is exercised on what is essentially a pretence-situation into which other pretences are introduced and exposed. But it does not go very deep; at the end Davoren the romantic pretender is still as unchanged as the cynical Shields. *Juno and the Paycock* goes deeper. Here Boyle is the great pretender, comically exposed as much by himself as by others. Irrepressible and incurable like his parasite, Joxer, he is an immortal comic type; but Juno is one of the great tragic heroines of drama and through her, as she echoes the sorrowful words of the bereaved Mrs Tancred, the positive human values of the play are asserted as Synge's Maurya asserts them, in a similar tragic and harmonic pattern.

The Plough and the Stars* is probably O'Casey's greatest play. It is centred around the Clitheroes but they are knit into a group of tenement-dwellers of great vividness and variety, conveying in their reactions to each other and to the Rising a sense of width and of depth. War is the catalyst that reveals their real values and that causes them to display new and sometimes deeper facets of their characters. There are few final acts more tragically powerful than Act IV of this play with the subdued comedy of its opening, succeeded by the deep tragedy of Nora's madness, the death of Bessie Burgess and the quiet ironic ending, as the tired British tommies drink tea and sing the sentimental ditty 'Keep the home-fires burning' in a home of death in a burning city. O'Casey dedicated this play 'To the gay laugh of my mother at the gate of the grave', a dedication that would have appealed to Synge.

O'Casey's language is based on the Dublin speech of his own time. Since Dublin is constantly fed by rural population streams, its speech reflects rural speech; it is often racy and idiomatic, alliterative, rhythmically phrased and has an urban quality in its oratorical Georgian phrases or its cynical witticisms. O'Casey used selectively its colourful images, its rising rhythms of rhetoric; but the fact that it is meant to be more realistic speech than Synge's makes it flatter, less delicately-wrought in cadence. When Uncle Peter says to the Covey, 'I'll be waiting for the day when the all-powerful, all-merciful, all-loving God 'll be burnin' and blastin' you, thwartin' and tormentin' you, rievin' and roastin' you!', he is speaking in language which is heightened but not far from natural speech-rhythms or vocabulary. Song is used sparingly in O'Casey's Dublin plays, but in the hymns of Bessie Burgess, the overheard oratory of the Speaker, the last chorus of the soldiers, we may see an anticipation of his later style. *The Plough and the Stars* was about as far as he could go in his first manner of poetic realism.

'The Big House'. Powerscourt, Enniskerry, Co. Wicklow. Bord Fáilte photograph.

CHAPTER XVII
Prose Fiction

Meanwhile, independently of the Irish literary revival, other Irish fiction-writers had begun to appear on the literary scene. Notable among them was a number of talented women who belonged to the ascendancy class and who tried to get to grips with Irish life as a whole. They wrote independently about contemporary Ireland, sometimes trying to probe back into her history, sometimes producing books of sketches and impressions. The quality of their writing is uneven, partly because of this diversification, partly because of the unsettled nature of public taste and the lack of proper artistic models for fiction in Ireland. If one reads Emily Lawless's *Hurrish* (1886) today, for example, one reads it more for its quiet descriptions of the Burren area of County Clare, based on a trained naturalist's observation, than for its melodramatic tale of murder and revenge during the Land League days; similarly *Grania* (1892), a slow-moving study of island lovers and a better novel, has more vitality in its Aran scenery than in its characters. Jane Barlow, who won some reputation with *Irish Idylls* and *Bogland Studies,* both published in 1892, was not without talent in her descriptions of rural Ireland and its people but did not really progress beyond sketch-writing in the many books which she wrote subsequently. The work of Edith Somerville and Violet Martin ('Somerville and Ross') is in a somewhat different category.

These ladies of Castletownshend, County Cork, began with a melodramatic tale, *An Irish Cousin* (1889), which was based on Le Fanu's *Uncle Silas,* and followed it with an uneven story of the Land League days, *Naboth's Vineyard* (1891). Then in 1894 they collaborated in an excellent novel, *The Real Charlotte.* Its plot centres around Charlotte Mullen, money-lender and dealer, a vulgar and callous woman driven by a lust for possession which causes her to wreck several lives, including her own. Her victims are members of the ascendancy class towards which she aspires and of the Protestant middle-class to which she belongs. The real theme of the book is the decline of the ascendancy, crumbling from its own decay, and the passing of land and power to the 'gombeen' type. Its power comes from its precise realism, the controlled relationship of plot to character and the occasional symbolism which helps to give it moral and philosophical depth. There is also an artistic use of the tensions underlying the whole question of land in Ireland.

The Silver Fox (1898) has something of the same tragic power but is a slighter and less sustained work, the symbolism of the witch-fox, the fatal lure of the gentry, being but poorly integrated with a realistic study of landlords and tenants. One year after its publication the partners published their first volume of stories about the fictional experiences of an Irish Resident Magistrate. It had an immediate success with the reading public and really determined the pattern of their collaboration until the death of Violet Martin in 1915. The *R.M.* stories are comic and well-told; they convey vividly types and characters both inside and outside the hunting set; and they are written intelligently with an extremely accurate sense of Irish dialogue. The time has passed when their evaluation inevitably becomes involved with discussions about how far they were designed for English consumption or how far they are typical of 'ascendancy writing'. In technique they have a competence which probably owes much to the influence of Kipling; they are comic enough to have some lasting quality; but this achievement, considerable though it may be, is slight enough when compared with that of *The Real Charlotte,* their one artistic triumph.

Later, Edith Somerville, who continued to publish over their joint pseudonym, tried to get back to this serious vein of novel-writing with *Mount Music* (1919) and *The Big House of Inver* (1925), both concerned with the theme of the downfall of the landed class. In the first of these, through the intermarriage of a decaying ascendancy family wth a rising Catholic middle-class one, possession of the estate passes into the hands of a Catholic doctor. The ebullient, genial and scheming Doctor Mangan has something of Charlotte Mullen's lack of scruple but is created much more sympathetically; it is noticeable that, shortly after he acquires Mount Music, he meets with a sudden accidental death, as if he too had inherited the doom of the antediluvian Talbot-Lowreys from whose effete hands he has wrested it. In this novel the technique is slacker, the style less sure. The powerful and disciplined edge of the writing has disappeared with Violet Martin; yet certain scenes and characters have considerable power. *The Big House of Inver* has more, although it was published when Edith Somerville was nearly seventy. In 1912 Violet Martin had suggested a novel based on one of the big houses brought to ruin by a proud, dissolute and snobbish family who had held it since the eighteenth century. It ended in the possession of an old spinster, sprung from some casual union of the family with their tenants; she lived nearby but would never enter the house or its beautiful old garden. Edith Somerville created such a character in Shibby Pindy, an illegitimate descendant of the Prenderville line, whose simple mind is obsessed with the idea of restoring its imagined dignity. The pathos of her futile attempts to do so by arranging a rich marriage for her half-brother and by filling the house with an assortment of hideous furniture is deepened by the family portraits which dominate the scene until the carelessness of the last Prenderville sends all up in flames.

This is a notable historical novel which deserves comparison with and sometimes goes deeper than *Castle Rackrent* in its study of the self-caused cycle of doom of a family through several generations. It might have been a great novel if the partners had undertaken it before success diverted them from such serious work; but professional writers usually follow public taste and Castletownshend had somehow to be paid for. Although the partners took their profession seriously they had not in fact a very high opinion of the artist's calling; their avoidance of contact with the literary movement may have been due to a professional wish to stick to their own last as well as to a distrust of the idea of 'a return to the people' on any but their own restricted terms.

A novelist of more constant purpose was Shan F. Bullock, whose first important book, *By Thrasna River* (1895), was a series of loosely co-ordinated sketches of Ulster rural life. It was followed by a series of novels which treat of the strong farmers of County Fermanagh, chiefly of Protestant planter stock, dour and hard-working, their horizons often narrowed by possession. Martin Hynes, the central figure of *The Squireen* (1903), is such a man: to preserve his property he jilts a loving woman and marries for money. The novel is a quiet, deliberate study of his deterioration and self-destruction, classical in its exact observation and in its close understanding of the life of its people. Bullock was strongly tied to his area by affection for its beauty and its inhabitants but he was also conscious of their hardness, which had driven him to a clerk's life in London. This gave him a detachment which enabled him to handle objectively the themes of home and of exile.

In *Dan the Dollar* (1905) Dan Ruddy returns home after twenty years of exile in America. Wealthy, he proceeds to take the neighbourhood in hand, sets up his poor parents, buys and improves land, plans to marry. But when his business in America fails, the mainspring of his life, indicated by his nickname, causes him to desert the affection which is at home for an attempt to build up another American fortune. There is no solution; the exile will never quite fit into the settled pattern of home; the settled life gives the people a quality and a happiness of their own, which he can appreciate, but sometimes finds infuriating in its narrowness. It is this repellent quality which is brought out in Richard Jebb, scheming farmer of *Loughsiders* (1924), Bullock's best novel. Jebb operates love, marriage and land in his own acquisitive interest, with something of the skill of Charlotte Mullen in *The Real Charlotte*. Yet even this unloveable character is presented with more human insight than Somerville and Ross display. They tend to treat all middle-class aspirants to power with insensitivity or hostility.

Bullock's devotion to his craft gives some of his many novels about Ireland considerable creative force, often vitiated by a certain flatness of style. His *Ring o' Rushes* (1896) and *Irish Pastorals* (1901) showed that he could also write serious sketches about Ulster people. Had his temperament been different, he might have been much more popular. The Donegal writer, Seumas MacManus, was capitalising on the demand for 'humorous and engaging' Irish fiction about the same time with books like *'Twas in Dhroll Donegal* (1897) and other whimsicalities which wear very badly with the years. His novel *A Lad of the O'Friels* (1903) was a more serious attempt at fiction but fails through its lack of structure and its saccharine quality.

In general the Irish novel of the period was a light-weight affair. The novels of George A. Birmingham (Canon Hannay) enjoyed a great vogue but today perhaps only *Spanish Gold* (1908) and *General John Regan* (1913) are still readable. Birmingham had a nimble wit but was usually inept in treating a serious subject. *The Northern Iron* (1907) had an interesting theme, the struggle of the Ulster Presbyterians under Jimmy Hope for Ireland's freedom in

1798, but became a schoolboy's yarn. *Hyacinth* (1906) had more interesting possibilities as a contemporary novel; an Ulster parson's son goes to Trinity College, Dublin, to study divinity, gravitates towards the politico-literary groups around Maud Gonne, toys with the idea of fighting for the Boers, becomes instead a commercial traveller and ends as a parson who will continue his father's work in the same district. Unfortunately there is scarcely any depth to his motivation; the young man is shunted around to different sidings of the author's interest and the possibility of developing the tensions of a real psychological dilemma is lost. It called for a deeper sense of artistic purpose than this writer possessed.

The novels of Canon Sheehan, parish priest of Doneraile, County Cork, are an interesting contrast. They tried to deal seriously with Catholic clerical life and its relationship to the problems of the rural people of that area. *My New Curate* (1899) was a series of clerical sketches given some unity by the character of Father Letheby, the zealous reforming curate to an old parish priest whom experience has convinced that 'nothing on earth can cure the inertia of Ireland'. *The Graves at Kilmorna* (1914), a Fenian tale, and *Glenanaar* (1905), which traced the history of an informer's family through three generations, were historical novels dealing with the effects of misgovernment and the dangers of revolution in rural Ireland. *Luke Delmege* (1901) and *The Blindness of Dr. Gray* (1909) return to the contemporary clerical scene. All of them are hampered by the author's care to avoid giving offence, his homiletic purpose and his failure to control his narrative style, which is rambling, moralistic and stilted. Here it was not triviality but the wrong kind of purpose which prevented that penetration in depth towards which the best European writers were striving all through the nineteenth century and which Proust later defined as the only possible line of progress in the novel. Sheehan remains interesting for his exploration of the rural and clerical society of his time. He showed a realisation of the chief dilemma of Ireland: the collapse of the landed system, the absolute necessity of reform and the impossibility of change until the landlords and the British government altered their whole approach to the Irish question. *Lisheen* (1907), written under the influence of Tolstoy, considered the values of socialism and tried, in a kindly way, to abstract its virtues and to reconcile them with Catholicism. *Luke Delmege* and *The Blindness of Dr. Gray* demonstrated the need for a change of perception on the part of the priesthood and for an improvement in their training.

The best models for novelists then were either French or Russian. In 1900 *Madame Bovary* was over forty years old and the followers of Flaubert's method of realism, his avoidance of sentiment and didactic purpose, had opted for the presentation of life in a detached and impersonal way. Gautier, Maupassant and Zola had swung the French novel away from Hugo's romanticism to the other extreme of realism and by the turn of the century the reaction against realism had prepared the way for Proust. Where French fiction had passed into a phase twice removed from romanticism; Irish fiction, limited by its environment, was in a half-baked condition: romantic, sentimental, didactic, lacking form, clinging to the tale, the sketch, the anecdote, the yarn, the stock fare of the circulating libraries. The freedom, form and temper of French fiction were missing. Russian fiction from Gogol to Gorky could have provided a variety of appropriate examples and challenges. The very factors which nourished it — awareness of the decay of a feudal system, strong national feeling, the probing of moral, social and political values, an urgent sense of regenerative purpose — all had their Irish counterparts during the revival years. But the work of the great Russians was almost unknown, although some of the reviews occasionally published them in translation. French novelists were known better but French realism, especially Zola's *tranches de vie,* seems to have scared Somerville and Ross almost as much as Canon Sheehan.

George Moore's *The Untilled Field* (1903) was a deliberate attempt to change the course of Irish fiction. Its thirteen stories were written in English and were intended for publication in Irish translations so that models would be provided for writers in Irish. Their common theme was to be the depopulation of Ireland through emigration — Moore said that the real hero of his book was the emigrant ship — and his general aim was to help the literary development of a country which he regarded as 'intellectually unwashed'. His own model for these stories was, appropriately, Ivan Turgenev, who a half-century before had written a remarkable series of studies, sketches and novels of the Russian landlords and peasants; observant, imaginative, he had conveyed with powerful impressionism the picture of a collapsing system, of a doomed aristocracy that had become superfluous and knew it, and of tenants who were restive and critical. His work owed its power to a firm narrative style, in which realism and impressionism were blended in describing character and landscape, and to the artistic objectivity of the presentation.

Moore had read Turgenev in Paris, where he was the best-known of the Russian writers, and had published an appreciation of him in 1888; mention of his name in a casual conversation with John Eglinton in Dublin now gave him the incentive for his book of Irish short stories. Yeats and A.E., and the example of Hyde had influenced the return of this established writer, chiefly known at that time as the author of the realistic novel *Esther Waters* (1894), to participate in the literary revival. Initially, at the turn of the century, he was full of enthusiasm, had even seen himself as an almost Messianic leader who would restore the Irish language and the national ethos. The writing of English, he believed or affected to believe, had finished with Walter Pater and the 'small languages' had a chance to succeed. His return, however, had exemplified the Irish exile's dilemma; the Gaelic League, the Catholic clergy and the Irish nationalists in general regarded with suspicion this Catholic landowner, author of *Parnell and his Island* (1887) which was not only anti-landlord but anti-clerical, and this attitude was shared by conservative Protestants, especially when, shortly after the publication of *The Untilled Field,* Moore announced his conversion to Protestantism. Moore's enthusiasms, like his conversion, were often febrile but there was a genuine streak of idealism in the motives for his return. His main incentive was fundamentally an artistic one and that is why the decade which he spent in Ireland did not result merely in frustration but led to several notable books.

In his preface to *The Lake* Moore has described the happy inspiration which produced the stories of *The Untilled Field:*

> one that could hardly fail to beget stories in the mind of anyone prone to narrative — the return of a man to his native land, to its people, to memories hidden for years, forgotten, but which rose suddenly out of the darkness, like water out of the earth when a spring is tapped.

This kind of Proustian sensibility tends to operate in terms of reminiscence and impressionism. Moore's affection for the French impressionist painters had already begun to influence his novels, which belonged generally to the realistic tradition; and the actual experience of return, of renewal of intimacy with the Irish landscape, Irish speech and characters, helped him to preserve the realistic base of his art. In dialogue he followed the method which he had praised in Turgenev, a rather flat, unemphatic style;

> where no one phrase is remarkable or striking when read separately, but when taken with the context continues the picture — a picture tense with emotion, a well-nigh fabulous photograph of the mind.

The stories of *The Untilled Field* deal for the most part with exile and with the frustration of Irish life which makes exile necessary or desirable. This frustration is seen as the result of clerical Puritanism, which in its institutional rigidity enforces a Roman discipline and has failed to adapt itself to human progress or to the nature of the people. The authoritarian priest succeeds, the kindly one fails; the young man or woman of spirit emigrates or is broken; the intellectual or the artist is forced out of a community which has surrendered to a dreary submissiveness, which has no real culture, only a vague aspiration. And yet the exile is haunted by the loss of something dear and intimate, by the feeling 'that no man ever wanders far from his grave sod'.

By the time that these stories appeared in book form, Moore's original aims had changed. Although an Irish version of them appeared in the same year, he had lost his enthusiasm for the revival cause. This desire for social reform had also become more obtrusive than Turgenev would have allowed; Moore himself recognized this by deleting several of the polemical passages when the work was being published in Germany. As it stands, the best stories are those in which Moore keeps to Turgenev's manner; James Bryden, who returns full of nostalgia from the Bowery to his native village, only to find that he is really an exile from the Bowery, Father MacTurnan, who wants priests to marry to prevent Ireland becoming Protestant, are more lasting characters than Ned Carmady, who becomes a mouthpiece of Moore himself. But even the more polemical stories have some touch of true observation of character or landscape, some lyrical quality which saves them.

Moore's novel *The Lake* (1905) was begun as a short story for *The Untilled Field*. In theme it might appear to conform to the general pattern of the stories; Father Gogarty, parish priest of Tinnick, cannot forget Rose Leicester, the schoolmistress whom he had driven from the village when he learned of her pregnancy; eventually he realises his love for her then and the shock of this realisation causes a soul-searching which convinces him that he has no vocation and leads to his decision to swim across the nearby lake and to begin life again in America. Exile is thus chosen as the result of unfeeling authoritarian action; but the action is remembered in guilt and reflected upon, the priest's thinking is developed by correspondence with Rose, who has found a full life of her own in London and Europe, and its whole train is one of self-discovery and development. Thus, while the theme involves a conflict of Irish Catholicism with life, it is wider than that conflict. Moore himself wrote to a friend in 1905 that Rose

> represents the spring tide and her breath awakens Gogarty; he gets up and goes in search of life. The story is no more than a sun myth, the earth is frozen in dogma and the spring comes and warms it into life.[1]

The difficulty of this novel was that its chief event, Rose's departure, had taken place before the story opens. Moore overcame this by seeing it through the reminiscences of Father Gogarty as he walks by the lake and through his correspondence with Rose, and by blending his weaving recollections with memories of his own past and with impressions of the surrounding countryside and of its historical associations. The theme is thus internalised in a psychological novel. The book is a curious artistic paradox; it is close to Moore himself in a personal way; the scene is undoubtedly the district of Moore Hall — Tinnick is Ballinrobe, the lake is Lough Carra — and Moore uses the memories of his youth as well as the experience of apostasy to provide the realistic basis; at the same time it is objective and told with a sense of artistic distance. There is much to be said for his opinion that *The Lake* has as much life as *Esther Waters* — 'a different kind of life, not so wide a life, perhaps, but what counts in art is not width but depth'.

Moore's most permanent Irish contribution, however, was the trilogy *Ave* (1911), *Salve* (1912) and *Vale* (1914), which make up *Hail and Farewell*. This work came straight out of his experience of the revival. It is given unity by his own arrival from Paris, after Yeats and Russell had urged him to play a part in it, and his departure over a decade later, a disillusioned man. Not unlike James Bryden in *The Untilled Field*, Moore found himself in exile from exile; rejected alike by the Gaelic League under the cautious Hyde, by Lady Gregory in whose protective custody Yeats's friendship for him gradually waned, and by most of the literary set apart from Russell and Edward Martyn, he painted his picture of the revival with many feline strokes, putting himself well in its centre and using even his disillusionment creatively, holding a balance between caricature and reality in depicting his characters and interweaving fact, fiction, reminiscence and description of Irish scenes and types with great skill. Even Moore's prejudices which led to a deep breach with his brother help to make the picture real, if at times somewhat tedious. The theme of the book is really the author himself, the fall of his house and of Irish feudalism, his problem as an artist in society. Yeats, nettled by the second part of the trilogy, referred to 'George Moore's disfiguring glass', but Moore's portraits of Russell, Yeats, Lady Gregory, Edward Martyn, Hyde, John Eglinton and other figures of the revival are unforgettable, they have enough truth and perception to engage the reader in an interplay of personalities who become universal types, conceived in the spirit of comedy and relieved by nostalgia and regret.

Just as Moore's early realism and impressionism helped him to write *The Lake*, the technique of introspective and retrospective analysis used in that book made *Hail and Farewell* possible. His real farewell to Ireland was *A Story-teller's Holiday* (1918), published five years before he died in London. This was a series of tales interchanged between Moore and a Mayo shanachie and chiefly about the conflict of love and sanctity in mediaeval Ireland. Here Moore, with the assistance of James Stephens, reverted to a simple narrative manner which engagingly used Irish-English idiom in a style which is more authentic than Lady Gregory's and bears comparison with Synge's, thus suggesting a method which might have proved extremely fruitful when, a quarter of a century before, he had set out to provide Irish models for fiction in *The Untilled Field*.

If *The Untilled Field* marks the beginning of the process of developing Irish fiction along the lines of the contemporary European tradition, James Joyce's *Dubliners* (1914) and *Portrait of the Artist as a Young Man* (1916) represent its culmination during the period up to the Rising.

In the decade before these works appeared, however, the two most notable writers to emerge were not part of that process. Lord

Dunsany began his long and prolific literary career with two books, *The Gods of Pegana* (1905) and *Time and The Gods* (1916), based on a mythology which was not Celtic but entirely of his own devising. Their setting was vaguely oriental, their theme the war of Time on gods and men, and they were told in the manner of fairy-tales but with an art that linked their remote splendours to natural settings of desert and mountain, wind and stars. Dunsany continued to work this vein of fantasy in his fiction as in his plays and had published eight books by 1916. Yeats, who made a selection from them for the Cuala Press in 1912, liked to fancy Dunsany's work as part of the revival's return to the imaginative world of dream and fairy-tale but acknowledged that this was perhaps mere superstition on his part.

The work of James Stephens, on the other hand, came straight out of the revival. Influenced by Arthur Griffith in politics and by A.E. in mystical pantheism, he wrote articles for the *United Irishman* and *Sinn Fein* and was one of the group of poets of *New Songs*. Three years after the publication of his first book of poems he appeared in the literary limelight with two prose works, *The Charwoman's Daughter* and *The Crock of Gold* (both 1912). These two books, with *The Demi-Gods* (1914), represent Stephen's best work in fiction. All three show the working of a highly original creative mind, speculative and imaginative, exercising itself in the blending of realism and fantasy in a most individual manner. *The Charwoman's Daughter* is about the passing of Mary Makebelieve from childhood to adolescence, her attraction for a large, solemn and possessive policeman and her preference for an idealistic young man. She and her mother, the charwoman, compensate for the hardship of their life in a Dublin slum by romantic fantasies about the way life might be; this conflict of illusion and reality conditions the girl's development and that of her mother, who passes from a fierce maternal custody of her daughter to a recognition that freedom is part of the condition of maturity. The setting is contemporary Dublin; leading figures of the revival pass through it as well as a colourful procession of its workers and tenement-dwellers, and the scenes and morals of the city are sketched with a vivid charm.

This subtly simple tale illustrates some of Stephens's ideas about creative writing. His chief interest was in the psychology of character, character being most interesting to him when explosive, variable and complex, like life itself: the static character, like most institutions, is dead; the ideal story 'is not one in which a person strives and conquers external enemies', he wrote, 'but that in which a human being is both the battlefield and the battle'. Life itself is enough of an adventure for the novelist to dispense with all but the minimum of happenings which provide situations for his characters. This is true of *The Charwoman's Daughter;* Mary Makebelieve seems to have issued from Stephens's conviction that youth is good, while to grow up is to be bewildered by rational distinctions. Thus she is an ideal centre of psychological conflict in her transition from youth to adolescence.

The *Crock of Gold* is a fantasy of a much more diffuse structure, consisting of two interwoven tales; the first a folk-tale about the confiscation of the gold of the leprechauns of Gort na Cloca Mora, their revenge on the Philosopher they hold responsible and the return of their treasure; the second, an allegorical story of the love of Caitilin for Pan, god of nature and of sensual love, whom she eventually leaves for Angus Og, the Celtic nature-god whose idealism and unselfish love she prefers. Interspersed are serio-comic philosophical disscussions, meetings with trinities of demi-gods, with policemen and tinkers, and anecdotes told by various minor characters. The book culminates with the invasion of Dublin by the joyous host of the supernatural world, who free the city-dwellers from the fetters of reason and habit.

What gives this book its extraordinary charm is its gay, speculative thought, which sees all life as valuable, good and evil as its fundamental interacting factors, free intuition tempered by spiritual energy as superior to formalised reason. Believing as he did that the myths are 'studies in experimental psychology', Stephens uses gods and demi-gods to deepen the human characters who meet them by recalling the old forgotten finenesses of thought of which they are the emblems. Dialogue, whether of humans or of animals (for asses, cows, spiders and flies have their say), is handled with a very sure grasp of Irish idiom, which helps to root the fantasy in reality. The result is an engaging story as well as a *tour de force* of an original mind. 'In every book there are two stories,' Stephens wrote in the *English Review* in 1914

> one is the tale which has been written for the reader, the other is the story which the writer has not been able to keep out of his pages ... the more interesting part of any book.

The same combination was seen in *The Demi-Gods* (1914), a fantasy in which three angels descend to earth and fall in with a tinker and his family. At the end of the tale, which follows the diffuse method of *The Crock of Gold,* the youngest angel takes off his wings, having decided to stay with the tinker's daughter. The book of short stories, *Here are Ladies* (1913), returns to a more realistic method for its subtle investigation of the nuances of relationships between men and women. Stephens was less successful in this manner; his characters tend to be mere demonstrations of a point of view which, although whimsical and attractive, becomes obtrusive. Later with *Irish Fairy Tales* (1920), *Deirdre* (1923) and *In the Land of Youth* (1924), he returned to legendary themes which he treated more objectively than in his earlier books. In the essay referred to, Stephens had written of authors, 'We reproduce ourselves: our characters live and move on our own mental plane solely. . . . Every book written is the creation of incest.' While this is in a sense true of his earlier handling of legend, his later retelling of legends which were already formed was disciplined by their form and provided less room for speculative invention; but his sense of appropriate style in the tales and his interest in the psychology of such characters as Deirdre give these later books a quality which is memorable, though different from that of the earlier works.

An interesting contrast with James Stephens was the contemporary Belfast writer Forrest Reid (1875-1947), who wrote a perceptive book on Yeats (1915) but stands apart from the revival. Reid had some affinity with AE but his own mysticism was closer to that of Wordsworth, being largely based upon the idea that all art harks back to the paradisial state of childhood. His best novels, *Peter Waring* (1937), a rewritten version of *Following Darkness* (1912), and the trilogy *Uncle Stephen* (1931), *The Retreat* (1936) and *Young Tom* (1944) continually probe that state of innocence and wonder and its relationships to myth and dream. *Peter Waring* set the pattern of Reid's protagonists, who prefer dreams to harsh reality and the memory of boyhood friendships to the difficulty of adult relationships, but he has more reality because his background is more tangible. Reid's introverted nature often made him lack the touch of external reality in his writings which would have strengthened the psychological reality of his characters. Although he spent a long life in Belfast, the city figures little in most of his novels. His autobiographies, *Apostate* (1926) and *Private Road*

(1940), are worth reading and his writing as a whole is distinguished by its clear and sensitive style.

A less known author of this period was Seumas O'Kelly (1875-1918), minor poet and dramatist, whose talent as a short story writer was recognised after his early death. His stories, first published in various newspapers and periodicals, range in quality from the slight and uneven *By the Stream of Kilmeen* (1906) and *Waysiders* (1917) to his best work in *The Golden Barque* and *The Weaver's Grave* (1919). The bargees who cross the Bog of Allen in *The Golden Barque* take on life and reveal their friendships and antagonisms through quiet, precise, controlled writing. The two old men who search an ancient graveyard for the exact place where the dead weaver had his traditional right of burial, reveal through their contentions the traditions of a whole community and eventually seem like standing stones in the background of the young widow's flirtation with a gravedigger.

If O'Kelly is remembered for these short stories, Gerald O'Donovan (1871-1942) is remembered for his first novel *Father Ralph* (1913), a harsh realistic study of a young man's domination by his mother and his decision to leave the priesthood. It reflects the author's own experience, of which George Moore had some knowledge before creating Father Gogarty in *The Lake*. O'Donovan, an idealistic liberal priest, was baffled by church policy which he debated in other novels, none of which had the power of his first. He left Ireland for England in 1904 about a month before James Joyce departed for the continent.

The year in which the last volume of *Hail and Farewell* and *The Demi-Gods* appeared was also the year in which James Joyce's *Dubliners* (1914) was published. Born in Dublin in 1882 and educated by the Jesuits, Joyce had an international view of literature from the start, as his interest in Ibsen and his pamphlet on the Irish Literary Theatre indicate. He was in many ways hostile to the revival, which he regarded as too concerned with the past, too parochial in outlook. He graduated by examination of the Royal University of Ireland after attending courses run by the remnants of Newman's Catholic University in St Stephen's Green. He had already begun to formulate the aesthetic ideas, derived mainly from Aristotle and Aquinas, which were to guide his writing, and he had read widely in the best European literature of the time. When he left Ireland in 1904, determined to fulfil his career as a writer, he had completed most of the stories in

Dubliners, which he regarded as a chapter of the moral history of Ireland, with Dublin as the centre of its paralysis.

The book, published after many difficulties with publishers and printers, consisted of fifteen stories of Dublin life arranged in order of the aspects of childhood, adolescence, maturity and public life. Its basic method was that of the 'epiphany' by which Joyce appears to have meant the symbol of the search for truth as well as the revelations which the trained artistic mind can discern in the casual details of observed life — nuances of speech, gesture, situation — and which it can shape into a form conveying the essential quality of life itself. The general theme of the book is paralysis, which runs through the stories, from the paralysed priest in the first to the frustrated Gabriel Conroy in the last. The method of revelation is, on the whole, ironic. Romantic attitudes are gradually confronted with drab disillusioning facts; sentimental songs or poems are presented in ironic contexts; the sense of entrapment, a form of paralysis, is frequent.

According to James Joyce these stories were 'written for the most part in a style of scrupulous meanness'; while it has something of Moore's deliberate flatness, its irony is more delicate: 'He lived his spiritual life without any communion with others, visiting his relatives at Christmas and escorting them to the cemetery when they died.' But Joyce's qualification should be noted, as is shown by the Pateresque lyrical style which ends 'The Dead', or the ironical echoes of Dante's great work in 'Grace'.

Joyce, although perhaps implying a moral judgement upon his native city, avoided Moore's overt polemics. His aim was primarily the precision which is necessary to an objective fidelity to the subject in hand and which carries conviction to the reader; but while this stems from the naturalistic movement, his use of symbolism, perhaps most obvious in 'Araby', and 'Clay', his delicate sense of nuance, and his use of parody, extend his style into further reaches. The technique is a breakaway from the contrived narrative which centres around plot and 'significant character'; like Chekhov's stories it reveals the essential quality of life shaped by an individual vision. Although Dublin is the locale, the vision lights up many cities.

If this work placed him in the forefront of contemporary short-story writers, *A Portrait of the Artist as a Young Man* (1916) heralded his power as a novelist. Its original plan was naturalistic, as is shown by *Stephen Hero,* part of an early draft, published in 1944;

James Joyce. Courtesy of Bord Fáilte.

the final form substitutes for third-party narration the revelation of the mind of the central character by an epiphanic process of illumination from within. It conveys an extraordinary impression of organic growth. Its five chapters treat respectively of Stephen Dedalus's childhood, his adolescence and early sexual experiences, his repentance, his rejection of a call to the priesthood in favour of an artistic vocation, and his university years during which he formulates his aesthetic theory, defines the obstacles to it and the instruments of its fulfilment. This has a natural order involving a psychological as well as a chronological progression from the child's first impressions of words to the artist's consciousness of the mastery of words, from sensation to sensitivity, from passivity to the exercise of will, but it is the result of a very careful art. The interior monologue, the flash-back of memory and the dramatic episodes are skilfully integrated into the general structure. Language is sometimes used in conventional form, with literary echoes of Pater or of Newman, but often becomes more psychologically contextual, adopting the forms of baby-talk, of schoolboy slang or the heightened realism of political anecdote, sermon or academic discourse. Symbolism is used in a variety of gradations, from the overt symbolism associated with the developing artist to the colour symbolism of Irish-English political conflict.

The result is a portrait not only of the growth of an artist's mind from its embryonic form to maturity but of the various influences which have shaped it, as well as the obstacles ('nationality, language, religion') which the artist must avoid by 'silence, exile and cunning' if he is to fulfil his destiny; once that mind has reached maturity the influences recede into the background and the spotlight is on the artist as he prepares for flight. This process is not without its drawbacks, including the reduction of the subsidiary characters in the final section to almost supernumerary roles, tame geese surrounding a young eagle, and the obscurity of motivation in some of Stephen's human relationships. While the title of the book and its partly fictional nature justify this, this treatment produces the effect of a *Künstlerroman* in which the *Künstler* is over-romanticised; yet the development of the *young* man (Joyce later called attention to the neglected adjective) is so finely conveyed that the reader accepts even his lengthy aesthetic homilies as part of its flowering, balanced as they are by that passage in which Stephen expresses his feeling about art in more human terms:

to try slowly and humbly and constantly to express, to press out again, from the gross earth or what it brings forth, from sound and shape and colour which are the prison gates of our soul, an image of the beauty we have come to understand — that is art.

The maturity of Joyce's art can be judged by the fact that he completed the book in 1914, when he was thirty-two, the year after Proust at forty-two had published the first section of *À la recherche du temps perdu.*

CHAPTER XVIII
Poets of the Easter Rising

The troubled years 1912 to 1924 were years of upheaval unfavourable to creative writing in Ireland. The close approach of Home Rule led to the formation in 1912 of the Ulster Volunteers, pledged to resist it by force of arms, and of the National Volunteers, who supported it. In the following year came the Larkin strike and the consequent formation of the Irish Citizen Army in Dublin. The outbreak of the First World War and the shelving of Home Rule were followed by the Easter Rising of 1916, the guerilla war of independence, the Anglo-Irish Treaty of 1922 and the Irish Civil War. When it ended in 1923, a new, partitioned Ireland had emerged. Since the Easter rising in effect ended the Irish Literary Revival, it is appropriate to consider its poets at this point; afterwards Irish writing took new directions.

This dislocated period saw the engagement of many active minds in political and military affairs. Its events are reflected in the history of the *Irish Review,* which at its inception in 1911 attracted the serious attention of older writers of the Irish literary revival (Yeats, A.E., Moore, O'Grady, John Eglinton and Seumas O'Sullivan) and younger writers (Colum, Stephens, Pearse, MacDonagh and Plunkett). Colum, Mac Donagh, Stephens and David Houston were prominent in starting it, Colum having chief editorial responsibility from about March 1912 to August 1913, when the review was bought by Joseph Plunkett. Its policy began to shift from purely literary to social and political concerns about the time that Connolly's first contribution appeared. There was no issue for July 1914, the month of the Howth gun-running by the National Volunteers; and its cessation in November 1914 is an index of the involvement of its interest with that body. Brief as its career had been, it first seemed to provide an answer to Yeats's question of 1892 — 'Can we not build up a national tradition, a national literature which shall be none the less Irish in spirit for being English in language?' — and to have shown that Pearse's statement that freedom is the first condition of any real living effort was a necessary qualification to any answer.

The Easter Rising was part of that qualification; the resultant execution of Pearse, MacDonagh and Plunkett, who had signed its proclamation, inextricably linked their writing with it in the Irish consciousness.

MacDonagh's work was the most considerable in quantity. By his twenty-eighth year he had published three books of verse, *Through the Ivory Gate* (1902), *April and May* (1903) and *The Golden Joy* (1906); as he suppressed most of their contents, it was by *Songs of Myself* (1910) and *Lyrical Poems* (1913) that he wished to be remembered. Yeats's judgement in 'Easter 1916' that MacDonagh was 'coming into his force' seems true enough; most of his poetry is so conventional in form and language that it is stilted, often rhetorical, literary rather than natural in diction, but in a few poems of his last volume, as in his translations of Catullus and of some Irish poems, he breaks free of these bonds and achieves directness and precision of image:

> The stars stand up in the air,
> The sun and the moon are gone,
> The strand of its waters is bare,
> And her sway is swept from the swan.

MacDonagh wrote three plays of slight merit but it was in criticism that he perhaps achieved most. His *Thomas Campion and the Art of Poetry* (1913) showed a good deal of critical sensitivity and his *Literature in Ireland* (1916) did pioneer work in discussing the nature of Anglo-Irish literature and of the 'Irish mode' in English verse. The latter work was the first modern critical attempt in Ireland to hazard a systematic analysis of the distinctive nature and scope of Anglo-Irish literature; of the linguistic struggle of two languages and of their eventual unity in a language which, while chiefly English in its characteristics, was often Irish in syntax, rhythm, pronunciation, vocabulary and idiom.

While MacDonagh's view that a distinctively Anglo-Irish literature could come only when the English-speaking Irish, mainly Gaelic in stock, produced a literature that 'was from, by, of, to and for the Irish people' might be challenged on various counts, his contention, that the influences working on that literature produced important differences from the literature of England and that these differences gave it individuality, is true.

MacDonagh chose the 'Irish mode' in poetry as the chief ground of his demonstration, discussing its musical, wavering rhythm, its use of delicate patterns carried over from Gaelic poetry, and its preference for direct colloquial speech and simple concrete images. While most of these ideas had been touched upon or demonstrated previously by Hyde, Yeats, A.E., Synge and others, MacDonagh synthesised them into a general critical work which, although rather hurriedly put together, provides a central core of positive argument and definition. The dedication of the work to George Sigerson showed its author's sense of literary continuity.

Pearse's poetic output was comparatively small and rests upon a score of poems, mostly translations from the Irish. In them the touch is sure, the language precise:

O lovely head of the woman that I loved,
In the middle of the night I remember thee:
But reality returns with the sun's whitening,
Alas, that the slender worm gnaws thee tonight.

The themes are usually childhood, death, lament; and in a few more deeply personal poems in blank verse the linking theme is renunciation of common sense and of beauty for the vision of a free people:

And now I speak, being full of vision;
I speak to my people, and I speak in my people's name to the masters of my people.
I say to my people that they are holy, that they are august, despite their chains,
That they are greater than those that hold them ...

Technically the influence here is probably Whitman, whose work Pearse may have known through Rolleston; the spirit is that of self-dedication which imbued everything that he wrote. Like MacDonagh, he believed that propaganda should be kept out of poetry and this is as near as he came to it; a rhetorical, impassioned cry of dedication which is to be found also in his plays *The Master* and *The Singer*. It has its appropriate place in his oratory, notably in his speech at the graveside of O'Donovan Rossa, which O'Casey drew upon in the second act of *The Plough and the Stars*.

To understand the basis of his political thinking one must read his pamphlets, especially the five which appeared in 1916. These are *Ghosts, The Murder Machine, The Separatist Idea, The Spiritual Nation* and *The Sovereign People,* which combine the mystique of revolutionary idealism with the logic of hard fact and affirm the principles of independence and of social justice — that core of thought which was at the centre of Tone's writings a century and a half before.

The third poet executed with Pearse and MacDonagh was Joseph Plunkett, who was almost a decade younger. He too was a member of the I.R.B. and was its contact with Casement in Germany during the summer of 1915. He believed strongly that in his day what was necessary to save nationalism was 'a formal rising and as much military success as possible'.

Plunkett was a delicate young man whose education, privately and at Stonyhurst, gave him a wide conversance with classical and European literature. He was greatly influenced by the mystical and romantic writers. His poetry also carries something of a literary burden and is full of echoes of Blake, Thompson, the early Yeats; but its craft is more deliberate than MacDonagh's, and its form, though conventional, frequently conveys a strong mystical urgency:

> All pathways by his feet are worn,
> His strong heart stirs the ever-beating sea,
> His crown of thorns is twined with every thorn,
> His cross is every tree.

His best poems (in *The Circle and the Sword,* 1911; *Poems,* 1916) have a Caroline quality of simplicity, of meditative music, or sometimes a romantic beauty:

> My lady has the grace of Death,
> Whose charity is quick to save ...

but too often he does not do what Yeats did when about his age, set himself to rid his work of literary diction and that verbal imprecision which is often the trap of the mystical poet.

Certain themes linked these poets together: the poet as seer, as custodian of the spark that is the seed of a nation's fire; the deliberate renunciation of life's attractions that comes with self-dedication to a cause; the loneliness that goes with this choice. Desmond Ryan, who edited a good selection of their work in *The 1916 Poets* (1963), recalled Pearse revising his writings in the early spring of 1916 and joking that if they did nothing else they would 'rid Ireland of three *bad* poets'. That must have been shortly before their three names appeared on the 1916 Proclamation of Independence. The words of MacDonagh's *Literature in Ireland* apply to all three and to Roger Casement, who also was a minor poet as well as a vigorous political writer: 'the cause which has been the great theme of our poetry may any day call the poets to give their lives in the old service.'

With these three poets is sometimes associated the name of Francis Ledwidge, who was born in the same year as Plunkett and died in 1917. He was a farm-labourer and road-worker who supported the Labour movement and the Volunteers; when the majority of the latter followed Redmond's advice to defend Home Rule by joining the British army, Ledwidge opposed it at first but joined up later and died in action in France. Before his death he had written several poems of lament for the Easter leaders, notably that for Thomas MacDonagh, whom he admired most:

> Nor shall he know when loud March blows
> Thro' slanting snows her fanfare shrill,
> Blowing to flame the golden cup
> Of many an upset daffodil.

Ledwidge was at his best in such poems of simple harmony and images. Lord Dunsany, who helped to bring his work to notice wrote that the keynote of his work was devotion to the fields of Meath; but it had a wider scope, through his interest in the associations of the Boyne valley with its old mythology. Although he admired the Georgian poets, his real affinity was with the romantics and there is a strong element of romantic escapism in his war poetry, which contrasts oddly with the work of such English contemporaries as Wilfred Owen and Siegfried Sassoon, who wrote of the grim horrors of mass-slaughter. This romantic element led to the inflation of Ledwidge's reputation, like that of Rupert Brooke, during the war period. His best poems survive in anthologies:

> Ay! soon the swallows will be flying south,
> The wind wheel north to gather in the snow,
> Even the roses spilt on youth's red mouth
> Will soon blow down the road all roses go.

'Ratification of the Irish Treaty' by John Lavery. Courtesy of the National Gallery of Ireland.

PART V
After the Revival

CHAPTER XIX
Poetry

The work of Yeats (1865-1939) went on for almost three decades after the close of the revival, accompanied by a rising tide of books of critical assessment which are readily available. The best possible introduction to him is to read through the *Collected Poems* before turning to the explanations of them by himself or others, for they have a power to arrest the mind. Any great poet's work does not admit of very rigid divisions. The tree may be divided into sections but the same concentric circles run throughout its length, showing its organic growth, an aspect which is vital to literary criticism. If, for convenience, the poetry of Yeats has to be considered in sections or phases, it may be that the poems from 1889, when his first volume appeared, to 1904, when Yeats was thirty-nine and the great love of his life, Maud Gonne, had recently married, might form the first group. The poetry, on the whole, is that of a good lyrical poet, mystical, dreamy and subjective in temperament, at first obviously indebted to the poets of the great period of English Romanticism, to the French Symbolists, the pre-Raphaelites and the world-weary *fin de siècle* poets. The idea of escape from materialism, from the grey truth of science or the grey pavements of London, the belief in the mystical life, in the value of poetic utterance are juxtaposed.

As the revival proceeds the themes of the older Irish heroic literature and of Irish folklore are used increasingly. Relevant poems reflect the same temperament; King Goll, Fergus, Oisin, all escape from reality to a world of dream and of transfigured nature. Cuchulainn first appears in one rather inferior short narrative poem, which mishandles the legend upon which it is based. He has not yet become the powerful symbol or character used to such effect in later poems and plays. The fairy world lures child or bride away to a world of supernatural beauty. The 'Rose poems', with their multiple symbols, demonstrate both the richness of the Symbolists, stirring the imagination by evocative association and harmonic tone, and the cult of the private symbol which deliberately and sometimes disastrously befogs communication by its use of the arcane. While it is not unjust to call these early poems 'the poems of escape', there is much to be said for escape from 'this preposterous pig of a world', as the poet saw it at certain times; but this is not the only element in this early work, which has a delicate musical charm. Its ballads, the beginning and end of *The Wanderings of Oisin,* and many lines and phrases show a hard, concrete directness which owes something to Irish literature, folklore and popular ballads, and something to the characteristics of Irish speech in English.

But the central artistic drive was Yeats's increasing determination to achieve perfection in his poetry by greater precision, by 'that stern colour and that delicate line' of the disciplined poet. Synge's example and the practical business of writing for the theatre, where words must have an immediate impact, also spurred him in this direction. The realities of life — the marriage of Maud Gonne, involvement in public controversies — increased its force from about 1904. Later came the inescapable events of the First World War, the Rising, the Civil War. While his lyrics gained in pared strength, it was notable that a harder, more meditative element characterised his poetry. His marriage in 1917 gave more order to his life. He read much in history and philosophy, became for a few years a Senator, a 'smiling public man', in the new partitioned Ireland. In 1923 he received the supreme recognition of the Nobel Prize for Literature.

The poems of this middle period (1904-25) are full of variety and richness; there are meditative poems about Ireland and her history, about the First World War and the upheaval of Western civilisation, poems in which he uses some of the ideas of *A Vision* — the cycles of history, recurrent types of personality, the passing of the soul through phases like the moon, the transmigration of souls — common to ancient Irish and Indian thought. At times he fiercely questions the values of society or, by allowing different aspects of himself to speak in the same poem, questions his own; or by use of the dramatic lyric expresses through a mask some dominant mood or idea. His symbols are used sparingly but with depth; Sato's sword, fashioned by Montashigi, is a symbol of enduring art, achieved by toil and pain. A constant idea is that for him art is the way of solving the riddle of existence. The smithies or workshops of the artist break the flood of transient life, endure, are timeless through what they create.

This line of thought, enriched by further reading and speculation, continues in his later and last poems (1926-39). These also show the same variety of techniques, themes and attitudes. They have been called individual stars forming clusters of intent. The 'Supernatural Songs' reflect his renewed interest in Indian philosophy and in its correspondences with early Irish Christian thought. The political or historical ballads express his belief in 'the indomitable Irishry' and its great figures, or sometimes turn fiercely upon the politicians of the present for being unworthy of their tragic past. Old age is often the theme but it is notable that Yeats is less troubled by it than he was in middle age, probably because of his belief in art and in the cycles of time, which will bring again the beauty that has faded. Out of the caverns of mystery the old man hears the mystical command, 'Rejoice!'. The eyes of the old Chinamen carved in lapis-lazuli are gay; for art, the result of meditation and measurement, laughs and sings forever. At the same time the artist is, perhaps in the Zen sense, indifferent, can 'Cast a cold eye/On life, on death' as Yeats's own epitaph on the plain limestone slab over his grave in Sligo commands.

Yeats's work made him the greatest 'classic' poet of the English-speaking world of his time, for in mode he was essentially a traditionalist and always preserved a sense of harmonic form, even when expressing many of the dissonances of a chaotic modern world. This gave his work, whether lyrical, reflective or rhetorical, a supple intensity and clarity. His clear diction and syntactical strength contrasted with the new modes in poetry which came in with the great experimental poets of the last two decades of his life, Eliot, Pound and Auden, whom he never quite understood and who largely supersede him in their influence on contemporary poetry.

Ireland, where he was born and where he rests, gave him 'a centre where to fix the soul', an old and valued well-spring of inspiration, the tensions of love and hate, greatness and littleness, a tragic past and the 'casual comedy' of ordinary life, an aristocratic sense and the pressures of a new democracy. In return, besides contributing to and influencing the mainstream of English poetry, Yeats blended two cultures and so helped to form and to provide standards for the newer of Ireland's two indigenous literatures.

Yeats's main prose writings are of three kinds: fiction, essays and philosophical writings. The fiction includes *John Sherman and Dhoya* (1891), a short novel and tale, and the unfinished novel, *The Speckled Bird.* Of these the first is more important; its two main characters represent opposing aspects of Yeats's personality. The unfinished novel, while also concerned with character and setting, anticipates the visionary types who appear in *The Secret Rose* (1897). The latter is a collection of stories with the dominant theme of the opposition between the world of science and common sense and the world of the spiritual and intuitive. The rose image stands for the spiritual. The stories are suffused with symbol and motif, with visionary beings, including Hanrahan. Yeats also edited a number of collections and tales, such as *Fairy and Folk Tales of the Irish Peasantry* (1888), *Representative Irish Tales* (1891) and *The Celtic Twilight* (1893), that show his immersion in Irish culture and his attempts to make the public more aware of a native heritage.

His essays have been issued in a number of collections of which *Ideas of Good and Evil* (1903) is of special relevance to his poetry. It contains some of his most important essays: 'Magic', 'The Symbolism of Poetry', 'The Celtic Element in Literature', 'The Galway Plains', 'Poetry and Tradition' and 'A General Introduction for my Work'. In 'Magic' he explains his concept of the *anima mundi* or collective unconscious and explains his belief that the 'borders of our mind are ever shifting, and that many minds can flow into one another, as it were, and create or reveal a single mind, a single energy'; that the 'borders of our memories are as shifting, that our memories are a part of one great memory, the memory of Nature herself', and that 'this great mind and great memory can be evoked by symbols'. In general, as Joseph Hone has written, the collection 'opposed the primitive to the popular, the subtleties and obscurities of ancient doctrine to the products of ratiocinating intellect. . . . Poetry is regarded . . . as a positive truth and contrasted with the illusions of history and politics.'[1] The essays have a close relationship with his early poetry, they define some of his critical points of view, they express his interest in symbolism and the occult and his views on various writers. In addition, the essay on 'The Symbolism of Poetry' contains his much-quoted comment:

> All sounds, all colours, all forms, either because of their preordained energies or because of long association, evoke indefinable and yet precise emotions, or, as I prefer to think, call down among us certain disembodied powers, whose footsteps over our hearts we call emotions; and when sound, and colour, and form are in a musical relation, a beautiful relation to one another, they become, as it were, one sound, one colour, one form, and evoke an emotion that is made out of their distinct evocations and yet is one emotion.

While *Ideas of Good and Evil* is central for the study of his poetry, two other collections of previously uncollected material, *Uncollected Prose,* vol. 1 (1970) and vol. II (1975), are also of interest, as are his letters. His essays on the theatre, originally collected in *Plays and Controversies,* are to be found in *Explorations* (1962).

Yeats's *Autobiographies* (1955) contains some of his most important work: *Reveries over Childhood and Youth* (1914), *The Trembling of the Veil* (1922), *Dramatis Personae, 1896-1902* (1936) and three other essays, including 'The Death of Synge'. The book as a whole is valuable as a biographical, historical and literary document. 'Art, Irish nationalism, and the occult', as Joseph Ronsley points out, 'provide themes which contribute some sense of unity.'[2] In *Reveries* he writes of his family, his own early years, his literary interests, his interest in the occult, his conflict with his father, and the importance of his meeting with the old Fenian, John O'Leary. *The Trembling of the Veil* points forward to the more famous *A Vision* (1926) in its classification of personality types. In this essay he first describes how his friends tried to achieve fullness of being and how he also sought it through images taken from the great memory. From an early stage in his career Yeats wanted to hammer his thoughts into unity; he wanted to systematize them and unify them with his feelings. To counter the dominance of nineteenth century rationalism he argued for a unity of being. He returned to the idea of the *anima mundi*, the universal mythic memory, upon which everyone could draw. He also defined his idea of the mask and the anti-self which he had already discussed in *Per Amica Silentia Lunae* (1918). *Dramatis Personae* describes the beginning of the Irish Literary Theatre, goes further into the subjects of personality and culture, the idea of the antinomies of the self and the anti-self. In fact the discussion here is clearer than it is in *A Vision*.

In *Per Amica Silentia Lunae* (1918) Yeats introduces his famous theories of the mask, the anti-self and the daimon; this long essay develops and brings together many of the ideas he had absorbed from his reading of the occult writers. Its ideas receive more elaborate treatment in his most important prose work, *A Vision* (1926, 1937). In its final form, as A.G. Stock has written, it

> amounts to a summing up of Yeats's own sense of values in a system of thought about the soul in and beyond life, and also about the meaning of history, all worked out in a geometrical symbolism, based on the esoteric doctrine in which he and his wife had both become adepts.

The book, she goes on to say, contains 'an abstract idea of two movements, one towards perfect self-realisation, the other towards perfect self-abnegation'.[3] The lunar cycle of twenty-eight phases is central. These are represented as periods of history, stages in human life, a series of incarnations, degrees of subjectivity or objectivity, and types of human characters. In addition to the image of the great wheel on which the twenty-eight phases are spokes, the book also uses the image of the interpenetrating gyres, one subjective, the other objective. History and the individual are considered to pass through a cycle from subjectivity to objectivity; the gyres are seen as whirling around inside one another, so that each age or personality type, or phase of an individual's life is made up of a tension of opposites, a pull between the subjective and the objective. Yeats's reflections on human nature or on history were enriched by these metaphors of complex antinomies. Some of his greatest poems drew upon the system which he worked out in *A Vision,* which, as far as he formulated one, expresses his philosophy.

George William Russell (1867-1935) published his *Collected Poems* in 1913. Yeats thought his early poems the most delicate and subtle of any Irish contemporary, distinctive in their visionary belief and simplicity. A.E.'s vision of men, influenced by Platonic and Indian thought and by poets from Blake to Emerson and Whitman, was transcendental. He saw this life as a preparation for eternal beauty and wrote of its abstractions in words of changing subtle charm:

Its edges foamed with amethyst and rose,
Withers once more the old blue flower of day:
There where the ether like a diamond glows
Its petals fade away.

This has a touch of the early Yeats but Russell's style did not grow in precision like that of the developing Yeats. He wrote poetry mainly because he believed that its flashes of divine truth could lead its readers to form a nobler vision of themselves than materialism could, and his vision was essentially private. He could be clear enough when the occasion demanded, as in his poem 'On Behalf of Some Irishmen not Followers of Tradition':

No blazoned banner we unfold
One charge alone we leave to youth,
Against the sceptred myth to hold
The golden heresy of truth.

Russell's visionary ideas were stated in prose in *The Candle of Vision* (1918), his practical ideas for the future of Ireland chiefly in *The National Being* (1916); his work for Sir Horace Plunkett's co-operative movement convinced him that a democracy could only work properly if based upon an organised co-operative system. His constructive economic thinking was expressed also as editor of *The Irish Homestead* and *The Irish Statesman,* and influenced the thought of Gandhi in India and of the New Deal in America. In politics he was moderate and strove vainly to reconcile the opposing forces of the Civil War which, he thought, had reversed the process of Yeats's play by turning a beautiful Cathleen ni Houlihan into a withered crone. Though his benign personal influence and his constructive positive thought were long remembered, his poetic influence had waned before he died in England in 1935.

Although the revival's influence began to wane with the Troubles, several of the poets associated with it continued its tradition well into this century. Padraic Colum (1881-1972) was the most notable, while Joseph Campbell (1879-1944) had a similar poetic aim and temper. The main strength of both is in their ballads. While both were influenced in this form by Yeats, stronger influences were Hyde's translations of Irish love songs and religious poetry, their own knowledge of the people of rural Ireland, more intimate than Yeats ever achieved, and their familiarity with traditional Irish music. Some of their ballads are still accepted as traditional folk-songs. Colum's 'She moved through the fair' and Campbell's 'My Lagan love' followed a similar process to Yeats's 'Down by the Salley Gardens'. All three poets shared the revival's aim of a return to the people which made the ballad an appropriate form, but where Yeats's poetic development diverted him from it, Colum and Campbell experimented with combinations of ballads with narrative verse forms and poetic prose. These experiments were not particularly successful and their ballad poetry remained their best achievement. It often took the form of the dramatic lyric; their early work in the theatre, Colum's in Dublin, Campbell's in the Ulster Literary Theatre movement in Belfast, probably helped to incline them towards this form, which has older traditional roots. Both used it successfully to present a variety of country types who speak for themselves rather than as a persona of the poet. They felt, like the folklorists, that many of these types — country fiddlers and singers, stone-cutters and ploughers — were dying out and should be recorded. In both the sense of history and of tradition was strong; Colum's tin-whistle player has the long face 'Sculptured on a cross of stone'; Campbell's modern fighting-man becomes a Gaelic warrior; but Colum carried his associations more skilfully, so that they deepened many of his poems without becoming obtrusive as they did with Campbell.

For many decades their work was known chiefly through anthologies. Colum's old woman of the roads, his poor scholar of the forties, his cattle drover with his thoughts on 'White ships and the King of Spain's daughter', or Campbell's dancer,

> Clay in his thoughts
> And lightning in his tread

were yet to become revival clichés to the younger poets.

Colum's *Poems* (1932) showed a wider range of interest; besides versions of translations by Hyde, Kuno Meyer and David ap Gwyllam, were poems and prose-poems on Tahitian themes and on the animals and flowers of different lands. Yet the older poems included seemed to have weathered best: this is confirmed by *The Poet's Circuits* (1960) in which Colum used the idea of the early Irish poets' traditional rounds to make his own imaginative circuit of Ireland by linking his ballads with his poems on mythological and historical themes, thus placing them in the imaginative perspective of the revival which had shaped him.

Most of the poetry which had established Campbell as a writer of strong, direct ballads, skilfully shaped to traditional Irish tunes, was published before 1917. The publication of *Poems by Joseph Campbell*, which Austin Clarke edited in 1963, shows a greater variety of subjects and forms; it contains realistic prison poems in blank verse, a long choral ode and a number of poems whose themes and modes are Elizabethan, as well as mythological poems and adapted street-ballads. There is also a long poem in blank verse about the monastic settlement of Glendalough and the history of its site from the ice age on; a poem which shows how scholarly knowledge can weigh a poem down, for the hard direct individual note of the ballads and lyrics, while not entirely lacking, is submerged by expository learning. The technique of his poetry, which is interesting for the clarity of the images in his best passages, was not entirely from ballad sources but owed something to the Imagist movement, while the influence of the symbolists is evident in his religious poetry.

After the Civil War Campbell went to America, returning after twelve years' academic activity to Glencree, County Wicklow, where he lived a scholar-hermit's life in a cottage full of old books and heraldic devices. His last years were saddened by his isolation and by the slaughter in Europe. He died a lonely death in Glencree in 1944. Colum, cheerfully preoccupied with poetry to the last, shuttled between Irish and American literary circles for thirty years after that, dying in New York in 1972. Each poet was in his own way like Oisin after the Fianna, although Campbell, lacking Colum's exuberance, was more in tune with the dour mood of that durable warrior.

Meanwhile their contemporary, James Stephens, continued to publish his poems sporadically during the twenties and thirties. He was already known as an excellent writer of dramatic lyrics, ballads, versions of Keating, O'Bruadair, O'Rahilly and other Irish poets in all of which he showed a strong individuality. His interest through A.E. in theosophy and in nature-mysticism, partly derived from Blake, made him unconventional in his approach to accepted values; he viewed gods and devils, weeds and flowers, on equal terms as complementary to each other in the scheme of things. His main theme was himself as a microcosm of the universe, as a participant in the vast processes of creation, which he celebrated with a joyful energy. In his best poems this enthusiasm was controlled by a tight lyrical style, direct in language, simple in image and swift in tempo, while at times simplicity was strained by elision, ecstatic utterance became too exclamatory, humour became too whimsical to achieve the intensity which he found in his Irish and Elizabethan models and accepted as the hallmark of poetry. He was a continual experimenter in the shorter lyric and always sought to preserve the sense of song.

Stephens's *Collected Poems* (1926) included most of his poems previously anthologised and its later editions contain most of his best poems published thereafter. In his preface Stephens stated his belief in the appropriateness of the lyric form to the tempo of a rapidly changing world and in intensity of song as its distinguishing feature. His later poems, particularly 'Demiurge', 'I Am Writer', 'The Pit of Bliss' and 'Strict Care, Strict Joy!', round out his poetics imaginatively; the poet's craft is the universal will which comes through his subconscious; his responsibility is to discipline his joys and sorrows into harmonic form.

Stephens, who died in London in 1950, was not as committed to the values and the limitations of the revival as Colum and Campbell: he was more speculative, more complex, delighted in standing accepted values on their heads; in this he was more modern. At the same time he shared with both men the idea of the poet as seer and singer and so preserved a valuable tradition in a world where poets had become increasingly introverted in thought, and dissonant in style.

He is an interesting contrast to Seumas O'Sullivan (1879-1958), three years his elder, a revival poet in his earlier books, *The Twilight People* (1905), *The Earth Lover* (1909), whose titles indicate the influence of Yeats and of A.E. during the first decade of this century; although their influence was at first overpowering, it helped to give his work a delicacy of rhythm and of cadence, while his interest in translating Catullus and Henri de Regnier preserved his precision from vague twilight abstraction, a work chiefly done for Stephens through Hyde and for Yeats through Synge. His *Collected Poems* (1940) contains his best poems; notably, quiet lyrics about Georgian Dublin and slight, impressionistic, sometimes sentimental glimpses of life's casual happenings. A line in his poem '1939' — 'The dread accidia of the soul' — hints at a melancholy underlying the delicate nostalgia of his poems.

Although O'Sullivan also published *belles lettres,* notably *The Rose and the Bottle* (1946), his chief service to literature in Ireland was his founding of *The Dublin Magazine* in 1923 and his editorship of it until his death in 1958. The policy of this periodical was strictly non-political. O'Sullivan regarded himself as a kind of protector of the 'intellectual remnant' and as a preserver of correct standards of literary taste. While this made the magazine somewhat eclectic, it also enabled it to act as a bridge between the older poets and the younger writers of a period of transition, much of whose work was encouraged and published by O'Sullivan, who also gave space to literary happenings in Europe. In some respects the scope of *The Dublin Magazine* was restrictive; its editor kept a wary eye on censorship and also reflected Yeats in his dislike of the Eliot-Auden school. By 1940 his rigid exclusion of social and political writing, the isolation of Ireland by the war and the establishment of *The Bell* had reduced its appeal considerably. Although its public was always small, it did succeed in attracting most of the literary talents of this period.

Three contemporary writers who wrote some poetry during and after the later stages of the revival were Oliver St John Gogarty, Lord Dunsany and James Joyce. Gogarty's *Collected Poems* (1952) contains the best of his work published over a stretch of some thirty years. He was well versed in the classics and learned from them a discipline of form which controlled his natural vivacity. His lyrics, whether expressing a kind of gay stoicism or joyful irreverence, are always well-wrought. This is the quality which Yeats admired; in his preface to the *Oxford Book of Modern Verse* he hailed Gogarty as one of the great lyric poets of the age, although he was careful to add that he never stayed long at his best; and indeed this many-sided man seems to have suffered from 'the cursed versatility of the Celt', putting into his conversation, his hasty books and his many activities most of the energy which might have made him a greater poet. In this he resembles Lord Dunsany, whose poems were published during the same period; *Fifty Poems* (1929) and *Mirage Water* (1938) represent his best. While these volumes of light verse contain some engaging lyrics, most of them recall James Stephens's remark that light verse tends to get heavier with the years.

James Joyce is in a different category, for everything he did was finely wrought. The poems of *Chamber Music* (1907) have the delicate Elizabethan cadences and the courtly language appropriate to lute-song although somewhat too contrived for modern ears. The later poems of *Pomes Penyeach* (1927) drop such mannerisms but preserve the clear images which made the imagists see some affinity between his work and theirs. Direct language and quick impressionistic strokes convey setting and feeling in a way which seems in line with Stephen Dedalus's description of the lyric as the simplest verbal vesture of an emotion, but the cadences are subtle. If Joyce's prose gradually works towards the condition of music, it should be remembered that his masterly lyricism was evident from an earlier period. His satirical power may be seen in 'The Holy Office' (1904) and 'Gas from a Burner' (1912); a controlled use of Swift's four-foot measure is used to ridicule the figures of the revival from whom he emphatically sets himself apart. The thrust of his satire is like that of Byron's *English Bards and Scotch Reviewers;* intensely personal, often unjust, always deft.

The long poetic career of Austin Clarke (1896-1974), stretching from the latter days of the revival into contemporary times, made him the most distinguished poet of this period apart from Yeats. His first publication, *The Vengeance of Fionn* (1917), appeared in his twenty-first year, his *Collected Poems* (1974) in the year of his death; in between there had been a steady flow of production: poetry, verse-plays, prose romances, autobiographies, a remarkable achievement, made possible only by a quiet integrity of personality and persistence of purpose, recognised at first by a limited circle in Ireland and England, later by a wider international audience.

Clarke's earliest work was chiefly in epic poetry. The revival themes were strong in these but there was also an individuality of treatment and a delicate lyricism sometimes overlain by elaborate description and intricate mythological reference, the traps of the revival poets and their predecessors, like Ferguson, who had attempted epic. Clarke, dissatisfied with the poetic mode of Ferguson, was also dissatisfied with the twilight atmosphere of the revival and found in some Irish literature a directness and a hard lyrical impressionism alien to it. Influenced by A.E., he studied Larminie's assonantal verse. Through Douglas Hyde and George Sigerson he became familiar with Gaelic poetic forms. From these he shaped his craft, learned to write poetry that was wrought with subtle cadences and was disciplined by form into a mode of individual expression. After *The Cattle-drive in Connaught* (1925) which is probably his most successful epic poem — it is based on the incident of the pillow-chat of Maeve and Ailill which introduces the *Táin* — Clarke found a strong attraction in mediaeval Ireland. Yeats had concentrated chiefly on the earlier Ulster cycle; Clarke found the mediaeval period closer to his taste; partly because of its legend and history and its Celtic Romanesque art, partly because it gave him many objective correlatives for the socio-religious conflicts of his own time, and for the personal dilemmas of conscience in which his waning Catholicism and his artistic growth involved him.

Such matters were the main themes of the poems and plays which he wrote during the next thirty years. *Pilgrimage and Other Poems* (1929) and the collection published in 1936 with Padraic Colum's preface show a strong, controlled lyricism, whether celebrating monastic art, the problems of celibacy, the sexy languor of the young woman of Beare or the beauty of the planter's daughter. The poems of *Night and Morning* (1938) are concerned with the problems of religion and reason, pride of intellect and faith, sexuality and conscience. They follow a confessional tradition in Gaelic poetry and reflect its technique but at the same time express in an immediate, poignant way the torn ambiguous, riddling mind of a modern poet, sure of his art but of little else. Clarke's style in this volume was less embellished, less burdened with learning; he was working towards a closer precision of language, although the subtle qualifications and ambiguities he expressed often made him a puzzling poet.

After 1938 Clarke published little poetry for seventeen years. His interest had turned to the writing of prose romances and of verse-plays, which he had begun in the twenties with *The Son of Learning* (1927).

Ancient Lights: Poems and Satires, his first book of poetry since
1938, appeared in 1955. About two-thirds of the poems in *Collected
Poems* (1974) belong to those twenty years, a prolific period of
poetry of varied form and temper. There are poems like 'Martha
Blake at Fifty-One', in which drab realism controls feelings of
despair and pathos, dream-poems blending fantasy with
reminiscence, satirical vignettes of politicians and churchmen,
poems which combine celebration of Dublin's beauty with lament
at its erosion, delicate lyrics which capture casual beauty in
impressionistic flashes or give new grace to the Irish harp-songs of
the eighteenth century by their haunting verbal music. Old
themes appear in new guises; the mental breakdown which was
the secret theme of Clarke's early poem, 'The Frenzy of
Suibhne', is given a new garb in that remarkable psychological
epic, 'Mnemosyne lay in Dust', in which Maurice Devane
becomes a closer personal surrogate than Mad Sweeney: the
young woman of Beare with modern dress does not sacrifice her
allure. Clarke now becomes a shape-changer, seer, satirical
commentator, recorder, stylistic exhibitionist, his language often
direct in address but as often difficult in reference, neologisms,
deliberate acrostics of meaning, displays of adjectival profusion
rivalling the Irish bardic poets or in telescoped meanings
reminiscent of the later Shakespeare or of Hopkins. The verse
technique is often roped into Gaelic forms or exasperatingly
experimental, calling undue attention to itself. Much of his poetry
hit the frustrated temper of the younger poets here and abroad.
They had been inclined perhaps to dismiss him as a poet trapped
in the Irish situation but now he had a new distinction in their
eyes and in his own peculiar way was expressing many of their
own feelings. So, in struggling out of his own chosen bonds, he
had helped to rid them of theirs, had made them conscious that
many of the dilemmas, metaphysical, religious, social or
otherwise, which they considered modern were in fact recurrent
through history and were assimilable into the poet's art.

The change in Clarke's poetry and its later accommodation to
the modern temper, as far as it went, indicates the transitional
state of Irish poetry in the thirties and forties. Yeats's influence
remained strong and a contemporary of Clarke, Yeats's protégé
F. R. Higgins (1896-1941), reflects it in his early work. *The Gap of
Brightness* (1940) contains some of his best lyrics, which have an
independent strength and vitality. Their rhythms are traditional;

those modelled on Gaelic have an assonantal grace not unlike Clarke's; [4]and the speech of others is at once conversational and harmonious:

> Only last week, walking the hushed fields
> Of our most lovely Meath, now thinned by November,
> I came to where the road from Laracor leads
> To the Boyne river . . .
> . . . where nothing stirs — only the shadowed
> Leaden flight of a heron up the lean air . . .

Higgins, whose other works (*Dark Breed*, 1927; *Island Blood*, 1925; *Arable Holdings*, 1933) are distinguished, collaborated with Yeats in the Cuala broadsides, showing a sense of vigorous song in his own ballads, of which the best known is probably 'Song for the Clatter bones', a ballad about Jezebel:

> And so she was thrown from the window;
> Like Lucifer she fell
> Beneath the feet of the horses and they beat
> The light out of Jezebel . . .

Higgins could control his vigour in his love poems, which have a tender strength. In others it propelled him towards a rather forced raciness, which younger poets saw as a kind of Irish posturing. They saw an obsession with 'the Irish thing' not only in Higgins but in Colum, Clarke and Stephens and looked for their models elsewhere, particularly to France, a country more alive to the modern dilemma and its effect on poetry.

In *The Bookman,* August 1934, Samuel Beckett (b. 1906) was expressing dissatisfaction with the comfortable traditional attitude of current Irish poets. He divided them into 'antiquarians', led by Yeats, who wrote on accepted themes and who had in common a desire to escape from self-awareness into the Celtic past or the surrounding Irish scenery, and those who showed a more modern approach in self-perception, perhaps under the influence of the Eliot-Auden school which Yeats had casually dismissed as 'fish that lie gasping on the strand'. Beckett saw some hope in Thomas MacGreevy whose *Poems* (1934) he reviewed in *The Dublin Magazine* the following year. MacGreevy, an art critic who later became director of the National Gallery of Ireland was two years older than Higgins and Clarke but had spent many years in France, where he became conversant with modern currents in thought and in technique; his thought reflects the metaphysical dilemma which he resolved in prayerful celebration in such poems as 'Nocturne of the self-evident presence', while his poetic method shows the influence of Eliot, whose work he had explored in *T. S. Eliot* (1931), and of the symbolists and surrealists of France. These influences are perceptible in 'Homage to Hieronymus Bosch', an apocalyptic vision set in Dublin and catching the nightmare quality of the Dutch painter. MacGreevy's poetic talent soon dried up but he had some significance as a forerunner of the modernist movement in Irish poetry.

This tendency was also evident in the impressionistic realism of Blanaid Salkeld (*Hello, Eternity,* 1933; . . . *the engine is still running,* 1937) and the free verse of Lyle Donaghy (*Selected Poems* 1939) in the thirties but it gained more force in a group of Irish poets who had closer associations with France. These were Samuel Beckett, Denis Devlin and Brian Coffey.

Collectively these three poets, although strongly individual in manner, represent the modernist movement in its reaction against romanticism and rhetoric, against materialism and logical positivism, and in the search for new forms to express the complexity of self-awareness. Beckett and MacGreevy both signed the verticalist manifesto which appeared in the March 1932 issue of *transition* and which proclaimed the value of the imagination and of the individual consciousness. Its praise of 'the hallucinatory irruption of images in the dream, the day-dream, the mystic-gnostic trance and even the psychiatric condition' is revealing, for the cult of the irrational and of the subconscious was linked to the aesthetic drive of its supporters. They tended to accept Ezra Pound's description of major form in poetry as a fallacy. Poetic expression was to be achieved mainly through images linked purely by associations which were often so private as to be obscure or so arbitrary as to produce a surrealistic dislocation. The chosen symbols were often hermetic, the syntax elliptical, the prosody irregular, avoiding fixed patterns.

Beckett's *Poems in English* (1961) are small in number and were written mainly in the thirties. They are comparatively slight in interest beside his novels and plays. They show that he could produce short lyrics of clear impact:

I would like my love to die
and the rain to be falling on the graveyard

> and on me walking the streets
> mourning the first and last to love me

where only the mood is complex. In most of his poems, especially in the longer 'Serena' and 'Enueg' series, the hermetic symbols, the arcane associations, the unusual syntax make perception of meaning difficult without considerable unravelling; yet some passages, although idiosyncratic, convey the feeling of despair or of suffering poignantly enough:

> Exeo in a spasm
> tired of my darling's red sputum
> from the Portobello Private Nursing Home
> its secret things
> and toil to the crest of the ridge of the steep perilous bridge

where suffering at the sight of a dying girl carries the *private* nightmare of a Dublin canal bridge which is neither steep nor perilous, except to one shaken by great stress.

Beckett had studied surrealists like André Breton, symbolists like Rimbaud, and had a deep knowledge of Dante and of French poetry from the Provencal poets to his own contemporaries. He is an erudite poet, like Eliot, but his style of associative images is less ordered, perhaps a reflection of the chaos of mankind's state, inducing either despair or the grim dianoetic laugh turned on oneself; so that in many of his poems a deep sensitivity is marked by a querulous bleakness and in others the syntactical structures seem barriers deliberately erected to protect the private grounds of feeling.

The problem of communication in a period when solipsism was the fashion can be seen also in the poetry of Denis Devlin (1908-1959). His early work was influenced by T.S. Eliot and by the French movements reflected by Beckett. An indefatigable recorder of his own dreams, he at first preferred the private fantasy of the surrealistic method, the allusive oblique style of the symbolists and their stance of detachment, in which the poet is a tired Tiresias who has foreseen it all and is not really concerned about the experiences he records. At first too derivative a poet to command an individual style, his work matured in the forties, during which he published *Lough Derg and Other Poems* (1946) and became known for his translations of St John Perse, a fellow-diplomat whose personal lyrical style successfully subsumed both symbolist and surrealist influences. His example probably helped

Devlin in his aim of writing poetry which would retain its personal note while expressing his own racial traditions and reflecting a wide range of European influences, an aim which he partly achieved in the fifties. In these poems there is a stricter form, poetry is not bound together merely by the self, and language is used fundamentally to communicate complex thought with considerable clarity.

Devlin's poetry was not widely known until after his early death in Dublin in 1959. The publication of his *Selected Poems* edited by Allen Tate and Robert Penn Warren (New York, 1963) and of *Collected Poems* edited by Brian Coffey (Dublin, 1964) gave a wider public a chance to recognise his merits.

It can be seen in these works that Devlin was a poet of considerable power in lyrical and meditative poetry. Some of his best poems are love poems, sometimes delicate and urgent:

> Brighten and be
> An amber dance of June's breath.
> Love's favourites are few
> Let him have me
> And you all instant you all of you!
> Nothing will need us after death.

In 'The Colours of Love', reflections on death and time blend with such passages, moving to the conclusion:

> Better no love than love, which, through loving
> Leads to no love. The ripples come to rest ...
> Ah me! how all that young year I was moving
> To take her dissolution to my breast!

His longest love poem, 'The Heavenly Foreigner', attempts a complex treatment of love in its relation to the changes of time, mood and spirit:

> The world glows with mortal divinity;
> The red turns gray,
> The ash creeps up on the flame,
> O heavenly foreigner! your price is high

But this poem shaped over some fifteen years is too full of the obscurity of his earlier manner to be fully successful. Devlin's later style, harder and more direct, suits alike the ironic Browningesque 'Memoirs of a Turcoman Diplomat' and the celebration of 'The Passion of Christ':

> What we have best imagined is the Mother
> Who, with the absolute, say Light, brought forth
> Self, without intervention of the Other,
>   The pure, the Virgin birth.

He was a poet whose full powers were coming into play during the decade preceding his death.

Brian Coffey (b.1905), a close friend of Devlin, with whom he published his first poems in *Poems* (1930), was subject to many of the same influences in Paris, where he studied philosophy under Maritain. He is a difficult poet of a similar hermetic style whose distinguishing feature is its broad metaphysical base of concern:

> What then is love for lovers mating
> with nought spoiled
> though all uprooted
> but completing natural skill
> forever giving him to her
> giving forever her to him
> for them joying
> in every difference
> love decrees

In *Missouri Sequence* (1962) a harder narrative style moves from the dilemmas of domestic life, exile and personal misfortune to an affirmation of faith in the equation of poetry, love and wisdom:

> Never was despair imperative,
> never are we grown so old
> we cannot start our journey
> bound to find
> an eternal note of gladness
> in loves true for men,
> the source whence they flow,
> the ocean whither they go.

A long later poem, 'Advent', explores the metaphysical reality of creation in a world of flux troubled by the unstable inheritance of history, in which 'Who opposes world world crucifies' and modern men, who learn nothing from history, expend 'all their resources drawn on/their planet gutted in the task'. This poem, although idiosyncratic in manner, has some true flashes of poetic insight, which strike suddenly out of obscurity. *The Death of Hector* (1979) is a moral and metaphysical meditation on that death and its implications.

Austin Clarke. Bord Fáilte photograph.

The thought and manner of these three poets make them appear very different from their home-based Irish or English contemporaries but they were writing close to a different tradition, that of France; all of them were international in their reading and in the range of their translations from European poets; although Ireland was often at the centre of their consciousness she was only one of a number of factors that by sympathy or by reaction sometimes nourished their work. The tradition of the revival and of its representatives, including Yeats, was regarded by them guardedly, sometimes with hostility, never with a sense of adherence. Their introversion, even in their most confessional poems, their eclectic interests and influence, partly account for their neglect in England and in Ireland but there is no doubt that in both countries generally there was little interest in these poets or discernment of their abilities until the fifties. Devlin's poem on Michael Collins, at once a tribute to and a qualifier of patriotism, and his 'Lough Derg', sceptical of Jansenism, evoking the wider view of Catholicism in its European context which he shared with MacGreevy and Coffey, commanded some attention in Ireland but the spiritual searchings which they shared with Claudel and the symbolist poets passed almost unnoticed and would have been shadowed in any case by the crack-up of Europe in 1939.

It was about this time that the poetry of Patrick Kavanagh (1904-1967) began to come to notice in Ireland. Kavanagh came of Monaghan small-farmer stock, was self-educated from the age of twelve, awkward, an eccentric self-assertion concealing an essential shyness. In youth his poetic instinct was encouraged by A.E. and by a variety of sporadic reading ranging from the romantics to *Poetry Chicago* and Ezra Pound. His first volume, *Ploughman and Other Poems,* published in 1936, contained simple impressionistic lyrics, sometimes written in free verse, reflecting the country life around him. His autobiographical book, *The Green Fool* (1938), drew greater attention, partly because of the successful libel action brought by St John Gogarty against it, which caused its suppression. In 1942 *The Great Hunger* established Kavanagh's reputation as a poet of primitive power and of poetic intensity. *A Soul for Sale* (1947) confirmed this impression. The bitter note of its concluding poems directed against adherence to an outworn tradition sounded louder in the poems of *Come Dance With Kitty Stobling* (1960) and is heard at its best and worst in his satires; but this volume also contained reflective lyrics of quiet beauty, somewhat akin to his earlier lyrics, different in their mood of indifference and resignation.

Collected Poems (1964) published four years before his death is confused in chronology but enables an assessment of his work as a whole. His best work belongs to the forties and is to be seen in his lyrics and *The Great Hunger*. The former show a power to transform the ordinary experiences of life into poetry; as in 'Spraying the Potatoes':

> And I was there with the knapsack sprayer
> On the barrel's edge poised. A wasp was floating
> Dead on a sunken briar leaf
> Over a copper-poisoned ocean.
>
> The axle-roll of a rut-locked cart
> Broke the burnt stick of noon in two . . .

This kind of magic, impressionistic, clearly imagined, is frequent in his poems, which often give locality and situation an extra dimension of space or of time; the black hills of Shancoduff lock in the poet-farmer but become imaginatively his Alps in winter; a row between pitchfork-armed farmers over a boundary brings him a whisper from Homer's ghost; at the dawn of spring the blackbird breaks 'the two-Minutes' silence/With a new poem's violence'. The vivid flashes come from a kind of primitive intensity, felt through all fourteen sections of *The Great Hunger,* which follows the farmer Patrick Maguire from youth to death. Mangan's line 'Mind is dungeon-walled by clay', is the story of Maguire's life; for the motif of clay which begins and ends the poem frames his doom of toil, of sexual frustration, of intervals of despairing self-realisation. The whole poem is beautifully knit to the passing of the seasons with their changing patterns of scene, activity and speech. Kavanagh lets the verse go free, occasionally intersperses lines of reflection, of ironic comment; the images drive home each mood:

> That was how his life happened.
> No mad hooves galloping in the sky,
> But the weak, washy way of true tragedy —
> A sick horse nosing around the meadow for a clean place to die.

Although Kavanagh later dismissed the poem because he felt that Maguire was really comic and that to have made him tragic was sentimental, it remains powerful, arresting, the product of an original mind.

This *arrière pensée* has some significance, for he was a poet with a fundamentally true poetic instinct, often torn by uncertainties; rural Ireland made him feel an outcast yet anchored his memories; London and Dublin literary circles, bohemian or conservative, at times repelled him, caused him to turn to satire's 'unfruitful prayer', which he rarely uttered with any real power for he lacked the exact rational control of language it demands. His last years, disturbed by illness, another adverse legal action and real or imagined slights, saw a decline in the quality of his work except for an occasional reflective lyric:

> Leafy-with-love banks and the green waters of the canal
> Pouring redemption for me, that I do
> The will of God, wallow in the habitual, the banal,
> Grow with nature again as before I grew ...

This nostalgic note is heard also in his autobiographical novel *Tarry Flynn* (1948), which like *The Green Fool* is uneven in quality but revelatory about his country background and how it fed his imagination, by giving it a fundamental base of reality. His occasional writings published in *Collected Pruse* (1967) are sketchy but often shot through with perceptive judgments: 'The great poets are those who burn in the smithy of their souls the raw material of life and produce from it this erotic-creative essence. . . . Almost any kind of the crude material of life can be burned to give us this intoxicating thing . . . all the poet does is to explode the atoms of our ordinary experience.'

It was Kavanagh who expressed most strongly a dislike of the revival tradition, which, he felt, had become too comfortable, too much of a vested interest to allow new poets to breathe. Yeats had died in 1939, critical standards were in the hands of literary cliques who believed in 'the Irish thing' and who preferred to remain parochial:

> Paddy of the Celtic Mist,
> Paddy Connemara West,
> Chestertonian Paddy Frog
> Croaking nightly in the bog.
> All the Paddies having fun
> Since Yeats handed in his gun.

Every man completely blind
To the truth about his mind.

Kavanagh himself preferred the poetry of George Barker or of
Ted Hughes, seeing in it a closer affinity with his own kind of
poetry. His ironic advice to Irish poets

Leave Christ and Christlike problems and you'll be
The synthesis of Gaelic poetry

probably expresses the feeling of the more reserved Devlin and
Coffey, his contemporaries. Yet, as sweeping satire must, it
ignores the achievement of other contemporaries.

During the thirties, while writers like Higgins and Fallon were
writing fairly close to the revival tradition and writers like Devlin
were taking a different line, a group of Ulster poets were choosing
another path. Louis MacNeice (1907-1963), the most
considerable of these, was associated with the English modernist
movement led by his friend Auden. At first he was concerned
chiefly with its social aspects; but he was also an original
speculative thinker, conscious of the metaphysical dilemma of
that disturbed period, and believing that poetry is 'a tentative
counter-attack upon the void'. Although some reflections of
Kafka's nightmare world and of the symbolists are found in his
poetry, his style was always governed by the aim of
communication; his probings of his own mind, his investigations
of the void were always expressed in an urbane, conversational
tone and in a disciplined classical form.

MacNeice's best lyric poetry appeared in the thirties during
which he wrote several eclogues remarkable for their acrid view of
contemporary urban society and *Autumn Journal* (1938), a long
poem whose blend of lyricism and didacticism, of speculation and
reminiscence, of the realistic image and the ironic cliché bears his
individual stamp. In 1939 the death of Yeats and the outbreak of
the war made him feel that realistic poetry was as unreal as
escapist poetry; that the poet should try to search for positive
values under the rubble of rejections. Thenceforth his poetry grew
more meditative, while his lyric power, though partly sapped by
his work as a broadcaster and lecturer, still remained
considerable. *Autumn Sequel* (1953), a long poem in *terza rima*,
attempted to unify his feelings about friends, places and poetry.
Although somewhat diffuse, it is a remarkable expression of a

poet's quest for truth and of his belief in art as the creative act which wrests meaning from the flux of life.

Born in Belfast, son of an Anglican archdeacon who supported Home Rule, repelled by the Orange bigotry of Belfast and by the complacency of Dublin, MacNeice reflected the dichotomy of Ireland in his character and poetry. The bitterness of rejection in 'Valediction' (1934) and in the sixteenth canto of *Autumn Journal* is balanced by the warmth of the tribute paid to F.R. Higgins in *Autumn Sequel* and of the lyrics associated with Irish places. Even in 'Valediction' he accepts his roots:

> I can say Ireland is hooey, Ireland is
> A gallery of fake tapestries,
> But I cannot deny my past to which my self is wed,
> The woven figure cannot undo its thread ...

and he is at his best when celebrating the incidental, casual things which form images, not opinions:

> ... the laughter of the Galway sea
> Juggling with spars and bones irresponsibly,
> I give you the toy Liffey and the vast gulls,
> I give you fuschia hedges and whitewashed walls ...
> And I give you the sea and yet again the sea's
> Tumultuous marble ...

At the time of his death T.S. Eliot described MacNeice as a poet of genius with 'the Irishman's unfailing ear for the music of verse'. Three years later his *Collected Poems* (1966) showed the full range of his achievement. Although Ireland figured on the periphery of MacNeice's concerns and rarely at their centre, MacNeice acknowledged the closeness of his 'near-far-country' whose name kept ringing 'like a bell/In an underwater belfry'. But his real kinship was 'With other solitary beings, with the whole race of men', which is probably the fundamental wish of the good poet anywhere.

The problem of cultural identity was more central to the work of John Hewitt (b.1907), whose *Collected Poems 1932-67* span a long period of poetic writing which continued into the seventies; in fact it is probably his major theme. He was of seventeenth-century Ulster planter stock and his family influences were liberal, Methodist and socialistic. Growing up after partition had been established he found his wish to identify with Ireland as a

whole frustrated by the defensive policy of the new six-county
state which regarded even the three counties of Ulster outside its
jurisdiction as having nothing in common with it and geared its
educational system to that of England. Hewitt's liberal and
socialistic convictions found some unity of purpose in the
'regionalist' poetry of his middle years which was influenced by a
variety of sources from Joseph Campbell and Louis Mumford to
Robert Frost, and which focused around his search for self-
realisation and his celebration of the countryside and people of his
native province:

> My region's Ulster. How can we afford
> to take the shouting politician's word,
> map-maker's frenzy, who with crazy line
> cut off three counties history marked our own?

From this standpoint Hewitt sought his themes in the healing
power of nature, the need for reconciliation, the quality of rural
people, sometimes observed with hard realism:

> I know my farmer and my farmer's wife,
> the squalid focus of their huxter life,
> the grime-veined fists, the thick rheumatic legs,
> the cracked voice gloating on the price of eggs,
> the miser's Bible, and the tedious aim
> to add another boggy acre to the name.

In 1957 Hewitt was victimised for his liberal and socialistic
beliefs by being denied promotion as an art director in Belfast.
This led to a fifteen-year period in Coventry, after which he
returned to Belfast, to continue writing and to lecture at Queen's
University.

In technique Hewitt was traditionalist and rarely experimental.
His strength lay chiefly in his clear and precise images, his
carefully chosen symbols united to positive statement:

> I have turned to the landscape because men disappoint me:
> the trunk of a tree is proud; when the woodmen fell it,
> it still has a contained ionic solemnity:
> it is a rounded event without the need to tell it.
>
> I have never been compelled to turn away from the dawn
> because it carries treason behind its wakened face:
> even the horned ram glowering over the bog-hole,
> though symbol of evil, will step through the blown
> grass with grace.

This blend of introspection with observed detail and rational statement marks his poetry at its best. Rationalisation or expanded detail often unite with conventionality of technique to produce verse of a monotonous flatness. There is sporadic intensity of the kind seen in 'An Irishman in Coventry' when a chance tune on a fiddle stirs the poet to a recollection of his nation:

... a people endlessly betrayed
by our own weakness, by the wrongs we suffered
in that long twilight over bog and glen,
by force, by famine and by glittering fables
which gave us martyrs when we needed men ...
This is our fate: eight hundred years' disaster,
crazily tangled as the Book of Kells;
the dream's distortion and the land's division,
the midnight raiders and the prison cells.
Yet like Lir's children banished to the waters
our hearts still listen for the landward bells.

This, however, is not the dominant element in the work of this quiet, disciplined craftsman whose continual dilemma was really the dilemma of any artist in a materialistic and antagonistic milieu.

The most notable Ulster poetic contemporary of Hewitt and MacNeice was born like them in Belfast; W.R. Rodgers (b.1909), after graduating at Queen's University, where he became a close friend of Hewitt, worked in County Armagh for twelve years as a Presbyterian minister. He left the ministry in 1946 and worked with the B.B.C. until 1966. He died in California, where he taught during his last few years, in 1969.

Rodgers published little poetry during his lifetime: *Awake! and Other Poems* in 1940, *Europa and the Bull* in 1952. *Collected Poems* (1971) contains little else of value. His work at its best has a delicate lyrical urgency:

Mary Magdalene, that easy woman,
Saw, from the shore, the seas
Beat against the hard stones of Lent,
Crying, 'Weep, seas, weep
For yourselves that cannot dent me more.

Its intensity is usually achieved by compressed imagery and a daring rhetoric, especially in his love poems:

> For though you were smoke, sucked up by a raging vent,
> I'd follow you through every flue of your fear,
> And over your faraway arms I'll mountain and cone
> In a pillar of carolling fire and fountaining stone.

This is a quality found in Hopkins but here it was primarily due to Rodgers' acute sense of sound and was partly derived from modernists like Auden and MacNeice. He believed that creative work springs from the conflict of opposites and that the word-play of the poet can be organised around this principle. His fondness for verbal acrobatics sometimes diverts attention from the genuine psychological spark in his poetry; but it is also true that hackwork and personal problems prevented the full development of a talent which is seen in his more intense and original passages.

MacNeice, Hewitt and Rodgers were among the northern poets who contributed to the Dublin-based literary magazine, *The Bell,* which started in 1940 under the editorship of Sean O Faolain. Its poetry-editor, Geoffrey Taylor, successfully encouraged their participation during the early years of *The Bell.* About the same time a group of them, led by Roy MacFadden and Robert Greacen, headed a movement to establish a distinctive 'Northern Irish' literary tradition. MacFadden *(Swords and Ploughshares,* 1943) and Greacen *(One Recent Evening,* 1944) were technically competent in verse but neither had enough poetic strength or individuality to sustain a movement and by 1949 their effort had failed. It was clear by then that the artificial nature of partition made it impossible in any case. Further, general indifference and Unionist hostility added to the climate of frustration. Another Ulster poet, Maurice James Craig,[5] said a satirical farewell to this in *Poems from Ulster* (1942):

> It's to hell with the future and live on the past
> *May the Lord in his mercy be kind to Belfast!*

On the other side of the border, many of his contemporaries were attacking a similar kind of parochialism marked by professional patriotism and a rigorous censorship. Where censorship in the north-east was mainly political and subterranean, censorship in the Free State was overt and puritanical. Both sets of poets were rather hostile to the aftermath of the Irish literary revival, the Ulster poets often because they did not understand the Gaelic tradition, the others because they felt that the use of Irish legendary themes and 'the Irish mode', which at that time the influence of Austin Clarke seemed to encourage, were interfering with the development of new approaches and a new idiom in poetry. The first, they believed, would be found by investigating and expressing the inner experience of the poet as a human being, the second in absorbing the influence of the modernist movement on idiom and rhythm.

During the forties and fifties, for example, Valentin Iremonger (b.1918), the best of the younger poets, was arguing in *The Bell* that the modern poet should make his poetry so perfectly personal that it should have universal validity and that 'the values of their own personalities are the girders upon which the younger Irish poets have formed their poems'. His own poetry dealt with the experience of life with a quiet detached recognition of its transience. One difference from Clarke's poetry of that time is observable in a number of poems in which figures from Greek mythology are treated in a style far removed from the 'Irish mode':

But star-chaser, big-time-going, chancer Icarus
Like a dog on the sea lay and the girls forgot him,
And Daedalus, too busy hammering another job,
Remembered him only in pubs ...

Iremonger's published work is small in quantity (*Reservations,* 1950; *Horan's Field,* 1972) and he did not quite fulfil the promise of his early poems. His articles in *The Bell* helped to draw the attention of his contemporaries to the moderns, including that delicate, intensely personal poet, Freda Laughton (*A Transitory House,* 1946).

The Bell provided a focal point for poetic criticism during these decades. Geoffrey Taylor, its poetry editor, also edited *Irish Poems of Today* (1948) and *Irish Poets of the Nineteenth Century* (1951). Anthony Cronin (*Poems,* 1958), whose early work was influenced by T.S. Eliot and Auden, supported and exemplified the modernist view. But the battle between traditionalist and moderns was largely artificial. Poets like Robert Farren continued to gather strength as well as restrictions from the Gaelic traditon; Padraic Fallon and Donagh MacDonagh remained open to both currents.

Padraic Fallon (1905-74) was the most accomplished of these in poetry. His work was difficult to assess during his lifetime; apart from *Lighting-up-Time* (1938), no collection of his work appeared until the year of his death *(Poems,* 1974) and his verse-plays for radio have not yet been published. Fallon was in theme and technique a very varied poet. He had absorbed modernist influences as well as that of Yeats; but the strongest influence on his work was probably that of the Gaelic poets and mediaeval story-tellers, reflected in his highly individual phraseology and metrics, in his vivid imagery, in the humorous extravagance of his love poems and in the spirit and verve of his 'Diarmuid and Grainne' (1950) and 'The Vision of Mac Conglinne' (1953) written for radio, both remarkable artistic achievements. In these and in his translations or adaptations of Raftery there is an obvious affinity with his subject. Austin Clarke noted his 'strong mythopoeic impulse'. This was particularly evident in his stage play for the Players' Theatre in 1945, *The Seventh Step,* which adapted the Agamemnon legend to an Irish setting. Fallon's reputation will grow as more of his work comes to light.

Robert Farren (Roibeard O Farachain) also came to attention in the thirties with *Thronging Feet* (1936) and *Time's Wall Asunder* (1939); they contain some excellent lyrics and some good versions of Irish poetry, as well as poems which suffer from a forced Chestertonian vehemence. His best service to poetry was to found with Austin Clarke in 1938 the Dublin Verse-speaking Society.

Donagh MacDonagh (1912-68), the son of Thomas MacDonagh, also wrote some excellent lyrics and some good verse-plays, of which *Happy as Larry,* a Dublin ballad-play, is easily the best. *Veterans* (1941) and *The Hungry Grass* (1947) contain his best poems.

The Bell was an outlet for these and other writers during the war and post-war years; it declined after O'Faolain left it in 1946 but continued until 1954 under the editorship of Peadar O'Donnell (b.1893), a good writer of socially engaged fiction *(Storm,* 1925; *Islanders,* 1928; *Adrigoole,* 1929) and of autobiographical writing *(The Gates Flew Open,* 1932; *Salud!* 1937; *There will be another day,* 1963), which reveal much about the social and political conditions of Ireland during and after the Troubles.

Other literary journals attracting creative and social writers were *Ireland Today* (1936-38), *Irish Writing* (1946-57) and *Envoy* (1949-51). Thus the gap left by *The Irish Statesman* (1919-30), which under Sir Horace Plunkett's patronage and A.E.'s editorship had attracted the best writers from Yeats to Patrick Kavanagh, was partly filled during a period when neither state nor church was friendly to writers on either side of the border.

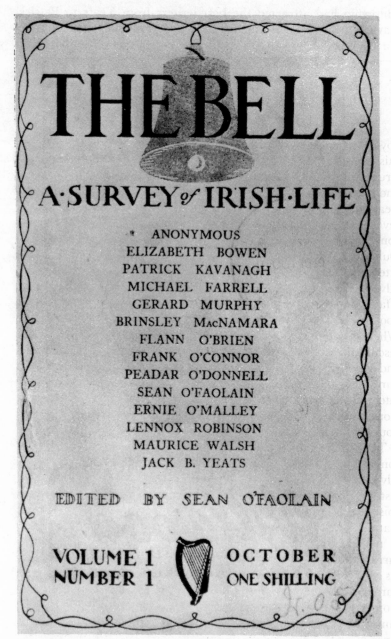

The Bell. *Courtesy of the National Gallery of Ireland.*

CHAPTER XX

Fiction

I

Joyce's *Ulysses* (1922) was probably the most important novel of this century in English. Its title implies not only its submerged structure of Homer's epic but the classical temper of acceptance and patience with which, in Joyce's aesthetic, the artist chooses to treat contemporary life, shaping it with such joyous skill that it reveals its secret meaning and essence. The surface 'story' concerns three principal characters during one day in the city of Dublin: Stephen Dedalus, who has returned from self-exile to attend his mother's deathbed, Leopold Bloom, a canvasser for advertisements; his wife, Molly, a concert-singer, who is having an affair with her manager. The eighteen episodes into which the book is ordered work towards the meeting of Bloom and Stephen. When it occurs it lasts only a few hours, during which Bloom rescues the drunken Stephen from a brawl, gives him hospitality and sends him on his way in the small hours; Molly never meets him but what her husband tells her of their encounter is woven into the flow of her half-awake soliloquy in the final episode. Roughly half of the book concerns the last three of its nineteen hours' imagined time.

The underlying structure which supports this casual day consists of a very deliberate reordering and adaptation of the adventures of Homer's Ulysses, as if to sustain the idea that history repeats itself but not in the same tone of voice. Each episode and character has some correspondence to Homer, but many differences. Stephen could do with a surrogate father but he is not seeking one, unlike Telemachus; Bloom, a potential surrogate father, has lost a son, is resourceful and has a courage of his own but he is no heroic Ulysses; Molly Bloom weaves and unravels her web of thought but she is no faithful Penelope. The Homeric epic affords Joyce a structure and clues to character; it can give the reader a continual sense of ironic contrast as well as a sense of order, even when the correspondences are submerged.

While the artifices of time, place and Homeric parallels are used to support the characters and events, the details of city life are used to anchor them in reality. The casual flow of Dublin surrounds them but it is based upon the minute observation of detail with exact relevance to chronology and topography; to the routes followed by Stephen, Bloom and the minor characters, and to the time of even the most incidental events. The sights, sounds, smells and associations of Dublin appear and recur, and their recurrences and coincidences are cross-stitched into a binding pattern. A mosaic of detail supports the general structure of the book and establishes its character.

To this one must add the tremendous insight into the individuality of the characters achieved by the use of the interior monologue, which Joyce borrowed from Edouard Dujardin and the psychologists but which has its remote origins in the Elizabethan convention of soliloquy. Since the interior monologue by its nature is not spoken, its literary treatment demands a special technique to convey how it operates largely by association, by half-formed sentences, by phrases or single words, sometimes achieving some fully-fashioned thought, but mostly proceeding in a disordered or chaotic way, like the jottings of some rambling diarist or the jerky speech of Mr Alfred Jingle. Joyce's skill is shown by his treatment of thought-processes which are essentially similar so as to convey individuality. Stephen, Bloom and Molly are all subject to normal interruptions, dislocations and contractions of subconscious thought; but Stephen's subconscious mind is continually speculating and shaping, Bloom's is more random and desultory, while Molly's has the flux of unpunctuated feminine loquacity. Thus the individuality inherent in the differences of their respective thought-associations is realised by their different modes and speeds of thought. Other characters, notably Malachi Mulligan and Blazes Boylan, appear and play their parts in life's casual comedy; but these three characters are known intimately, in essence as in detail, through the workings of their minds.

Part of the fascination of *Ulysses* comes from its variety of forms and styles. The Sirens episode is written in a musical form, the Polyphemus episode juxtaposes three kinds of inflated narrative, while for the Circe scene Joyce chose the form which he had not quite successfully used in his introverted Ibsenish play, *Exiles* (1918). Here a dramatic form of extravagant fantasy perfectly fits the presentation of the midnight hallucinations which take shape in Bella Cohen's brothel. Elsewhere shifts of style follow the growth of the human embryo or counterpoint the irony of unspoken thoughts in relation to uttered graveside platitudes. The vital human flow of Molly's personality is preceded by the impersonal catechetical method which inspects Bloom and Stephen as mere atoms in time and space. All through the book language accommodates itself to context, whether in describing the changing appearances of a mongrel dog in the Protean episode or the tired condition of Bloom and Stephen at night, where the narrative drags and falters. Rhythm is an essential part of technique; Dublin slang or casual conversation or Victorian rhetoric receives its appropriate and exact movement. Rhythm unites with linguistic skill in superb parodies of English literary styles.

The total effect is a vision of humanity in its multifarious aspects. The meeting of Stephen and Bloom is brief and casual enough on the surface and it is not intimate, yet we know them both in their strength and weakness, their aspirations and failures, their potentialities. Stephen is haunted by the ghost of his mother, whose dying request he has refused, Bloom by memories of his suicide father and stillborn son and by the knowledge of his wife's adultery. Both are lonely, the artist isolated by his vocation, Bloom by his Jewish ancestry. Yet their affinity results also from their presentation as detached observers of the human scene. Thus their meeting symbolizes the meeting of the artist's mind with ordinary human life which his work can shape into an aesthetic whole.

Finnegans Wake (1939) is the fictional dream of a Dublin family seen in terms of a universal history of mankind and of civilisation. While composing it, Joyce stated that he was trying to tell the story of this Chapelizod family in a new way.

Time and the river and the mountain are real heroes of my book |he wrote|. Yet the elements are exactly what every novelist might use: man and woman, birth, childhood, night, sleep, marriage, prayer, death. . . . Only I am trying to build many planes of narrative with a single esthetic purpose. . . . Did you ever read Laurence Sterne?

The family consists of a publican of Scandinavian origin, Humphrey Chimpden Earwicker, his wife, Anna Livia Plurabelle, two sons, Jerry and Kevin, and a daughter, Isobel;

but their associations, analogies and prototypes as imagined by the author give them many other names and shapes, under which their human identities are submerged but suggested. On the human plane nothing much happens. Book I of the four books into which *Finnegans Wake* is divided centres about the publican and his wife and their antecedents and indicates what their children are like. Book II deals mainly with the children, they play in front of their father's pub or study in the nursery; at night the customers drink downstairs; the publican falls drunk, clambers upstairs to bed, makes love, sleeps and dreams. In Book III he dreams of the future, of one son as a popular leader (in contrast to his scapegrace brother), who will transform the future and continue his father's personality, repeating him. Then day comes (Book IV), the usual tasks recur. All begins again.

Seen imaginatively, as in some universal dream, this family becomes Protean, representing many human types recurring through the flux of time, which brings everything around again. From the elemental aspect of man and woman they are transformed into the recurrent patterns of history or the universal ideas of human destiny. The publican's initials can stand for Here Comes Everybody; through association he can be Adam, Bacchus, and many other people; the conflicting brothers provide many associations of battles, confrontations and disputations; their sister can become the prototype of all young girls or of her mother, of whom she is a recurrence in time; together they repeat the fluid principle in nature, like the river or like the flux of life itself. Time has given their locale, city, river and mountains a myriad of associations. Fixed or fluid, they could have many tales to tell. Joyce gives them many voices.

The novel's dream-form makes this possible. A dream is outside time and therefore may mingle all times, centuries can shift, can be telescoped and telegraphed; buried monarchs may appear and disappear or dwindle into goblins, as in O'Grady's vision of Irish legend; unconsidered trifles (a pipe, an envelope) can take on strange associations and can jostle considered magnitudes (Swift, Waterloo, St Patrick); figures can become gigantic or diminutive, like Gulliver. They demand many planes of narrative. A single aesthetic purpose calls for great resources of structure and style.

For the general structure Joyce borrowed the idea of Giambattista Vico, an eighteenth-century Italian philosopher, that civilisation proceeds in a pattern of cycles; theocratic, aristocratic, democratic and chaotic; chaos ends in a return to theocracy, which begins another cycle. The four books follow this pattern. The book of the parents is followed in turn by the book of the sons, the book of the people and the comparatively brief *ricorso,* as the book flows back to its beginning, as river to sea. In this general cycle of mankind, many cycles of human birth, life and death, of nature, history and the universe are incorporated. The microcosm reflects the macrocosm; the story of man is reflected in the ballad about Tim Finnegan's fall, apparent death, wake and resurrection. Imagined as the mythical builder of Dublin he resurrects throughout the book.

Cycles involve recurrence and recurrences provide one of the organising factors of the book. Joyce had long been interested in the sixteenth-century philosopher, Giordano Bruno, in whose belief that the Divine intellect, working on matter, creates all things, he saw a parallel with his own conception of the artist. Every power in nature, Bruno argued, evolves its opposite in order to continue; out of the clash of opposites life renews itself. Joyce used this idea to pattern the many recurring contrasts in the book; so, for example, the two quarrelling sons of Earwicker can be Shem, the artist, and Shaun, the efficient organiser, St Patrick opposing the Druid, Wellington versus Napoleon, the Mookse and the Gripes, the Ondt and the Gracehoper, those fable figures of Irish Catholicism and Roman Catholicism, of the organisation man and the artist, and other opposing complementary forces. As in nature or in legal or scholastic disputation or in the dialectic process, the clash of opposites engenders some form of reconcilitation, unity and modified resurrection. So life goes on.

Joyce's reference to the eighteenth-century novelist, Laurence Sterne, indicates his own approach to the problem of weaving together many planes of narrative, mythological, historical, universal and human. Sterne's *Tristram Shandy,* written in a style of cultivated eccentricity, consists almost entirely of digressions from a scarcely existent plot. Dreams do not have plots and the multiple-association is itself a form of rapid, almost simultaneous digression from one theme to another. In orchestrating his word-score Joyce used the connotations rather than the denotations of language to correspond with the dissolving images of dream, their sense/nonsense meaning, their symbolism. He condensed language or expanded it by accretion, exalted the humble pun into a literary formula for joining incongruous meanings, and coined neologisms for a similar purpose. By these devices and many others he shaped a dream-language for his book, a language which exploited contemporary knowledge of the psychology of dreams and their connection with myth, which was based on English, but polyglot and innovative, a continuing puzzle to the reader. This makes the total aesthetic effect difficult to assess; the book continually rises by the skill of genius and sinks under its overload of elaborate accretion; but to hear its river-passages read aloud or to watch the word-play of its fabulous cosmic, comic animals often gives the incentive to dive into this circular narrative (at any point, the author suggested) and to join the fun of *Finnegans Wake*.[1]

It's meant to make people laugh, Joyce remarked, and anticipated in its course the solemn fun that academics and 'Joyce specialists' have had with it ever since (like farmers contesting a will, is one happy description). Some see in its solipsism and in its cult of the arcane the seeds of madness; others, a deliberate subordination of plot and character to design, as Joyce applied his basic aesthetic principles to the stuff of the dream, of life and of his own mind. *Finnegans Wake* might be described as a romance, primarily a romance with language, but in that sense Joyce went 'romancing through a romping lifetime', a playboy with and a master of style. 'I know it is no more than a game', he wrote to Harriet Weaver: 'Children may just as well play as not. The ogre will come in any case.' Two years after the publication of his last book he died of colitis in Zurich at the age of fifty-nine.

II

The writings of Daniel Corkery (1878-1964) are a good introduction to the post-revolutionary, home-based Irish writers of fiction of the next generation. Corkery was a national teacher who later became Professor of English at University College, Cork (1931-47). In literature he is primarily known as an excellent writer of short stories, which appeared in four volumes: *A Munster Twilight* (1916), *The Hounds of Banba* (1920), *The Stormy Hills* (1929) and *Earth out of Earth* (1939). His literary model was Turgenev, whose quiet revelatory method he applied to the poor people of Cork, clerks, slum-dwellers, sailors, and to the small farmers and fishermen of its hinterland. The theme of revolution runs through *The Hounds of Banba;* the young guerrilla fighters, 'on their keeping' with cliff and coastal dwellers, discover affinities and antagonisms which link past and present through a submerged consciousness of race. In *The Stormy Hills* the underlying theme is the land and the way in which it is knit to so many facets of Irish character; independence, conservatism, land-hunger, imagination, distrust, sacrifice. In stories such as 'Rock-of-the-Mass' Corkery's art is seen at its best: an old farmer, prosperous at the end of his days, strays back in memory to the Mass Rock of penal times, associated with his first hungry farm. It seems to have been a symbol of what his life was all about; but the quiet revelations of his present uncover the trail of sacrifice and of wrecked lives which has led from austerity to prosperity; and, unknown to him the Mass Rock itself has been dynamited in road-making. We are left, like the reader of Chekov's 'Gooseberries', asking what is human happiness?

This is the method of Corkery's one novel, *The Threshold of Quiet* (1917), which opens when the body of a local salesman is found in the river Lee and which gradually unfolds the complex web of family ties, friendships and estrangements with which he is involved. *The Threshold of Quiet* is the acceptance of life's harsh realities by gentle people 'whose endeavour it is to live on good terms with fate', and carries the penalty of frustration as well as the gain of self-realisation. The prefatory maxim of the book is Thoreau's aphorism that the mass of men lead lives of quiet desperation; its general impression is of loneliness and quiet resignation in an intellectually paralysed city, whose physical vitality is conveyed with a skill which owed something to Corkery's training as a painter. He had some affinity in his short stories with Moore and with Joyce and was particularly skilled in his use of what he called orchestration, the counterpointing of characters, and in capturing the racy idiom of Cork.

His direction in prose fiction was largely due to his interest in Russian literature, which seemed to him to reflect a pattern of life that had much in common with Ireland: an irresponsible aristocracy, which preferred foreign to native culture; an overloaded bureaucracy; a peasant nation, volatile in temperament and abounding in strange, interesting types; strong in religious faith, land-hungry and not lacking revolutionaries. A great modern national literature had been produced by Russian writers whose primary allegiance was to their own country. Ireland might do the same, Corkery thought, but Irish writers would have to realise that the intimate study of Irish life and character so far had been impeded by the prevailing ascendancy tradition in fiction which lacked intimacy with Irish people and their conditions.

He himself believed that Irish could be revived as a generally spoken language and hoped that it would become a medium for a national literature. His influence on Sean O'Faolain and Frank O'Connor is acknowledged in their respective autobiographies; both had him as a mentor and friend. It waned when Corkery followed *The Hidden Ireland* (1925), a good study of the Munster Gaelic poets of the eighteenth century, with *Synge and Anglo-Irish Literature* (1931). Corkery wrote appreciatively of Synge but fell short of admitting his greatness, perhaps because of his own dogmatism about the basic elements of the Irish consciousness — religion, nationality and the land — which should be reflected in the work of a national writer. This view seemed to the younger writers to be too restrictive and to ignore the individual nature of the artist; as for the three elements of Irish consciousness, which Corkery had ranked in the order above, was not land the primary element, which, as Corkery had shown in the *The Stormy Hills,* conditioned the other two? The controversy over Synge caused some of the younger writers to regard him as an obscurantist but his influence extended to other writers of the forties and fifties like Francis MacManus and Bryan MacMahon. He is chiefly remembered for his short stories and for the plays which he wrote for *An Dún,* a little theatre which he founded in Cork in the years before 1916. The latter were published in *The Yellow Bittern and other Plays* (1920).

Corkery helps us to understand some of the currents working in Irish writing at that time; the search for new directions in literature, the growing consciousness of continental models, the pull between nationalism and personal creativity. These all concerned the writers of the next generation. In a good if forgotten little novel, *The Gael* (1919) by Edward Lysaght, one character pauses during the Troubles to reflect: 'our own fight is not to reach the top of the ladder but to get our feet on the bottom rung. What will the new Ireland be like?' It was a question which the new writers would try to answer.

III

'There is no escape for a man from his own time . . . save in his own nature — in his use of memory and imagination.' So the writer Matt Considine reflects in Kate O'Brien's *Pray for the Wanderer* (1938). The fiction of this period grows out of the revolution. It is directly concerned with the kind of society that emerges, with the role of the individual in that society. The issues are at once personal and national, questions of identity and of definition. The preoccupations are social and reflect an east-west Irish dichotomy that is in part an urban-rural division. On the one hand urban writers are attracted to the rural, particularly the western background, to a way of life lived close to nature and the land, to an area in which habits of thought and ways of feeling are verified by tradition and custom. On the other hand they are repelled by life along the eastern seaboard, by the middle-class, by a way of life that reflects a mediocrity of mind and character and in which the spirit suffers restrictions. The division is not as clearly defined in the work of Liam O'Flaherty. Irish literature as a whole shrinks in these post-revolutionary years; its horizons are limited, its preoccupations are local; its social involvement is excessive. The writers are aware of the limitations, knowing they are intellectual and cultural, as well as social, and that the great days of the Irish Literary Revival are over.

Two of the new writers, Sean O'Faolain and Frank O'Connor, were born and raised in Cork city. Both were attracted by republican nationalism and both experienced the disillusion brought about by civil war and the feeling of diminished possibilities for the country and the individual that emerged in the twenties and thirties.

Sean O'Faolain wrote of his generation[2], 'they lived their most vital years at the peak of the excitement and they fell after that into the pit of disillusion.' Each of his first three novels, *A Nest of Simple Folk* (1934), *Bird Alone* (1936) and *Come Back to Erin* (1940), is concerned with the fate of the individual who is trapped within a restrictive environment. Each is set in the lower middle class and in each a rebellious hero turns against its values in order to forge a more satisfying destiny for himself. That rebellion is motivated by his contact with some dynamic older figure who embodies attractive forces of the past or of personal integrity. For Denis Hussey, the boy in the third book of *A Nest of Simple Folk,* the past is seen most forcefully in his uncle, Leo Donnell, who represents tradition, the best principles of Fenianism and a tough individualism. In *Bird Alone*, a *Bildungsroman* set in Cork, Philip Crone, the fierce Parnellite, is the decisive influence. Both Leo Donnell and Philip Crone resist restrictions placed on their lives by society, politics and Church; they strike out for a full life and face the consequences — disapproval, condemnation or imprisonment. Their impact on the young rebels is decisive. In the third novel the younger rebel is the middle-aged Frankie Hannafey and for him the past is represented most tangibly in the person of his Aunt Nell and her vivid memories of the Famine, O'Connell, the landlords — the burden of Irish history.

A Nest of Simple Folk is a slow-paced account of the progress of a family from the rural background, through the hardships of their struggle to 'rise in the world', to their final arrival in Cork. There the Husseys acquire the trappings of middle-class furnishings and middle-class values. Through its history the family is recurrently torn between opposing instincts — 'the instinct to strive violently, to erupt volcanically on the idealistic plane, the instict, as deep and as terrible, of self-preservation.' That tension is an integrating factor in the novel, which has many sensitive descriptions of rural and urban life, of the delicacies of feeling, and the beauty of settings, as well as the emphasis on economic hardship and struggle.

Bird Alone avoids the structural weaknesses of the first novel; the action is compressed and the influence of Phil Crone on the boy, Corney, is given concrete expression. Corney's education is related to specific influences that are expressed in parents and friends. Middle-class values, the compressed life of the city, submissive piety, personal independence are all manifested in actual persons and incidents. The novel is particularly successful in its portrayal of the pieties and restrictions.

Corney Crone's rebellion against middle-class values leads to his love affair with Elsie Sherlock, a girl from a pious, unquestioning Catholic family. Just as old Philip preyed on the boy's innocence, so Corney preys on Elsie's, forcing her away from her home and into his own 'sinful' state. The young people's inability to cope with her pregnancy is a reflection on the inadequacies of their backgrounds; her home is so pious and sheltered that it excludes the trust and compassion she now needs; his alienation from home results from the narrow pride he inherited from old Philip. Corney is driven from his home because of Elsie's pregnancy and death, he is shunned by society and becomes a bird alone.

In *Come Back to Erin* the old-fashioned Republican hero, Frankie Hannafey, is out of place in the post-revolutionary, middle-class society. Oppressed by the futility of his life in Ireland he goes to America where he enjoys the personal freedom it brings him, but is drawn further and further from the dedication that had inspired him in the past. His eventual return to Ireland provides no solution to the problems raised in the novel.

O'Faolain's misfit heroes remind us that the theme of exile, which is found throughout Irish literature, has particular prominence at this period, in which some novels present it as the only alternative to the frustrations of Irish life and others present life in Ireland itself as a kind of spiritual exile. The issue permeates the literature of the period.

Sean O'Faolain's fourth novel is free from the social and political issues that had occupied his attention in the earlier novels. *And Again?* (1979) is a playful consideration of a variety of related issues: the role of memory, the effects of time and change on human behaviour, the operation of chance, the intuitions of truth. At the age of sixty-five Mr James Younger is given the opportunity to live his life over again, journeying back through the years and getting younger as he does so. But since he is reborn without the benefit of memory, he has to try to understand each experience as it happens. His basic assumption, which experience tends to verify, is that a man is what he is no matter how many times he may live his life. This rueful conclusion establishes itself only through a sophisticated and complex series of relationships, mainly with a succession of women whom he finds compellingly attractive. O'Faolain's lively imagination creates an ironic portrait of an aged lover who becomes an increasingly younger but not necessarily a wiser lover as time goes by.

Apart from his fiction, O'Faolain's contribution to Irish life in this period, as biographer, editor and essayist, is of great importance. His historical biographies, *King of the Beggars* (1938), *De Valera* (1939) and *The Great O'Neill* (1942), are valuable studies in their own right, but are also attempts to find directions for Irish life in his own time through examining the personalities and achievements of these political leaders. His work as editor of *The Bell*, the most important periodical of the period, involved encouragement of potential writers, the provision of a medium for reflections of life and culture, and assessments, often polemical, of the hypocrisies and weaknesses to be found in church and state. O'Faolain's book, *The Irish* (1947), summarises some of his views and his autobiography, *Vive Moi!* (1964), analyses the shaping forces on his imagination. His contemporary, Arland Ussher, in *The Face and Mind of Ireland* (1949) and *Three Great Irishmen: Shaw, Yeats, Joyce* (1952), revealed a similar range of interests. Of the two the first has interesting reflections on the revolutionary period and on some of its leading figures and both books employ the method of the continually shifting point of view.

Frank O'Connor, who grew up in Cork city in the same period as Sean O'Faolain, wrote two novels, *The Saint and Mary Kate* (1932) and *Dutch Interior* (1940). His own background of slum poverty is reflected in their settings and in addition the former reveals several themes that are central to his work: eccentric piety, the 'natural' girl, and colourful characters. *The Saint and Mary Kate* is a formless novel about bewildered young people, that moves from a slum setting into a world of fantasy and fairy tale in which the unexpected can readily happen. The bewildered young lovers, Mary Kate and Phil Drinan, the saint of the title, follow a zig-zag path towards understanding and self-discovery, their progress being impeded as much by innocence in her case and by perverse piety in his as by external obstacles in family or social conditions. The novel resembles *Bird Alone* in its preoccupations with Cork as a setting for youth's development, but it is more optimistic. O'Connor's imagination is filled with the colourful chaos of his slum setting and its eccentric characters but his young lovers move away to Dublin and then to the countryside.

Dutch Interior, on the other hand, is 'a chronicle', as Thomas Flanagan observed, 'of spirit wasted and wasting in a provincial backwater'.[3] The difference between the two novels is striking. Cork is no longer a place of entertaining characters, but a place in which character has gone to seed and become personality; it no longer opens to a pastoral land of fantasy and freedom, but closes in upon itself, blighting human existence from childhood to manhood; the inhabitants are conscious of 'an air of hopelessness and doom'. The young hope against hope in a setting of rain and darkness; their aspirations are short lived, for the reality of unhappy marriage, gossip, emotional repression, hysteria and emigration soon destroys the notion of an individual happiness or fulfilment. Stevie Dalton, who endures, feels that he has been 'left among dead people, those for whom life held nothing'.

The frustration of the characters affects the structure of the novel, which is claustrophobic; the characters are undeveloped, the organisation of the plot is unclear, and the setting is not adequately realised. The novel expresses anger and frustration but lacks firm outline. It is effective in depicting family relationships, such as those between Peter Devane and his mother, and between Stevie Dalton and his family.

If Sean O'Faolain and Frank O'Connor reacted to the drastic social and political changes, the tensions and divisions of Irish life in the period are presented with remarkable clarity and power in the novels of Liam O'Flaherty who for two decades was the most prolific and the most promising of Irish novelists, writing six novels between 1923 and 1929 and five between 1932 and 1937. Born on the Aran Islands, he writes with unequalled authority and intimacy about peasant life, drawing naturally into his work the surviving, subliminal, cultural values of the West and instinctively shaping his notion of form, manner and characterisation in the light of traditional modes and ideals of Irish story-telling. At the same time and often within the same work, he reacted to forces of materialism and social revolution that affected this western society in the early years of this century, so that his accounts of the corrupting effects of an emerging middle-class, while related to a predominantly peasant community, parallels and illustrates similar processes of social transformation that were taking place in the country as a whole in the twenties, thirties and forties. Revolutionary activities are more prominent in O'Flaherty's novels than in anyone else's. They are central to *The Informer, The Martyr,* and *The Assassin,* studies of revolutionary types, as well as accounts of violence and of the turmoil in people's lives occasioned by such events. Finally, the east-west divisions are also important, in the visible tensions in his work between novels about his western/rural background, such as *The Neighbour's Wife, The Black Soul, Skerrett, Famine,* and novels about the city, *Mr. Gilhooley, The Puritan* and most of the novels of revolution, in which, as in his short stories, he bases his creation of character on the idea that man is at his best within his own natural-rural environment where he is undivided and in tune with nature; he is corrupted by contact with cities and 'civilisation'.

Liam O'Flaherty. Photograph Michael Barron.

O'Flaherty's reputation as a novelist rests upon three works: *The Informer, Skerrett* and *Famine.* The first is a powerful, fast-moving novel, full of action and dense with physical detail. The informer is Gypo Nolan, a man of enormous physical strength, who acts instinctively but has a low intelligence; he is unable to think clearly, to make plans for his own safety. When he turns informer he is hunted through the slum areas of north Dublin, preyed upon as much by his own fears as by the pitiless and cunning revolutionary Dan Gallagher, head of the revolutionary organisation. Gypo fears Gallagher, fears his cold, hard intelligence and fears the organisation, because it is 'all brain and no body'; it is not something he can attack physically. The naturalistic style of *The Informer* is its strength and ultimately its weakness. O'Flaherty describes his characters in crude detail and provides graphic pictures of Dublin streets and houses.

Despite the power of the language and the excitement of the action, the novel moves within a narrow range of conflict and is limited in human interest. Even the intrigue and conflict, since they emanate from two boldly contrasting types of revolutionary, are over-simplified. Both Gallagher and Nolan are monsters by nature, extreme, obsessive, one-sided, types of humanity rather than representative individuals. Of the two Gypo is the more appealing. He foolishly informs on the friend who used to help him to make plans, and has an immediate sense of being outcast. His sudden experience of alienation is characteristic of the main characters in all O'Flaherty's Dublin novels. The city and the people become strange and frightening once a crime has been committed, as though the moral state of the character received confirmation in the realities of place and people. Gypo's ultimate death is an undeserved fate, a punishment out of proportion to the initial crime except in the dictionary of revolution. Only the murdered man's sister and mother voice the idea that murders and counter-murders do not solve anything, The novel never faces larger issues of purpose and value.

In *Skerrett* (1932) O'Flaherty combines his clash of character with a realistic and controlled account of life on the island of Nara, i.e. Aran. In this case the conflict between the two antagonists, the subtle priest, Fr Moclair, and the courageous teacher, David Skerrett, is related to their position within the island community. The conflict is basically for power. The priest's spiritual leadership is less important to him than his temporal power. Skerrett is an instinctive man; he identifies with the people and tries to help them. But he is also capable of sudden shifts in allegiance: from being against the people to becoming their champion, from being an active supporter of the priest to being his fierce opponent. A proud man, stubborn in his pride, he reacts fiercely to misfortune — the death of his son, the drunkenness and eventual insanity of his wife, the alienation of the people. In crisis, he is seen as a primitive and elemental being, who issues 'the challenge of his strength to the rocky earth that had struck down his son' and is mastered by a demonic hatred of Fr Moclair, whom he once worshipped this side of idolatry.

The struggle between the two men forms the core of the novel, although the characterisation of Skerrett is more complete than that of the priest. He can be admirably brave and strong, he can be idealistic and selflessly devoted to causes, but has no guile and is impotent against the cunning priest. His fall from power is balanced by the priest's rise to greater authority. Skerrett's weapon is defiance, but while he is defeated by his more clever opponent, he becomes, after his death, a kind of folk hero to the people. He grows in their memories, while his opponent diminishes. In the long run he is seen to be on the side of heroic human value, courage, strength, pride, and these carry great weight in this community. Such men, inspiring and enthusiastic, lack the steel of practicality, but become legendary, symbols of what mankind may achieve.

In *Famine* (1937), O'Flaherty writes with authority and intimacy about peasant life with fidelity of detail, of incident, and of speech. He gives flesh and blood to the facts, records and statistics of history and recreates the event in a persuasive way. The violence and extremes of his other novels are reduced here, negated by the greater calamity of the Famine itself, so that O'Flaherty's emotive tendencies are held in check by his concentration on the event. The disaster is firmly grounded in the ordinary lives of the people and is realised within their range of experience. *Famine* is a true novel in the sense that O'Flaherty relates his narrative and his characters to a recognisable society; they have their being within a setting that is clearly defined and understandable. Historical explanations and accounts of the political background are absorbed into the narrative as part of the experience, often to ironic effect. He creates on a broad canvas, expanding from an initial concentration on one family, the

Kilmartins, to include their relatives on both sides, the people of the Black Valley, the village of Crom and the distant port-town of Clogher. At the end he returns to the place of origin, in the Black Valley, with old Kilmartin trying to dig a grave for his wife and falling lifeless on to the land he loves.

One of the great pleasures afforded by this book is the description of the familiar. O'Flaherty describes the daily, almost ritualistic doings of the Kilmartin family with a quiet accuracy. A life of natural ceremony and custom is quietly delineated, and there is gentleness and delicacy in personal relationships. But the famine destroys a way of life. By the end of the two years, for example, there are no wakes, just burials. Even old Kilmartin's deeply-rooted trust in the land and in the life of a landsman, is denied by the harsh effects of the potato blight. The young couple, Martin and Mary, flee from the catastrophe to a new life in the New World, abandoning what has turned deadly.

The young wife, Mary Kilmartin, is O'Flaherty's most successful portrait of a woman. Not alone is she beautiful and sensuous, but she is tough and practical, stubborn in the face of custom when she sees it as foolish. She becomes a dynamic force in the peasant cottage. Where her sister yields to the sexual eccentricities of the landlord, Chadwick, she rebels against the lop-sided social system that makes famine possible. Like other women in the novel she fights to feed her child and, as with them, starvation and the threat of death transform her: she determines to escape and to abandon the old couple. At the end of the novel there is a flicker of hope in the news of rebels gathering and in the suggestion that some emigrants will return to achieve 'future vengeance'. These are understandable illusions, but out of place in this masterly and realistic recreation of the famine experience.

Like Liam O'Flaherty, Francis Stuart is one of the most prolific Irish novelists of this century. Together with Kate O'Brien and Austin Clarke, he expresses a spiritual vision, being less concerned with social realities than with individual psychology. His literary career falls into three main divisions: in the thirties he published a novel each year, sometimes two, beginning well with *Women and God* (1931), *Pigeon Irish* (1932), *Coloured Dome* (1932) and *Try the Sky* (1933), then writing several undistinguished novels. The war, which he spent in Germany, interrupted this work, but then came a remarkable revival of energy with the publication of *The Pillar of Cloud* (1948), *Redemption* (1949), and the less effective *The Flowering Cross* (1950). He wrote five other novels in the fifties, but again his talent slackened and he seemed to repeat himself in work like *Good Friday's Daughter* (1952), *The Pilgrimage* (1955) and *Angels of Providence* (1959). The long silence that followed was broken with the publication of his masterpiece, *Black List/Section H* (1971), an autobiographical novel that had been foreshadowed in *Victors and Vanquished* (1958). This remarkable late flowering has continued with *Memorial* (1972), *A Hole in the Head* (1977) and *The High Consistory* (1981).

Even in his first novel, *Women and God,* Stuart showed the concerns his fiction would continue to have. Its fundamental issue is the search for meaning in a world singularly lacking in hope, and the solution is to be found in the realisation of God's presence in the world. *Pigeon Irish,* which has a pessimistic view of Irish society, contrasts the scientific and the mystical response to life; it introduces the idea of victory arising from apparent defeat which becomes more pronounced in later novels. It is central to *The Coloured Dome,* which is the most successful novel of the first period, its plot sustained, its characters credible, and with a less intrusive use of symbolism than the earlier novels.

For Garry Delea the threat of death gives intensity to experience. The first part of the book, in particular, registers his fine perception of external reality, but social concerns are subordinated to the idea that happiness is found only by 'agony and self-immolation'. He turns away from Tulloolagh, the girl he loves, to return to prison so that he can share humbly in the suffering of those he finds there. Stuart is somewhat over-insistent on the mystical peace that Delea achieves, but in *The Coloured Dome* shows that he uses social realities to express the mystery of human relationships and the possibility of the transforming experience. The ideal is an experience similar to that of mystics and saints.

These early novels are mainly allegorical; they rely less on external reality than on their vision of spiritual reality. In the novels which he published after the war, he succeeds in uniting a realism of place and person with his unremitting search for a Christ-like experience. The war makes the difference. War-torn Europe provides an ideal context for his interest in the redemptive possibilities of suffering. *The Pillar of Cloud* is in part a realistic novel; it is particularly effective in conveying poverty, hunger, loneliness and suffering. The heroines, Lisette and Halka, both victims of violence, find an inner faith on the brink of death and in the midst of suffering. Dominic, the Irishman who has deliberately sought these miserable conditions, is at the centre of a strange, transforming experience which is created by the catastrophe and by the saintly suffering of the two girls.

He is drawn by the idea of a new peace shaped from pain. He wants to be part of 'the great stream of suffering that was flowing across Europe'. By taking us into this abyss the novel tries to make manifest the redemptive nature of suffering:

> it was in such places that a new world was taking shape; in the hearts of the tormented a new world was born. A world in which there would be no more victims and no more executioners, without prisons and dungeons. Nowhere else was there such faith in a new peace, in the coming to earth of a liberty of spirit that would be like a new sun shining on men and women. No more suspects, no more hunted.

Together with the two girls Dominic creates a way of life that is simple, honest and Christ-like. Sex has no part in their small community. Both Lisette and Halka have experienced such horrors that neither want sex. Domnic loves Halka, but at her request marries the consumptive Lisette so that he can try to get her out of Germany for treatment. Only in prison, after Lisette's death, do he and Halka find sexual union and fulfilment. There his belief in a fragile blossoming of peace and love is confirmed when Halka forgives the executioner, Bergmann. The novel's radical meaning is conveyed in Dominic's defence of the innocence of women who have been purified by imprisonment and suffering.

In *The Pillar of Cloud* the Irishman gained direct, transforming experience from the war in Europe; in *Redemption* (1949) the Irishman returns to his own country. Ezra Arrigho has memories of the 'catastrophe' in Europe. Experiences are in sharp contrast to the small town complacencies of Altamont. He disrupts this world, particularly by influencing Fr Mellowes and the crude fishmonger, Kavanagh. The latter, moved by Ezra's account of the violence in Europe and angered by Altamont's disapproval of his affair with Annie, reacts by getting her to daub Fr Mellowes' holy pictures with her blood, by possessing her brutally and by killing her. This murder corresponds to the violence Ezra has talked about, and he in turn brutally possesses the priest's sister,

Romilly. Evil becomes part of Altamont as of Europe; suffering
enters the priest's life through Ezra. It is the priest who begins to
argue for forgiveness. Drawn by his Christ-like acceptance of
those who are carried away by emotion, Ezra says, 'like you,
Father, he sought the mad, the possessed, and the sick and dying;
they best understood the extravagance of what he would do at the
end'. Fr Mellowes sets up a little community, a 'little corner of
tangible peace', as Ezra calls it, where the relationships are
'simple' and 'true', 'a daring and delicate experiment'. The
members are the priest, Kavanagh, Romilly, the crippled
Margareta, who has risen from the rubble of Europe, and Ezra,
now joined happily with her in a union that is without sexual
intercourse. Romilly and Kavanagh marry so that they will have
each other through the ordeal of his trial and execution. In a series
of ceremonies and rituals of washing, dressing, confessing and
marriage, the novel prepares for the redemptive process, the
realisation of common humanity in the face of evil. *Redemption* is
less insistent on the vision of fraternity than other Stuart novels
and for that reason is artistically more satisfying.

The third period in Stuart's literary career began with the
publication of *Black List/Section H* (1971). It is an unusual novel in
the Irish context, since it transcends cultural, national and
religious roots, realising their presence as important elements but
appropriating them to the unifying theme of the growth of the
imagination, and enlarging them to include influences from the
contexts of British and European traditions, cultures and events.
H, the central, autobiographical hero, moves from an initial
involvement with W. B. Yeats, Iseult and Maud Gonne, the Civil
War and other specific Irish events and places to a wider horizon
gained by visits to London, journeys to Europe, and finally to an
extended stay in Germany before, during and after the war. The
novel is a private history, but recorded within and shaped by
public events. There is a foundation of realism, connections with
time, place, event and actual people, but these are selectively used
and at times, particularly during the German period, public
events, however major, are of much less importance than the
spiritual condition of H. His overriding faith, intuited in early life
and verified by successive incidents, is a belief in suffering and
endurance as redemptive agencies. One of the book's most
impressive achievements is that H's quest for redemption merges
with historical forces, that finally the collapse in Europe, so

appalling in its dislocation of people's lives and its disruption of old political and social orders, confirms his belief that suffering can be redemptive. Out of its horrors H emerges, renewed, stripped of false values, with his instinctive beliefs verified.

From the beginning H is against authority and established categories. He is drawn to the despised and threatened. Much of the novel's interest is derived from his intuitive and austere cast of mind.

> . . . he was absorbed by states of mind that appealed to him first because they ran counter to the familiar ones. He began to put his whole heart into trying to share this kind of consciousness, quite strange, in which intense emotion was joined to a daring imagination that seemed natural to him, though it was rare in contemporary literature.

In pursuit of these 'states of mind' he reads the writings of such mystics as Juliana of Norwich and St Catherine of Sienna. He identifies with Christ because He preferred isolated individuals and spoke in parables. He is particularly attracted by the figure of the crucified Christ, equating it with 'the longing of exposed, tormented beings' for the coming of darkness.

The story of H is an obscurely motivated spiritual quest. He stumbles through experience, from one ill-considered decision to another, led by an instinctive trust in the self. In 'surviving perilous situations . . . he'd gain the insights he needed to reach whatever degree of psychic and imaginative depths he was capable of, and be able to communicate these in his fiction'. He risks everything for the sake of some ultimate discovery and in Nazi Germany on the eve of the war he achieves a position that is both isolated and extreme, and one that will bring him close to suffering and persecution. Finally, he too becomes a displaced person, one of the thousands of victims of evil. Paradoxically, but in keeping with his imaginative faith, he finds precarious consolations in the midst of radical loss.

Like Francis Stuart, Kate O'Brien wrote about spiritual issues but she began her literary career as a social novelist. *Without My Cloak* (1931), her first study of Irish provincial middle-class, is an account of the rise of a merchant class; it follows the fortunes of the Considines and the Hennessys with interest and ironic detachment, as they move towards affluence, with the usual ups and downs of fortune. But her second novel, *The Ante-room* (1934), narrows its focus by concentrating on the remorse and fears of a dying woman; the change in emphasis indicates Kate O'Brien's strong interest in psychology. She knew the world of the small town, but in *Mary Lavelle* (1936), as in *That Lady* (1946), she moves beyond its horizons to the country that became a kind of second home. In Spain, with the objectivity and clarity that distance can bring, she found and created even clearer examples of remorse and self-discovery.

Pray for the Wanderer (1938), about the return of an exiled Irish writer to the provincial town of Mellick, is an argumentative novel in which there are clashes of ideas about Ireland, art, religion and ways of living. Matt Considine, suffering from rejection by his beautiful actress mistress in London, seeks out the security of his former home, falls in love with a local beauty who represents much of what he seeks, but is finally turned down by her. He has to follow his Muse abroad. This is a short novel, somewhat spoiled by Kate O'Brien's tendency to dissect and analyse human nature and to react to Irish politics of the thirties, but enlivened at times by a taut style that is sensitive to tense human relationships. It finally solves Matt Considine's dilemma a little too neatly, but what the novel clearly reveals is O'Brien's subtle and sophisticated sensibility.

Her keen intelligence is also evident in *The Land of Spices* (1941), a psychological portrait of a nun and a realistic, occasionally comic account of life in a boarding school for girls. The novel is perceptive in its analysis of human relationships and of the processes by which we gain understanding of our own behaviour and that of others. St Marie-Hélène Archer, Reverend Mother of an Irish convent, is an austere, self-critical English woman who feels ill-equipped to deal with Irish life and character. Regarded by some, with some justice, as a cold, even merciless person, she is also, as the novel slowly reveals, compassionate as well as just, and as honest in the assessment of self as of others. Her gradual recovery of feeling is central to the novel's development. At the age of eighteen, in an act of blind judgment, she rejected her beloved and loving father in order to enter a convent, driven to that decision by the shock of her discovery of his homosexuality. That experience froze her feelings, making her seem merciless. Now, in middle-age and faced with the complex task of being Superior to the nuns and girls under her care and obedient to the decisions of the Mother General of the Order in Brussels, she reassesses the past. That re-examination results not only from the maturity of her years, but from the mirroring of her early self, as child and girl, in the person of Anna Murphy, one of the boarders. The child's growth to girlhood is one major thread of the story in which another is the winding back of time in the subjective life of the nun. Once she hated her father. Now, wiser and more tolerant, she deplores that arrogant judgment and in small acts of understanding, kindness and obedience reveals the sympathetic nature that exists behind the surface coldness of her manner.

Kate O'Brien's psychological skill comes to full flower in *That Lady* (1946), which is a sustained and complex investigation of human motive. The setting is the strange court of Philip II of Spain. The central issue is the conflict between the king and Ana Mendoza, friend and confidante, because of her love affair with Antonio Perez, his secretary of state. In the background are the larger issues: Philip's political intrigues with other European countries, the expansion of his empire, the weakness of the Spanish nobility, the impoverishment of Spain, the clash of Catholic and Protestant interests abroad and at home the fierce rivalries between ambitious ministers who are close to the king.

At first Ana and Antonio Perez carry on their adulterous affair under the nose of the unsuspecting king, but their story is much more than another account of romantic passion. It is given an additional psychological interest by Ana's spiritual conflict: although she would seek salvation, she will not for the sake of her soul abandon Antonio in his need for her love and support. The novel moves from the ordinary realm of romance in its portrayal of a woman who sees clearly what she is doing and of whose moral greatness and integrity there is no doubt. She chose her lover in an act of personal freedom. Now, having gratified her senses, she lives in sin but is loyal to Antonio and too honest with God to seek either present or retrospective repentance.

She appreciates the feelings of loneliness and rage to which the king succumbs when he discovers her affair. In one of the novel's finest scenes the ageing monarch visits the woman he has loved, whose goodness and goodwill he does not doubt. He weeps in response to her generous appeal that he abandon his secretive ways of government. But he is a victim of the ugly, unassuageable passion that her love for another has roused and cannot match her generosity of spirit nor her transcendent love of country.

This is a deeply spiritual novel, its issues are never simply those of love and sensuality but of love inseparable from moral responsibility. Ana's stand against Philip and for Antonio is principled and without self-deception, asserting the right of the individual to private conscience and to public trial in the face of absolute monarchy and jealous kingship. Philip oversteps his powers in the domain of public justice and in the area of private relationships. In a country grown spineless, Ana stands to the bitter end, through humiliation, imprisonment and death itself, for the rights of the individual.

Kate O'Brien's studies of spiritual anguish are similar in some respects to Austin Clarke's more austere investigations of the conflict between love and repression. His prose romances, *The Bright Temptation* (1932), *The Singing Men at Cashel* (1936) and *The Sun Dances at Easter* (1952), are set in the Hiberno-Romanesque period. *The Bright Temptation,* a simple novel in structure and theme, is based on the story of Diarmaid and Grainne. It has a lyrical and romantic central narrative dealing with the journey of Aidan and Ethna and, in conflict with that, there are incidents and figures that threaten love or distort it into something shameful, such as the monstrous Prompolaun, the glen of the madmen, or the destruction of the monastic city of Cluanmore. But their story affirms the value of love in the face of the repressive laws of the Church.

The Singing Men at Cashel centres on the three marriages of Gormlai, daughter of the High King of Ireland — to Cormac Mac Cuilleanain, King of Munster, to Carroll Mac Muinenan, King of Leinster, and to Nial Glundubh, King of Ailech. The dichotomies between Gormlai and the first two and the contrasts between the two men are of primary importance. The first marriage joins the innocent Gormlai with the austere scholar king. Both are disturbed by the implications of sexual attraction.

In a world of learning and refinement at Cashel, Cormac and Gormlai almost transcend the physical. Nevertheless she sees how different from her Cormac is, his mind infused with spiritual purpose and without appreciation of the things that appeal to her — story-telling, poetry, music, the revival of the old fairs.

Ironically, her second marriage is as resolutely physical as her first was austerely spiritual. The conflict now is between her duties as wife and her longing for freedom from such submission. She and Carroll quarrel bitterly when he accuses Cormac of an ambition to make Cashel the primatial see of Ireland, instead of Armagh. Her meeting with Nial Glundubh is framed by their common imaginative response to the mythic past. Nial confesses his love for her. It is a moment of mystery, rising above her misery and full of promise. Book II, beginning in conflict and fear, surges towards this lyrical and passionate moment. Where Book I developed in an orderly progression, Book II is full of violence, encounters and intrigues. Gormlai's situation is eased when war breaks out between Carroll and Cormac. Cormac is killed and Carroll is wounded.

But the novel falters soon afterwards, turning the focus of attention away from Gormlai. In Book III she is happily married to Glundubh and recreates a period of cultural activity. But the book is unsatisfactory; one expects something that will balance against the first two, but in effect Gormlai's conflicts are over and her imagination finds release and opportunity for creative activity.

The structural weakness in *The Singing Men at Cashel* is not present in *The Sun Dances at Easter,* in which a number of parallel and complementary narratives are carefully worked out and sustained. In place of the moral fervour of the former, there is a lively, comic impulse that celebrates the unruly and the irreverent. The intermeshing of narratives dissolves reality, just as the characters from the main story and within the framed stories cross from the visible and real world into the invisible. Beyond the human world lies the divine race imagined by the old Irish imagination; beyond reality and the riddle of existence lies the paradise of Christian teaching. Mankind lives where 'everything is next to nothing'; they long for the certainty of the otherworld ideal, but exist precariously and in doubt. The novel tells of parallel journeys towards mystery and miracle. The spiritual pilgrimage to St Naal's well ends in a pagan bacchanalia; the fertility sought by Orla may be found at home, but her baby has curls that resemble those of her lover in the invisible world. The concern again is the conflict of soul and body, between the Christian and the pagan, but here the manner is irrepressibly light-hearted. Seriousness, authority and reserve are undermined and replaced by fun, self-reassessment and generosity of heart in the land where 'all that can be imagined is true' and 'every wish that belongs to the present' is granted.

The Irish literary revival had sponsored an enthusiastic

retelling of myth and legend, but in the post-revolutionary period there is a change of mood and approach. Austin Clarke, Mervyn Wall, Eimar O'Duffy have an ironic approach. On the whole the realistic tradition had little time for the mythic method and even less time for experimentation. Only in Francis Stuart does one find a vision that transcends, even as it absorbs and is shaped by, specifically Irish experience. Only in Flann O'Brien and Samuel Beckett does one find a vision that is allied to an experimental response to the form and conventions of the novel.

Flann O'Brien, whose real name was Brian O'Nolan, wrote three works of distinction: *At Swim Two Birds* (1939); *The Third Policeman,* written soon afterwards but not published until 1967; *An Beal Bocht* (1941), a complex satire on specific themes and modes in Irish literature, on characteristic aspects of modern Irish society; and a satirical and provocative newspaper column for the *Irish Times* called Cruiskeen Lawn which he wrote under the pseudonym, Myles na Gopaleen. Of these the first is the most effective. It has three main plots running parallel; each has its own narrative pace, its own world of action and its own cast of characters. In the first the narrator is presented as he is at home, at university, in the city; in the second he enters the mythical world of Finn MacCool and Sweeny, from the mediaeval tale Suibhne Geilt; in the third he is involved with the fictional world of Dermot Trellis, author. Outside of these is O'Brien, who moves freely from one to the other and draws as he wishes from the general literary tradition. He believes that characters may be moved from one book to another, as he himself accordingly moves characters from one plot to another. Characters can even be independent of their author, as Dermot Trellis discovers. O'Brien's theories may seem to be congenial to chaos, but in fact he constructs his novel carefully, creating parallels of plots and counterplots, recurrences of characters and incidents that mirror and reflect each other. Within each plot there are comic situations, characters and conversations; wild ideas exist side by side with mundane situations, and ordinary situations are transformed by extraordinary characters.

Clearly the novel is not representational and in this is different from most Irish fiction of the period; it is related to specific details of place or person only occasionally, and then for comic purposes. From the start it rebels against the convention of the single beginning by declaring that a book may have three openings entirely dissimilar and interrelated only 'in the prescience of the author'. Fiction is a product of the privacy of the mind. The 'I' persona appears to be lazy but is mentally active. Retiring to the kingdom of his mind, he produces from that darkness the Finn MacCool plot which imitates and parodies Fenian lays and romances. His own story has the closest connection with reality but, as in the mediaeval romance, the fictive world is outside society's norms; it has a landscape, or landscapes, of its own. The novel juxtaposes different worlds and leaves the incongruities to establish themselves. To these, as to much else, the reader can adjust his credibility as best he can. The important element throughout is language: conversations, description, poetry, parody, irony, pastiche; the imagination is concerned with fiction, with varieties of fictive worlds, with multiple perspectives and with their interaction. It is precisely this freedom from convention, and the expectations thereby aroused, that makes the reading of this novel, this self-evident sham, an exciting intellectual and imaginative experience.

The third plot concerns the author, Dermot Trellis, who compels his characters to live with him in the Red Swan Hotel so that he can watch them. They, as it happens, are drawn mainly from books by a writer called Tracy. The demarcation between fact and fiction becomes less clear. The chinese box effect increases with the discovery that Shanahan, a character in novels by Tracy, is also staying at the Red Swan and that he too is a story-teller. His story of the Ringsend cowboys is one of the novel's most entertaining sections. Shanahan's use of Dublin idiom is comic in itself and contrasts with the 'high' style of the Finn sections. Further contrast achieved by the manner of Finn's story of Sweeny and by the section on Jem Casey, poet of the people, whose world counters the mythic world of Sweeny.

The Third Policeman is less complicated in plot and has fewer characters; it too is an obvious fiction. The novel deals with retribution. The nameless narrator has killed Philip Mathers for the money which he is supposed to keep in a black box. As a punishment he is sent to a hell in which the rules of time and space, including that of gravity, do not prevail. With the money he had intended to publish a definitive edition of the works of de Selby. Appropriately his hell works according to the latter's crazy theories. Events in the novel tend to grow from de Selby; his habits of mind and of speech are imitated by the commentators on his work. In this unreal world reason is put to the test in bizarre conversations. The narrator's only aim throughout is to find the black box and this search represents the pursuit of truth, as do all the theories which are expressed. MacCruiskeen, the policeman, searches for *omnium,* which is absolute knowledge. There is a tension throughout the novel between the narrator's hold on reality, on reason, on his sense of what is normal and true, and what he encounters: the policemen, their theories, bicycles and fixations. Even eternity is a nightmare of mechanical devices and yet another mirror for the solipsistic universe.

The Third Policeman depicts a hell of recurring futility and frustration. *The Hard Life* (1961), while it has a number of successful comic characters, Mr Collopy, Father Kurt Fahrt, S.J., and 'the brother', is poorly organised and lacks the coherence that makes the disciplined complexity of *At Swim Two Birds* so satisfying. *The Dalkey Archive* (1964) resembles *The Third Policeman* in its attempts to parody concepts of time and space and in its re-use of characters, ideas and situations from the earlier novel. Here also O'Brien employs pedantry as a comic mode for his assault on religion and the religious life and for his portrayal of James Joyce and his work. *The Dalkey Archive,* a satire on presumptuous ignorance, is a tightly controlled and carefully worked out novel that combines most of the theories explored in the previous novels.

Joyce, Flann O'Brien and Samuel Beckett are the most experimental Irish novelists of the period. Beckett's literary career, while contemporaneous with those of Sean O'Faolain and Flann O'Brien, is unique in its sudden emergence in the fifties as a major literary phenomenon and in its pessimistic vision that reflected a contemporary feeling of malaise in western Europe. His concerns are metaphysical, his characters are isolated beings who find no intelligible purpose in existence. They are tormented physically by their own decrepitude and by the fact that they are unable to alleviate the miseries of their lives. For all of them mind and body are separate. They therefore hope to find release from bodily pain by entering a purely mental state. In the later novels this is seen as an illusory hope. Beckett's pessimistic outlook is made even more traumatic by his feeling that language is incapable of expressing what people feel; yet the writer has no alternative but to struggle with words if he is to give expression to his personal vision. In the course of that struggle Beckett handles the fictive conventions of the novel in a radically experimental manner.

His novels are unorthodox in form, but in themselves are closely interrelated in form and content; their settings and their characters undergo a process of increasing disintegration. Each character seems to be a reincarnation of those who were present in the preceding novels. All exemplify the same obsessions; they want to explain the unexplainable, they seek to impose order on what is meaningless, they are compelled to be active, mentally and physically, and they long to escape into mental silence but never succeed in doing so. If the characters resemble one another, recognisable fictional elements are less and less evident from one novel to the next. Beginning with *Watt,* Beckett discards the novel's conventional properties. The notion of character changes; for while the characters are alike in their physical condition and in their spiritual isolation, they eventually lose their individuality. At the beginning, in the earlier novels, they exist in a social world that we recognise; by the end they are nameless beings, without social definition, without identity. Nor does the idea that characters change, understand themselves or the nature of existence receive much support. While journeys and quests are recurrent elements, they lead nowhere; the characters are unchanged by experience, learn nothing, gain no insight. In the negative void in which they have their being, they fill space and time with fictions; they are story-tellers, inventors of illusions. Beckett's claim 'I am working with impotence, ignorance', is fully verified by his novels.

Beckett's fiction may be divided into three areas: the early work, written in English, including *More Pricks than Kicks* (1934), *Murphy* (1938) and *Watt* (1953); the novels written in French between 1947 and 1949, *Molloy, Malone Dies* and *The Unnamable;* and the short pieces published since 1960, in particular *Comment c'est* (1961).

In the first period the fiction is fairly conventional, characterised by a distorted social realism. The heroes, Belacqua Shuah, Murphy and Watt exist partly within society and partly within the world of illusion which they prefer. Belacqua, who is central to the stories in *More Pricks than Kicks,* is a self-centred, literary and intellectual show-off, who would like to escape from society. His isolation is due in part to Beckett's view of the difficulty of communication between any two people. Even in this early work Beckett distorts the conventions by ignoring the idea that there should be a beginning, middle and end, by paying little attention to characterisation or to plot and by using style to discredit style. Writing itself may be the real subject of these stories. *Murphy* brings us closer to the familiar Beckettian vision of human loneliness and failure. Its compressed opening captures the human predicament, as Beckett sees it: 'The sun shone, having no alternative on the nothing new. Murphy sat out of it, as though he were free, in a mew in West Brompton.' Murphy sits in his rocking chair with the sun, symbol of the cyclical, repetitious nature of time, shut out. He tries to withdraw from reality into the apparent freedom of his own mind, but fails; he cannot become totally independent of the external world. This novel has an omniscient narrator, a coherent form and illuminates experience. In its treatment of the dualism of mind and body it places one set of characters against another and embodies the ideal in Mr Endon, but the perfect harmony of mind, body, self and another is not achieved.

Watt, the most experimental of the early fictions, reveals how human reason cannot account for fiction's inability to express reality. Watt wants to find meaning; he wants to know. The account of his journey to Knott's house is the story of man's search for absolute knowledge. But the universe is meaningless. There is always, as Watt comes to realise, a chasm between reality and explanation. Watt experiences the failure of language to express meaning yet feels obliged to express meaning. In this novel, as H. Porter Abbott has shown, the form is imitative; it seeks to generate the experience that is its content. Watt's search for meaning is both encouraged and frustrated. The novel seems to invite interpretation but at the same time fails to reveal meaning, with the result that the reader feels compelled to interpret. Watt's obsessive search is re-enacted in the reader's futile attempts to derive meaning from a novel that both lures him on to do so and at the same time denies him success in that attempt.[4]

In the French novels Beckett changes to the subjective, first-person narrator. Freed from social realism, the characters create the world in which they exist and create fictions that embody their sense of loss and disintegration. Where Murphy and Watt struggled with the Cartesian duality of mind and body, these have the freedom to be themselves and in particular to place less and less trust in reason and external reality. They move from a concern with things outside themselves to a concern with the self, from a belief in the possibility of knowledge to a condition of uncertainty. As the novels progressively reveal human disintegration their form and language also undergo a corresponding deterioration. Yet paradoxically, the more nihilistic the characters are, the more likely they are to possess their fictive roles and thereby become indifferent to the human condition. Faced with its hopelessness, they live by fictions.

Molloy's two-part structure is a good example of Beckett's ability to suggest interpretations while denying any clear-cut significance. The two parts are apparently joined by parallels and cross-references, yet are really not connected. Molloy seeks his mother in part one; Moran seeks Molloy in part two. So the sense of parallel is unavoidable, even though it is not clear if the two quests take place at the same time. In its imitative form the novel gives a feeling of intimacy between the two stories but does not make the actual connection clear. The trilogy of French novels may have been pre-planned, but it may also be true that Beckett saw only the first two as companion pieces. They do seem to be closely related. In *Molloy* the subjective narrator deals with the world of reality and with the self. In *Malone Dies* the narrator just wants to tell stories, to avoid the problem of accurate reportage on the world. The dualism that *Murphy* portrayed is here embodied in two separate, but related books. Professor Abbott sums up as follows:

> ... in *Molloy* we have two narrators under strict orders to report a certain passage from each of their lives and who, in the process of reporting, become involved in the process of creating, of lying, of making up stories about themselves; in *Malone Dies* we have one narrator under no orders but those of his fancy who, in the process of making up stories, becomes involved in the process of reporting, that is, of telling stories very much in the image of what we imagine to have been his life. Thus *Molloy* depicts the impossibility of defining one's self, while *Malone Dies* depicts the impossibility of escaping one's self.[5]

The Unnamable narrows the focus even more: 'Where now? Who now? When now?.' In these opening words we hear the voice of the self lost in unknown space and time, without purpose, without identity, without a fiction to sustain it. The voice tries over and over and in repeated failure to make new beginnings, to find a way forward, and each new attempt is undertaken in the hope that it will lead the speaker to the self.

> Let us first suppose, in order to get on a little, then we'll suppose something else, in order to get on a little further, that it is in fact required of me that I say something, something that is not to be found in all I have said up to now. That seems a reasonable assumption. But thence to infer that the something required is something about me suddenly strikes me as unwarranted.[6]

To pass the time the Unnamable tells stories, but eventually begins to feel that they are not told by him, but by a voice he cannot control. He wants it to stop, but cannot make it stop. He wants desperately to escape into unconsciousness, but must face the fact that he is destined to go on thinking and talking.

The radical thrust of Beckett's fiction is strikingly evident in the ultimate goal of the ⹁Unnamable: 'silence'. As Beckett himself observed of this task, 'there's complete disintegration. No 'I', no 'have', no 'being'. No nominative, no accusative, no verb. There's no way to go on.' Speaking of this novel and of *Texts for Nothing*, written shortly afterwards, Professor Abbott writes, 'Without story, without people, without things, without space and time, the books become their words and syntax'. Beckett's task as a writer is not to seek the Unnamable; he is not concerned with expressing silence. But he presents the search and this he does in his own unique manner, in which verbal skill and control are beautifully employed and in which the most painful kinds of experience and the most absurd vision are transmuted into comedy.

Comment c'est may be seen as the end of the extended journey into fictional disorder; it is plotless, seems shapeless, has minimal characterisation. In it the human being is reduced to a creature crawling in the mud. Language is limited to the same set of expressions which reveal themselves in a syntax that lacks logical order. The novel does not try to project reality, but lives in abstractions and illusions. Yet it has a logical projection. Its structure is tightly wrought, its few verbal expressions gather meaning as they recur, and the act of writing becomes a metaphor for the novel itself. 'What is presented then', as Federman observes, 'is a controlled image of a world in chaos, a world in the process of disintegrating, in the process of *not* becoming'.[7]

Beckett's achievement has to be seen in more than national terms. The problems he copes with are those of expression, form, language, and the dilemma of existence. His novels seem to repeat the same story and his characters are virtually all one. The question of the connections between them involves that of identity. In *The Unnamable* this is inseparable from the question of the controlling voice: '... I have no voice and must speak, that is all I know ...' There is the suggestion that they may all be different levels of consciousness within one character, with the Unnamable at the deepest level of all. The development in the novels is in the reduction of fictional elements. In the process humans become less recognisable as social beings and less definable as individuals; they become anonymous, universal beings with little connection with specific societies or cultures. There is no simple answer to the question of identity. In Beckett's view man cannot establish an identity nor even be certain that there is a 'self' within. The confusion, as he has said, is all around us and our only chance now is to let it in. His novels try to find forms to express his vision of chaos.

Several other novelists of the period also deserve attention. Elizabeth Bowen (1899 - 1973) was the most distinguished woman novelist contemporary with these; she was one of the period's foremost writers in artistic achievement. *The Last September* (1929) is set in Ireland during the war of independence and conveys the reaction of a young woman in one of the Big Houses to the divided attitudes of its Anglo-Irish inhabitants to the Irish-English conflicts at the time. This is done most subtly through nuances of conversation, through feelings knit to the surrounding landscape and to the Big House itself, and through hinted reservations rather than what is actually said.

Elizabeth Bowen spent most of her adult life in England but lived in Bowen's Court, County Cork, which she inherited in 1928, for about a decade from 1952. *The Last September* and her books of reminiscences, notably *Bowen's Court* (1942) and *Seven Winters: Memories of a Dublin Childhood* (1942), are her best presentations of the Irish scene. The illumination of art characterises all her novels, which are written intelligently, combining exact observation with sensitivity of feeling and a careful discipline of expression that evokes by implication and symbol. She is particularly good at conveying children's minds, as she does in

The House in Paris (1935) and *The Death of the Heart* (1935), and in her novels and stories frequently uses the values of children or of odd people to test or to expose the values of conventional society. The best of her other novels are *To the North* (1932), *The Heat of the Day* (1949) and *Eva Trout* (1968). A continuing implication behind all of them is the necessity of illusion and the value of art in supplying it. Her short stories have been published in several collections, of which *Encounters* (1923) was the first and *Collected Short Stories* (1981) the most recent.

She was a writer who, like Joyce, won her reputation chiefly outside Ireland but unlike him was not preoccupied with her memory of it. Both Ireland and England played a part in her formative years, which probably helps to account for the bifurcated attitude of Lois in *The Last September* and for the impression of loneliness detectable in Elizabeth Bowen's work as a whole, though it is the artist's lot in any case.

Other women writers include Janet MacNeill, Maura Laverty, and Mary Colum. Janet MacNeill's best work, *The Maiden Dinosaur* (1964) deals with failure amid the apparently successful world of middle-class respectability; she is particularly concerned with marital breakdown. Maura Laverty's best novel, *Lift Up Your Gates* (1946), also called *Liffey Lane* (1947), is a naturalistic work about the progress of a young girl through a part of Dublin, bordering on the river. Mary Colum's *Life and the Dream* (1947) gives a romantic view of the Irish Literary Revival; her better known, *From These Roots* (1937), is an account of the origins of modernism.

Francis MacManus (1909-65) was a novelist of steady production and of considerable status during this period. He began his career as a novelist with three historical novels, *Stand and Give Challenge* (1934); *Candle for the Proud* (1936) and *Men Withering* (1939); they are set in the eighteenth century and centre around the wandering Gaelic poet, MacConmara, who is the focus of native life. This trilogy captured something of the terror, dislocation and hopelessness of that time and was a promising beginning. MacManus then continued the line of more realistic fiction based on life in his native Kilkenny, which he had begun with *This House Was Mine* (1937). *Flow on, Lovely River* (1941) and *Watergate* (1942) do not quite fulfil the expectation aroused by *This House was Mine,* a good study of a man obsessed and destroyed by land-hunger; it has a depth of penetration which MacManus rarely achieved elsewhere, except in *The Wild Garden* (1940), a fine study of a young girl. He was perhaps too conventional a writer to explore realistically the deeper causes of Irish adult frustration, as can be seen in the sentimentality which mars his treatment of clericalism in *The Greatest of These* (1943). In *The Fire in the Dust* (1950) he faced the issue of the puritanical aspects of Irish Catholicism and wrote one of his best novels.

His Ulster counterpart was Michael MacLaverty (born 1907), who wrote novels and short stories over the same period, reaching in *Call my Brother Back* (1939) and in *The Game Cock and other stories* (1947) a level of excellent writing which he never surpassed but frequently equalled. His fiction presents the Catholic people of Ulster in a deliberately quiet, restrained style which conveys effectively their relationship to the land, their docility in religious matters and the subtle nexus of affiliation which binds them. Political issues are kept vaguely in the background so that the characters lack a dimension almost inescapable in recent times; but this frees MacLaverty for concentration on purely human local observation. His art is seen at its best in his first novel *Lost Fields* (1941) and *Collected Short Stories* (1978).

Brief mention should be made here of two other Northern Ireland writers, Lynn Doyle and Patrick Boyle. The former is remembered for his humorous stories about an imaginary village — *Ballygullion* (1918) and *Back to Ballygullion* (1953). The latter, who began writing late in life, has written some very good short stories and one powerful novel about a middle-aged, hard-drinking bachelor, *Like Any Other Man* (1966).

Brinsley MacNamara (1890-1963) was the pseudonym of James Weldon, who is better known as a playwright but wrote several novels. The first of these, *The Valley of the Squinting Windows* (1918), had a *succès de scandale,* for its satirical picture of his village in Delvin, County Westmeath, caused his expulsion therefrom. Today it would be regarded as rather tame and not particularly well written. *The Mirror in the Dusk* (1921) and *The Various Lives of Marcus Igoe* (1929), a fantasy, are worthier works.

Eimar O'Duffy (1893-1935) wrote on a wide variety of subjects and wrote a good realistic novel about the Easter Rising, *The Wasted Island* (1919), and two satirical novels, *King Goshawk and the Birds* (1926), in which Cuchulain's son leads a revolt against capitalism, and *The Spacious Adventures of the Man in the Street* (1928), which satirises the conventions of earth by inverting them on Planet Rathé, Both these fantasies are largely successful but the third book of the trilogy, *Asses in Clover* (1933), is quite inept. Darrell Figgis (1882-1925) wrote a satirical version of the Oisin legend, *The Return of the Hero* (1923), and several novels — *Children of Earth* (1918), a study of island people, is a minor classic.

One has to be equally selective with some later writers. Mervyn Wall wrote two moderately good plays (*Alarm among the Clerks*, 1940; *The Lady in the Twilight*, 1941) but deserves to be remembered chiefly for *The Unfortunate Fursey* (1946), a very good satirical fantasy in which a simple monk encounters all the terrors of the mediaeval Irish world, from devils to authoritarian bishops. Fursey did not return successfully in *The Return of Fursey* (1948) but in *Leaves for the Burning* (1952) Wall satirised Irish prejudices and ineptitudes in a serious vein; he had much experience of Irish frustration as a civil servant and as secretary of the Arts Council. He retained his sense of wry, rather despondent humour and his excellent sense of style.

IV

A considerable number of writers wrote short stories in this period; four who achieved international stature were Sean O'Faolain, Frank O'Connor, Liam O'Flaherty, and Mary Lavin. The troubles and the society that emerged are again the prominent issues. O'Faolain's first collection, *Midsummer Night Madness* (1932), reflects the turbulence of Anglo-Irish and Civil War, but suggests disengagement. The earliest story, 'Fugue', is a lyrical account of the rebel on the run, but the final story is a realistic choice of love before war; even the title of the collection indicates an attitude. If it marks a turning aside from romantic nationalism, *Purse of Coppers* (1937) shows the emergence of a distinctive vision and the hammering out of a more compact style. The theme now is the survival of the individual in an inhibiting society. The prologue story, 'A Broken World', carefully outlines the relevant social and historical circumstances. Its theme of loneliness, announced in the first line, permeates the stories and includes all the various kinds of frustration that appear. The interplay in the prologue story between three men, artist, priest and peasant, becomes a drama of increasing response to the priest's account of the forces that have made Irish life what it is.

Two visions emerge: one by the priest through his story of a broken world, one by the artist who has been inspired by the priest's vision of wholeness, but the reality is the apathy of the peasant. In the frustrated, lonely priest, a compulsive talker and a man haunted by his vision of a different and better kind of life, O'Faolain introduces one of the central figures in the collection. Everyman, as Hanafan exclaims in 'Admiring the Scenery', lives out his own imagination of himself and every imagination must have a background; if it does not, he is doomed to loneliness. O'Faolain's stories of frustration, written with increasing technical skill, are punishingly bleak.

By the time he published his next collection, *Teresa and other Stories* (1947), O'Faolain had developed a different approach. In writing his biographies of Daniel O'Connell, Hugh O'Neill and Eamon De Valera, he had explored the complicated nature of the Irish character. His acceptance of its complications may be seen in 'One True Friend', in which the repetitive elements illuminate Mrs Moore's inconsistencies and contradictions. Distancing himself now from his subjects, he writes with humour and compassion about the ambivalent nature of his countrymen. The new detachment may be seen in 'The Man Who Invented Sin', which deals with the effects of narrow clericalism. It places the innocent pleasures of two nuns and two Christian Brothers in a liberating and beautiful setting in the West. Into this Eden there intrudes the satanic figure of the local curate whose disapproval interprets innocent freedom as deliberate wrong.

The opening of this story evokes the beauty of the West to which many went to learn Irish and to come into contact with their racial origins. In 'The Silence of the Valley' the death of the story-teller breaks the links between the old and the new. By descriptions of the beauty of the valley, by accounts of the carefree activities of the visitors, by the portrayal of the simple dignity of the cobbler's bedroom, and by the sense of an ending that comes with his burial the story moves ever closer to the realisation of that loss.

O'Faolain's interest in human nature and his fascination with the hidden forces within it developed steadily. 'Lovers of the Lake' and a succession of related stories are humorous investigations of the complexity of Irish character. There is an ironic balance in the story between man and woman, between rationality and impulsiveness, between honest self-awareness and

evasive self-deception. The lovers, surgeon Flannery and his mistress, Angela, live in the world and enjoy their sensuality. Only in remote regions, like the penitential island of Lough Derg to which they go on pilgrimage, can they transcend these conditions and then, ironically, that transcendence is achieved by means of isolation, mortification and humility. O'Faolain's handling of the theme is masterly — balanced, sympathetic, precise in characterisation, appropriating details of landscape, weather and human appearance to reveal human nature, and the hidden recesses of the self.

All the later collections, from *I Remember! I Remember!* (1961) to *Foreign Affairs* (1976), deepen and extend his portrayal of human nature. The later stories are of two main kinds: some, like 'The Planets of the Years' or 'The Talking Trees', deal delicately and tenderly with human feelings; others, like 'Hymeneal' or 'In the Bosom of the Country', are more broadly comic, expose inconsistencies and contradictions. The latter depend on plot, incident, progression, discovery, realisation and resolution. 'Hymeneal' reverses the myth of the West, that recurrent dream that west of the Shannon is a more attractive way of life.

The later stories are the work of a mature, complex and very subtle personality. To express this subtlety O'Faolain has evolved a technique of understatement and of meaning achieved through the interrelation of elements within the story, a resonance of moods, images and incidents. He also has a style that occasionally makes use of exaggeration and stereotype. People are made to reveal themselves with an honesty and a clarity rarely achieved in ordinary life; they become representative, symbolic.

Frank O'Connor's response to rural life is more emotional and romantic than O'Faolain's. This appears, for example, in 'The Majesty of the Law', in Dan Bride's dignified response to the sergeant, his traditional shaming of his enemy, and in his lament for the 'secrets' that have been lost. It appears in 'Peasants', a colourful story composed of a series of confrontations between the parishioners and the priest. In the process their atavistic response to Old Irish law based on community clashes with his adherence to English law, under which the individual is the liable unit. This idea is given more serious treatment in 'In the Train', which illustrates the divisions in Irish life between east and west, city and country, 'foreign' law and 'Irish' law. As their train moves westward, the travellers are freed from the restraints that they felt in the court of law in the city. They were brought there to give evidence in a murder trial of one of their own community, but refused to inform on her. Nevertheless in accordance with tradition they will drive her from their midst, which is the traditional form of punishment.

Stories like 'Uprooted' and 'The Long Road to Ummera' depict a way of life that was attractive, different and disappearing. 'Uprooted' deals most fully with the price paid when one leaves one community and culture for another. When the two brothers return for a week-end to the cottage in which they were raised, everything speaks to them of what has been lost.

Again O'Connor has written a story that reaches out beyond itself, beyond the immediate issue of uprootedness, to poignant and vivid evocation of a place, a people and a culture. Like 'The Long Road to Ummera' the story moves from the drabness of the city to the magic of the West. Among O'Connor's many portrayals of the West is the delicate and poetic 'Bridal Night', a story of madness, loss and pain in which an old woman tells how she lost her only son to the mental asylum. Using a dialect narrator, O'Connor allows her to tell her story so that syntax, idiom and the rhythms of speech define her distinctive voice — compassionate, grateful, muted, sorrowing.

The other major area of O'Connor's stories, the people of the towns, has a bleaker and more satirical quality; it includes the middle class — shopkeepers, clerks, teachers, priests, solicitors — usually respectable and ignorant. Several of his best stories are relevant here; 'The Luceys', 'The Mad Lomasneys', 'The Custom of the Country', 'News for the Church', 'Darcy in the Land of Youth', 'The Holy Door'. Many illustrate how respectability restricts freedom of expression and of decision, moulds people to fixed pattern of social convention.

Of these 'The Luceys' is a probing illustration of middle-class attitudes, how these affect character, and how their presence in a small town can exert pressure on the individual person. It is a story about bitterness, about the hatred that can develop in a family, originating in some particular disagreement and then hardening into fixed attitudes and even passing on into the next generation. The added dimension in the context of small-town Irish life is that these family quarrels are conducted in public, since they cannot be hidden, and are therefore even harder to resolve, since public opinion as to what a person should or should not do affects the decision. The tensions are therefore both private and public, familial and communal.

O'Connor's presentation of this kind of situation is well developed, carefully worked out and fully understood. His judgment is made in terms of wholeness or deficiency; the decent man, who makes the right kind of response, has sympathy and effective consideration; the deficient man is a source of distortion and wrong, for himself and for others.

In 'The Custom of the Country' Irish piety and respectability are again put to the test through the device of the outside observer faced with local values. In a number of stories, such as 'The Idealist' and 'Darcy in the Land of Youth', O'Connor contrasts Irish ways with English ways, the former muddled and unreliable, the latter clear-cut and responsible. But whereas English ways may be more admirable from a moral point of view, Irish ways are imaginatively more attractive. In 'The Custom of the Country' Mrs Martin is a typical middle-class Irish Catholic. Her influence over her daughter, Anna, is strong, until Anna meets the Englishman, Ernest, whose air of good manners and refinement make him acceptable to Mrs Martin. The conflict is between English rationality and belief in a man's right to have a mind of his own and Irish emotionalism, unquestioning faith in the Church, and a determination not to offend against social respectability for fear of what the neighbours might say. The story develops by a series of comic complications until Ernest and Anna marry. Then she discovers that he has a wife and family already. She returns home at once, endures local gossip for a while, then realising her good fortune in having a man who loves her and whose child she carries, goes off to join him in England.

In a succession of stories O'Connor mocks and satirises the life-style and values of middle-class people. 'The Mad Lomasneys' is a portrait of an Irish girl who has been defined by their attitudes to the point where the restrictions on her behaviour cause her to react recklessly, to choose a husband by chance rather than by love, so that an otherwise likeable, courageous girl ruins her chance of happiness. O'Connor's satirical stories are entertaining, but they can be repetitive. The comic element in 'The Holy Door', a story that provides a small-scale panorama of post-revolutionary, small-town life, is strong, as it is in 'Legal Aid', 'The House That Johnny Built', and many others, but the inventiveness of the plot, usually proceeding through a chronological succession of incidents, sometimes tends to limit the possibilities of characterisation; the figures tend to be caricatures, types of humanity, rather than individuals. At the same time O'Connor has a compassionate understanding of the conditions that produce such people.

Frank O'Connor's stories of children run throughout his career, and includes 'First Confession', through the much-loved 'My Oedipus Complex', 'The Drunkard' and 'The Babes in the Wood', a sharp, poignant story about illegitimate children. The real feeling evoked in this story shows up the over-clever humour and irony of 'My Oedipus Complex' and similar stories, which are weakened by sentimentality and ingenious manipulation of incident.

Unlike O'Faolain and O'Connor, Liam O'Flaherty was not an urban writer. His first collection of stories, *Spring Sowing* (1924), contained thirty-two stories, including some of his best — 'Spring Sowing', 'The Cow's Death', 'His First Flight', 'Three Lambs' and 'Going into Exile'. It was a remarkable contribution to modern Irish literature. The stories were written with intensity and directness, and in a style that was precise. In this first collection, as in *The Tent* (1926), *The Mountain Tavern* (1929), *Two Lovely Beasts* (1948), and *The Pedlar's Revenge* (1976) — a collection of previously uncollected stories — O'Flaherty celebrates pure energy and the old virtues of strength, courage and vitality, whether found in humans, animals or the creatures of sea and air. He admires the tramp who is free, self-reliant and responsive to nature. He writes with equal skill of the cow that leaps blindly over a cliff after her calf, of the goat who fights fiercely to protect her kid, of the young seagull who finds the courage of his wings, of the mother suckling her child, of the wave attacking the cliff, of the man exulting in his horsemanship.

Unlike the country people of Frank O'Connor and Sean O'Faolain, his peasants are diggers of the earth, or fishermen: they live in real places and are not just embodiments of habits. When he wants to reflect the presence of older beliefs, he does so in an unselfconscious way, as in 'The Fairy Goose'. The story excels not only in its creation of the clash between pagan and Christian forces, but in its provision of a realistic milieu within which the supernatural exists.

O'Flaherty's stories of animals are unique — vivid, pictorial, unsentimental and written with extraordinary sensory immediacy. 'Three Lambs' has his gifts of fidelity to reality, economy of language, objectivity, precision in detail and directness. It is so seemingly unsophisticated in technique, so apparently artless, that it is easy to miss the skill with which it was written.

'The Wild Goat's Kid' describes the beauty and bravery of the goat; she is wild and, in O'Flaherty's view, is therefore naturally brave and beautiful, possessed of an instinctive grace of form and movement; the story is lovingly detailed in its descriptions of the goat and her kid and of her maternal responses. By contrast the dog from the village, degraded by his contact with society, is ugly and treacherous. 'The Tent' is a parallel story in the human world; here the natural grace and vitality of the tinker, who fights to protect his women, are contrasted with the sly manner of the soldier. In both cases the wilder creatures defeat the ugly enemy and in the same manner.

'The Mountain Tavern' is O'Flaherty's outstanding story of the revolution. Everything in it functions as a metaphor against war — the bleak, indifferent snowy landscape, the burnt-out tavern, the dejected and defeated Republican soldiers, the suffering of the ordinary people and the death of the leader. It is a grim scenario in which incident after incident passes as uncompromising evidence of human misery. At the end, as at the beginning, nature remains — hugely indifferent to these puny humans and their little wars.

This story is characteristic of O'Flaherty's second kind of story — the consecutive narrative. His sense of form is less sophisticated than O'Faolain's, less concerned with its organic nature. He likes to tell a good story, to complete an action, and he does not lay down a judgment on the story, as O'Connor does in his formula stories. O'Flaherty tells his story directly, with careful use of incident, setting and characterisation, making it fresh and vivid being more important than making it oblique or ambivalent.

It can be said of much of his work that it lacks a social sense; 'Two Lovely Beasts', 'Galway Bay' and 'The Post Office' prove otherwise. 'Two Lovely Beasts' is concerned with social forces and with explaining how they work. It focuses on the man who migrates from one class to another without actually moving from the same area. When Colm Dirrane decides to raise a second calf, he sins against the communal law of his people, and when he succeeds and becomes capitalistic in his thinking, he becomes a gombeen man. Instead of treating this figure with ridicule or contempt, O'Flaherty presents it in a detached, analytical manner and puts it in its proper social setting. The burden of sympathy is with the peasants, but the story shows the effects of the struggle Colm undergoes, its good results in terms of money, its less attractive effects on his character.

'Galway Bay' is O'Flaherty's hymn of praise to his own people, but it is also a lament. It laments the passing of a special 'breed' of men in its characterisation of Old Tom, in its account of his journey to the mainland fair, in the fading of light from the scene, in the palpable diminishing of energy. O'Flaherty's sensitive awareness of Aran life, expressed in his vivid imagery and descriptions of men and creatures, is present here, in the fierce, old man, raging against the dying of the light. The story is buoyed on the succcessive waves of his encounters with the people on the boat, the sergeant, the young man, the native woman, the tourists, and sinks gradually to the final picture of man and cow walking dejectedly side by side. Similarly in 'The Post Office' O'Flaherty, in a manner that is unusual for him, plays with the central metaphor of confusion, through which he portrays the presence in the West of the new and the old, as three visitors — an elegantly dressed young man and two exotic and dazzling girls — enter a local post office in order to send a telegram to Los Angeles. That the place is called Praiseach, which means 'confusion', is entirely appropriate to what follows. Martin Conlon, the postmaster, hates having to use the telephone, as he must now to send a telegram. From that one simple task the story develops. The theme of confusion insinuates itself into the story, becomes rampant as the complications grow, and finally triumphs. O'Flaherty works here in comic manner, detached, observant, fully in control, his energy for once channelled into hearty, impersonal laughter.

Mary Lavin is a very different kind of writer. In 'The Will', first published in *The Long Ago* (1944), the issues that permeate much of her subsequent writing are revealed in the clash between Kate Conroy and her younger sister, Lally; the latter is condemned by her middle-class family for 'lowering' herself, for living at a social level inferior to theirs. Their comments are belittling and offensive. But Mary Lavin's sympathies are on the side of the romantic Lally, who married against her mother's wishes and has been left out of her will. Despite the hardship of the years Lally has not regretted her choice. The stubborn independence that characterised her in the past enables her to refuse their offer of financial assistance now. The will of the title refers not only to the legal document that showed her moth unrelenting bitterness, but to the courage and self-reliance of the daughter. The final proof of Lally's generosity of spirit comes when she insists that masses must be said with her money for the repose of her mother's soul. In that final impulsive act Lally rises above the petty, demeaning values of the Conroys.

Another target for Mary Lavin's criticism is the sentimentalist. In 'The Cemetery in the Demesne' the garrulous carter is reduced to silence by the shock of his meeting with the woman and the dying child. In 'Sunday Brings Sunday' adults — priest, parents, employers — are condemned for their failure to prepare the inexperienced and romantic Mona for the facts of life. In 'The Long Ago' Hallie's nostalgia for the past is bluntly condemned when she offers the spurious consolation of a return to their girlish pasts to the woman whose husband has just died. In 'The Little Prince' Bedelia Grimes ruthlessly drives her brother, Tom, from their home so that she and the shop-boy, Daniel, can get the family business; then she foolishly searches for him in America, seeking not the dead pauper she actually finds but the beautiful boy, the little prince that Tom once was in her eyes. An even more monstrous example of self-deception comes in 'A Happy Death', in which Ella pursues her obsessive dream of a better future, despite the reality of the squalor in which she and Robert live. The story exposes the inhuman insensitivity of this self-driving, destructive woman.

The dangers of illusions are also expressed in the long title story of *The Becker Wives* (1946), in which Flora, newly married into the stolid and respectable middle-class family of the Beckers, brings lightness and imaginative excitement into their lives. The tragedy is that Flora's flair for impersonation is a form of schizophrenia; beneath the sophisticated performances lies a failure of identity; she can live only in the illusion of another's being. The whole collection concentrates on such figures whose make-believe always results in misfortune. But the title story brings together two sources of potential failure — those who fail by virtue of what they are and those whose middle-class background produces failure. The next collection, *A Single Lady* (1951), brings these two sources of failure together. Here the single lady of the title story is a product of her background — educated, refined, class conscious, dependent on her father. She has a restless, questioning mind that is puzzled by her father's infatuation for the slovenly servant. At the heart of this mystery is the inability of the unmarried woman to understand the sensuality involved. She has never asserted herself. Her attempt to do so now by means of a pretence is further evidence of her evasion of responsibility.

Many characters are guilty of self-deception and of the cruelty to others that sometimes results. Daniel in 'Posy' is one example. So is the surgeon in 'A Woman Friend', a self-centred and ambitious man who is insensitive to the feelings of his friend, Bina. No wonder Mary Lavin points out in 'The Widow's Son' that it is only by careful watching and absolute sincerity that we follow the path which is destined for us, and that, no matter how tragic that may be, it is better than the tragedy we bring on ourselves. When we fail to be honest with ourselves the consequences are made clear in story after story, including 'A Gentle Soul' in which the girl-narrator's hatred of her sister who compelled her to go against her own feelings and to adhere to her own class is shown in reality to be hatred of herself for her cowardice.

The idea that Mary Lavin's fiction deals only with the comfortably well-off, the middle-class, is not true. Her real concern is not with social position or mercenary values, although these are sometimes used as metaphor or as shaping forces on behaviour, but with what she has called the 'vagaries and contrarieties' of the human heart. These include a wide range of feelings, from Ella's destructive progress in 'A Happy Death' to Liddy's tremulous happiness in 'Frail Vessel'; in between are the quiet heartache of the young nun in 'Chamois Gloves' or the honest self-assessment of the woman in 'A Nun's Mother'.

The change in Mary Lavin's work in the 1960s is signalled by the character of the widow, Mary, in the story 'In a Cafe'. She is an attractive woman — hesitant, responsive, sensitive to the feelings of others as to her own. Accustomed to depending on Richard for her feelings and ideas, she moves in the course of the story to a self-reliant identity. She has the alert, analytical mind of an Ella or a Bedelia, but has an appreciation of the physical, sensual relationship between men and women. 'Dry love and barren longing' are the widow's lot. But so too are maturity and the ability to assess human nature. If the widow in 'The House in the Fields' is afraid of the dark, she is not afraid to do business with men. If she is lonely for her dead husband, she remembers their love with gratitude. Having lived through that satisfying relationship she can cope unsentimentally when Bartley Crosson tries to kiss her. So too in 'The Cuckoo Spit', Vera Traske copes firmly with Fergus, whose youthful attraction she finds both touching and rash. In these later stories Mary Lavin deals with the psychology of love; it is typical of their changed mood that there is a greater use of natural imagery and that the narrative voice is mature, sympathetic.

Central to the question of love and loss is the larger issue of happiness, what it is, how it is created, why it is lost. Honesty and independence are still essential, but the larger question of the nature of happiness remains. The story 'Happiness' embodies this indefinable, elusive quality in the figure of the mother. To the daughters the issue is tantalisingly problematical, though frequently discussed. Language cannot account for it; action cannot illustrate it convincingly. It is a force discernible in the mother's vitality, her zest for life; it is present in the dynamism of her response to experience, in her relationships with family and friends, in her devotion to love, even in her assertion that one may be happy when in pain or dying. The issue has lurked within all Mary Lavin's work, visible in Liddy's mysterious smile, even in Ella's tormented quest, in the spirit of all the impulsive and generous characters, in Renee's warmth and courage in 'The Lost Child'. It is implied in the many allusions to the happiness that marriage can bring; its absence is a reason for loneliness in widows and at the same time explains their resourceful sympathy and understanding.

The semi-autobiographical nature of many Irish novels may remind us that autobiography itself has an important place in Anglo-Irish literature. Many writers have written autobiographies, memoirs, reminiscences, or recollections — the term used varies — and there are times when autobiography reads like a novel of revenge. Nevertheless, as was evident in the case of George Moore and W.B. Yeats, autobiography is of considerable interest in itself and can be of particular help in enabling us to understand the writer's work. Sean O'Faolain's *Vive Moi!* (1963), together with Frank O'Connor's *An Only Child* (1961) and *My Father's Son* (1968) provide insights to their growing up in Cork before, during and after the revolution. Austin Clarke's *Twice Round the Black Church* (1962) is essential background reading to his own work and subtly counters the view of north Dublin presented by James Joyce. Stephen Gwynn's *Experiences of a Literary Man* (1926) shows what a varied public and literary life he had; he was a moderately good literary historian, e.g. *Irish Literature and Drama* (1920).

Nor is autobiographical writing confined to literary figures. Ernie O'Malley's *On Another Man's Wound* (1936) is the best of several accounts of revolutionary activities. Maud Gonne's *A Servant of the Queen* (1940) should also be read, and Francis Hackett's *I Choose Denmark* (1940) and perhaps Ella Young's *Flowering Dusk* (1945), although it is disappointing from a woman who contributed many poems and books of Celtic Wonder-tales to the revival period. Gogarty's semi-autobiographical *As I was Going Down Sackville Street* (1937) and *Tumbling in the Hay* (1939) give some vivid impressions of life in Joyce's Dublin.

The most detailed autobiographical work is that written by Sean O'Casey. It may be that his six volumes (1939-1954) will prove of more enduring interest than most of his later plays. They are written in a highly individual style, combining realistic impressionistic and fantastic presentation of his own life, of the things that made him, and of the various people and events which affected him. Although sometimes marred by unsuccessful attempts to follow Joyce's associative thought-stream technique or by the rhetoric of opinion, they give much insight into his life, work and time.

Chapter XXI

Drama

For the next twenty or thirty years after the revival O'Casey was still the Irish dramatist whose work attracted most international expectation. Living in post-war London he became interested in the expressionistic drama of Toller, Kayser and the Capek brothers, whose influence had affected some of the plays of Eugene O'Neill and of Elmer Rice. Expressionism sought, by the use of stylised characters and movement, by chant, chorus, symbol and dance, to express the tragedy and comedy of spiritually fragmented and physically regimented man. It was often overtly or implicitly didactic (anti-war, anti-capitalist) in approach. Toller once noted two of its tendencies which he disliked: 'the tendency to produce a black and white drawing, showing men on one side as devils, on the other as angels', and 'the tendency to worship the great proletarian, to carry on an inverted byzantine cult in his honour'.

O'Casey at first did not display either tendency strongly, though his play, *The Silver Tasie* (1928), marked an approach in style to the expressionistic manner. In the first naturalistic act young Harry Heegan goes gaily off to war, cheered by his friends and kissed by his sweetheart Jessie, who drinks with him from the cup, the Silver Tassie, which his football team has won. In Act II the war itself is conveyed expressionistically: a huge gun and a broken crucifix are focal points between which move and chat the tired soldiers, the stretcher-bearers, the fatuous visitors to the front. Reverting in the last acts to the opening style, O'Casey shows Harry paralysed by war, crippled from the waist down. Embittered by the loss of Jessie to his best friend and by the futility of the efforts of his loquacious father and friends to cheer him up, he destroys the Silver Tassie and accepts his fate.

Although Shaw thought this 'literally a hell of a play', it was rejected by the Abbey Theatre. This led to a temporary breach between O'Casey and Yeats, which was only partly healed when the Abbey produced the play in 1935. O'Casey, who had left

Ireland in 1926 to receive the Hawthornden Prize and had decided to remain in England after the rejection of *The Silver Tassie,* settled in Devon and continued to write plays until his last years. *Red Roses for Me* (1942) was in the mixed style of *The Silver Tassie.* It is about a young railway worker who leads a strike for better wages, which he sees as 'the shining emblem of a larger life', and is killed by strike-breakers. The third act is expressionistic: as Ayamonn Bredon goes through the 'bleak, black and bitter city' for his final confrontation, its drab flower-sellers, its despondent down-and-outs take on a new dignity, are transformed in dress, the city comes to life and dances. Dance, mass movement, chant and song are used to show what changes the spirit of self-sacrifice may cause. This theme is counterpointed by stylised Orange and Catholic bigots, comic but with the sinister overtones of 'mechanick people', who fail in human sympathy and frustrate his vision.

The Star Turns Red, completed in 1939 on the edge of the Second World War, is more of a message play. Its idea, which O'Casey had been thinking out for some twenty years, was that of 'a communist following in the footsteps of Christ'. Dramatically this was expressed by a series of confrontations — between the reactionary Red Priest and Red Jim, a labour leader, between fascists, workers and trade-union officials, whose conflicts the Brown Priest (O'Casey's chief mouthpiece) tries to reconcile. The result is a fine pageant, with dance, song and chant, rather than a play. *Oak Leaves and Lavender* (1946), written while England was at war, is even more didactic and is dramatically weaker. Both contain excellent passages of poetic rhetoric but on the whole O'Casey's new manner was hampered by his message. *Within the Gates* (1933) was written entirely in the expressionistic mode; it has the setting and characters of an imagined kind of Hyde Park and centres on the search for faith by the Young Whore, whose death startles the complacent bishop into self-discovery; for all its melodrama, including the final revelation that she is the bishop's daughter, it has considerable poetic and dramatic power and probably represents the best union of O'Casey's genius with expressionistic manner, though his individual style of dialogue often seems at variance with expressionism's abstract aims and objective style.

Writing to an American critic in 1939 O'Casey said (of his autobiography in progress): 'I do get tremendous joy out of the writing of fantasy, more than out of anything else. . . .' His last plays, *Cock-a-Doodle Dandy* (1949), *The Bishop's Bonfire* (1954) and *The Drums of Father Ned* (1958), are largely satirical fantasies in the manner of an earlier play, *Purple Dust* (1940). All of them are set in Ireland and are satirical expositions of the backward, conservative forces in Irish society set against human kindliness, decency and humour. The characters are often near-stereotypes — poor young women with wider horizons, comic workmen, puritanical and kindly priests, hypocritical blatherers and pious frauds. Behind O'Casey's gleeful destruction of fixed, dead attitudes is a positive plea for imagination, vitality and change, chiefly addressed to the next Irish generation, which perhaps was maturing more rapidly than he thought.

O'Casey defended his change of style in an article, 'Tender Tears for Poor O'Casey' (*Irish Writing,* June 1947).

> . . . the time has passed for a drama to devote its expression to one aspect of life alone, and to consider that aspect of life as dominant for the time the play takes to unfold itself |he wrote|. Consistency of mood and of manner isn't always, indeed, not even often found in life, and why should it then be demanded in a play? . . . A jewel moved about in the hand shows many flashes of light and colour; and the human life, moved about by circumstances of tragedy and comedy, shows more than many flashes of diversity in the unity of its many-sided human nature. . . .

Whether the course of O'Casey's plays bears this out is questionable; but a playwright cannot go on forever writing in the same manner. O'Casey left a legacy of daring experimentation, curiously analogous to that of Yeats in the use of chant, dance, stylisation and symbol, in an effort to unite the arts of the theatre; but he also made use of the burlesque and clowning of the music-hall, thus anticipating in some respects the work of Samuel Beckett.

During the period 1926 to 1951 the playwrights whose work dominated the Abbey Theatre were Lennox Robinson and George Shiels. Robinson, who began his contribution in 1908, showed by 1916 with *The Whiteheaded Boy* that his true bent lay in comedy. By 1950 some twenty of his plays had been produced at the Abbey. He had a gentle ironic view of life's illusions and realities, a keen and intimate appreciation of character and an excellent practical sense of construction, helped by his experience as a producer. It is these qualities which make enduring his best comedies of Irish small-town life; *The Whiteheaded Boy, Crabbed Youth and Age* (1922), *The Far-off Hills* (1928) and *Drama at Inish* (1933). Many of the others have a certain sameness, as if tailored for repertory, but *The Big House* (1926) is an unusually deep study of an ascendancy family during the First World War and the Troubles, with the contrasting allegiances of its older and younger members, while the obsolescence of such a house was presented in *Killycreggs in Twilight* (1937).

George Shiels (1886-1949), who wrote over twenty plays for the Abbey between 1921 and 1946, was probably the most popular playwright of that period. His work seemed specifically geared to the popular taste of Abbey audiences and of the amateur dramatic societies; the characters were usually few and stereotyped, the scene the same throughout, the plot frequently revolved about family disputes concerning land, legacies, auctions, social pretensions; the dialogue, although racy enough, abounded in what came to be known as P.Q. or 'peasant quality'. Shiels drew his characters strikingly but predictably and showed good craftsmanship in contriving stock situations. His most popular successes in comedy were *Paul Twyning* (1922), *Professor Tim* (1925) and *The New Gossoon* (1930); his directly didactic tragi-comedy, *The Rugged Path* (1940), a plea for law and order in rural Ireland, had the longest run of this period. In retrospect his work seems thin and banal, his influence heavily on the side of the formula piece; yet his plays, with O'Casey's and Robinson's, undoubtedly saved the theatre, that victim of changing taste, at a difficult time.

Other contributions of realistic plays were made by Brinsley MacNamara, in comedy with *The Glorious Uncertainty* (1923) and *Look at the Heffernans!* (1926), in tragedy with *Margaret Gillan* (1933); and by Louis Lynch D'Alton with a play about the poet, J. C. Mangan, *The Man in the Cloak* (1937), a melodrama, *Tomorrow Never Comes* (1939) and a comedy, *The Money Doesn't Matter* (1941). Both writers had other plays produced during that period but these were their most effective.

The most promising discovery of the thirties was Paul Vincent Carroll who followed a strong naturalistic drama, *The Things That are Caesar's* (1932), with *Shadow and Substance* (1937), probably the best new play produced in Ireland since O'Casey's *The Plough and the Stars*. It deals with the conflict between a cultured but authoritarian Catholic canon and an idealistic reforming teacher. Both are united in their affection for the Canon's maid, a simple girl who sees visions of her namesake St Brigid, the patron saint of the district. The conflict, in which the Canon enlists the services of the village philistines he despises, leads to the death of Brigid. Carroll wrote other plays, notably *The White Steed* and *The Strings are False*, but never quite recaptured the dramatic power of this play, which concerned not only deep contemporary Irish dilemmas but the universal problem symbolised in its title. This dimension was sadly lacking in the average Abbey play; Carroll, influenced by Ibsen, went deeper.

During the thirties the quiet artistry of Teresa Deevy was also seen in a number of plays, notably *Temporal Powers* (1932), which shared an Abbey Theatre prize with *The Things That are Caesar's* in 1933, *The King of Spain's Daughter* (1935) and *Katie Roche* (1936). Her forte was the subtle revelation of inner personality under a naturalistic domestic surface, her consistent theme the heroic acceptance of ordinary life, but her art was uneven in developing stronger conflicts.

T.C. Murray continued to write during this period and probably achieved his best work in *Autumn Fire* (1924), a tender and delicate treatment of love of father and son for the same woman, the theme which Eugene O'Neill handles with greater dramatic power in *Desire Under the Elms*. After that came *The Blind Wolf* (1928), a tragedy of a returned exile son who is unwittingly murdered by his peasant father. While it had considerable dramatic power, Murray's placing of the scene in Hungary robbed him of his main strength, convincing location and dialogue. *Michaelmas Eve* (1932) had these but is perhaps too didactic in its theme of the misery caused by 'made matches' in rural Ireland.

Other notable writers wrote for the Abbey in the thirties; Peadar O'Donnell, *Wrack* (1932), F.R. Higgins, *A Deuce of Jacks* (1935), Sean O'Faolain, *She Had to Do Something* (1937), Francis Stuart, *Men Crowd Me Round* (1933). None of these plays achieved popular or artistic success, although Stuart's second play, *Strange Guest* (1940), had considerable merit.

In 1938 the poet F.R. Higgins, who was then a director of the Abbey Theatre, complained that, although hundreds of scripts were submitted each year, they were 'mere inbreeding of Abbey successes' they rarely had any literary quality and were undistinguished in speech, although Irish speech in English was still colourful and distinctive. In the forties the work of M.J. Molloy showed in the Abbey the kind of distinction that Higgins sought. *Old Road* (1943) was a Chekhovian type of play set in western Ireland; it had strong yet subtle characterisation and rich dialogue. The old road was the road to the emigrant ship, enforced upon young people by necessity and yet, as in the plays of Padraic Colum, symbolising the path to wider horizons. Molloy followed it with *The Visiting House* (1946), a study of a declining institution in the West, where 'visiting houses' were ports of call for colourful local story-tellers, musicians and wandering men. This too was a work of quality, although it displayed Molloy's weakness in construction. *The King of Friday's Men* (1948) was a tauter play set in the West during the time of faction fighters, tally-women and ascendancy landlords who claimed the *droit de seigneur;* it is the attempt to exact that 'right' which leads to a young girl seeking the protection of a tough faction-fighter, Bartley Dowd, who is one of 'the King of Friday's Men', victims of misfortune. The strong portrayal of Bartley and the girl did not save the play from melodrama, but clearly showed that Molloy had found his basic theme, misfortune and the reactions of human beings to its pressure. It was sounded again in his next play, *The Wood of the Whispering* (1953), which reverted to the loose construction of his first play but contained many memorable vignettes of simple people, twisted into comic, pathetic and terrible shapes by the neglect of governments and by relentless exploitation. It was in effect an indirect indictment of Ireland's social system but the Abbey audiences of that time reacted mostly with the 'Abbey laugh'; they were conditioned, partly by Shiels's plays, to regard rural types as essentially comic. Although Molloy wrote other plays, these were his best. Other promising plays of that decade were written by Walter Macken *Mungo's Mansion*, (1946) and by Bryan MacMahon *The Bugle in the Blood,* (1949). Macken had an excellent ear for Galway dialect and his play was a good study of a Galway docker who dominated a tenement having some of the characteristics of a 'visiting house' in the Claddagh area. MacMahon's play showed the pull of traditional patriotism against that of family security. Myles na gCopaleen's *Faustus Kelly* (1943) about a minor official who sells his soul to the devil in exchange for a seat in parliament, was a good farcical comedy. Edwards and MacLiammoir produced his *Rhapsody in Stephen's Green,* a version of *The Insect Play,* about 1943.

More important to the Abbey was the work of Frank O'Connor who, like F.R. Higgins, was sponsored by Yeats as a new director of the board in 1935. His short story 'In the Train' was dramatised successfully by Hugh Hunt in 1937. This led to their collaboration in a historical play, *The Invincibles* (1937), a powerful study of the men who carried out the 'Park murders' in 1882; they were portrayed as simple men determined to call a halt to evictions and coercion, and desperate at the ineptitude of politicians in post-Fenian times; the tricking of their leader, Carey, into informing on his comrades provided the powerful climax of the play. The collaboration also produced *Moses' Rock* (1938), a more creative but dramatically weaker play about the effect of the 'Parnell split' upon an Irish family. O'Connor subsequently wrote *Time's Pocket* (1938) and *The Statue's Daughter* (1941), but his work in collaboration with Hunt was stronger.

Part of O'Connor's purpose was to use the material of history to illuminate the present and to show the recurrence of idealistic and venal types in situations in which confrontations were inevitable. During the Second World War this appealed to some of the younger writers. The neutrality of the Irish Free State provided Ireland with a tenuous security, but it also produced the feeling of being locked into the *status quo* for the duration. The time seemed suitable for assessing the past and perhaps for providing some touchstones for the future.

The historical play flourished. *Trial at Green Street Couthouse* (1914) and *Rossa,* which won the Abbey prize for an historical, play in 1945, were both plays about Fenian times by Roger McHugh, Andrew Ganly's *The Cursing Fields* (1942) dealt with landlords and tenants during the land agitation, Sigerson Clifford's *The Great Pacificator* (1947) with Daniel O'Connell and Seamus Byrne's *Design for a Headstone* (1950) with the treatment of political prisoners in more recent times. On the whole the historical plays fitted in with the dominant current of realism in the Abbey Theatre.[1] Meanwhile some important developments were occurring outside it.

Although most of W. B. Yeats's later plays were produced at the Abbey Theatre up to his death, verse-drama had been given little scope there. After 1939 the production of *Black Fast* (1941) by Austin Clarke was a reminder that poetic drama had continued a somewhat precarious existence outside the Abbey. In 1938 Clarke and Robert Farren had founded the Dublin Verse-speaking Society which kept it alive by radio recitals and then by short seasons at the small Peacock theatre, started within the Abbey premises in 1925. From 1944 to 1950, the Society's dramatic arm, the Lyric Theatre Company, appeared regularly in similar seasons on the Abbey stage, presenting international verse-plays, revivals of Yeats and Fitzmaurice, and new plays by Clarke, Farren and Donagh MacDonagh.

Clarke had written his first play, *The Son of Learning*, some twenty years before; it had been rejected by Yeats but produced at the Cambridge Theatre Festival of 1932. It was a lively comedy based on an Irish mediaeval tale of a king cured of the hunger demon in his belly by a wandering poet-scholar. Exuberant speech in flexible blank verse invigorated the scholar's praise of food and edged his satire of the antagonistic monks. Clarke set his next two plays, *The Flame* (1929) and *Sister Eucharia* (1939), in convent settings, which enabled him to use costume, movement, chant, chorus and ritual with poetic effect. In both plays the individual vision of a nun is set against the thought and custom of a community. Clarke in his own way was facing not only the technical problems of Yeats in his later plays but also the dilemma which Yeats was handling about the same time — 'what if the irrational return?' But where Yeats brings the irrational back to pose and answer the question, Clarke ends these plays equivocally with an event which may be miraculous, may have a rational explanation; when the poet disappears in a thunderclap at the end of *The Son of Learning*, it may be that, as the monks interpret it, the demon has carried him off, or it may be more than a coincidence that the king's collar of gold is also missing.

These plays had been produced outside the Abbey. *Black Fast*, a poetic farce, was a lively play about mediaeval times; the king of Ulster is preparing an Easter feast, his wife objects that it is still Lent; their conflict is caused by the difference between the Irish Church's dating of Easter as falling a month before the date observed by Rome; this discrepancy, which Joyce puts to good comic effect in *Finnegans Wake*, is used here for one of Clarke's best plays. During the following decade Lyric Theatre productions on the Abbey or Peacock stages included *The Plot is Ready* (1943) based on a mediaeval tale of a king whose abbot foresees his death and digs his grave-plot, urging him to forsake his mistress. The king's wife forgives him, the abbot will not. But when the king is killed by accidentally falling into his grave, his spirit rises in a blaze of glory to summon his mistress to the other world. Like *The Moment Next to Nothing* (Players Theatre, Trinity College, Dublin, 1958) this is a drama of conscience in which past events are given contemporary significance; it is about a young cleric and a river-goddess of the Boyne who discover the appeal of each other's creeds — a theme also of Clarke's prose romance, *The Sun Dances at Easter*. Both were based upon a mediaeval tale which is also found in Irish folklore; Clarke's poetry in this play finely blends the natural setting of the hermit — river, oak and hazel, iris and reed — with the mythological associations of the Boyne and its gods. *The Kiss* (1942), *The Second Kiss* (1946) and *The Third Kiss* (1976) were short, pierrot, verse-plays, *The Viscount of Blarney* (1945)and *The Plot Succeeds* (1950) entertaining medleys of folklore and mythology.

Clarke's *Collected Plays* (1963) enables one to assess the strength of his verse-plays as a whole. His verse shows an admirable range of dexterity and flexibility, accommodating itself as much to witty dialogue as to descriptive passages. Imagery is rapid, condensed, vivid. Clarke's close familiarity with his legendary themes sometimes makes his work too complex or erudite for audiences not 'trained to catch the allusion' but it is usually saved by the progression of the human situation that is being developed. His prevailing theme is the drama of conscience, specifically that of the Irish conscience and its pull between natural instinct and institutional thought, but taking on a wider extension of meaning into the conflict between art and morality. His characters are less abstract, give more of a sense of human play than Yeats's, which are wider in material and in speculation, but fundamentally abstract. Both poets demand fine speaking, disciplined movements and gesture in the theatre but ritual is more important to Yeats in his later plays. Clarke was in practice more of a man of the theatre than Yeats; his plays, although, like Yeats's, concerned with deep problems of human existence, have not the same tendency towards abstraction. Yeats, of course, sought an esoteric audience from 1917, Clarke did not.

The antagonism between Yeats and Clarke was unfortunate; if Clarke had been appointed to the Abbey board, poetry might have held its place in the national theatre. As it was, the naturalistic movement dominated. Discontent with this policy grew stronger after the death of Yeats. The new managing director, Mr Ernest Blythe, had certain limitations in artistic sensibility and, being an enthusiast for the revival of Irish speech, insisted on recruiting his players on the basis of their fluency in Irish rather than on their acting ability. The main result was large-scale expenditure on an annual Abbey pantomime in Irish of doubtful quality, rather than the production of worthwhile plays or translations into Irish of foreign masterpieces. Standards of production and acting went down noticeably about this time and caused a public protest against the Abbey's artistic policy in 1947, led by the younger writers. The subsequent controversy did something to clear the air but led to little more than a temporary improvement in production. Four years later the Abbey Theatre, which had opened its doors almost half a century before, was destroyed by an accidental fire.

The production of international masterpieces had long been neglected by the Abbey. Apart from Lady Gregory's three translations of Molière, the company had staged only some dozen translations of international plays between 1906 and 1928. This was partly remedied by the Dublin Drama League, which gave performances at the Abbey some Sunday and Monday nights during 1918 to 1928. Then in 1928 the Gate Theatre group, led by Hilton Edwards and Michael MacLiammoir, began its production of world drama. MacLiammoir had been the first director of Ireland's first Gaelic-speaking theatre in Galway and was an excellent designer and actor; Edwards, a versatile actor of considerable power, was a director of genius. They launched their productions in the Peacock Theatre with *Peer Gynt* in 1928 and from 1930 functioned as Dublin Gate Theatre Productions at the Gate Theatre. From 1936 they shared this theatre with Longford Productions, a company formed by their associate, the Earl of Longford. The latter company specialised in revivals of Sheridan, Goldsmith, Wilde and Shaw, but the Earl of Longford was also a collaborator with his wife in the Greek classics[2] and wrote a good play about Swift, *Yahoo* (1933). Longford Productions lasted until about 1953, when the Earl of Longford died. The Gate Theatre, despite many vicissitudes, won fame by its international tours and since 1968 has received an annual grant from the Irish Arts Council.

Coincidental with the artistic decline of the Abbey Theatre, the Gate Theatre became a true centre of international drama presented with great artistry by two men interested in the whole gamut of the theatre. While this was the main achievement of the Gate, it also attracted native playwrights, some like T.C. Murray and Lennox Robinson were established, others like Mary Manning (*Youth's the Season?* 1931), were new. MacLiammoir contributed a translation into English of his own play, *Diarmuid and Gráinne* (1928), which had been staged at the Galway theatre in Irish, and several original plays in English, of which *Where Stars Walk* (1940) and *Ill Met by Moonlight* (1946) have been repeatedly revived. Both were entertaining blends of fantasy and reality; the first was based on the legend of Etain and Midir, the second has the folk theme of the changeling, both given a modern context. Other new dramatists include Donagh MacDonagh, who contributed a verse-play about tinkers, *God's Gentry* (1951) and *Step in the Hollow* (1957), a comedy about an eccentric judge. His best play, a lively Dublin ballad-drama, *Happy as Larry,* had been produced by Clarke's Lyric Theatre in 1947.

The most interesting new playwright associated with the Gate Theatre was Denis Johnston, whose play, *The Old Lady Says 'No',* rejected by the Abbey, was produced at the Gate in 1929. This was a dream-play about Robert Emmet's romantic conception of Ireland set against the social and political pretensions of contemporary reality; it hit the prevailing mood of reaction against the conservatism which had affected the Abbey Theatre since in 1926 it had rejected O'Casey's *The Silver Tassie.* The critical temper of Johnston's play was accentuated by its technique of expressionism which he had observed in a London experimental theatre frequented by O'Casey.

The Old Lady Says 'No' was influenced by the expressionistic technique of Kaufman and Connolly's *Beggars on Horseback* and by Capek. Johnston used a similar style in the less successful *A Bride for the Unicorn* (Gate Theatre, 1939). Meanwhile his second play, *The Moon in the Yellow River,* had been produced by the Abbey in 1931. This has a different style; its human 'frame' is a father's alienation from his daughter but its central concern is the problem of the right of a government to execute members of an armed minority, a very real problem in Ireland during the Civil War. Translated into many languages, this is probably Johnston's best-known play abroad. The publication of his *Complete Plays* (1978-79) shows that his dramatic talent was considerable and that he had an interesting range of style; both qualities are manifest in *The Dreaming Dust* (Gate Theatre Company, 1940), a play about Swift, Stella and Vanessa, which has something of Pirandello's style in *Six Characters* and which makes credible, as well as dramatically powerful, the theory that Swift and Stella were closely related by blood.

There were of course smaller and more sporadic little theatre groups in Ireland during this period which are relevant here in so far as they produced some new plays of artistic merit. Gerard Healy, whose naturalistic play *Thy Dear Father* (1943) was produced at the Abbey Theatre, wrote *The Black Stranger* for the promising but short-lived Players' Theatre in 1945. Of all plays set in historical times in Ireland, this play about the Irish Famine was probably the best to date; its style was naturalistic but it had a quiet poetic quality and a simple dramatic strength reminiscent of Colum's early plays. Somewhat later a young dramatist, Maurice Meldon, whose *House Under Green Shadows* (Abbey Theatre, 1951) was a promising naturalistic play on the theme of the decline of the ascendancy house, advanced in style in the satirical fantasies of *Aisling* and *The Purple Path to the Poppy Field,* both produced by the 37 Theatre Club in 1953. Unfortunately both these dramatists died young and had no chance to fulfil their undoubted artistic talent at a time when it was so badly needed on the Irish stage.

Mairtín Ó Cadhain. Photograph Dept. of Foreign Affairs.

CHAPTER XXII

Writing in Irish: Fiction and Poetry

Writers in the Irish language were just as frustrated by the circumstances of this period as were writers in English, but they had even more serious disadvantages to contend with, such as the absence of a fictive tradition, the need to discover a modern idiom in poetry and the even more fundamental problem that their language was endangered. The haunting question for them was and is how would a tradition of writing in Irish survive the disappearance of the Irish-speaking areas?

The origins of fiction in Irish go back to Fr Peadar O Laoghaire's *Séadna* (1894), the first novel, or rather folk-novel, about a country shoemaker who sold his soul to the devil. O'Laoghaire used the language of Munster speakers and despite some unevenness of style achieved character and plot development. It was over ten years later before Padraig Pearse encouraged Irish writers to write in the short story form and to seek a more elevated style, something beyond the peasant simplicities to be found in *Séadna*. He himself wrote *Iosagán* (Jesukin) as an example. His lead was followed by Pádraig O'Conaire, the one writer of the period who was capable of producing work of a high literary standard. He was the first writer in Irish to describe urban life convincingly, although his characters have a varied social background. He brought the kind of literary awareness of European literature, specially French and Russian, into Irish writing that George Moore had brought into Anglo-Irish writing with *The Untilled Field* and *The Lake*. O'Conaire's stories have a fine sense of form. He wrote one good novel, *Deoraíocht* (Exile), which is a bizarre, picaresque account of Irish exiles in London, centred on a love affair between a crippled emigrant and a big red-haired woman. The lack of available Irish models was compensated for by O'Conaire's understanding of French and Russian Literature.

If Anglo-Irish fiction tended to reflect nostalgically on the rural backgrounds, specially as found in western and Gaelic-speaking areas, writers in Irish produced a number of works that are first-hand accounts of that life. Some of these are read more as social documents. Padraic Og O'Conaire wrote *Ceol na nGiolcach* (Music of the Reeds) about Connemara, Seamas MacGrianna wrote about Donegal in *Caisleán Oir* (Golden Castles) as did his brother Seosamh MacGrianna in *An Druma Mór* (The Big Drum), a political novel, and Eamonn MacGiolla Iasachta wrote *Cúrsaí Thomais* (1927) about West Clare. Even more remarkable were the autobiographical accounts of life on the Blasket Islands off the south coast: Tomas O'Criomthain's *An tOileánach* (The Islandman) (1929), Peig Sayer's *Peig* (1936) and Muiris O Suilleabhain's *Fiche Bliain ag Fás* (Twenty Years a-Growing) (1933). These are intimate memoirs. All have considerable narrative skill, but the first is a masterpiece. It has real feeling for the people and their culture and is written with marvellous lucidity and directness. O'Criomthain's philosophy of life enhances his account; he draws naturally and instinctively upon his feeling for family life, he appreciates the joys of simple living and accepts the harsh realities and the misfortunes that are part of existence in this pre-industrial community. In no other work is the life-style and the sense of landscape so vividly evoked and so deeply realised.

The tradition of autobiographical writing, so prevalent in Anglo-Irish literature, is also a feature of writing in Irish. Seosamh MacGrianna wrote *Mo Bhealach Féin* (My Own Way) (1940), in which the sense of division between a nobler way of life in Donegal and the meaner life of Dublin is particularly strong. Donall Mac Amhlaidh's *Saol Saighdiura* (A Soldier's Life) and *Dialann Deorai* (Journal of an Irish Navvy) are more recent examples of the genre. The autobiographical novel and the Gaeltacht memoir received satirical treatment in Brian O'Nolan's *An Béal Bocht* (The Poor Mouth).

After the Second World War Irish fiction was represented by Séamas O'Néill's *Tonn Tuile* (Floodtide) (1947), an attempt to deal with modern life in Dublin, Eoghan O Tuairisc's two novels — *L'Attacque* (1962), which is about the landing of the French in 1798 and *De Luain* (Monday) which is an imaginative documentary about the 1916 Rising, and Diarmuid O Suilleabhain's *Uain Bheo* (Live Moment) (1968), which is an experimental novel about the drab side of urban life. These last two novelists deal with human nature in a mature and sophisticated manner, and are aware of the work of contemporary French novelists, Malraux and Camus in particular. The supreme novel in Irish is Mairtin O Cadhain's *Cré na Cille* (The Graveyard Earth) (1949), a Rabelaisian comic novel written in a richly textured prose that reveals the ways of thought and of conversation of people in south Connemara. O Cadhain also produced a number of collections of short stories, which are among the finest in the language. His stylistic achievements in both forms brought, as he intended, a new richness into Irish speech. He had a sense of responsibility towards the language, towards its preservation and improvement. His essay *Páipéir Bhána agus Páipéir Bhreaca* (lit. 'white papers and speckled papers') (1969) is an important discussion of the problems confronting the writer in Irish.

During this period also Liam O'Flaherty collected his stories in Irish in *Dúil* (Desire) (1953), about Aran life and written in his characteristic direct and uncomplicated style. Brendan Behan's *An Giall* (1958), better known as *The Hostage,* perhaps calls attention to the absence of a tradition of plays in Irish. Although there were actors available and at least one theatre, in Galway, no dramatist of stature emerged.

Poetry revived during and after the Second World War. The poets, as Máirtín O Direáin pointed out, were also hampered by the fact that there was no authoritative poet attempting to deal with contemporary problems in a contemporary style. The new poets wanted to find a fresh idiom. Instead of traditional styles, they used the language as they had absorbed it. O'Direáin's first collection has simple lyrics written in the language he himself spoke. At the same time, as he developed, O Direáin became experimental in his use of language. Like O Cadhain he wanted to enrich the language and to purify it. His contemporary, Seán Ó Riordáin, can also be simple and direct in style, but he is concerned with moral and philosophical issues. Finally, Máire Mhac an tSaoi is particularly noted for her first collection *Margadh na Saoire* (1956), in which there are a series of short, intense poems that reflect on a dying passion.

The number of writers of merit is naturally small, smaller than the number writing successfully in English during the same period, and unfortunately there is not very much interaction between the two traditions. The remarkable thing about writing in Irish in this century is that it has developed so well despite the adversities. It has acquired a sophisticated literary awareness and a linguistic range that are impressive. At the same time it has maintained its connections with native life and native traditions. Whereas a writer like Sean O'Faolain might give up writing in Irish for the simple reason that it is not his native language and that he feels it lacks historical linguistic resonance, a writer like Mairtin O Cadhain, also for simple and fundamental reasons, has to write in Irish:

> . . . I feel a satisfaction in handling my native language, the speech handled by generations of my ancestors. I feel I can add something to that speech, make it a little better than it was when I got it. In dealing with Irish I feel I am as old as New Grange, the Old Hag of Beare, the Great Elk. In my eyes, in my ears, in my head, in my dreams, I carry around two thousand years of that dirty old sow which is Ireland.[1]

Perhaps no other statement by a writer in Irish is so remarkably in tune with the feeling of contemporary Anglo-Irish writers. It is precisely this powerful instinctive and intuitive relationship with the past that motivates and stimulates their imaginations. While there is not much evidence of a two-way assimilative process between the two traditions, in the sense of direct influence from one writer to another, although parallels may be seen, there is considerable evidence of a common sense of tradition, a common awareness of the problems they face and a similar attempt to strengthen and enrich the present from native and non-native sources. Writing in Irish and Anglo-Irish writing are parallel growths from the same source.

PART VI

Chapter XXIII

Contemporary Writing

A new generation of writers began to emerge in the fifties. Born about 1930 and growing up in the period that Austin Clarke and Sean O'Faolain had found restrictive, they were largely unaffected by the problems and aspirations that had characterised their immediate predecessors. They were affected not by nationalism or the divisions of the Civil War but by the Second World War, the bombings in England and Europe, news of the concentration camps, and the possibility of atomic destruction. A new cosmopolitanism entered Irish life and reached its peak in the reversal of national policy that came about with the introduction of a new economic programme in the late fifties.

In this period, during which Austin Clarke re-emerged with sustained energy, Sean O'Faolain wrote a succession of good stories, Mary Lavin wrote her best stories, Francis Stuart wrote his masterpiece *Black List, Section H,* and Denis Johnston wrote *The Brazen Horn* (1976), reflections on metaphysical and philosophical issues involving space, time and the nature of existence. A number of new novelists and poets made their appearance and gradually created a sense of a continuing tradition.

The feeling among the young writers that they belonged to a new, less isolationist and more liberal Ireland is explicit in John Montague's poem 'The Siege of Mullingar', where it is given an exact historical and theological placing, since the music festival it describes takes place at the time of the death of Pope John XXIII. The outlook is also reflected in Thomas Kinsella's deflating use of names once celebrated by Yeats, 'MacDonagh & MacBride,/Merchants; Connolly's Commercial Arms . . .', or in Richard Murphy's reflections on the 'Rebels in silk hats' who attended the reburial of Roger Casement.

Initially the new writers wanted to be regarded not as Irish writers, but as writers. They felt their peripheral involvement in the calamities and enormities of war in Europe, but they were not

Thomas Kinsella. Photograph S. Cashman.

indifferent to them. As John Montague pointed out in 'Auschwitz, Mon Amour', subsequently retitled 'A Welcoming Party', the realisation came late. In *Langrishe, Go Down* Aidan Higgins parallels the final destruction of an Irish Big House with Hitler's invasion of Austria. Thomas Kinsella's 'Old Harry' renders the nightmarish consequences of atomic destruction, including the expulsion of myth from the poetic imagination. In 'Downstream' he connects his vision of evil with his understanding of its presence in Europe during the war. It was, he observed,

> no news that the human mind was an abyss, and that the will, just as much as the imagination, was capable of every evil. But it was something new that in Nazi Germany creatures out of Hieronymus Bosch should have materialised into the world.

The result, he felt, was an isolation of the individual, who became 'conscious of a numbness and dullness' in himself.

> Everywhere in modern writing the stress is on personal versions of the world . . .The detailed explorations of private miseries is an expedition into the interior to find what may guide us in the future. It is out of ourselves and our wills that the chaos came, and out of ourselves that some order must be constructed. [1]

The statement holds true for most writers of his generation, novelists as well as poets. They explore their own natures and backgrounds, their families, their personal pasts, their historical and mythical antecedents and share in a common effort to find meaning and direction for their lives. Whereas the aim in O'Faolain's time was to investigate the past in order to find directions for the present, the emphasis now was on personal understanding; the graph of individual feeling curves at the centre of long meditative poems by Kinsella, Richard Murphy and John Montague, and in a succession of novels by John McGahern, Aidan Higgins, Brian Moore, Edna O'Brien and others; it is present also in plays by Thomas Murphy and Brian Friel. A generation that had started with the determination not to be labelled 'Irish' writers became, in their preoccupation with definitions of the self, notable for their involvement with Ireland. To discover who they are they study the influences that have helped to shape them and their times; they find a place and this includes a sense of history and of heritage.

I

The Irish novel since the fifties has been concerned not so much with society as with private and personal issues. Edna O'Brien's early novels deal with the break from the orthodoxies of home and education; later novels explore the consequences of that leaving and return searchingly to the childhood world. John McGahern returns again and again to familiar scenes and events within which the individual responds to and is shaped by experiences of love, death and separation. Brian Moore uses his Belfast background in his first three novels and subsequently examines the clash of cultures in the experiences of the Irishman in North America.

Brian Moore has a gift of making ordinariness interesting and creates a credible social context for his characters. His theme of man's encounter with himself is easily recognisable. His first novel, *The Lonely Passion of Judith Hearne* (1955), is unusual in that it studies the problem of the loss of religious faith in an ordinary Belfast woman who is driven into the loneliness of disbelief and becomes an alcoholic. *The Feast of Lupercal* (1956) introduces the theme of the later novels: the responsibility for one's own existence and for one's influence on others. In 1960, with *The Luck of Ginger Coffey,* Moore moved to a wider moral horizon and to the subject of marriage under stress. Then, with *An Answer from Limbo* (1962), he wrote about a number of interrelated issues — the fragile marriage, the dissatisfactions of modern life, the difficulty of living without a fixed set of beliefs, casual human evil, and apathy. The novel was all the more powerful for this greater density of concern. In it the expatriate Irish writer, Brendan Tierney, tries to survive in the alien milieu of Madison Avenue, pulled between artistic integrity and the lure of commercial success, only to find that such success means the wreck of his private life.

In *Fergus* (1971) Moore moved away from the realistic mode. Now the writer is put on trial by his past through a series of hallucinatory encounters with parents, family, friends and an earlier self, none of which reveal more than he already knows. Moore's attraction to non-realistic methods became more pronounced in *The Great Victorian Collection* (1975), in which Anthony Maloney dreams a huge display of Victorian objects into existence, and in *The Mangan Inheritance* (1979), which is a gothic tale about a Canadian's search for ancestry in west Cork. Moore's best novels are *The Lonely Passion of Judith Hearne, An Answer from Limbo* and a remarkable study of a woman's psychology, *I Am Mary Dunne* (1968). He is the most prolific Irish novelist of this period, successful, skilful, disciplined.

He is a clear example of the emphasis on the pursuit of private issues. John McGahern is another. Looked at in the order of composition, McGahern first produced a predictable kind of Irish novel, *The Dark* (1965), a story of adolescence on a small farm. The boy-hero is surrounded by an inhibiting world — a frightening father, a perverted priest, a shopkeeper who tries to seduce his sister. He seeks release in sexual fantasies and in masturbation, and these result in anxiety and guilt. His ultimate hope is to escape from this dark world. *The Dark* is an imperfectly realised account of his development; it is an honestly realistic story. *The Barracks* (1963), a more accomplished work, shows McGahern writing with compassion, distance and understanding about a woman in the crisis of dying. Elizabeth Regan's journey into that final separation is beautifully realised; dying of cancer, she lives through periods of enduring silence, which are alleviated by occasional moments of tenderness with her family — her stepchildren and awkward husband — and by memories of her one illuminating love-affair that had put windows into her life and whose sweetness has helped to sustain her in her remote Irish town. In its mingling of sadness and joy, past love and present pain, *The Barracks* shows the more mature McGahern. In its background, seen mainly in the range and resentment of Elizabeth's husband, is the frustration of the small town, the loss of idealism since 1922, the repressed lives, the puritanical mind, the loneliness. These are part of the novel's texture, but Elizabeth's ordeal is primary.

The Irish imagination in this period is sometimes reflective, addicted to a return to favourite landscapes and figures. McGahern's third novel, *The Leavetaking* (1974), returns to his preoccupations with mother and father, death, the search for love, and in this case the discovery of a love to replace lost mother-love. The leavetaking is twofold; in the first half of the novel McGahern establishes the bonds that join mother and son and shows too how destructive they are for him. To escape, the young man enters into a new love and this in turn requires a leavetaking, not only of home but of country. In the second part of the novel McGahern does what other recent novelists have done: he joins the Irish and the non-Irish. If the hero is emotionally handicapped by his background, so too is his American girl by hers. For her, too, love is a transcendence of pain. The parallel helps to universalise experience. A similar concentration on intimate personal relationships is present in *The Pornographer* (1979), in which a hack writer responds with compassion and tenderness to the death of his aunt, refuses to be trapped into marriage by one woman and risks happiness with another. His capacity for real feeling is clearly not confined to sexuality.

John McGahern remains the most promising of the contemporary novelists. He is also an accomplished writer of short stories, as *Nightlines* (1970) and *Getting Through* (1978) clearly show. He writes with a poet's concern for language; one reads his prose attentively for its implications and verbal associations. In his best stories he blends setting, imagery and event in a bond of quiet illumination.

Aidan Higgins, although a very subjective writer, is more concerned with the external world outside his characters than McGahern. In *Langrishe, Go down* (1966), a three-part novel about the decline of a Big House, he brings two figures together from different backgrounds and suggests parallels between European and Irish events. But the love-affair between Imogen Langrishe and Otto Beck is doomed and the novel ends with her final misery and with the death of her sister, Helen. The novel's structure emphasises the brief blossoming of Imogen's love. The transitory beauty of her affair is made poignant by being framed by Part 1. While we follow its rise and decline, we have in mind the subsequent depressive isolation of Imogen and her spinster sisters in their decayed house. Furthermore, the Irish events are set against the larger destructions in Europe, first the attacks on Spain in the opening months of the civil war, then the German invasion of Austria. These parallel signs of violence intensify our response to Imogen and Otto, whose different racial origins make their relationship more difficult.

Higgins, while consciously European, is much concerned with Irish contexts. He draws carefully from newspaper records and is faithful to the details of place. He also has a sense of history, but in *Langrishe, Go Down* the past provides no solutions to distress: Imogen rummages desperately among her father's papers, Helen searches in vain among the headstones in the graveyard. The past leaves little for the present — for Imogen, the fading memory of her love affair, for Helen, the bleak revelation of nothingness, even amid the once great eighteenth-century associations of Celbridge: 'I hear nothing, remember nothing, am nothing.' The 'old impossible life' of the Big House is in a state of decay and impoverishment. For Higgins historical re-examination may make the present more understandable, but not more palatable. He presents a number of perspectives — Ireland and Europe, various views of Ireland from previous observers. The novel focuses on particular scenes, particular conversations, individual occasions, and these become part of a general pattern of vivid contrasts, a composite of interacting perspectives and images. The novel is memorable for its evocative portrayal of the decayed world of a Big House, for its creation of the doomed love of Otto and Imogen, and for its slow-motion technique of vividly realised scenes and images.

Higgins's ability to evoke a sense of place, and of time and memory, is an important element in *Langrishe, Go Down*, in his first collection of stories, *Felo de Se* (1960), in his account of life in Africa, *Images of Africa* (1971) and in *Scenes from a Receding Past* (1977), which is an exploration of the nature of memory. This novel is comprised of a series of memories, more or less in chronological order, and include those of the girl, Olivia, whom the narrator marries. Not that memory can be trusted; it has fleeting images that are not focused always. Higgins's longest novel is *Balcony of Europe* (1972), set mainly in the Spanish town of Nerja, which it evokes with remarkable accuracy. It is a radical change from his previous work, relying on a continuous first person narrative and a restricted point of view. Here, too, as in *Langrishe, Go Down*, Higgins is not concerned with plot, but with isolated tableaux, with what one critic called 'stationary picaresque', an apparent contradiction in terms that is nevertheless appropriate. Higgins himself called the form of the novel 'a spider web of cross references'. The characters, none of whom are allowed to emerge as fully-rounded figures, are restlessly peripatetic people. The main focus of the novel is on Dan Ruttle's love for Charlotte Bayless; once again, as with Imogen and Otto, his pursuit of the promiscuous Charlotte seems obsessive and ill-judged, a wasteful erotic dependence. Once again, as so often in Higgins's work, love is destructive, although it is not fatal. His view of these matters is not optimistic, but neither is it despairing. The book as a whole is rich in incident and in literary and political allusion, it is constructed with considerable ingenuity, but its energy is dissipated by its over-complicated narrative.

Aidan Higgins is one kind of experimental novelist, John Banville is another, more modern in the sense that he writes about writing itself and about the connections between the act of writing and its subjects. He is a self-conscious stylist with an obsessive interest in time, memory, the creation of a fictive timelessness, and death. *Birchwood* (1973), his third novel, places him within the Irish tradition is so far as it may be said to be 'about' a Big House and contains a large element of fantasy but his major work is *Doctor Copernicus* (1976), which could be said to be a novel about science, about the Polish scientist's view of the universe. But it is more interested in creating a work of fiction in which what is said and how it is said are one. The self-conscious art is seen in the over-inventive ingenuity with which the book creates its own inner echoes, repeats sentences, deploys haunting, recurrent images, proceeds by means of a circular pattern of incidents. The prose has power and concentration and, like *The Balcony of Europe*, patiently accumulates details of place and person. Banville does not tell a story; he works through moods and images, creating the moment from inside. The novel's stylistic achievements are impressive, but the importance of Copernicus and his views, including his love-hate relationship with his no-good brother, Andreas, are not sufficiently compelling. Nevertheless, Banville is the most exciting novelist of the present period. His *Kepler* (1981), while not as profound and penetrating as *Doctor Copernicus,* is artistically his most accomplished work.

That loss of intellectual focus is not found in Thomas Kilroy, whose novel *The Big Chapel* (1971) is about freedom from authoritarianism. It deals with a quarrel between a priest and his bishop in Callan, County Kilkenny, in 1871, and with the sectarian violence that erupted in the town, dividing families and resulting in killings, burnings and bitterness. *The Big Chapel* is a powerful novel in its recreation of past events; it is well constructed and has a variety of styles. The central issue is to find truth, but between Butler, the scientist who will not act responsibly on his convictions, and Fr Lannigan, whose training has instilled into him a respect for authority, Nicholas, the young man in search of truth, remains baffled: science and religion fail to provide a credible answer.

Other novelists of the period are James Plunkett, Benedict Kiely, Michael Farrell, John Broderick, Richard Power, Kevin Casey, Anthony Cronin, Jennifer Johnston and Julia O'Faolain. Plunkett, who began as a short-story writer with *The Trusting and the Maimed* (1955), has written two novels about Dublin and its surroundings, *Strumpet City* (1969) and *Farewell Companions* (1977) one historical, the other drawing upon personal memories. He is particularly interested in the story of the workers and of the trade-union movement. His novels suffer from being somewhat too symmetrical in organisation and too subservient to the social panoramas and the historical record. Of the two, *Strumpet City* is the more interesting for its vivid recreation of the turbulent period of the 1913 Workers' Strike and the dynamic figure of James Larkin, the labour leader.

Benedict Kiely, a prolific writer of novels, short stories and essays, began with several realistic novels about his Ulster background, of which *Land without Stars* (1946) and *In a Harbour Green* (1949) were the best. Later he developed a freer, more inventive kind of fiction with *The Captain with the Whiskers* (1960) and *Dogs Enjoy the Morning* (1968). His new mode is partly gothic and partly picaresque. Kiely is a story-teller with a good sense of ironic comedy, but lacks the necessary discipline in form, tending as he does to be too anecdotal and reminiscent.

Author of one successful novel, *Thy Tears Might Cease* (1963), Michael Farrell gives a clear picture of life in Ireland from about 1910 to 1920, the country balls and sodality meetings, the narrow puritanism of some of the clergy, Catholic education, the gentry, the revolution and its aftermath.

John Broderick, a novelist from the midlands, is a more severe critic of the middle class and the Catholic Church, the one for its snobberies and pretensions, the other for its corruption. He is somewhat shrill in his attack, as may be seen in *Apology for Roses* (1973) and *Fugitives* (1962). He has a good sense of style and of what the realistic novel should be, but his work often suffers by the intrusion of personal opinions and a concomitant tendency to make his characters illustrate them. *The Waking of Willie Ryan* (1965) and *The Pride of Summer* (1976) are perhaps his best novels. Richard Power died prematurely just when his technical skills had matured. In *The Hungry Grass* (1969) he wrote a compassionate portrait of a priest who is self-critical, lonely, unsure of his value as a priest, yet capable of earning the love of his people and the grudging respect of his colleagues. Kevin Casey is an intelligent novelist, with a restrained, detached style and a good sense of form. Of his three novels, *The Sinner's Bell* (1968), *A Sense of Survival* (1974) and *Dreams of Revenge* (1977), the last has the more sensitive treatment of personal relationships in its account of the feelings that arise when a love affair fails.

Anthony Cronin wrote the *Life of Riley* (1964), a comic and satirical novel about literary life in Dublin. His *Identity Papers* (1979) is an even more sustained work. Jennifer Johnston has written a sequence of successful novels, of which *Shadows on Our Skin* (1977) and *The Old Jest* (1979) are of particular interest. Julia O'Faolain's *Women in the Wall* (1975), set in sixth-century Gaul, is a powerful psychological study, rather than a conventional historical novel. *No Country for Young Men* (1980) is a satirical updating of her father's *Come Back to Erin*, in that it analyses the legacy of republicanism in an intelligent and dispassionate manner by studying its effects on one family.

A more light-weight kind of fiction was provided by Walter Macken, who also wrote historical novels, a popular type in recent years. He likes to place his work in rural settings, as does Bryan MacMahon, who has written two novels, *Children of the Rainbow* (1952) and *The Honey Spike* (1967), and a number of collections of short stories. He has a romantic attachment to rural life and a colourful imagination. Social comedy of a light sub-acid type is to be found in the work of Terence de Vere White, novelist and man of letters. *The March Hare* (1970) and *Mr. Stephen* (1971) are good examples of his comedy of manners kind of fiction. His autobiographical *A Fretful Midge* (1959) is notable for its critical portrayal of the early years of the new state. William Trevor is also a novelist and short story writer. His novel, *Mrs. Eckdorf in O'Neill's Hotel* (1969), recreates the atmosphere of Dublin with remarkable success. He is particularly interested in the psychology of misfits and delights in bizarre characters and situations, as may be seen in *The Boarding House* (1965) and *The Love Department* (1966). *The Ballroom of Romance* (1972) shows his skill in the short story form. Molly Keane's account of ascendancy life, *Good Behaviour* (1981) is a witty and moving elegy on that class.

On the whole Irish literature remains conservative and non-experimental, although playwrights like Brian Friel, Thomas Murphy and Stewart Parker have a flexible, experimental quality. The emergent fiction writers, such as Bernard

MacLaverty, Maeve Kelly, Gillman Noonan or Desmond Hogan, use traditional narrative techniques and are interested in human psychology and the drama of inner life. Most of the new writers write in a detached sometimes humorous and ironic manner about ordinary people and events. But Niall Quinn's first collection of stories, *Voyovic* (1980) — the American edition (1981) is retitled *Brigitte* — has an unusual range of experience of which he writes in a vivid and uncompromising manner. Of the younger writers Neil Jordan seems to be the most promising. His first collection of stories, *Night in Tunisia* (1976), has a distinctive vision, an elemental approach to character and a personal style. His work resembles that of his contemporaries in its avoidance of nationalism, its indifference to social and religious concerns, and in its unembarrassed treatment of sexual matters. His first novel, *The Post* (1981) is a skilful and experimental work. The spoken word, memory and imagination are, as the narrator says, all 'frighteningly elastic'. The narrative tries to focus the flux, uncertainty and opacity of past experience as precisely as possible. In the process Jordan also tests the resources of narrative technique. His affinity with South American writers, like Borges, is characteristic of the international awareness that has informed Irish novelists during the last twenty-five years and that we find also in the poets.

II

Irish poetry since the fifties has also been concerned with private and personal themes. Like the novelists the poets have also wanted to avoid being consciously Irish writers and have aimed at giving their work a wider dimension. Thomas Kinsella's early work owes as much to Auden as to Yeats and its thematic concern with erosion and death owes little to specifically Irish antecedents. He recognised the peculiarity of the situation of the Irish poet, whose predecessors were mainly Yeats and the lesser poets of the nineteenth century, unless he could avail of the rich and extensive traditions which were available in the Gaelic and Old Irish cultures. Throughout his literary career he has pursued two aims: on the one hand, through translation, he has deepened his understanding of the Gaelic and Old Irish heritage; on the other, he has kept an alert critical contact with modern poetry in England and America, and he has read European literature. Not that he is unique in his attempt to make connections in his work between Irish and non-Irish experience. John Montague, Seamus Heaney, Derek Mahon and others inherit the modernist idiom. Richard Murphy has affinities with the neo-modernist poetry of England. The poets of this period absorb influences from other literatures and other cultures, while they develop their own work.

At the beginning of his literary career Thomas Kinsella's poetry was lyrical and musical, but his first important poem, 'Baggot Street Deserta', is grave and sombre. From the beginning Kinsella has felt the precariousness of existence, but that tragic vision is countered by his belief in love and in poetry itself, which can be sustained by love. While he can write poems about a harmonious and fulfilled life, such as 'The Laundress', he more frequently writes of suffering, violence, death and the figure of the artist. 'Cover Her Face', about the death of a young girl, is an example; it registers the facts in an uncompromising manner. The ability to accept is fundamental in Kinsella's view. His outlook may be depressive, but is alleviated by the instinct to understand clearly and by his belief in a creative evolutionary process. The ethic of suffering that informs his work is related to his conviction that renewal may come from suffering. The theory is articulated most fully in 'Phoenix Park' and is central to the 'Wormwood' sequence and several related lyrics, such as 'Landscape and Figure' and 'The Secret Garden'.

In a number of long, reflective poems — 'A Country Walk', 'Downstream', 'Phoenix Park' and 'Nightwalker — Kinsella places a questioning figure within defining settings so that the progress of the poem is a movement towards understanding. 'Nightwalker' marks a change in his work to poetry of the first voice. In it Kinsella identifies with Irish contexts which the poem explores in detail.

Poems about artist figures indicate his fascination with the processes of growth. *Notes from the Land of the Dead* handles the subject in a variety of ways — through the encounters between boy and grandmother, through the imagery of eating, through allusions to the classical myth of Proserpina and to the Celtic myths about the arrivals of early settlers in Ireland. Those poems that bring child and grandmother together establish the polarity of youth and age, innocence and experience. What the child finds in her, could he but digest all she has experienced and represents, is his own future; she is his source of knowledge by virtue of her capacity to endure and absorb experience to the edge of darkness and nothingness. She is frightening, associated with the smell of decay, with blackness, with predatory birds, but when he faces her she becomes the source of renewal and growth. The encounter is figured in the book's larger designs, in its myths, imagery, recurrent situations and linguistic transformations.

Kinsella's poetry, since this collection, has pursued his interest in psychic myth. 'Finistère', an other-world journey in reverse, celebrates man's capacity for discovery. It enacts the movement of people from Brittany to Ireland; in response to an inner urge they seek out a new land in which they will rebuild the megalithic culture they leave behind. That the speaker should repeat Amergin's hymn of creation affirms Kinsella's belief in the creative act and expresses his need to connect his work with the memory of the race.

In recent poems he has reflected on contemporary events; the death of Seán O Riada, the assassination of John F. Kennedy, the links that bind him to his own family and through them back into Irish history and prehistory. His poetry has gained in strength with the years, from its initial lyricism, through its bleak notations of reality and through its longer ambulatory poems. Then comes the turning inwards to poetry of the first voice, in *Nightwalker* and the poems that follow. Now he writes with force and precision in use of language and control of rhythm. *One of the Other Poems* (1979), in his words, leans towards 'the accurate perception of reality and the allegorical, but away from the metaphysical'.

Richard Murphy's poetry springs from his ascendancy background and his attempts to bridge the gap between that and the native Irish world. Aware that he had an almost entirely British education, he would connect the formalism and traditionalism of his training with the wilder, imaginative, instinctive life of the people who live outside the walls of the big estate. The concern with ancestry is evident in a number of poems, in 'Woman of the House', in 'The God Who Eats Corn', in the historical meditation, 'The Battle of Aughrim'. The concern with bridging the gap may be seen in the earlier poems about the sea, 'Sailing to an Island', 'The Last Galway Hooker', 'The Cleggan Disaster'. The first is an account of an actual journey he and his brother made in search of the legendary island of the pirate queen, Grainne Maol; it begins in mythic quest, encounters testing storms, concludes in the haven of Inishbofin's harbour. 'The Last Galway Hooker' relates his buying of the *Ave Maria;* it gives the history and accomplishments of the boat and concludes with her spring-like renewal when the poet buys her and employs the best local craftsmen to fit her out again.

> Her skilful sailmaker,
> Her inherited boatwright, her dream-tacking steersman
> Picked up the tools of their interrupted work,
> And in memory's hands this hooker was restored.

It is in keeping with Murphy's detached and accurate use of language that he should allow the terms of the crafts to stand unadorned, the denotative use of language being sufficient to the dignity of the calling. His poems also respect good workmanship; they respect the conventions of line and form, they employ the binding power of rhyme; their voice is low-keyed, tactful, making no demands upon us. In these ways they reflect Murphy's wish to retain the civilised procedures of his background and education while he finds a place for his imagination within the landscapes and the seascapes of Connemara.

Murphy is attracted by narrative; he respects the truth of event and is drawn by the drama of what happened in particular places. For all its diversity of incident, character and time, *The Battle of Aughrim* is a drama of a single consciousness. The poet, characteristically, wants to strip away the myths that time, tradition and conflicting attitudes have imposed on the event so that its truth may shine through the faithful, almost documentary narrative. Aughrim becomes a stage, a drama of contrasting voices, figures, events, observations, focused by a presiding, detached narrator so that he may present the battle as the centre of a vital conflict which determined the destiny of Ireland and of himself.

Subsequently, Murphy's poetry became more personal. The *High Island* collection, with its three separate, complementary worlds, indicates the discovery of another centre — the area close to Cleggan, comprising Omey and High islands and the ocean. 'Seals at High Island' marks a new development in the poetry in that it not only describes and observes, but enjoys the music of its own making. Throughout this book there is a freeing of the poetic voice. There is also a respect for the world of nature — seals, storm petrels, their freedom and grace; the poet bears witness to the activities of the landscape. The central figure is still an observer, but the poems are recognitions of community, of integration, of the renewal of the past. It is a poetry of metaphor, simile and onomatopoeia, expressive of feeling.

John Montague has always been concerned with social and cultural contexts, particularly with those forces that have shaped his relationship with Ireland:

> Ancient Ireland, indeed! I was reared by her bedside,
> The rune and the chant, evil eye and averted head,
> Formorian fierceness of family and local feud.

Trusting in the validity of his own region, he has rooted his work in its landscape, deepening and extending his personal experience with historical and mythical associations. Much of this material is gathered into *The Rough Field* (1972), an historical meditation which reveals his preoccupation with landscape and people, with historical divisions and cultural losses. The cosmopolitan self returns to Garvaghey, an Irish name meaning 'rough field', explores his own origins, recreates past experience and reflects on the forces that have been at work within his own family, within the community, within Ulster. The poem's structure is symphonic; it has a unifying theme of loss and change, a central consciousness.

Montague's poetry alternates between love and lament. *The Rough Field* is an expression of love for the childhood world, it is also a lament for what has been destroyed:

> Like shards
> Of a lost culture, the slopes
> Are strewn with cabins, deserted
> In my lifetime

Some of his best poems are tender portraits of old women, tributes to their fragility, their lives of service and of love. Often in Montague's work there is a numinous imaginative presence behind the poem. Many convey a sense of a hinterland of archetypal reference, as does 'All Legendary Obstacles', in which the relationship of the lovers is menaced by mythical and other -worldly forces.

Montague's poetic aim is to express things as clearly and luminously as possible, 'ritualising the details', seeking 'a slow exactness'. An early example is 'The Trout':

Bodiless lord of creation
I hung briefly above him
Savouring my own absence
Senses expanding in the slow
Motion, the photographic calm
That grows before action.

In the love poems the precision of language, the chaste diction and the finely controlled rhythm and syntax can be effective. While expressive at times of great gentleness, they also respond to the complex emotional range that may exist in a relationship.

In recent collections, *A Slow Dance* (1975) and *The Great Cloak* (1978), his work has become more earthy; where earlier poems move towards epiphany by indirection and intuition, these move more directly and more explicitly. The concerns are still landscape and people, a landscape enriched by archaeology and myth, and people seen quizzically and with affection.

Such a development in its sense of place and past, as well as in its use of language, points towards the achievement of other Northern poets, such as Seamus Heaney and Derek Mahon and a number of other poets, including Michael Longley and Paul Muldoon.

Seamus Heaney's early poetry respects craftsmanship. Asserting his ancestry within a farming community, he shows the validity of his claim in the skill of his own work, in poetry that is tidy and well-made. Following on Kavanagh's trust in the validity of the parish, he was also influenced by a Hopkinesque delight in the sensuous possibility of words and by Robert Frost's careful delineation of country life. But he sees beyond the immediate realities of the farm. Planting his feet firmly on the land he continued to deepen his awareness of the historical and mythical possibilities of the region. Like Kinsella and Montague he writes a poetry in which psychic and historical myth have a vital place. His Jungian sense of a layered past is affirmed in 'Bogland':

Our pioneers keep striking
Inwards and downwards,

Every layer they strip
Seems camped on before.

The bogholes might be Atlantic seepage.
The wet centre is bottomless.

This centre holds, as he says in another poem, echoing Yeats in a counter-echo. Part of his territorial claim is linguistic, the ability to read the landscape so that the vocables of place are miniscule signs of race and culture. His sense of the bogland was confirmed and enriched when he read P.V. Glob's account of the discovery of the bog people of Denmark, early iron-age victims of sacrificial rituals to the goddess of the earth. He was deeply moved both by the book's illustrations of the recovered bodies and by the account of the rediscovery; he found satisfying imaginative parallels between the violence in his own time in Northern Ireland and violence in Northern Europe. In a succession of 'bog poems' he responded to the parallels, declaring, in one of intended pilgrimage, that:

Out there in Jutland
In the old, man-killing parishes
I will feel lost,
Unhappy and at home.

The power of this parallel, so economically made, is characteristic of Heaney's skill. His collection, *North* (1975), explores these parallels: its poetry is aural, textured, delighting in the sensuous possibilities of language. 'Viking Dublin: Trial Pieces' is a free-wheeling excursion from the design on a particular artefact through allusions to Viking culture and trade, to the arrival of a longship in Dublin. 'Kinship', a declaration of faith in the bogland, is similar in its release of feelings, its joyful affirmation of origins, its self-delighting linguistic fluidities. *Field Work* (1979) marks a change to a plainer style. The 'I' figure speaks with authority. Heaney's 'Casualty' has, for example, the rhythms of Yeats's 'The Fisherman' and is also about a fisherman and about a life-style. The context of several poems is still the divisions and violence of Northern Ireland, but there are also poems of love and a sequence of complex sonnets about art and personality. The love poems and the elegies, together with the more direct mode of address, suggest that Heaney is moving to a more personal kind of poetry.

The titles of Derek Mahon's poems indicate his range and

aspirations: on the one hand are what one has come to expect form a Northern Irish poet, poems of place and of people, definitions of a personal context — the tradition runs from MacNeice, Hewitt, through Montague and Heaney; on the other hand are poems in which the definition is by literary allusions and cultural contexts. Mahon's aspiration towards a modernist idiom and an international scope is also recurrent in several modern Irish poets; in his case it is achieved by a skilful appropriation more than by imitation or technical influence. The filtering of Beckett's universe, for example, through images, rhythm and tone in 'Image from Beckett' is a good example of his controlled use of a literary connection; the poem takes the texture of Beckett's plays and creates a modern, bleak and unlocalised landscape. Just as Heaney takes the heritage of the Danish bog people and turns it back upon his own landscape, so Mahon, in creating the outlines of an apparently distant and non-Irish region, emphasises his own Northern world. His achievement in poems like this is to balance neatly between the local and the cosmopolitan; such poems touch fleetingly upon his childhood environment which remains the founding element in his work. There is also the tendency for the subliminal to surface through the concrete images and personal references as in 'A Disused Shed in Co. Wexford' or 'The Sea in Winter'. He is often close to Heaney in his sense of the deposits of the past affecting the present, although he is more responsive to the deterioration of civilisation. He has more wit than Heaney and a touch of mockery is characteristic of much of his work. Beginning as a romantic he has developed a shielding irony of manner, which is controlled by a lively intelligence, a fine ear for language, and a unique lightness of touch and tone.

The neo-realism of Mahon's work, with its exacting attention to detail and its refined use of language, is a characteristic of much contemporary poetry in Northern Ireland, where there is a strong sense of literary tradition. In part this is due to the concentration on fundamental personal and political issues that the continuing violence has brought about. While some poets have reacted grossly to the brutalities, and others with an uneasy levity, many have sought to view experience in a detached and sometimes oblique manner. They have pruned their work of linguistic excess, developed their technical skills and have been concerned with the well-made poem. Central to their work is the determination to analyse the situation in an intelligent, often ironic manner. Michael Longley, for example, has been less concerned with history than John Montague or Seamus Heaney. While tending to write about experience in an oblique manner and through the use of mythic and literary allusion, he can also write directly about love and family relationships. Poets are saddened by the tragedies of the North; naturally the issue runs through all of their work. At the same time, and again it is pervasive in their tradition, they are attracted to their own places of origin. The tension between revulsion and love results sometimes in a remarkable poignancy, heard in Montague, Heaney, Mahon, Muldoon and many others. Mahon's sense of the destruction of civilisation involves, as it does in others, the awareness of the destruction of human decencies. Poetry for him, as for Longley and Muldoon, gives witness to civilised procedures. The poets try to make themselves heard in a situation in which perhaps a numbed, inarticulate silence is the only general response.

In the South there is also evidence of some regionalist groupings, but there is greater individual diversity of manner, such as Patrick Galvin's poetry of dramatic self-awareness, Brendan Kennelly's belief in poetry as inseparable from fable, Eilean Ni Chuilleanáin's natural metaphysics, Eavan Boland's notations of feminist concerns, or Eugene Watters' visionary tone. Pearse Hutchinson and Michael Hartnett, in particular, respond positively to individuals whom they see as embodiments of folk traditions or culture. They are concerned with threatened ethnic groups and this includes a concern for the loss of a distinctive language. Hartnett's decision to write in Irish, after years of writing in English, is a manifestation of a widespread concern for the disappearance of the native language. A number of poets, but particularly Hutchinson, Hartnett and Watters, (who writes in Irish as Eoghan O Tuairaisc) write in both languages and translate from the Irish. Hutchinson, apart from his response to peripheral cultures, also writes of love and of a private grief, sometimes in appropriately disjointed syntax.

Sean O'Faolain used to explain the inhibiting conditions within which Irish literature was written and the generation that followed also felt isolated. Now conditions have improved. There is a wider and more perceptive public. Young writers, looking back at the course of Irish literature, particularly in the twentieth century, have a sense of a viable literary tradition.

III

It was in 1953 that Samuel Beckett's play, *En Attendant Godot,* was produced in Paris. It appeared in England as *Waiting for Godot* in 1955. Since then his principal stage-plays have been *Fin de Partie* (1956), *Endgame,* (1958), *Krapp's Last Tape* (1959), *Happy Days* (1961), *Play* (1962) and *Not I* (1971). He was awarded the Nobel Prize for literature in 1970.

Beckett began to write these plays as a relaxation from novel-writing, finding the dramatic form and its discipline a relief from the difficulty of searching for form in the novel. Their basis is metaphysical. They are explorations into the chaos of life by a writer who cannot see any trace of a system in it, who sees mankind as mainly impotent and ignorant in coping with it and who, while realising the probable futility of language to deal with it, must express his individual consciousness in artistic form. Perhaps the artistic success of some of his plays may contradict most of these assumptions and the ability of others to move international audiences may prove the validity of communication. Their author has said that the key-word in his plays is 'perhaps', that they deal with distress but that they have no message about or explanations of life. But if he has refused to provide exegesis he has given a general indication of what he is at by remarking that he is trying to chart a whole zone of being in the individual, the zone of distress, impotence and failure.

The principal characters are usually trapped by a situation. In *Godot* the two tramps must wait for Godot who may never come, if he exists. Hamm and Clov in *Endgame* have various forms of physical disability but, although the play seems to move towards their parting, they cannot part. In other plays the nature of the entrapment — by memory, age or guilt — is manifest, sometimes physically portrayed. There is never a resolution of the situation. It repeats itself, specifically or by implication.

The characters themselves, although presented in an arresting and surprising way, are ordinary and undistinguished. They are at once generalised, like the characters of morality plays, symbolic in their suggestive overtones, yet given such specific patterns of human behaviour, such marks of human suffering and humour, of frailty and aspiration, that they have a fundamentally human impact. By skilfully orchestrating their patterns of behaviour Beckett gives an effect of ritual, of mythology. His art is a very precise one, using analogy and repetition as its basis and the relationship of every detail of speech, acting, lighting and other elements of 'total theatre' in the whole design. Thus failure, entrapment, human misery and humour are given dramatic expression, although the total effect is sometimes too abstract and intellectual to register on a human audience.

This is the barest introduction to a body of highly complex individual dramatic work. The reader should experience the impact of the plays before seeking further information from the considerable body of commentary and exegesis which has gathered about them.

In Ireland the drama during the same period proceeded on less adventurous lines. The main event of the 1950s at first appeared to be the arrival of Brendan Behan (1923-64). His autobiography, *Borstal Boy* (1958), relates the circumstances of his Dublin life, his enlistment in the I.R.A., his imprisonment in England and Ireland, all of which gave him the material for his first play *The Quare Fellow* (1956). The title is a euphemism for a condemned man and the play is a study of the inmates of a Dublin prison as they await his execution. The method is naturalistic; the movement in time towards the execution gives a tension which braces the contrasting attitudes of the prisoners, the warders and the officials towards the event, whose horror is accentuated by the trivialities of routine and by many touches through which the shadow of the condemned man, who does not appear, seems to lie over the play. Graphic realism lit by flashes of poetry, song, gallows humour and biting wit gave a powerful impact to *The Quare Fellow*. Behan's next play, *The Hostage* (1958), was originally written for an Irish-speaking theatre and was a comparatively simple naturalistic play about a young girl's love for a captured British soldier, held hostage by a republican group. This he transformed, with some assistance, into a vaudeville entertainment, with many additions of characters, songs, dances and topical jokes. Deliberately rewritten for the commercial theatre, it succeeded on an international scale before Behan's premature death|in 1964.

That year saw the first performance of *Philadelphia, Here I Come!* The author, Brian Friel, was born in County Tyrone in 1929 and taught school until 1960, when he became a professional writer, publishing two volumes of short stories, *A Saucer of Larks* (1926) and *The Gold in the Sea* (1966). In *Philadelphia,* Friel used two characters to present the public and private selves of Gareth O'Donnell, a small shopkeeper's son, on the eve of his emigration from Donegal. The clash of the two selves brought out the usual pull between far horizons and loved certainties, village and urban life, but its deeper problem concerned Gareth's love for his father and their failure to communicate. This is a delicate and humorous comedy which was internationally successful. It marked the beginning of a series of worthwhile plays by a committed dramatist, which continued throughout the 1970s. *The Loves of Cass Maguire* (1966) was a sympathetic study of an ageing woman who returns from America to Ireland, to settle down with relatives whose respectable standards, clashing with her irrepressible lust for life, cause them to banish her to an old people's home. Here, as in *Lovers* (1967), Friel's strong talent for character drawing compensates for his tendency to use the explanatory devices of the flashback or the narrator. Characterisation was the strong point of *The Freedom of the City* (1973), a play based upon Derry's 'Bloody Sunday' in 1972, and of *Aristocrats* (1979), which showed a new strength in using a Chekhovian manner to reveal the characters and background of a Catholic family of property in Ulster. *The Faith Healer* (1979) and *Translations* (1980), a considerable artistic success, show an interesting range of experiment.

Friel's contemporary, Hugh Leonard, steadily produced adaptations and plays during the same period. His most successful adaptation was *Stephen D* (1960), based on James Joyce's *Portrait;* his plays, although they lack depth, are witty and entertaining, the work of a very competent dramatist. *Da* (1972) the nostalgic study of a father-son relationship, contained a deeper personal emotion and is his best play to date. It has been successful both in Ireland and abroad.

Looking back over the last twenty-five years one recalls some individual works of power; Tom Coffey's *Them* (1962), Eugene McCabe's *King of the Castle* (1964), Thomas Murphy's *A Whistle in the Dark* (1070) and *Morning after Optimism* (1971), Heno Magee's *Hatchet* (1972), Thomas Kilroy's *Talbot's Box* (1977) and Tom McIntyre's *Find the Lady* (1978). These dramatists are still writing and it remains to be seen whether a great dramatist emerges from their number. In some ways the *ambience* of the Irish theatre is favourable to this development. The Abbey Theatre has widened its scope considerably; the Arts Council encourages training; the amateur drama movement is more organised and has better standards; there is a lively ferment of dramatic activity among the younger groups.

In Belfast the fate of drama proved very uncertain after the Ulster Literary Theatre faded. In the twenties and thirties it was kept alive sporadically by the National Drama League, in the forties by the Ulster Group Theatre and, after its collapse, by the Belfast Arts Theatre. A continual difficulty was the lack of a permanent theatre in Belfast. Things began to change in 1951 through the foundation of the Lyric Players in 1951 by Mary and Pearse O'Malley. The formation of this dedicated group, guided mainly by Yeats's principles and a sense of the importance of international standards, led in 1968 to the opening of the Lyric Players' Theatre, now a respected dramatic and cultural centre. The work of this group in perspective can be seen to have repeated the pattern of the early Abbey Theatre and to have preserved its ideals, under the most difficult circumstances. That is an earnest of the survival of the imagination and ideas of Yeats and his companions; but only dedicated groups can achieve them.

Stamps commemorating Irish authors.

APPENDIX

The Irish-English Dialect of Synge's Plays

Synge used the characteristics of Irish-English speech more than any other Irish writer. Consequently his dramatic prose illustrates all its major distinctive qualities and its differences from standard English. The examples chosen are principally from *Riders to the Sea,* where Synge's writing is at its most austere.

In an English sentence subject, predicate and object are the normal order. In Irish the verb comes at the beginning of a sentence. Irish, like Spanish, has two words for 'is' ('is' and 'tá'). It has therefore a more flexible word-order than English, which relies upon a fixed word-order in the sentence. In English the fixed word-order is not changed by emphasis; in Irish it is, since the emphatic word is placed close to the verb at the beginning of a sentence: *Is it Bartley it is?; Will she see it was crying I was?; It's little the likes of him knows of the sea; It's getting old she is, and broken.*

Irish, unlike English, has no perfect and pluperfect tenses; Irish-English substitutes constructions with 'after'. *Isn't it nine days herself is after keening and crying? his body is after being found, I'm after seeing him this day.* The pluperfect equivalent would be conveyed by putting the verb into the past tense.

Irish, unlike English, has an habitual tense, expressed in Irish-English by 'do be'; *the young men do be leaving things behind them; the black hags that do be flying on the sea.*

Irish-English tends to drop relative pronouns, to substitute 'that' for all forms of the relative pronoun and to substitute Gaelic usages for English prepositional usages; *There was a man in here a while ago; the man sold us that knife; the black hags that do be flying; what way was he drowned?; I looked up then and I crying; there's no man in it to make the coffin; if it wasn't found itself; Isn't it sorrow enough is on everyone in this house.*

Another notable characteristic is the preference of Irish-English for the emphatic imperative; *Let no one say a word; let you not be afraid, let you and Nora get up weed, Let you go down now.*

In vocabulary there are several old English survivals inherited from the English speech of planters: *God speed you, It's hard set we'll be, I'll have no call to be up, What is it ails you?* There are also words borrowed from the Irish, 'keen', 'poteen'. Such borrowings widen the vocabulary of Synge and make it more individual.

In general the flexible word order of Irish-English, the cavalier treatment of relative clauses, the emphatic imperative, the vocabulary and idiom, promote a form of speech which lends itself to dramatic treatment. Synge's use of such characteristics is selective; it is heightened and moulded into a form which suits his own personal style but at the same time it has a basis in real speech. In *Riders to the Sea* the language is deliberately kept austere and simple to suit the nature of the primitive elements of the conflict between man, woman and the sea; *that wind is raising the sea, and there was a star up against the moon, and it rising in the night.* But one notices the artistic cadence of the following sentence: *If it was a hundred horses or a thousand horses you had itself, what is the price of a thousand horses against a son where there is one son only?* Such cadences are a repeated feature of Maurya's speeches.

One may turn from this quietly poetic prose to the exuberant lyrical prose of Christy's love-passage with Pegeen in Act III of the *Playboy*. All the speech characteristics already exemplified are to be found in it but there is a heightened vivid quality in the concrete, colourful phrases used to give reality to the play of the lovers' imaginations; *and I squeezing kisses on your puckered lips, till I'd feel a kind of pity for the Lord God is all ages sitting lonesome in His golden chair; if the mitred bishops seen you that time, they'd be the like of the holy prophets I'm thinking, do be straining the bars of paradise to lay eyes on the Lady Helen of Troy, and she abroad pacing back and forward with a nosegay in her golden shawl; And myself a girl was tempted to go sailing the seas till I'd marry a Jewman with ten kegs of gold.* Synge's belief that 'in a good play every speech should be as fully flavoured as a nut or apple' is strikingly exemplified. His cadences are not obtrusive but one discovers them easily at the end of sentences; *on the sides of Neifin, when the night is down; your like for eloquence or talk at all; drawing all times nearer to this holy day; in the Owen or the Carrowmore.* However intricate they are, they are never far removed from Irish-English cadence in speech.

Other features of Irish-English exploited by Synge are the habit of exaggeration (particularly in the *Playboy*) and the habit of answering one question by another. Amongst other characteristics which will be noted are the use of *will* in preference to *shall,* of *would* in preference to *should;* the use of *himself* or *herself* for the man or woman of the house. In many cases the departure from standard English is due to direct borrowing from Irish idiom; for example, the sentence *isn't it sorrow enough is on everybody in this house?* retains the Irish idiom of sorrow being *on* the sufferer like a burden.

For the closer study of Synge's language the following books will be found helpful; Alan Price, *Synge and Irish Drama* (1961); Alan Bliss, 'The Language of Synge' in *J.M. Synge Centenary Papers 1971* (ed. Harmon, 1972) and 'A Synge Glossary' in *A Centenary Tribute to J. M. Synge* (ed. Bushrui, 1970); Albert Favre, 'Le Langue Anglo-Irlandaise' in *Annales Universitaires,* Avignon (Mars 1978).

Notes

PART I

Chapter 1

1 'Early Irish History and Pseudo-History'. *Studia Hibernica*, 3, 1963, p.118.

2 *Buile Suibhne*, ed. J.G. O'Keeffe. Irish Texts Society, vol. XII. (London: David Nutt, 1913), p.153.

3 Quoted in part by Myles Dillon in *Early Irish Literature*, p.172.

4 Myles Dillon, 'Literary Activity in the Pre-Norman Period' in *Seven Centuries of Irish Learning*, p.24

Chapters 2, 3, 4 and 5.

1 All the quotations may be found, sometimes slightly modified, in Cross and Slover, *Ancient Irish Tales*.

2 See Myles Dillon, *Early Irish Literature, p.43*.

Chapter 6

1 All the quotations may be found in Kuno Meyer, *Ancient Irish Poetry*.

2 Samuel Ferguson, *Poems*, (Dublin: Talbot Press, 1916), p.182.

PART II

Chapter 7

1 Ó Cuív, Brian. *Seven Centuries of Irish Learning 1000-1700*, p.40.

2 Alspach, Russell K. *Irish Poetry from the English Invasion to 1798*, p.14.

3 Hoagland, Kathleen. *1000 years of Irish Poetry*, p.316-17.

4 Hoagland, p.319.

5 Alspach, p.23; Hoagland, p.306.

6 Spenser, Edmund. *View of the Present State of Ireland*, p.104

7 Spenser, p.75.

8 Ó Cuív. *Seven Centuries*, chapter III, p.42; Alspach, p.68.

Chapter 8

1 Clarke, Austin. *Collected Poems*, Dublin: Dolmen, 1974, p.318.

2 Quoted in Alan Bliss, *Spoken English in Ireland 1600-1704*. Dublin: Dolmen, 1979, pp.164-5.

3 Alspach, p.40.

4 Edited by Thomas Wall, Dublin: Gill, 1960.

5 *Poetical Works*, edited by Herbert Davis, London: Oxford University Press, 1967.

6 *Collected Works*, ed. Arthur Friedman, vol. III, p.119.

Chapter 9

1 On the other hand Johnson dedicated his *Journey to the Hebrides* to Edmund Malone, the Irish Shakespearean scholar.

PART III

Chapter 13

1 Standish O'Grady. *History of Ireland: Critical and Philosophical,* vol.1. London: Sampson Low, 1881, p.43.

PART IV

Chapter 14

1 W.B. Yeats. *Autobiography.* Garden City, N.Y.: Doubleday, 1958, p.67.

2 Katharine Tynan. *The Wild Harp; a selection from Irish Poetry.* London: Sidgwick & Jackson, 1913, p.xiii.

3 Douglas Hyde in *The Revival of Irish Literature,* ed. Charles G. Duffy. London: T. Fisher Unwin, 1894, p.118.

4 Lionel Johnson in *Poetry and Ireland: Essays by W.B. Yeats and Lionel Johnson.* Dublin: Cuala Press, 1908, p.37.

5 *Letters from AE.* Selected and edited by Alan Denson. London: Abelard-Schuman, 1961, p.13.

6 Austin Clarke. *Poetry in Modern Ireland.* Dublin: Sign of the Three Candles. 1951, p.18.

7 W.K. Magee, whose critical essays were published in *Two Essays on the Remnant* (1894) and *Pebbles from a Brook* (1901). His friendly criticism was unusually objective and is well worth reading.

8 George Russell. *Imaginations and Reveries.* Dublin: Maunsell, 1915, pp.43-44.

Chapter 15

1 See also Dan H. Lawrence and David H. Greene, eds. *The Matter with Ireland.* New York: Hill & Wang, 1962.

2. Miss Horniman was the lessee. As she was not resident in Ireland, Lady Gregory became the official patentee.

3 Gerard Fay. *The Abbey Theatre. Cradle of Genius.* Dublin: Clonmore and Reynolds, 1958, p.109.

4 W.G. Fay and Catherine Carswell. *The Fays of the Abbey Theatre.* London: Rich and Cowan, 1935, p.231.

Chapter 16

1 Synge's observations, quoted in this chapter, are to be found in *Collected Works.* London: Oxford University Press, vol. II Prose, 1966 and vol. IV, ii Plays, 1968.

2 See Appendix: "The Irish-English Dialect of Synge's Plays".

3 F. R. Higgins "Yeats and Poetic Drama in Ireland" in Lennox Robinson. *The Irish Theatre*. London: Macmillan, 1939, p. 73.

Chapter 17

1 Quoted in Joseph Hone, *The Life of George Moore*. London: Gollancz, 1936, p. 262.

PART V

Chapter 19

1 Joseph Hone. *W. B. Yeats 1865-1939*. London: Macmillan, 1942, p. 185.

2 Joseph Ronsley. *Yeats's Autobiography: Life as Symbolic Pattern*, Cambridge, Mass: Harvard University Press 1968, p. 3.

3 A. G. Stock. *W. B. Yeats. His Poetry and Thought*. Cambridge: University Press, 1964, pp. 122-123.

4 See also the best lyrics of Patrick Macdonogh (1902-61) which appear in *A Leaf in the Wind* (1929) and *One Landscape Still* (1958).

5 *Twelve Poems* (1942) shows his early promise as a poet, but he is chiefly known for his elegant *Dublin 1660-1860* (1952).

Chapter 20

1 Sean O'Faolain, "Emancipation of Irish Writers," *Yale Review*, 23 (Spring, 1934), 492.

2 Sean O'Faolain, "Autobiographical Sketch," *Wilson Bulletin*, 8, 6 (March, 1934), 380.

3 Thomas Flanagan, "The Irish Writer" in *Michael/Frank*, ed. Maurice Sheehy. New York: Knopf, 1969, p. 162.

4 H. Porter Abbott. *The Fiction of Samuel Beckett; Form and Effect*. Berkeley: University of California Press, 1973, p. 67.

5 Abbott, p. 114.

6 Abbott, p. 131.

7 Raymond Federman. *Journey to Chaos, Samuel Beckett's Early Fiction*. Berkeley: University of California Press, 1965, p. 9.

Chapter 21

1 It did, however, produce Jack B. Yeats's *La La Noo* in 1942, while his *In Sand* was performed by the Abbey Experimental Theatre in 1949. Jack Yeats's plays were highly individual, inconsequential and associative, often more conversation than plays. They were not collected until 1971 (ed. Skelton).

2 They were a versatile couple. He wrote poems, translations from the Irish, and plays. She wrote novels, historical plays and slight comedies. She died in 1980.

Chapter 22

1 Mairtin O Cadhain, "Irish Prose in the Twentieth Century" in J.E. Caerwyn Williams. *Literature in Celtic Countries*. Cardiff: University of Wales Press, 1971, p. 151.

PART VI

Chapter 23

1 Thomas Kinsella in *Directions*, Springfield, Illinois, 1966-67.

Bibliography

The bibliographies provided for each Part are selective, relating
mainly to works mentioned in the text. More complete bibliographies
may be found by consulting the books listed below.

GENERAL

The British National Bibliography.
London: British Library, 1950 —.

Contemporary Authors: a bio-bibliographical guide to current authors and their work.
Detroit: Gale Research Co., 1963
—. Vol. 1 —. Semi-annual.

Contemporary Writers of the English Language. 3 vols. London: St. James Press, 1970 — 1973. Triennial revision.

Eager, Alan. *A Guide to Irish Bibliographical Material.* London: Library Association. 2nd edition, 1980.

Finneran, Richard. *Anglo-Irish Literature. A Review of Research.* New York: Modern Language Association, 1976. Five year supplement in preparation.

Harmon, Maurice. *Select Bibliography for the Study of Anglo-Irish Literature and its Backgrounds. An Irish Studies Handbook.* Dublin: Wolfhound, 1977.

Hogan, Robert. *The Macmillan Dictionary of Irish Literature.* New York: Macmillan, 1980.

The New Cambridge Bibliography of English Literature. Cambridge: Cambridge University Press, 5 vols., 1969-1975. Volumes not published in numerical order. Vol. 3 has Anglo-Irish nineteenth century literature; vol. 4 includes twentieth century Irish writers, 1900-1950.

Modern Language Association of America. *International Bibliography of Books and Articles on the modern languages and literature.* New York: Modern Language Association, 1922 —. Since 1970 has a separate fascicle on English, Anglo-Irish and American literature.

McKenna, Brian. *Irish Literature 1800-1875. A Guide to Information Sources.* Detroit: Gale Research Co., 1978. Vo. 2 will cover 1876-1950.

HISTORY: GENERAL

History books for particular periods are listed in the bibliographies for each Part.

Beckett, J.C. *The Making of Modern Ireland 1603-1923.* London: Faber, 1966 (reprint, 1969).

Curtis, Edmund. *A History of Ireland.* London: Methuen, 1936 (reprint, 1960).

Freeman, T.W. *Ireland, its Physical, Historical, Social and Economic Geography.* London: Methuen, 1950.

Moody, T.W. and F.X. Martin. *The Course of Irish History.* Cork: Mercier, 1967.

Moody, T.W., F.X. Martin and F.J. Byrne. *A New History of Ireland.* 9 vols. Oxford: Clarendon, 1976. In progress.

Lydon, James and Margaret Mac Curtain, *The Gill History of Ireland.* 10 vols. Dublin: Gill and Macmillan, 1972-75.

PART 1

HISTORY

Bieler, Ludwig. *Ireland: Harbinger of the Middle Ages.* London: Oxford University Press, 1963.

Byrne, Francis John. *Irish Kings and High-Kings.* London: Batsford, 1973.

de Paor, Maire and Liam. *Early Christian Ireland.* London: Thames and Hudson, 1958.

Hughes, Kathleen. *The Church in Early Irish Society.* London: Methuen, 1966.

O'Rahilly, T.F. *Early Irish History and Mythology.* Dublin: Dublin Institute for Advanced Studies, 1946.

Otway-Ruthven, A.J. *A History of Medieval Ireland.* London: Benn, 1968.

LITERARY STUDIES

Bergin, Osborn. *Irish Bardic Poetry.* Dublin: Dublin Institute for Advanced Studies, 1970.

Dillon, Myles. *The Cycles of the Kings.* London: Cumberlege, Oxford University Press, 1946.

Dillon, Myles. *Early Irish Literature.* Chicago: University of Chicago Press, 1948. (reprint, 1969).

Dillon, Myles. *Early Irish Society.* Dublin: The Sign of the Three Candles, 1954. (reprint, 1959).

Dillon, Myles. *Irish Sagas.* Dublin: Stationery Office, 1959. (reprint 1968).

Flower, Robin. *The Irish Tradition.* Oxford: Clarendon Press, 1947. (reprint, 1978).

Jackson, Kenneth. *The Oldest Irish Tradition: a window on the Iron Age.* Cambridge: Cambridge University Press, 1964.

Jackson, Kenneth. *Studies in early Celtic Nature Poetry.* Cambridge:

Cambridge University Press, 1935. (reprint, 1977).

Knott, Eleanor. *Irish Classical Poetry.* Dublin: The Sign of The Three Candles, 1957. (reprint, 1960).

MacCana, Proinsias. *Celtic Mythology.* London: Thames and Hudson, 1970.

Murphy, Gerard. *The Ossianic Lore and Romantic Tales of Medieval Ireland.* Dublin: The Sign of the Three Candles, 1955. (reprint, 1971).

Murphy, Gerard. *Saga and Myth in Ancient Ireland.* Dublin: The Sign of the Three Candles, 1961. (reprint, 1971).

Ó Cuív, Brian. *Seven Centuries of Irish Learning 1000 — 1700.* Dublin: Stationery Office, 1961. (reprint, 1971).

Rees, A. and B. Rees. *Celtic Heritage: ancient tradition in Ireland and Wales.* London: Thames and Hudson, 1961.

COLLECTIONS

Carney, James. *Medieval Irish Lyrics.* Dublin: Dolmen Press, 1967.

Cross, T.P. and C.H. Slover. *Ancient*

Irish Tales. London: Harrap, 1935. (reprint, 1969).

Flower, Robin. *Poems and Translations.*

London: Constable, 1931.

Greene, David and Frank O'Connor. *A Golden Treasury of Irish Poetry, A.D. 630 — 1200*. London: Macmillan, 1967.

Jackson, Kenneth. *A Celtic Miscellany: translations from the Celtic Literatures*. London: Routledge and Kegan Paul, 1951. (reprint, 1971).

Kinsella, Thomas. *The Tain*. Dublin: Dolmen Press, 1969. (reprint, 1980).

Knott, Eleanor. *Irish Syllabic Poetry*

1200-1600. Dublin: Dublin Institute for Advanced Studies, 1957, (revised ed. 1974)

Meyer, Kuno. *Ancient Irish Poetry*. London: Constable, 1911. (reprint, 1959).

Murphy, Gerard. *Early Irish Lyrics*. Oxford: Clarendon Press, 1956.

O'Connor, Frank. *Kings, Lords and Commons*. New York: Knopf, 1959. London: Macmillan, 1961.

O'Faolain, Sean. *The Silver Branch*. London: Jonathan Cape, 1938.

PART 11

HISTORY

Bagwell, Richard. *Ireland under the Stuarts 1603-91*. 3 vols. London: Longman's Green, 1909-16.

Barrington, Jonah. *Personal Sketches*. London: Colburn, Colburn & Bentley, 1827-32.

Barrington, Jonah. *The Rise and Fall of the Irish Nation*. Paris: Bennis, 1833.

Dolley, Michael. *Anglo-Norman Ireland* Dublin: Gill and Macmillan, 1972.

Dowling, P.J. *The Hedge Schools of Ireland*. Dublin: Talbot, 1935.

Froude, J.A. *The English in Ireland in the Eighteenth Century*. 3 vols. London: Longman's Green, 1887.

Johnston, Edith Mary. *Ireland in the Eighteenth Century*. Dublin: Gill and Macmillan, 1974.

Keating, Geoffrey. *History of Ireland,* Irish · Texts Society, 1 — 1V. London: Nutt, 1902-1914.

Lecky, W.E.H. *Ireland in the Eighteenth Century*. 5 vols, London: Longmans, 1892.

Lecky, W.E.H. *Leaders of Public Opinion in Ireland*. 2 vols. London: Longmans, Green, 1912.

Lydon, James. *Ireland in the Late Middle Ages*. Dublin: Gill and Macmillan, 1973.

Nicholls, Kenneth. *Gaelic and Gaelicised Ireland in the Middle Ages*. Dublin: Gill and Macmillan, 1972.

Moody, T.W., F.X. Martin and F.J. Byrne. *Early Modern Ireland 1534-1691*. Oxford: Clarendon, 1976.

Orpen, G.H. *Ireland under the Normans 1169-1333*. 4 vols. Oxford: Clarendon, 1911-20.

Otway-Ruthven, A.J. *A History of Medieval Ireland*. London: Benn, 1968.

Spenser, Edmund. *View of the Present State of Ireland,* ed. W.L. Renwick. Oxford: Clarendon, 1934. (reprint 1970).

Young, Arthur. *Tour in Ireland, 1776-9,* ed. A.W. Hutton, 2 vols. London: Bell, 1892.

LITERARY HISTORY

Alspach, Russell K. *Irish Poetry from the English Invasion to 1798.* Philadelphia; University of Pennsylvania, 1943. 2nd. ed. 1959, 1964.

Bliss, Alan. *Spoken English in Ireland 1600-1740.* Dublin: Dolmen, 1979.

Corkery,| Daniel. *The Hidden Ireland.* Dublin: Gill, 1924 (reprint |1970).

De Blacam, A. *Gaelic Literature Surveyed.* Dublin: Talbot, 1929 (rev., 1973).

Hyde, Douglas. *A Literary History of Ireland from the earliest times to the present day.* London: Unwin, 1899.

(rev., 1967).

Mercier, Vivian. *The Irish Comic Tradition.* Oxford: Clarendon, 1962. (rev., 1969).

Ó Cuív, Brian. *Seven Centuries of Irish Learning 1000-1700.* Cork: Mercier, 1961. (reprint, 1971).

Power, Patrick. *A Literary History of Ireland.* Cork: Mercier, 1969.

Ryan, Desmond. *The Sword of Light from the Four Masters to Douglas Hyde, 1636-1938.* London: Barker, 1939.

Seymour, St. John D. *Anglo-Irish Literature, 1200-1582.* Cambridge: University Press, 1929 (reprint, 1973).

COLLECTIONS

Brooke, Charlotte. *Reliques of Irish Poetry.* Dublin: G. Bonham, 1789. 2nd. ed., 1816.

Hardiman, James. *Irish Minstrelsy.* 2 vols. London: J. Robins, 1831. (reprint, 1971).

Hoagland, Kathleen. *1000 Years of Irish Poetry.* New York: Devin-Adair, 1947.

Joyce, P. W. *Irish Music and Song.* Dublin: Gill, 1888.

O'Lochlainn, Colm. *Irish Street Ballads.* Dublin: Sign of the Three Candles, 1939.

O'Lochlainn, Colm. *More Irish Street Ballads.* Dublin: Sign of the Three Candles, 1965.

Ó Tuama, Seán and Thomas Kinsella. *An Duanare 1600-1900: Poems of the dispossessed.* Dublin: Dolman, 1981

TEXTS

Berkeley, George. *Works,* edited by A. C. Fraser, Oxford: Clarendon, 1871.

Burke, Edmund. *Letters, Speeches and Tracts on Irish Affairs,* edited by Mathew Arnold. London: Macmillan, 1881.
Fussell, Paul. *The Rhetorical World of Augustan Humanism: Ethics and Imagery from Swift to Burke.* London:

Oxford University Press, 1965
Mahoney, Thomas H. D. *Edmund Burke and Ireland.* Cambridge: Harvard, 1960.

Dunkin, William. *Select Poetical Works.* 2 vols. Dublin: W. G. Jones, 1767-70.

Farewell, James. *The Irish Hudibras.* London: Richard Baldwin, 1689.

Goldsmith, Oliver. *Collected Works,* edited by Arthur Friedman. Oxford: Clarendon, 1966.

Sells, A. Lytton. *Oliver Goldsmith, His Life and Works.* London: Allen & Unwin, 1974.

Grattan, Henry. *Speeches of the Right Honourable Henry Grattan,* edited by his Son. London: Longmans, Hunt; Dublin: Milliken, 1822. See also Henry Grattan, *Memoirs of the Life and Times of Henry Grattan.* London: H. Colburn, 1839-46.

Swift, Jonathan. *Poetical Works* edited by Herbert Davis. London: Oxford, 1967.

Swift, Jonathan. *Prose Writings,* edited by Herbert Davis, vols. IX, XI, XII. Irish Writings. Oxford: Blackwell, 1948, 1951, 1955.

Ferguson, Oliver. *Jonathan Swift and Ireland.* Urbana: University of Illinois, 1962.

Teerink, Herman. *A Bibliography of the Writings of Jonathan Swift,* 2nd ed. revised by A. H. Scouten. Philadelphia: University of Pennsylvania, 1963.

Tone, Wolfe Tone. *Autobiographies,* edited by R. B. O'Brien, 2 vols. Dublin: Phoenix, 1893.

Tone, William T. Wolfe. *Life of Theobald Wolfe Tone.* Washington: Gales and Seaton, 1826.

Wadding, Luke. *A Pious Garland being the December letters and Christmas carols* of Luke Wadding, bishop of Ferns 1683-1688, edited by Thomas Wall. Dublin: Gill, 1960.

Whyte, Laurence. *Original Poems on Various Subjects.* Dublin: Powell, 1740.

PART 111

HISTORY

Connell, K. H. *The Population of Ireland 1750-1845.* Oxford: Clarendon, 1950.

De Freine, Sean. *The Great Silence.* Dublin: Foilseacháin Náisiúnta Teo., 1965.

Edwards, R. Dudley and T. D. Williams. *The Great Famine.* Dublin, 1956.

Lyons, F. S. L. *The Fall of Parnell.* London: Routledge & Kegan Paul, 1960.

Lyons, F. S. L. *Ireland since the Famine.* London: Weidenfeld & Nicolson, 1971, (rev. 1973).

McDowell, R. B. *Public Opinion and Government Policy in Ireland, 1801-1846.* London: Faber, 1952.

Mansergh, Nicholas. *The Irish Question, 1840-1927.* London: Allen & Unwin, 1965, (rev. 1975).

O'Faolain, Sean. *King of the Beggars* London: Nelson, 1938.

Woodham-Smith, Cecil. *The Great Hunger.* London: Hamish Hamilton, 1962

LITERARY HISTORY

Brown, Malcolm. *The Politics of Irish Literature from Thomas Davis to W. B. Yeats.* London: Allen & Unwin, 1972.

Cronin, John. *The Anglo-Irish Novel.* Vol. 1: The Nineteenth Century. Belfast: Appletree, 1980.

Flanagan, Thomas. *The Irish Novelists 1800-1850.* New York: Columbia, 1959.

MacDonagh, Thomas. *Literature in Ireland: Studies Irish and Anglo-Irish.* Dublin: Talbot, 1916.

Power, Patrick C. *The Story of Anglo-Irish Poetry. 1800-1922.* Cork: Mercier, 1967.

Welch, Robert. *Irish Poetry from Moore to Yeats.* Gerrard's Cross: Smythe, 1980.

COLLECTIONS

Brooks, S. A. and T. W. Rolleston. *A Treasury of Irish Poetry.* New York: Macmillan, 1932.

Cooke, John. *The Dublin Book of Irish Verse. 1728-1909.* Dublin: Hodges & Figgis, 1909.

Hoagland, Kathleen. *1000 Years of Irish Poetry.* New York: Devin-Adair 1947.

Kennelly, Brendan. *Penguin Book of Irish Verse.* Penguin: Harmondsworth, 1970.

Montague, John. *Faber Book of Irish Verse.* London: Faber, 1974.

Taylor, Geoffrey. *Irish Poets of the 19th Century.* London: Routledge & Kegan Paul, 1951.

TEXTS

Allingham, William. *Laurence Bloomfield in Ireland.* London: Macmillan, 1864.
Poems, ed. John Hewitt. Dublin: Dolmen, 1967.
Warner, Alan. *William Allingham: an Introduction.* Dublin: Dolmen, 1971.

Banim, John and Michael Banim. *Tales of the O'Hara Family.* London: Colburn, 1825-29.
Crohoore of the Billhook. London: Simpkin & Marshall, 1825.
The Boyne Water. London: Simpkin & Marshall, 1826.
The Croppy. London: Colburn, 1828.
The Nowlans. London: Colburn,

1826
The Last Baron of Crana. London: Colburn & Bentley, 1830.
The Conformists. London: Colburn & Bentley, 1830.
Hawthorne, Mark D. *John and Michael Banim (the O'Hara Brothers).* Salzburg: Institüt für Englische Sprache und Literatur, 1975.

Berkeley, George. *The Works of George Berkeley.* London: Nelson, 1948-1975. See in particular *The Principles of Human Knowledge* and *Three Dialogues.* ·

Callanan, Jeremiah Joseph. *The Poems of J. J. Callanan.* Cork: Bolster, 1847.

Carleton, William. *Traits and Stories of*

the Irish Peasantry. Dublin: Wakeman, 1830-33.

Fardorougha, the Miser. Dublin: Curry, 1839.

Valentine M'Clutchy, the Irish Agent. Dublin: Duffy, 1845.

Art Maguire or the Broken Pledge. Dublin: Duffy, 1845.

Parra Sastha or the History of Paddy-go-Easy. Dublin: Duffy, 1845.

The Black Prophet. Belfast: Simms & McIntyre, 1847.

The Emigrants of Ahadarra. London Simms & McIntyre, 1848.

The Tithe Proctor. London: Simms & McIntyre, 1849.

The Life of William Carleton, ed. D. J. O'Donoghue 2 vols. London: Downey, 1896.

Boué, André. *William Carleton, 1794-1869, romancier Irlandais.* Villeneuve D'Ascq: Université de Lille, 1973.

Kiely, Benedict. *Poor Scholar.* New York: Sheed & Ward, 1948.

Wolff, Robert Lee. *William Carleton, last Peasant Novelist.* New York: Garland, 1980.

Croker, Thomas Crofton. *Fairy Legends and Traditions of the South of Ireland.* London: Murray, 1825.

Darley, George. *Selected Poems,* ed. Anne Ridler. London: Merrion Press, 1979.

Davis, Thomas. *The Poems of Thomas Davis.* Dublin: Duffy, 1846.

Literary and Historical Essays. Dublin: Duffy, 1846.

De Vere, (Sir) Aubrey. *The Lamentation of Ireland and Other Poems.* London: Pickering, 1847.

De Vere, Aubrey. *Poetical Works.* London: Kegan Paul, 1898.

Reilly, Mary Paraclita. *Aubrey De Vere, Victorian Observer.* Lincoln: University of Nebraska, 1953.

Edgeworth, Maria. *Castle Rackrent.* London: Johnson, 1800.

Ennui. London: Johnson, 1909.

The Absentee. London: Johnson, 1812.

Ormond. London: Hunter, Baldwin, Cradock & Joy, 1817.

McWhorter Harden, O. Elizabeth. *Maria Edgeworth's Art of Prose Fiction.* The Hague: Mouton, 1971.

Newby, Percy H. *Maria Edgeworth.* London: A. Barker, 1950.

Ferguson, Sir Samuel. *Lays of the Western Gael.* London: Bell & Daldy, 1865.

Congal. Dublin: Ponsonby, 1872.

Poems. Dublin: McGee, 1880.

Brown, Malcolm. *Sir Samuel Ferguson.* Lewisburg, Pa.: Bucknell University Press, 1973.

O'Driscoll, Robert. *An Ascendancy of the Heart: Ferguson and the Beginnings of Modern Irish Literature in English.* Dublin: Dolmen, 1976.

Griffin, Gerald. *Tales of the Munster Festivals.* London: Saunders & Otley, 1826-27.

Holland Tide. London: Simpkin & Marshal, 1827.

The Collegians. London: Saunders & Otley, 1829.

The Christian Physiologist. London: Bull, 1830.

The Rivals. London: Saunders & Otley, 1830.

Tracy's Ambition. London: Saunders & Otley, 1829.

The Invasion. London: Saunders & Otley, 1832.

Tales of My Neighbourhood. London: Saunders & Otley, 1829.

The Duke of Monmouth. London: Bentley, 1836.

Tales of the Jury Room. London: Maxwell. 1842.

Adventures of an Irish Giant. Boston: Donahoe, 1854.

Cronin, John. *Gerald Griffin.* London: Cambridge University Press, 1978.

Kennedy, Patrick. *Legends of Mount Leinster*. Dublin: Kennedy, 1855.
Legendary fictions of the Irish Celts. London: Macmillan, 1866.
Banks of the Boro. Dublin: M'Glashan & Gill, 1867.
Evenings in the Duffrey. Dublin: M'Glashan & Gill, 1869.

Kickham, Charles. *Sally Cavanagh*. Dublin: Kelly, 1869.
Knocknagow. Dublin: Duffy, 1879.
Comerford, R. V. *Charles J. Kickham*. Dublin: Wolfhound, 1980.

Lalor, James Fintan. *Collected Writings*. Dublin: Maunsel, 1918.

Larminie, William. *Fand and Other Poems*. Dublin: Hodges & Figgis, 1892.

Leadbeater, Mary. *The Leadbeater Papers*. London: Bell & Daldy, 1862.

Le Fanu, Joseph Sheridan. *The House by the Churchyard*. London: Tinsley, 1863.
Uncle Silas. London: Bentley, 1864.
Wylder's Hand. London: Bentley, 1864.
Begnal, Michael. *Joseph Sheridan Le Fanu*. Lewisburg, Pa.: Bucknell Univesity Press, 1971.
McCormack, W. J. *Sheridan Le Fanu and Victorian Ireland*. London: Oxford University Press, 1980.

Lever, Charles. *The Confessions of Harry Lorrequer*. Dublin: Curry, June, 1839.
Charles O'Malley, The Irish Dragoon. Dublin: Curry, 1841.
Jack Hinton. Dublin: Curry, 1843.
Tom Burke of Ours. Dublin: Curry, 1844.
Arthur O'Leary. London: Colburn, 1844.
The O'Donoghue. Dublin: Curry, 1845.
St. Patrick's Eve. London: Chapman & Hall, 1845.

The Knight of Gwynne. London: Chapman & Hall, 1847.
The Martins of Cro Martin. London: Chapman & Hall, 1856.
Stevenson, Lionel. *Dr. Quicksilver: The Life of Charles Lever*. London: Chapman & Hall, 1939.

Lover, Samuel. *Legends and Stories of Ireland*. Dublin: Wakeman, 1831.
Handy Andy. London: F. Lover, 1842.

Maginn, William. *Miscellaneous Writings of the Late Dr. Maginn*, ed. R. Shelton Mackenzie. New York: Redfield, 1855-1857.

Mahony, Francis Sylvester. *The Reliques of Father Prout*. London: Fraser, 1836.
Mannin, Ethel. *Two Studies in Integrity*. London: Jarrolds, 1954.

Mangan, James Clarence. *Poems*, ed. D. J. O'Donoghue. Dublin: Gill, 1903.
Donaghy, Henry J. *James Clarence Mangan*. New York: Twayne, 1974.

Maturin, Charles. *The Fatal Revenge; or Family of Montorio*. London: Longman's Hurst, Rees & Orme, 1807.
The Wild Irish Boy. London: Longman's Hurst, Rees, & Orme, 1808.
The Milesian Chief. London: Colburn, 1812.
Melmoth the Wanderer. Edinburgh: Constable, 1820.

Mitchel, John. *The Life and times of Aodh O'Neill*. Dublin: Duffy, 1845.
Jail Journal. New York: The Citizen, 1854.
The Last Conquest of Ireland (Perhaps). Dublin: *The Irishman* Office, 1861.

Moore, Thomas. *Irish Melodies*. London Power, 1808-1834.
Lalla Rookh. London: Longman, Hurst, Orme & Brown, 1817.

deFord, Miriam Allen. *Thomas Moore*. New York: Twayne, 1967.

Morgan, Lady. *The Wild Irish Girl*. London: Phillips, 1806.
Florence MacCarthy. London: Colburn 1818.
O'Donnel. London: Colburn, 1814.
The O'Briens and the O'Flahertys. London: Colburn, 1827.
Stevenson, Lionel. *The Wild Irish Girl*. New York: Russell & Russell, 1936.

O'Curry, Eugene. *Lectures on the Manuscript Materials of Ancient Irish History*. Dublin: Duffy, 1861.
On the Manners and Customs of the Ancient Irish. London: Williams & Norgate, 1873.

O'Donovan, John. *Annals of the Kingdom of Ireland by the Four Masters*. Dublin: Hodges, Smith, 1848-51.

O'Grady, Standish James. *History of Ireland: Heroic Period*. London: Sampson Low, Searle, Marston & Rivington, 1878.
History of Ireland: Cuchulain and his Contemporaries. London: Sampson Low, 1880.
The Bog of Stars. London: Fisher Unwin, 1893.
The Flight of the Eagle. London: Lawrence & Bullen, 1897.
Marcus, Phillip. *Standish O'Grady*. Lewisburg, Pa.: Bucknell University Press, 1970.

Petrie, George. *The Ecclesiastical Architecture of Ireland*. Dublin: Hodges & Smith, 1845.
The Petrie Collection of the Ancient Music of Ireland. Dublin: University Press, 1855-1882.

Walsh, Edward. *Reliques of Irish Jacobite Poetry*. Dublin: Machen, 1844.

PART IV

HISTORY 1890-1920

Caulfield, Max. *The Easter Rebellion*. London: Muller, 1963: New York: Holt, Rinehart, Winston, 1964.

Holt, Edgar. *Protest in Arms. The Irish Troubles. 1916-1923*. London: Putnam, 1960; New York: Coward, McCann, 1961.

Kain, Richard. *Dublin in the Age of W. B. Yeats and James Joyce*. Norman, Oklahoma: University of Oklahoma Press, 1962.

Larkin, Emmet. *The Roman Catholic Church and the Creation of the Modern Irish State, 1878-1886*. Philadelphia: American Philosophical Society. 1975.

Lee, J. J. *The Modernisation of Irish Society 1848-1914*. Dublin: Gill and Macmillan, 1963.

McHugh, Roger. *Dublin 1916*. London: Arlington, 1966.

Mansergh, Nicholas. *The Irish Question 1840-1921*. London: Allen & Unwin, 1965.

O'Brien, Conor Cruise. *The Shaping of Modern Ireland*. London: Routledge & Kegan Paul, 1960.

O'Hegarty, P. S. *Ireland Under the Union 1800-1922*. London: Methuen, 1952.

Williams, T. D. *The Irish Struggle, 1916-26*. London: Routledge & Kegan Paul, 1966.

LITERARY HISTORY

Bell, Sam Hanna. *The Theatre in Ulster: a survey of the dramatic movement in Ulster from 1902 to the present day.* Dublin: Gill and Macmillan, 1972.

Boyd, Ernest.*Ireland's Literary Renaissance.* Dublin: Maunsel, 1916; Allen Figgis, 1969.

Costello, Peter. *The Heart Grown Brutal. The Irish Revolution in Literature from Parnell to the death of Yeats 1891-1939.* Dublin: Gill and Macmillian, 1977.

Ellis-Fermor, Una. *The Irish Dramatic Movement.* London: Methuen, 1939.

Fallis, Richard. *The Irish Renaissance.* Syracuse: Syracuse University Press, 1977.

Hogan, Robert and James Kilroy. *The Modern Irish Drama.* Dublin: Dolmen, 1975- in progress.

Howarth, Herbert. *The Irish Writers. 1880-1940.* London: Rockliff, 1958.

Hunt, Hugh. *The Abbey: Ireland's National Theatre. 1904-1978.* Dublin: Gill and Macmillan, 1979.

Loftus, Richard. *Nationalism in Modern Anglo-Irish Poetry.* Madison University of Wisconsin Press, 1964.

Malone, A. E. *The Irish Drama.* London: Constable, 1929.

Marcus, Phillip L. *Yeats and the Beginnings of the Irish Renaissance.* Ithaca and London: Cornell University Press, 1970.

Thompson, William. *The Imagination of an Insurrection: Dublin, Easter 1916.* New York: Oxford University Press, 1961.

Watson, G. J. *Irish Identity and the Literary Revival.* London: Croom Helm, 1979.

TEXTS

AE (George Russell). George. *Homeward Songs by the Way.* Dublin: Whaley, 1894.
The Earth Breath. London: John Lane, 1896.
New Poems. Dublin: O'Donoghue, 1904
Deirdre. Dublin: Maunsell, 1907.
Collected Poems. London: Macmillan, 1913.
Imaginations and Reveries. Dublin & London: Mansel, 1915.
The National Being. Dublin & London: Mansel, 1915.
The Candle of Vision. London: Macmillan, 1918.
Collected edition in preparation by Colin Smythe, London, 1980-.
Summerfield, Henry. *That Myriad-Minded Man: A Biography of G. W. Russell — "A.E."* Totowa, N.J.: Rowman & Littlefield, 1975.
Denson, Alan. *Printed Writings of George Russell (AE).* Evanston, Ill.: Northwestern University Press, 1961.
Barlow, Jane. *Irish Idylls.* London: Hodder & Stoughton, 1892.
Bogland Studies. London: Unwin, 1892.
Birmingham, George. *Hyacinth.* London: Edward Arnold. 1906
The Northern Iron. Dublin: Maunsel, 1907.
Spanish Gold. London: Methuen, 1908.
General John Regan. London: Hodder & Stoughton, 1913.

Boucicault, Dion. *London Assurance.*
London: private printing, 1841.
The Dolmen Press Boucicault. Dublin:
Dolmen Press, 1964; contains *The
Colleen Bawn, Arrah-na-Pogue,* and
The Shaughraun.
Hogan, Robert. *Dion Boucicault.*
New York: Twayne, 1969.

Boyle, William. *The Building Fund.*
Dublin: Maunsel, 1905.
The Eloquent Dempsy. Dublin: Gill,
1911.

Bullock, Shan F. *By Thrasna River.*
London: Ward, Lock & Bowden,
1895.
Ring O'Rushes. London: Ward,
Lock & Bowden, 1896.
Irish Pastorals. London: Grant
Richards, 1901.
The Squireen. London: Methuen,
1903.
Dan the Dollar. Dublin: Maunsel,
1905.
The Loughsiders. London: Harrap,
1924.

Campbell, Joseph. *The Mountainy Singer.*
Dublin: Maunsel, 1909.
Irishry. Dublin & London:
Maunsel, 1913.
Poems, ed. Austin Clarke. Dublin:
Figgis, 1963.

Casement, Roger. *Some Poems.* Dublin:
Talbot Press, 1918.

Carberry, Ethna. *The Four Winds of
Erin.* Dublin: Gill, 1902.

Casey, W. F. Plays are unpublished.

Colum, Padraic. *The Land.* Dublin:
Abbey Theatre, 1905.
Wild Earth. Dublin: Maunsel,
1907.
The Fiddler's House. Dublin:
Maunsel, 1907.
Thomas Muskerry. Dublin: Maunsel,
1910.
Collected Poems. New York: Devin
Adair, 1953.
Poems. London: Macmillan, 1932.

*The Poet's Circuits: Collected Poems of
Ireland.* London: Oxford University
Press, 1960. Dublin: Dolman,
1981.
Bowen, Zack. *Padraic Colum.* Car-
bondale, Ill.: Southern Illinois
University Press, 1970.

Connolly, James. *Labour, Nationality
and Religion.* Dublin: Harp Library,
1910.
Labour in Ireland. Dublin: Maunsel,
1917.
Edwards, Owen Dudley. *The Mind
of an Activist.* Dublin: Gill and
Macmillan, 1971.

Cousins, James. *Collected Poems, 1894-
1940.* Adyar, Madras: Kalakshetra,
1940.
Dumbleton, William. *James
Cousins.* New York: Twayne, 1980.
Denson, Alan. *James H. Cousins and
Margaret E. Cousins, a Bio-
Bibliographical Survey.* Kendal: Alan
Denson, 1967.

Dunsany, Lord. *The Gods of Pegana.*
London: Elkin Mathews, 1905.
Time and the Gods. London:
Heinemann, 1906.
Five Plays. London: Grant
Richards, 1914. Includes *The
Glittering Gate.*
50 Poems. London & New York:
Putnam, 1929.
Mirage Water. London & New York:
Putnam, 1938.
Amory, Mark. *A Biography of
Lord Dunsany.* London: Collins,
1972.

Eglinton, John. *Two Essays on the
Remnant.* Dublin: Whaley, 1894.
Literary Ideals in Ireland. London: T.
Fisher Unwin, 1899.
Pebbles from a Brook. Kilkenny &
Dublin: Standish O'Grady, 1901.

Ervine, St. John. *Four Irish Plays.*
Dublin: Maunsel, 1914; contains
Mixed Marriages and *The
Magnaminous Lover.*

John Ferguson. Dublin: Maunsel, 1915.

Fitzmaurice, George. *Five Plays.* London: Maunsel, 1914; contains *the Country Dressmaker* and *The Pie Dish.*
The Plays of George Fitzmaurice. 3 vols. Dublin: Dolmen Press, 1967-1970.
McGuinness, Arthur E. *George Fitzmaurice.* Lewisburg, Pa.: Bucknell University Press, 1975.

Gore-Booth, Eva. *Poems.* London: Longmans, Green, 1929.

Graves, Alfred Percival. *Father O'Flynn and other Irish Lyrics.* London: Swan Sonnenschein, 1889.

Gregory, Lady. *Coole Edition of Lady Gregory's Writings.* Gerrard's Cross: Smythe, 1970-.
Adams, Hazard. *Lady Gregory.* Lewisburg, Pa.: Bucknell University Press, 1973.

Hopper, Nora. *Ballads in Prose.* London: John Lane, 1894.

Houston, David. Unpublished.

Hyde, Douglas. *Beside the Fire.* London: David Nutt, 1890; 1973.
Love Songs of Connacht. Dublin: Gill, 1893; 1969.
Religious Songs of Connacht. Dublin: Gill, 1906; 1972.
Casadh an tSugáin. Baile Atha Cliath: Cló Chumainn, n.d.
Daly, Dominic. *the Young Douglas Hyde.* Totowa, N.J.: Rowman & Littlefield, 1974.

Johnson, Lionel. *Twenty-one Poems.* Dundrum: Dun Emer Press, 1904.

Joyce, James. *Chamber Music.* London: Elkin Mathews, 1907.
Dubliners. London: Grant Richards, 1914.
A Portrait of the Artist as a Young Man. New York: W. B. Huebsch, 1916.
Ulysses. Paris: Shakespeare and Co., 1922

Exiles. London: Jonathan Cape, 1918.
Pomes Penyeach. Paris: Shakespeare and Co., 1927.
Finnegans Wake. London: Faber, 1939.
Stephen Hero. London: Jonathan Cape, 1944.
The Critical Writings of James Joyce. New York: Viking, 1959.
Adams, Robert Martin. *James Joyce: Common Sense and Beyond.* New York: Random House, 1966.
Adams, Robert Martin. *Ulysses: Surface and Symbol.* New York; Oxford University Press, 1967.
Ellmann, Richard. *James Joyce.* New York & London: Oxford University Press, 1959.
Goldberg, S. L. *The Classical Temper: a Study of James Joyce's Ulysses.* London: Chatto & Windus, 1961.
Hart, Clive. *Structure and Motif in Finnegans Wake.* Evanston, Ill.: Northwestern University Press, 1962.
Hart, Clive. *James Joyce's Dubliners.* New York: Viking, 1969.
Hayman, David. *Ulysses. The Mechanics of Meaning.* Englewood Cliffs, N.J.: Prentice-Hall, 1970.
Kain, Richard. *Fabulous Voyager: James Joyce's Ulysses.* Chicago, Ill.: University of Chicago Press, 1947.
Levin, Harry. *James Joyce: a Critical Introduction.* London: Faber, 1941; rev., 1960.
Litz, A. Walton. *James Joyce.* New York: Twayne, 1966.
Magalaner, Marvin and Richard M. Kain. *Joyce: The Man, The Work, The Reputation.* New York: New York University Press, 1959.
Slocum, John J. and Herbert Cahoon. *A Bibliography of James Joyce.* New Haven, Conn.: Yale University Press, 1953.
Lawless, Emily. *Hurrish.* Edinburgh:

Blackwood, 1886.
Grania. London: Smith, Elder, 1892.

Ledwidge, Francis. *Complete Poems.* London: Martin Brian & O'Keeffe, 1972.

Curtayne, Alice. *Francis Ledwidge: A Life of the Poet* London: Martin Brian & O'Keeffe, 1972.

Macdonagh, Thomas. *Through the Ivory Gate.* Dublin: Sealy, Bryers & Walker, 1902.
April and May. Dublin: Sealy, Bryers and Walker, 1903.
The Golden Joy. Dublin: O'Donoghue, 1906.
Songs of Myself. Dublin: Hodges, Figgis, 1910.
Lyrical Poems. Dublin: *Irish Review,* 1913.
Thomas Campion and the Art of English Poetry. Dublin: Hodges, Figgis, 1913.
Literature in Ireland: Studies Irish and Anglo-Irish. Dublin: Talbot, 1916.
Poetical Works, ed. James Stephens. Dublin Talbot, 1916.
Norstedt, Johann. *Thomas Mac-Donagh. A Critical Biography.* Charlottesville, Va.: University of Virginia Press, 1980.

MacManus, Seamus. *'Twas in Dhroll Donegal.* London: Downey,1897.
A Lad of the O'Friels. New York: McClure, Phillips, 1903.

Martyn, Edward. *The Heather Field: A Play in Three Acts and Maeve.* London: Duckworth, 1899.
An Enchanted Sea with A Tale of a Town. Kilkenny: Standish O'Grady, 1902.
Courtney, Sr. Marie-Therese. *Edward Martyn and the Irish Theatre.* New York: Vantage, 1956.
Setterquist, Jan. *Ibsen and the Beginnings of Anglo-Irish Drama. II: Edward Martyn.* Upsala: Lundquist, 1960.

Milligan, Alice. *The Last Feast of the Fianna.* London: David Nutt, 1900; 1967.
Poems. Dublin: Gill, 1954.

Mitchell, Susan. *The Living Chalice.* Dublin: Maunsel, 1908.
Aids to the Immortality of Certain Persons in Ireland: Charitably Administered. Dublin: New Nation, 1908.
Kain, Richard. *Susan L. Mitchell.* Lewisburg, Pa.: Bucknell University Press, 1972.

Moore, George. *Parnell and his Ireland.* London: Swan Sonnenschein, Lowrey, 1887
The Strike at Arlingford. London: Walter Scott, 1893.
Esther Waters. London: Walter Scott, 1894.
The Bending of the Bough. London. T. Fisher Unwin, 1900.
The Untilled Field. London: T. Fisher Unwin, 1903.
The Lake. London: Heinemann, 1905.
Hail and Farewell. London: Heinemann, 1911-1914.
A Storyteller's Holiday. London: Cumann Sean-eolais na h-Eireann, 1918.
Collected editions: Carra, New York: Boni and Liveright, 1922-24; Ebury, London: Heinemann, 1937.
Diarmaid and Grania, with W. B. Yeats, *Dublin Magazine,* April-June, 1951.

Brown, Malcolm. *George Moore: A Re-consideration.* Seattle: University of Washington Press, 1955.
Noël, Jean C. *George Moore: l'Homme et l'Oeuvre (1852-1933).* Paris: Didier, 1966.
Gilcher, Edwin A. *Bibliography of George Moore.* De Kalb, Ill.: Northern Illinois University Press, 1970.

Murray, T. C. *Birthright*. Dublin: Maunsel, 1911.

Maurice Harte. Dublin: Maunsel, 1912.

Autumn Fire. London: Allen & Unwin, 1925.

Michaelmas Eve. London: Allen & Unwin, 1932.

O'Casey, Sean *The Shadow of a Gunman* in *Two Plays*. London: Macmillan, 1925.

Juno and the Paycock in *Two Plays*. London: Macmillan, 1925.

The Plough and the Stars. London: Macmillan, 1926.

The Silver Tassie. London: Macmillan, 1928.

Within the Gates. London: Macmillan, 1933.

The Star Turns Red. London: Macmillan, 1940.

Purple Dust. London: Macmillan, 1940.

Red Roses For Me. London: Macmillan, 1942.

Oak Leaves and Lavender. London: Macmillan, 1946.

Cock-a-Doodle Dandy. London: Macmillan, 1949.

Collected Plays. London: Macmillan; New York: St. Martin's Press, 1949-1951.

The Bishop's Bonfire. London and New York: Macmillan, 1955.

The Drums of Father Ned. London Macmillan; New York: St. Martin's Press, 1960.

The Autobiographies of Sean O'Casey. 2 vols. New York: Macmillan, 1956. Reprinted as *Autobiographies*, 2 vols. London: Macmillan, 1963.

Ayling, Ronald. *Sean O'Casey*. London: Macmillan, 1968.

Hogan, Robert. *The Experiments of Sean O'Casey*. New York: St. Martin's Press, 1960.

Kilroy, Thomas. *Sean O'Casey*. Englewood Cliffs, N.J.: Prentice-Hall, 1975.

Krause, David. *Sean O'Casey. The Man and his Work*. London: Macmillan, 1960.

Ayling, Ronald and Michael Durkan. *Sean O'Casey, a Bibliography*. London: Macmillan, 1978.

O'Kelly, Seumas. *The Shuiler's Child*. Dublin: Maunsel, 1909.

By the Streams of Kilmeen. Dublin: Talbot, 1916. *Waysiders*. Dublin: Waysiders*. Dublin: Talbot, 1917.

The Golden Barque and the Weaver's Grave. Dublin: Talbot, 1919.

Saul, George Brandon. *Seumas O'Kelly*. Lewisburgh, Pa.: Bucknell University Press, 1971.

O'Neill, Moira. *Songs of the Glens of Antrim*. Edinburgh & London: Blackwood, 1901.

Pearse, Patrick. *The Murder Machine*. Dublin: Whelan, 1916.

Tracts for the Time, Nos. 10, 11, 12, 13. Dublin: Whelan, 1916.

The Singer. Dublin: Maunsel, 1918.

Political Writing and Speeches. Dublin: Talbot, 1952.

Plays, Stories, Poems. Dublin: Talbot, 1958.

Edwards, Ruth Dudley. *Patrick Pearse: The Triumph of Failure*. London: Gollancz, 1977.

Plunkett, Joseph Mary. *The Circle and the Sword*. Dublin: Maunsel, 1911.

Poems. Dublin: Talbot, 1916.

Collected Poems. Edinburgh & London: Blackwood, 1933.

Ray, R. J. Plays not published.

Robinson, Lennox. *Crossroads*. Dublin: Maunsel, 1909.

The Clancy Name. Dublin: Maunsel, 1911.

Harvest. Dublin: Maunsel, 1911.

Patriots. Dublin: Maunsel, 1912.

The Dreamers. Dublin: Maunsel, 1915.

The Whiteheaded Boy. London: Putnam's, 1912.

O'Neill, Michael J. *Lennox Robinson.* New York: Twayne, 1964.

Rolleston, T. W. *Myths and Legends of the Celtic Race.* London: Harrap, 1911.

Ryan, Desmond. *The 1916 Poets.* Dublin: Figgis, 1963.

Shaw, G. B. The Bodley head Collected Shaw. *Collected Plays with Their Prefaces.* London: Max Reinhardt, 1970-74.

Crompton, Louis. *Shaw the Dramatist.* Lincoln: University of Nebraska, 1969.

Evans, T. E. Shaw: *The Critical Heritage.* London: Routledge, 1976.

Pearson, Hesketh. *Bernard Shaw.* McDonald & Jane's, 1942; 1975.

Sheehan, Canon. *My New Curate.* Boston: Marlier, 1899.

Luke Delmege. London: Longmans, 1901.

Glenanaar. London: Longmans, 1905.

Lisheen. London: Longmans, 1907.

The Blindness of Dr. Gray. London: Longmans, 1909.

The Graves at Kilmorna. London: Longmans, 1914.

Sigerson, Dora. *Collected Poems.* London: Hodder & Stoughton, 1907.

Sigerson, George. *Poets and Poetry of Munster.* Dublin: John O'Daly, 1860.

Bards of the Gael and Gall. London: T. Fisher Unwin, 1897.

Somerville, Edith and Martin Ross. *An Irish Cousin.* London: Bentley, 1889.

Naboth's Vineyard. London: Spencer Blackett, 1891.

The Silver Fox. London: Lawrence and Bullen, 1898.

The Real Charlotte. London: Ward & Downey, 1894.

Some Experiences of an Irish R.M. London: Longmans, Green, 1899.

Mount Music. London: Longmans, Green, 1919.

The Big House of Inver. London: Heinemann, 1925.

Berrow Robinson, Hilary. *Somerville & Ross: A Critical Appreciation.* Dublin: Gill & Macmillan, 1980.

Stephens, James. *Insurrections.* Dublin: Maunsel, 1909.

The Hill of Vision. New York: Macmillan, 1912.

The Charwoman's Daughter. London: Macmillan, 1912.

The Crock of Gold. London: Macmillan, 1912.

Here are Ladies. London: Macmillan, 1913.

Songs from the Clay. London: Macmillan, 1915.

The Demi-Gods. London & New York: Macmillan, 1915.

Adventures of Seumas Beg. London: Macmillan, 1915.

Here Are Ladies. London: Macmillan, 1915.

The Insurrection in Dublin. Dublin & London: Maunsel, 1916.

Irish Fairy Tales. London & New York: Macmillan, 1920.

Deirdre. London: Macmillan, 1923.

In the Land of Youth. London & New York: Macmillan, 1924.

Collected Poems. London & New York: Macmillan, 1926; 2nd edition, 1954.

McFate, Patricia. *The Writings of James Stephens.* London: Macmillan, 1979.

Martin, Augustin, *James Stephens: A Critical Study.* Dublin: Gill, 1977.

Bramsbäck, Birgit. *James Stephens. A Literary and Bibliographical Study.* Upsala: A. B. Lundequistska Bokhandeln; Dublin: Hodges, Figgis, 1959.

Synge, J. M. *Collected Works.* London:

Oxford University Press, 1962-68.

Gerstenberger, Donna. *John Millington Synge*. New York: Twayne, 1964.

Harmon, Maurice. *Synge Centenary Papers 1971*. Dublin: Dolmen, 1972.

Price, Alan. *Synge and Anglo-Irish Drama*. London: Methuen, 1961.

Todhunter, John. *The Banshee and Other Poems*. London: Kegan Paul, 1888.

Tynan, Katharine. *Louis de la Valliere*. London: Kegan Paul, 1885.

Shamrocks. London: Kegan Paul, 1887.

Irish Love Songs. London: T. Fisher Unwin, 1892.

The Wild Harp. London: Sidgwick & Jackson, 1913.

Collected Poems. London: Macmillan, 1930.

Waddell, Sam. *The Turn of the Road*. Dublin: Maunsel, 1907.

The Drone. Dublin: Maunsel, 1909. Includes *Red Turf*.

The Troth. Dublin: Maunsel, 1909.

Bridgehead. London: Constable, 1939.

Wilde, Oscar. *Complete Works*. London: Collins, 1948.

Yeats, W. B. *The Wanderings of Oisin*. London: Kegan Paul, Trench, 1889.

Representative Irish Tales. London: Putnam's Sons, 1891.

John Sherman and Dhoya. London: T. Fisher Unwin, 1891.

Irish Fairy Tales. London: T. Fisher Unwin, 1892.

The Celtic Twilight. London: Lawrence & Bullen, 1893.

A Book of Irish Verse. London: Methuen, 1895.

The Secret Rose. London: Lawrence & Bullen, 1897.

The Tables of the Law. London: Elkin Mathews, 1904.

Per Amica Silentia Lunae. London: Macmillan, 1918.

A Vision. London. Warner Laurie, 1926.

Collected Plays. London: Macmillan, 1952.

Collected Poems. London & New York: Macmillan, 1956.

Essays and Introductions. London & New York: Macmillan, 1961.

Mythologies. London & New York: Macmillan, 1962.

Explorations. London & New York: Macmillan, 1962.

Autobiographies. London & New York: Macmillan, 1966.

Uncollected Prose. 2 Vols. New York: Columbia University, 1970 & 1975.

Donoghue, Denis and J. R. Mulryne. *An Honoured Guest: New Essays on W. B. Yeats*. London: Arnold, 1965.

Ellmann, Richard. *Yeats: The Man and the Masks*. London & New York: Macmillan, 1948.

Ellmann, Richard *The Identity of Yeats*. London: Macmillan, 1954; 2nd edition. 1964.

Hall, James and Martin Steinmann. *The Permanence of Yeats: Selected Criticism*. New York: Macmillan, 1950.

Henn, T. R. *The Lonely Tower: Studies in the Poetry of W. B. Yeats*. London: Methuen, 1950; 2nd edition, 1965.

Rajan, Balachandra. *W. B. Yeats: A Critical Introduction*. London: Hutchinson, 1965; 2nd edition, 1969.

Unterecker, John. *A Reader's Guide to W. B. Yeats*. New York: Noonday, 1959.

Ure, Peter. *Yeats the Playwright: A Commentary on Character and Design in the Major Plays*. London: Routledge & Kegan Paul, 1963.

Wade, Allen. *A Bibliography of the Writings of W. B. Yeats;* revised by Russell K. Alspach. New York: Oxford University Press, 1968.

PART V

HISTORY 1920-1950

Arensberg, C. and S. T. Kimball. *Family and Community in Ireland.* Cambridge, Mass.: Harvard University Press, 2nd ed., 1968.

Bowyer Bell, J. *The Secret Army.* Dublin: Academic Press, 2nd. ed., 1980.

Coogan, T. P. *Ireland Since the Rising.* London: Pall Mall Press, 1966.

Chubb, Basil. *The Government and Politics of Ireland.* Stanford: Stanford University Press, 1970.

Kee, Robert. *The Green Flag.* London: Weidenfeld and Nicolson, 1972.

Lyons, F. S. L. *Ireland since the Famine.* London: Weidenfeld and Nicolson, rev., ed., 1973.

MacDonagh, Oliver. *Ireland.* Englewood Cliffs: Prentice Hall, 1968.

MacManus, Francis. *The Years of the Great Test. 1926-39.* Cork: Mercier, 1967.

Meenan, James. *The Economic History of Ireland since 1922.* Liverpool: Liverpool University Press, 1970.

Moody, T. W. *The Ulster Question 1603-1973.* Cork: Mercier, 1974.

Murphy, John A. *Ireland in the Twentieth Century.* Dublin: Gill, 1975.

O'Sullivan, Donal. *The Irish Free State and its Senate.* London: Faber, 1940.

Rose, Richard. *Governing Without Consensus. An Irish Perspective.* London: Faber, 1971.

Whyte, John. *Church and State in Modern Ireland 1923-1979.* Dublin: Gill, 2nd ed., 1980.

LITERARY HISTORY

Brown, Terence. *Northern Voices: poets from Ulster.* Dublin: Gill & MacMillan, 1975.

Clarke, Austin. *Poetry in Modern Ireland:* Dublin: Sign of the Three Candles, 1951.

Dunn, Douglas. *Two Decades of Irish Writing: a critical survey.* Manchester: Carcanet Press, 1975.

Foster, John Wilson. *Forces and Themes in Ulster Fiction.* Dublin: Gill & Macmillan, 1974.

Harmon, Maurice, 'Introduction' to *Irish Poetry after Yeats: Seven Poets,* Dublin Wolfhound, 1979; Boston. Little Brown, 1981.

Hogan, Robert. *After the Irish Renaissance: a critical history of the Irish Drama since 'the Plough and the Stars'.* Minneapolis: University of Minnesota Press, 1967.

Hunt, Hugh. *The Abbey; Ireland's National Theatre, 1904-1978.* Dublin: Gill & Macmillan, 1979.

Kiely, Benedict. *Modern Irish Fiction: a critique.* Dublin: Talbot, 1950.

Lucy, Sean. *Irish Poets in English.* Cork: Mercier, 1973.

O'Connor, Frank. *The Backward Look: a survey of Irish Literature.* London: Macmillan, 1967.

Rafroidi, Patrick and Maurice Harmon. *The Irish Novel in Our Time*. Villeneuve d'Ascq: Universite de Lille III, 1975.

Rafroidi, Patrick and Terence Brown. *The Irish Short Story*. Villeneuve d'Ascq: Universite de Lille III, 1979.

WRITING IN IRISH

De Blacam, Aodh. *Gaelic Literature Surveyed*. Dublin: Talbot, 1929, rev., 1974.

Jordan, John. *The Pleasures of Gaelic Literature*. Cork: Mercier, 1977.

TEXTS

A.E. See Part IV above.

Beckett, Samuel. *More Pricks than Kicks*. London: Chatto & Windus, 1934.
Murphy. London: Routledge, 1938 /Trans. into French by Beckett and Alfred Péron, Paris: Bordas, 1947.
Molloy. Paris: Editions de Minuit, 1951/Trans. into English by Beckett and Patrick Bowles, Paris: Merlin/Olympia, 1954/New York: Grove, 1955.
Malone Meurt. Paris: Editions de Minuit,1951/Trans. into English as *Malone Dies* by Beckett, New York: Grove, 1956/London: Calder & Boyars, 1958.
En Attendant Godot. Paris: Editions de Minuit, 1952/Trans. into English as *Waiting for Godot* by Beckett, New York: Grove, 1954/London: Faber, 1956.
Watt. Paris: Merlin/Olympia, 1953 /New York: Grove, 1959/London: Calder & Boyars, 1961.
L'Innommable. Paris: Editions de Minuit, 1953/Trans. into English as *The Unnamable by Beckett*, New York: Grove, 1958.
Nouvelles et Textes pour Rien. Paris: Editions de Minuit, 1955/Trans. into English as *Stories and Texts for Nothing* by Beckett, New York: Grove, 1967/collected edition under the title *No's Knife*, London: Calder & Boyars, 1966.
Fin de Partie. Paris: Editions de Minuit, 1957/Trans. into English as *Endgame* by Beckett, New York: Grove, 1958/London: Faber, 1958.
Krapp's Last Tape. London: Faber, 1959/New York: Grove, 1960/trans. into French as *La dernière bande* by Beckett and Pierre Leyris, Paris: Editions de Minuit, 1959; *Krapp's Last Tape and Other Dramatic Pieces*, New York: Grove, 1960.
Happy Days. New York: Grove, 1961/London: Faber 1962/Trans. into French as *Oh les beaux jours* by Beckett, Paris: Editions de Minuit, 1963.
Comment C'est. Paris: Editions de Minuit, 1961/Trans. into English as *How It Is* by Beckett, New York: Grove/London: Calder & Boyars, 1966.
Play. London: Faber, 1964/in *Cascando and Other Short Dramatic Pieces*, New York: Grove, 1967.
Not I. London: Faber, 1973/in *First Love and Other Shorts*, New York: Grove. 1974
Collected Poems in English and French. London: J. Calder, 1977.
Abbott, H.P. *The Fiction of Samuel Beckett; Form and Effect*. Berkeley:

University of California Press, 1973.

Cohn, Ruby. *Back to Beckett*. New Jersey: Princeton University Press, 1973.

Federman, Raymond. *Journey to Chaos, Samuel Beckett's Early Fiction*. Berkeley and Los Angeles: University of California Press, 1965.

Fletcher, J. *The Novels of Samuel Beckett*. London: Chatto & Windus, 1964.

Webb, Eugene. *Samuel Beckett. A Study of his Novels*. Peter Owen, 1970.

Federman, Raymond and John Fletcher. *Samuel Beckett His Works and His Critics: An Essay in Bibliography*. Berkeley and Los Angeles: University of California Press, 1970.

Boyle, Patrick. *Like any Other Man*. London: MacGibbon & Kee, 1966.

Bowen, Elizabeth *Encounters*. London: Sidgwick & Jackson, 1923/New York: Boni & Liveright, 1925/republished in *Early Stories*, New York: Alfred A. Knopf, 1950.

The Last September. London: Constable/New York: Dial, 1929.

To the North. London: Gollancz, 1932/New York: Alfred A. Knopf, 1933.

The House in Paris. London: Gollancz, 1935/New York: Alfred A. Knopf, 1936.

The Death of the Heart. London: Gollancz, 1935/New York: Alfred A. Knopf, 1936.

Bowen's Court. London: Longmans, Green/New York: Alfred A. Knopf, 1942/2nd ed. with Afterword, London: Longmans, Green/New York: Alfred A. Knopf, 1964.

Seven Winters: Memories of a Dublin Childhood. Dublin: Cuala, 1942/republished as *Seven Winters:*

Memories of a Dublin Childhood and Afterthoughts: Pieces on Writing, New York: Alfred A. Knopf, 1962.

The Heat of the Day. London: Jonathan Cape/New York: Alfred A. Knopf, 1949.

Eva Trout or Changing Scenes. New York: Alfred A. Knopf, 1968/London: Jonathan Cape, 1969.

Collected Stories, London: Cape, 1981.

Glendinning, Victoria. *Elizabeth Bowen*. London: Weidenfeld & Nicolson, 1977.

Byrne, Seamus. *Design for a Headstone*. Dublin: Progress House, 1956.

Campbell, Joseph. *The Poems of Joseph Campbell*, ed. and with an Introduction by Austin Clarke. Dublin: Allen Figgis, 1963.

Carroll, Paul Vincent. *Things That Are Caesar's*. London: Rich & Cowan, 1934.

Shadow and Substance. New York: Random House, 1937/London: Macmillan, 1938.

The White Steed and Coggerers. New York: Random House, 1939.

The Strings, My Lord, Are False. *In Three Plays: The White Steed, Things That Are Caesar's, The Strings, My Lord, Are False*. London: Macmillan, 1944.

Doyle, Paul A. *Paul Vincent Carroll*. Lewisburg, Pa.: Bucknell University Press, 1971.

Clarke, Austin *The Vengeance of Fionn*. Dublin & London: Maunsel, 1918.

The Cattledrive in Connaught. London: Allen & Unwin, 1925.

The Son of Learning. London: Allen & Unwin, 1927.

Pilgrimage and Other Poems. London: Allen & Unwin, 1929.

The Flame. London: Allen & Unwin, 1930.

The Bright Temptation. London: Allen & Unwin, 1932.

The Singing Men at Cashel. London: Allen & Unwin, 1936.

Night and Morning. Dublin: Orwell, 1938.

Sister Eucharia. Dublin: Orwell/London: Williams & Norgate, 1939.

Black Fast. Dublin: Orwell, 1941.

The Kiss. In *Dublin Magazine*, Vol. XVII, N.S., No. 3, pp. 5-18, July-Sept., 1942.

The Plot is Ready. 1943.

The Viscount of Blarney and Other Plays. Dublin: Bridge/London: Williams & Norgate, 1944.

The Second Kiss. Dublin: Bridge/London: Williams & Norgate, 1946.

The Plot Succeeds. Dublin: Bridge, 1950.

The Sun Dances at Easter. London: Andrew Melrose, 1952.

The Moment Next to Nothing. Dublin: Bridge, 1953.

Ancient Lights. Dublin: Bridge, 1955.

Twice Round the Black Church. London: Routledge & Kegan Paul, 1962.

Collected Plays. Dublin: Dolmen, 1963.

Collected Poems. Dublin: Dolmen, 1974.

The Third Kiss. Dublin: Dolmen, 1976.

Liberty Lane. Dublin: Dolmen, 1978.

Halpern, Susan. *Austin Clarke. His Life and Works*. Dublin: Dolmen, 1974.

Harmon, Maurice, *ed. Irish University Review*, Vol. 4, No. 1, (Spring 1974). An Austin Clarke Special Issue.

Tapping, G. Craig. *Austin Clarke: A Study of his Writings*. Dublin: Academy Press, 1981.

Clifford, Sigerson. *The Great Pacificator* (1947).

Coffey, Brian *Selected Poems*. Dublin: New Writers' Press, 1971.

Irish University Review, Vol. 5, No. 1, (Spring 1975). A Brian Coffey Special Issue.

Death of Hektor. Wiltshire: Circle, Press, 1979.

Colum, Mary. *From These Roots*. New York: Scribners, 1937.

Life and the Dream. Garden City, N.Y.: Doubleday, 1947.

Colum, Padraic. See Part IV.

Corkery, Daniel. *A Munster Twilight*. Dublin & Cork: Talbot, 1916/New York: Stokes, 1917.

The Threshold of Quiet. Dublin & Cork: Talbot/London: Unwin, 1917.

The Hounds of Banba. Dublin & Cork: Talbot, 1920/New York: Huebsch, 1922.

The Yellow Bittern and Other Plays. Dublin: Talbot/London: Unwin, 1920.

The Hidden Ireland. A Study of Gaelic Munster in the Eighteenth Century. Dublin: Gill, 1925.

The Stormy Hills. Dublin: Talbot London: Jonathan Cape, 1929.*Synge and Anglo-Irish Literature*. Cork: Cork University Press, London: Longmans, Green, 1931. Reprinted Cork: Mercier Press, 5th impression, 1966.

Earth Out of Earth. Dublin & Cork: Talbot, 1939.

Saul, George Brandon. *Daniel Corkery*. Lewisburg, Pa.: Bucknell University Press, 1973.

Craig, Maurice (James) *Twelve Poems*. Dublin: Privately printed, 1942.

Dublin 1660-1860. London: Cresset, 1952/Dublin: Figgis, 1969.

Cronin, Anthony. *The Life of Riley*. London: Secker & Warburg, 1964.

Collected Poems. 1950-1973. Dublin:

New Writers' Press, 1973.
Identity Papers. Dublin: Co-op Books, 1979.

D'Alton, Louis 'The Man in the Cloak.' In *Two Irish Plays.* London: Macmillian, 1938.
Tomorrow Never Comes. Dublin: Duffy, 1945.
The Money Doesn't Matter. Dublin: Duffy, 1957.

Deevy, Teresa. Katie Roche. In *Famous Plays of 1935-6.* London: Gollancz, 1936. And in *Three Plays.* London: Macmillan, 1939.
The King of Spain's Daughter. In *Three Plays.* London: Macmillan, 1939.

Devlin, Denis *Lough Derg and Other Poems.* New York: Reynal & Hitchcock, 1946.
Selected Poems. Robert Penn Warren and Allen Tate, *eds.* New York: Holt, Rinehart & Winston, 1963.
Collected Poems. Brian Coffey, *ed.* Dublin: Dolmen, 1964.

Donaghy, John Lyle. *Selected Poems.* Dublin: Orwell, 1939.

Doyle, Lynn. *Ballygullion.* Dublin: Maunsel, 1918.
Back to Ballygullion. London: Duckworth, 1953.

Dunsany. See Part IV.

Fallon, Padraic. *Lighting-up Time.* Dublin: Orwell, 1938.
The Seventh Step (1954). One of several unpublished plays.
Poems. Dublin: Dolmen, 1974.

Farren, Robert (Roibeard Ó Faracháin)
Thronging Feet. London: Sheed & Ward, 1936.
Time's Wall Asunder. London: Sheed & Ward, 1939.

Figgis, Darrell. *Children of Earth.* Dublin: Maunsell, 1918.
The Return of the Hero. London & Sydney: Chapman & Dodd, 1923. Published under the pseudonym of Michael Ireland/New York: C. Boni, 1930, published under his own name with Introduction by James Stephens and a second unsigned Introduction, probably by Padraic Colum.

Ganly, Andrew. *The Cursing Fields* (1942). Unpublished.

Gogarty, Oliver St. John. *As I Was Going Down Sackville Street.* London: Rich & Cowan/New York: Reynal & Hitchcock, 1937.
Tumbling in the Hay. London: Constable/New York: Reynal & Hitchcock, 1939.
The Collected Poems of Oliver St. John Gogarty. London: Constable, 1951/New York: Devin-Adair, (1954).
O'Connor Ulick. *Oliver St. John Gogarty: a Poet and His Times.* London: Cape, 1964.

Gonne, Maud. *A Servant of the Queen.* London: Gollancz, 1938.

Greacen, Robert. *One Recent Evening.* London: Favil, 1944.

Gwynn, Stephen *Irish Literature and Drama in the English Language.* London: Nelson, 1920.
Experiences of a Literary Man. London: Thornton Butterworth, 1926.

Hackett, Francis. *...I Chose Denmark.* New York: Doubleday, Doran, 1940. *The Green Lion,* 1936.

Healy, Gerard. *The Black Stranger.* Dublin: James Duffy, 1950.
Thy Dear Father. Dublin: P. J. Bourke, 1957.

Hewitt, John. *Collected Poems 1932-67.* London: MacGibbon & Kee, 1968.
Selected Poems ed. A. Warner. Belfast: Blackstaff, 1981.

Higgins, F. R. *Island Blood.* London: J. Lane, 1925.
The Dark Breed. London: Macmillan, 1927.

Arable Holdings. Dublin: Cuala, 1933.
The Gap of Brightness. London: Macmillan, 1940.
The Deuce of Jacks—Unpublished

Iremonger, Valentin. *Reservations*. Dublin: Envoy, 1950.
Horan's Field and Other Reservations. Dublin: Dolmen, 1972.

Johnston, Denis. *The Brazen Horn*. Dublin: Dolmen, 1977.
Collected Plays, Vol. 1. Gerrards Cross, Buckinghamshire: Colin Smythe, 1977.
Collected Plays, Vol. 2. Gerrards Cross, Buckinghamshire: Colin Smythe, 1979.
Barnett, Gene A. *Denis Johnston*. New York: Twayne, 1978.
Ferrar, Harold. *Denis Johnston's Irish Theatre*. Dublin: Dolmen, 1973.

Joyce, James. — See Part IV.

Kavanagh, Patrick. *Ploughman and Other Poems*. London:Macmillan, 1936. *The Green Fool*. London. Michael Joseph, 1938.
The Great Hunger. Dublin: Cuala Press, 1942.
A Soul for Sale. London: Macmillan, 1947.
Tarry Flynn. London: Pilot, 1948.
Come Dance With Kitty Stobling and Other Poems. London: Macmillan, 1960.
Collected Poems. London: MacGibbon & Kee, 1964.
Collected Pruse. London: MacGibbon & Kee, 1967.
Nemo, John. *Patrick Kavanagh*. New York: Twayne, 1979.
O'Brien, Darcy. *Patrick Kavanagh*. Lewisburg, Pa.: Bucknell University Press, 1975.

Laughton, Freda. *A Transitory House* London: Cape, 1946.

Laverty, Maura. *Lift Up Your Gates*.

London: Longmans, Green, 1946.
Liffey Lane. New York: Longmans, Green, 1947.

Lavin, Mary. *The Long Ago and Other Stories*. London: Michael Joseph, 1944.
The Becker Wives and Other Stories. London: Michael Joseph, 1946.
The Stories of Mary Lavin, Vol. 1. London: Constable, 1964 (reprint, 1970); Vol. 11, 1974.
Kelly, A. A. *Mary Lavin: Quiet Rebel*. Dublin: Wolfhound, 1980.
Irish University Review, Vol. 9, No. 2 (Autumn 1980). A Mary Lavin Special Issue, with Bibliography.

Longford, Lord. *Yahoo*. Dublin: Hodges, Figgis, 1934. Reprinted in *Plays of Changing Ireland*, ed. Curtis Canfield, New York: Macmillan, 1936.

Lysaght, Edward. *The Gael*. Dublin: Maunsel, 1919.

MacDonagh, Donagh. *Veterans and Other Poems*. Dublin: Cuala, 1941.
Happy as Larry. Dublin: Maurice Fridberg, 1946. Included in *Modern Verse Plays*, ed. E. Martin Browne, Harmondsworth, Middlesex. Penguin, 1958. Dublin: Fridberg & Dolman. 1967.
The Hungry Grass. London: Faber & Faber, 1947.
God's Gentry, (1951).—Unpublished
Step-in-the-Hollow. In *Three Irish Plays*, Harmondsworth, Middlesex: Penguin, 1959.

MacFadden, Roy. *Swords and Plough-shares*. London: Routledge, 1943.

MacGreevy, Thomas. *Collected Poems*, ed. Thomas Dillon Redshaw, with a Foreword by Samuel Beckett, Dublin: New Writers' Press, 1971.

McHugh, Roger. *Trial at Green Street Courthouse*. Dublin: Browne & Nolan(1945).
Rossa. Tralee: Kerryman (1946?).

MacLaverty, Michael. *Call My Brother Back*. London & New York: Longmans, Green, 1939/reissued Dublin: Allen Figgis, 1970.
Lost Fields. New York & Toronto: Longmans, 1941. Dublin: Poolbeg, 1980
The Game Cock and Other Stories. New York: Devin-Adair, 1947.

MacLiammoir, Micheal. *Diarmuid agus Grainne*. Baile Atha Cliath: Oifig Dialta Foillseachain Rialtais, 1935.
All for Hecuba. London: Methuen, 1946/revised, Dublin: Progress House, 1961.
Where Stars Walk. Dublin: Progress House, 1962.
Ill Met by Moonlight. Dublin: Duffy, 1964.

MacMahon, Bryan. *The Bugle in the Blood* (1949).
Children of the Rainbow. London: Macmillan, 1952.
The Honey Spike. London: Bodley Head, 1967.

MacManus, Francis. *Stand and Give Challenge*. Dublin: Talbot, 1934.
Candle For the Proud. Dublin: Talbot, 1936.
This House Was Mine. Dublin: Talbot, 1937.
Men Withering. Dublin: Talbot, 1939.
The Wild Garden. Dublin: Talbot, 1940.
Flow On, Lovely River. Dublin: Talbot, 1941.
Watergate. Dublin: Talbot, 1942.
The Greatest of These. Dublin: Talbot, 1943.
The Fire in the Dust. London: Jonathan Cape, 1950.

MacNamara, Brinsley. *The Valley of the Squinting Windows*. London: Sampson Low, Marston, 1918; as "Oliver Blyth", *The Irishman*, London: Everleigh Nash, 1920.
The Mirror in the Dusk. Dublin & London: Maunsel & Roberts, 1921.
Look at the Heffernans! Dublin & Cork: Talbot, n.d.
The Various Lives of Marcus Igoe. London: Sampson Low, Marston, 1929.
Margaret Gillan. London: George Allen & Unwin, 1934.
The Glorious Uncertainty. Dublin: P. J. Bourke, 1957.

MacNeice, Louis. *Autumn Journal*. London: Faber, 1939; New York: Random House, 1940.
Autumn Sequel. London: Faber (1954).
The Collected Poems of Louis MacNeice, ed. E. R. Dodds. London: Faber (1966)/New York: Oxford University Press, 1967.
Brown, Terence. *Louis MacNeice: Sceptical Vision*. Dublin: Gill and Macmillan/New York: Barnes & Noble, 1975.
Armitage, Christopher. *A Bibliography of the Works of Louis MacNeice*. London: Kaye & Ward, 1973.

MacNeill, Janet. *The Maiden Dinosour*. London: Geoffrey Bles, 1964.

Macken, Walter. *Mungo's Mansion*. London: Macmillan, 1946.

Manning, Mary. *Youth's the Season-?* In *Plays of Changing Ireland*, ed. Curtis Canfield, New York: Macmillan, 1936.

Meldon, Maurice. *Purple Path to the Poppy Field*. In *New World Writing*, Fifth Mentor Selection, New York: New American Library, 1954.
Aisling. Dublin: Progress House, 1959.
House Under Green Shadows. Dublin: Progress House, 1962.

Molloy, M. J. *The King of Friday's Men*. Dublin: James Duffy, 1953.
Old Road. Dublin: Progress House, 1961.
The Wood of the Whispering. Dublin:

Progress House, 1961.
The Visiting House. In *Seven Irish Plays 1946-1964*. Minneapolis: University of Minnesota Press, 1967.

Murray, T. C. *Autumn Fire: A Play in Three Acts*. London: G. Allen & Unwin, 1925.
The Blind Wolf (1928), (afterwards titled The Karavoes). Unpublished.
Michaelmas Eve: A Play in Three Acts. London: G. Allen & Unwin, 1932.

O'Brien, Flann. *At Swim-Two-Birds*, London: Longmans, Green, 1939; MacGibbon & Kee, 1960.
The Third Policeman London: MacGibbon & Kee, 1967.
An Béal Bocht Dublin: National Press, 1941; Dublin: Dolmen, 1964.
Faustus Kelly. Dublin: Cahill, 1943.
The Hard Life. London: MacGibbon & Kee, 1961.
The Dalkey Archive. London: MacGibbon & Kee, 1964.
Clissman, Anne. *Flann O'Brien: A Critical Introduction to his Writing*. Dublin: Gill and Macmillan, 1975.
O'Keeffe, T. *Myles*. London: Martin, Brian & O'Keeffe, 1973.

Kate O'Brien *Without My Cloak*. London: Heinemann/Garden City, N.Y.: Doubleday, Doran, 1931.
The ante-Room. London: Heinemann/Garden City, N.Y.; Doubleday, Dublin: Arlen, 1980.
Mary Lavelle. London: Heinemann, Garden City, N.Y.: Doubleday, Doran, 1936.
Pray for the Wanderer. London: Heinemann/Garden City, N.Y.: Doubleday, Doran, 1938.
The Land of Spices. London: Heinemann, 1941.
That Lady. London: Heinemann, 1946/Published in the U.S. as *For One Sweet Grape*, Garden City, N.Y.: Doubleday, 1946.

O'Casey, Sean — See Part IV.

O'Connor, Frank. *Guests of the Nation*. London: Macmillan, 1931.
The Saint and Mary Kate. London: Macmillan, 1932.
The Invincibles (1937) with Hugh Hunt. Unpublished.
Moses' Rock (1938) with Hugh Hunt. Unpublished.
Time's Pocket (1938). Unpublished.
Dutch Interior. London: Macmillan, 1940.
The Statue's Daughter (1941). Unpublished.
Stories. New York: Knopf, 1952; London: Hamish Hamilton, 1953.
More Stories. New York: Knopf, 1954, 1967.
An Only Child. New York: Alfred A. Knopf, 1961/London: Macmillan, 1963.
Collection Two. London: Macmillan, 1964.
My Father's Son. London: Macmillan, 1968/New York: Alfred A. Knopf, 1969.
Collection Three. London: Macmillan, 1969.
Sheehy, Maurice. *Michael/Frank. Studies on Frank O'Connor*. New York: Knopf, 1969.

O'Donnell, Peadar. *Storm*. Dublin: Talbot Press, 1925.
Islanders. London: Jonathan Cape, 1928/Published in the U.S. as *The Way It Was With Them*. New York: Putnam's 1928.
Adrigoole. London: Jonathan Cape/New York: Putnams, 1929.
The Gates Flew Open. London: Jonathan Cape, 1932.
Wrack. London: Jonathan Cape, 1933.
Salud! An Irishman in Spain. London: Methuen, 1937.
There will be another day. Dublin: Dolmen, 1963.

O'Donovan, Gerald. *Father Ralph*.

London: Macmillan, 1913.

O'Duffy, Eimar. *King Goshawk and the Birds.* London: Macmillan, 1926.

The Spacious Adventures of the Man in the Street. London: Macmillan, 1928.

The Wasted Island. Dublin: Martin Lester, 1919/revised ed. London: Macmillan, 1929.

Asses in Clover. London: Putnam's, 1933.

O'Faolain, Sean. *Midsummer Night Madness and Other Stories.* London: Jonathan Cape, 1932.

A Nest of Simple Folk. New York: Viking, 1934.

Bird Alone. London: Jonathan Cape, 1936.

A Purse of Coppers: Short Stories. London: Jonathan Cape, 1937.

She Had To Do Something: A Comedy in Three Acts. London: Jonathan Cape, 1938.

King of the Beggars, A Life of Daniel O'Connell. Dublin: Poolbeg, 1980. New York: Viking, 1938.

De Valera. Harmondsworth, Middlesex: Penguin, 1939.

Come Back to Erin. New York: Viking, 1940.

The Great O'Neill, A Biography of Hugh O'Neill, Earl of Tyrone. New York: Duell, Sloan & Pearce, 1942.

The Irish. West Drayton, Middlesex, 1947. Harmondsworth: Penguin, 1969.

Teresa and Other Stories. London: Jonathan Cape, 1947.

Vive Moi! Boston: Little, Brown, 1964.

I Remember! I Remember! Boston: Little, Brown, 1961.

Foreign Affairs, and Other Stories. London: Constable, 1976.

And Again? London: Constable, 1979.

Collected Stories. London: Constable, 3 vols. 1980-

Harmon, Maurice. *Sean O'Faolain.*

South Bend: University of Notre Dame Press, 1966.

O'Flaherty, Liam *The Neighbour's Wife* London: Jonathan Cape, 1923/New York: Boni & Liveright, 1925/Bath: Lythway, 1972.

The Black Soul. London: Jonathan Cape, 1924/New York: Boni & Liveright, 1925. Dublin: Wolfhound, 1981.

Spring Sowing, London: Jonathan Cape, 1924.

The Informer. London: Jonathan Cape/New York: Alfred A. Knopf, 1925.

The Tent. London: Jonathan Cape, 1926.

Mr. Gilhooley. London: Jonathan Cape, 1926/New York: Harcourt Brace, 1927.

The Assassin. London: Jonathan Cape, 1926/New York: Harcourt Brace, 1928.

The Mountain Tavern. London: Jonathan Cape, 1929.

The Puritan. London: Jonathan Cape, 1931/New York: Harcourt Brace, 1932/Bath: Lythway, 1973.

Skerrett. London: Gollancz/New York: Long & Smith 1932. Dublin: Wolfhound, 1977.

The Martyr. New York: Macmillan, 1933/London: Gollancz, 1935.

Famine. London: Gollancz, 1948/New York: Random House, 1937. Dublin: Wolfhound, 1979.

Two Lovely Beasts. London: Gollancz, 1948. New York: Devin Adair, 1950.

The Pedlar's Revenge. Dublin: Wolfhound, 1976.

The Ecstasy of Angus. (privately 1931) Dublin: Wolfhound, 1978.

The Wilderness. Dublin: Wolfhound, 1978.

Kelly, A.A. *Liam O'Flaherty: The Storyteller.* London: Macmillan 1976.

Sheeran, Patrick F. *The Novels of*

Liam O'Flaherty. Dublin: Wolfhound, 1976.

O'Malley, Ernie *On Another Man's Wound.* London: Rich & Cowan, 1936.

O'Sullivan, Seumas *The Twilight People.* Dublin: Whaley/London: Bullen, 1905.
The Earth-Lover and Other Verses. Dublin: New Nation 1909.
Collected Poems. Dublin: Orwell, 1940.
The Rose and the Bottle. Dublin: Talbot Press, 1946.

Reid, Forrest *The Bracknels.* London: Edward Arnold, 1911.
Following Darkness. London: Edward Arnold, 1912.
Uncle Stephen. London: Faber, 1931.
The Retreat. London: Faber, 1936.
Peter Waring. London: Faber, 1937.
Young Tom. London: Faber, 1944.
Denis Bracknel. London: Faber, 1947
Bryan, Mary. *Forrest Reid.* Boston: Twayne, 1976.
Burlingham, Russell. *Forrest Reid. A Portrait and a Study.* London: Faber, 1953.

Robinson, Lennox *The Whiteheaded Boy A Comedy in Three Acts.* London: Putnam's, 1921.
Crabbed Youth and Age: A Little Comedy. London: Putnam's, 1924.
The Big House: Four Scenes in Its Life. London: Macmillan, 1928.
The Far-Off Hills: A Comedy in Three Acts. London: Chatto & Windus, 1931.
Drama at Inish: An Exaggeration in Three Acts (retitled *Is Life Worth Living?*, London: Macmillan, 1 9 3 3 .
Killycreggs in Twilight and Other Plays. London: Macmillan, 1939.

Rodgers, W.R. *Awake! and Other Poems.* London: Secker & Warburg, 1941.

Europa and the Bull and Other Poems. London: Secker & Warburg, 1952.
Collected Poems. London: Oxford University Press, 1971.
O'Brien, Darcy, *W.R. Rodgers.* Lewisburg, Pa.: Bucknell University Press, 1970.

Salkeld, Blanaid *Hello Eternity!* London: Elkin, Mathews & Marot, 1933.
... the engine is still running. Dublin: Gayfield, 1937.

Shiels, George. *Paul Twyning.* In *Three Plays* (Professor Tim, Paul Twyning, The New Gossoon). London: Macmillan, 1945.
Professor Tim. In *Three Plays* Professor Tim, Paul Twyning, The New Gossoon). London: Macmillan, 1945.
The New Gossoon. In *Three Plays* (Professor Tim, Paul Twyning, The New Gossoon). London: Macmillan, 1945.
The Rugged Path London: Macmillan, 1942.

Stephens. See Part IV.

Stuart, Francis. *Women and God.* London: Jonathan Cape, 1931.
Pigeon Irish. London: Gollancz/New York: Macmillan 1932.
The Coloured Dome. London: Gollancz, 1932/New York: Macmillan, 1933.
Try the Sky. London: Gollancz/New York: Macmillan, 1933.
Men Crowd Me Round (1937). Unpublished.
Strange Guest (1940). Unpublished.
The Pillar of Cloud. London: Gollancz, 1948.
Redemption. London: Gollancz, 1949/New York: Devin-Adair, 1950.
The Flowering Cross. London: Gollancz/Toronto: Longmans, 1950.

Good Friday's Daughter. London: Gollancz/Toronto: Longmans, 1953.

The Pilgrimage. London: Gollancz/Toronto: Bond Street Publishers, 1955.

Victors and Vanquished. London: Gollancz, 1958/Cleveland, Pennington Press, 1959.

Victors and Vanquished. London: Gollancz, 1958/Cleveland, Pennington Press, 1959.

Angels of Providence. London: Gollancz/Toronto: Doubleday, 1959.

Black List, Section H. Carbondale, Edwardsville: Southern Illinois University Press/London; London: Martin, Brian & O'Keeffe, 1975.

A Hole in the Head. London: Martin Brian & O'Keeffe, 1973.

Memorial. London: Martin Brian & O'Keeffe, 1977

The High Consistory. London: Martin, Brian & O'Keeffe, 1981.

Natterstad, J.H. *Francis Stuart.* Lewisburg, Pa.: Bucknell University Press, 1974.

Taylor Geoffrey, Ed. *First Poems of Today.* London: Routledge &

Kegan Paul, 1951.

Irish Poets of the Nineteenth Century, London: Routledge, 1951.

Ussher, Arland, *Three Great Irishmen: Shaw, Yeats, Joyce.* London: Gollancz, 1947.

The Face and Mind of Ireland. London: Gollancz, 1949.

Wall, Mervyn, *Alarm Among the Clerks.* Dublin: Richview, 1940.

The Unfortunate Fursey. London: Pilot, 1946/New York: Crown, 1947.

The Return of Fursey. London: Pilot, 1948.

Leaves for the Burning. London: Methuen/New York: Devin-Adair, 1952.

The Lady in the Twilight. Newark, Del. Proscenium, 1971.

Yeats, Jack B. *In Sand.* Dublin: Dolmen, 1964.

The Collected Plays of Jack B. yeats, ed. Robin Skelton. London: Secker & Warburg, 1971.

Yeats, W.B. See Part III.

Young, Ella. *Flowering Dusk.* New York: Longmans, 1945.

WRITING IN IRISH

Mac Amhlaidh, Donall. *Dialann Deoraí.* Baile Átha Cliath: An Clóchomhar, 1960.

Saol Saighdiúra. Baile Átha Cliath: An Clóchomhar, 1962.

Mhac an tSaoi, Máire. *Margadh na Saoire.* Baile Átha Cliath: Sáirséal agus Dill, 1956.

Mac Giolla Iasachta, Eamonn. *Cúrsaí Thomáis.* Baile Átha Cliath: Hodges & Figgis, 1927.

Mac Grianna, Seamus. *Caisleán Óir.* Dun Dealgan: Preas DhúnDealgan, 1924.

Mac Grianna, Seosamh. *Mo Bhealach Féin.* Baile Átha Cliath: Oifig an tSoláthair, 1940.

An Druma Mor. Baile Átha Cliath: Oifig tSoláthair, 1969.

Ó Cadhain, Mairtín. *Cré na Cille.* Baile Átha Cliath: Sáirséal agus Dill, 1949.

Páipéir Bhána agus Páipéir Bhreaca. Baile Átha Cliath: An Clóchomhar a d'fhoilsigh do Chumman Merriman, 1969.

Titley, Alan. *Mairtín Ó Cadhain: Clár saothair.* Baile Átha Cliath: An

Clóchomhar Tta., 1975.

Ó Conaire, Padraig. *Deoraíocht.* Baile Átha Cliath: Cló Talbot, 3ú éag, 1973.

Ó Conaire, Padraig Óg. *Ceol na nGiolcach* Baile Átha Cliath: Oifig an tSoláthair, 1939.

Ó Criomthain, Tomás. *An tOileánach.* Baile Átha Cliath: Oifig an tSoláthair, 1929.

Ó Direáin. *Rogha Dánta.* Baile Átha Cliath Sáirséal agus Dill, 1949.

O'Flaherty, Liam. *Dúil.* Baile Átha Cliath Sairséal agus Dill, 1953.

O'Neill, Seamus. *Tonn Tuile.* Baile Átha Cliath: Sáirséal agus Dill, 1947.

Ó Laoghaire, Peadar. *Seadna.* Dublin: Irish Book Co., 1904.

O'Nolan, Brian. *An Béal Bocht.* Baile Átha Cliath: An Preas Naisiunta, 1941.

Ó Riordáin, Seán. *Eireaball Spideoige.*

Baile Átha Cliath: Sáirséal agus Dill, 1970.

Taréis mo bháis agus dánta eile. Baile Átha Cliath: Sáirséal agus Dill, 1978.

Ó Tuama, Seán. *Seán Ó Riordáin: Saothar an fhile.* Corcaigh agus Baile Átha Cliath: Oideas Mercier, 1975.

Ó Suilleabhain, Diarmuid. *An UainBheo.* Baile Átha Cliath: Sáirséal agus Dill, 1968.

Ó Suilleabhain, Diarmuid. *An Uain Bheo.* Baile Átha Cliath: Sáirséal agus Dill, 1968.

Ó Tuairisc, Eoghan. *L'Attacque.* Baile Átha Cliath: Figgis, 1962. *De Luain.* Baile Átha Cliath: Figgis, 1966.

Pearse, Padraig. *Iosagán.* Baile Átha Cliath: Connradh na Gaedhilge, 1907.

Sayers, Peig. *Peig.* Baile Átha Cliath: Clólucht an Talboidig, 1936.

PART VI

HISTORY

Edwards, Owen Dudley. *Conor Cruise O'Brien Introduces Ireland.* London: Andre Deutsch, 1969.

Lee, J.J. *Ireland 1945-70.* Dublin: Gill & Macmillan, 1979.

Nowlan, Kevin B. and T. Desmond Williams. *Ireland in the War Years and After 1939-51.* Dublin: Gill and Macmillan, 1969.

See also under Part V. *History.*

LITERARY HISTORY

See works listed under *Literary History* Part V.

TEXTS

Banville, John. *Birchwood.* London: Secker & Warburg, 1973.
Doctor Copernicus. London: Secker &

Warburg, 1976.
Kepler. London: Secker & Warburg, 1981.

Harmon, Maurice *Irish University Review,* Vol. II, No 1 (1981), A John Banville Special Issue.

Boland, Eavan. *The Wall Reader.* Dublin: Arlen, 1979.

Beckett, Samuel. *See Part V.*

Behan, Brendan. *The Quare Fellow.* Dublin: Progress House, 1956.
Borstal Boy. London: Hutchinson, 1958.
The Hostage. London; Methuen, 1958.
O'Connor, Ulick. *Brendan Behan.* London: Hamish Hamilton, 1970.

Broderick, John. *The Fugitives.* London: Weidenfeld & Nicolson, 1962.
The Waking of Willie Ryan. London: Weidenfeld & Nicolson, 1965.
Apology for Roses. London: Calder and Boyars, 1973.
The Pride of Summer. London: Harrap, 1976.

Coffey, Tom. Them. Unpublished.

Casey, Kevin. *The Sinner's Bell.* London: Faber, 1968.
A Sense of Survival. London: Faber, 1974.
Dreams of Revenge. London: Faber, 1977.

Cronin, Anthony. See Part V

de Vere White, Terence. *The March Hare.* London: Gollancz, 1970.
Mr. Stephen. London: Gollancz, 1971.
A Fretful Midge, London: Routledge, 1957.

Farrell, Michael. *Thy Tears Might Cease.* London: Jonathans Cape, 1963.

Friel, Brian. *A Saucer of Larks.* London Gollancz, 1962.

Philadelphia, Here I Come! London: Faber, 1965.
The Gold in the Sea. London: Gollancz, 1966.
The Loves of Cass McGuire London: Faber, 1967.
Lovers. London: Faber, 1968.
The Freedom of the City. London: Faber, 1974.
Aristocrats. Dublin: Gallery, 1980.
Translations. London: Faber, 1981.
Maxwell, D.E.S. *Brian Friel.* Lewisburg, Pa.: Bucknell University Press, 1973.

Galvin, Patrick. *The Wood Burners.* Dublin: New Writer's Press, 1973.
Man on the Porch. Selected Poems. London: Martin & Brian O'Keeffe, 1980.

Hartnett, Michael. *Selected Poems.* Dublin: New Writer's Press, 1970.
A Farewell to English. Dublin: Gallery Press, 1975; enlarged edition, 1978.

Heaney, Seamus. *Death of a Naturalist.* London: Faber, 1966.
Door into the Dark. London: Faber, 1969.
North. London: Faber, 1975.
Field Work. London: Faber, 1979.
Buttel, Robert. *Seamus Heaney.* Lewisburg, Pa.: Bucknell University Press, 1975.

Higgins, Aidan. *Felo de Se.* London: Calder & Boyars, 1960.
Langrishe, Co. Down. London: Calder & Boyars, 1966.
Images of Africa. London: Calder & Boyars, 1971.
Balcony of Europe. London: Calder & Boyars, 1972.
Scenes from a Receding Past. London: Calder & Boyars, 1977.

Hogan, Desmond. *The Diamonds at the Bottom of the Sea*. London: Hamish Hamilton, 1979.

Hutchinson, Pearse. *Tongue Without Hands*. Dublin: Dolmen, 1963. *Watching the Morning Grow*. Dublin: Gallery, 1972. *The Frost is All Over*. Dublin: Gallery, 1975.

Johnston, Denis. See Part V.

Johnston, Jennifer. *Shadows on Our Skin*. London: Hamish Hamilton, 1977. *The Old Jest*. London: Hamish Hamilton, 1979.

Jordan, Neil. *Night in Tunisia*. Dublin Irish Writers' Cooperative, 1976. *The Past*. London. Cape, 1980.

Keane. Molly. *Good Behaviour*. London: Andre Deutsch, 1981.

Kelly, Maeve. *A Life of Her Own*. Dublin: Poolbeg Press, 1976.

Kiely, Benedict. *Land Without Stars*. London: Christopher Johnson, 1946. *In a Harbour Green*. London: Jonathan Cape, 1949. *The Captain with the Whiskers*. London: Methuen, 1960. *Dogs Enjoy the Morning*. London: Gollancz, 1968. Casey, Daniel J. *Benedict Kiely*. Lewisburg, Pa.: Bucknell University Press, 1974.

Kilroy, Thomas, *The Big Chapel*. London: Faber, 1971. *Talbot's Box*. Dublin: Gallery, 1979

Kinsella, Thomas. *Nightwalker*. Dublin Dolmen, 1967. *The Táin*. Dublin: Dolmen, 1969. *Notes from the Land of the Dead*. Dublin: Cuala, 1972.

Finistère. Dublin: Cuala, 1972. *A Technical Supplement*. Dublin: Peppercanister, 1976. *Poems 1956-1973*. Winston-Salem: Wake Forest University Press, 1979. *Peppercanister Poems 1972-1978*. Winston-Salem: Wake Forest University Press, 1979. *Fifteen Dead*. Dublin: Dolmen, 1979. *One and Other Poems*. Dolmen, 1979. Harmon, Maurice. *The Poetry of Thomas Kinsella*. Dublin: Wolfhound Press, 1974.

Leonard, Hugh. *Stephen D*. London: Evans, 1964. *Da*. Newark: Proscenium, 1975.

Longley, Michael. *The Echo Gate*. London: Secker & Warburg, 1979.

McCabe, Eugene. *Victims*. London: Gollancz, 1976. *Heritage*. London: Gollancz, 1978. *King of the Castle*. London: Gollancz, 1978.

McGahern, John. *The Barracks*. London: Faber, 1963. *The Dark*. London: Faber, 1965. *Nightlines*. London: Faber, 1970. *The Leavetaking*. London: Faber, 1974. *Getting Through*. London: Faber, 1978. *The Pornographer*. London: Faber, 1979.

McIntyre, Tom. Find the Lady. One of several unpublished plays.

McLaverty, Bernard. *Secrets*. Belfast: Blackstaff, 1977. *Lamb*. Belfast: Blackstaff, 1979.

Macken, Walter. *Seek the Fair Land*. London: Macmillan, 1959. *The Silent People*. London:

Macmillan, 1962.
The Scorching Wind. London: Macmillan, 1964.

MacMahon, Bryan. See Part V above.

Magee, Heno. *Hatchet.* Dublin: Gallery Press, 1978.

Mahon, Derek. *Poems 1962-1973.* London: Oxford University Press, 1979.
Courtyards in Delft. Dublin: Gallery, 1981.

Montague, John. *Forms of Exile* Dublin Dolmen, 1958.
A Chosen Light. London: McGibbon and Kee, 1967.
Tides. Dublin: Dolmen, 1970; 1978
The Rough Field. Dublin: Dolmen, 1972.
A Slow Dance. Dublin: Dolmen, 1975.
The Great Cloak. Dublin: Dolmen, 1978.
Kersnowski, Frank. *John Montague.* Lewisburg, Pa.: Bucknell University Press, 1975.

Moore, Brian. *The Lonely Passion of Judith Hearne.* London: André Deutsch, 1955.
The Feast of Lupercal. London: André Deutsch, 1956.
The Luck of Ginger Coffey. London: André Deutsch, 1960.
An Answer from Limbo. London: André Deutsch, 1962.
I Am Mary Dunne. London: Jonathan Cape, 1968.
Fergus. New York: Holt, Rinehart & Winston, 1970.
The Great Victorian Collection. London: Cape, 1975.
The Mangan Inheritance. London: Jonathan Cape, 1979.

Dahlie, Hallvard. *Brian Moore.* Toronto: Copp Clark Publishing Co., 1969.
Flood, Jeanne. *Brian Moore.* Lewisburg, Pa.: Bucknell University Press, 1974.

Muldoon, Paul. *Mules.* London: Faber, 1977.
Why Brownlee Left. London: Faber, 1980.

Murphy, Richard. *The Battle of Aughrim* London: Faber, 1968.
High Island. London: Faber, 1974.
Selected Poems. London: Faber, 1979
Harmon, Maurice. *Richard Murphy: Poet of Two Traditions.* Dublin: Wolfhound, 1978.

Murphy, Thomas. *The Morning after Optimism.* Dublin and Cork: Mercier Press, 1973.
A Whistle in the Dark. Unpublished.

Ní Chuilleanáin, Eiléan. *The Second Voyage.* Dublin: Gallery, 1977.

Noonan, Gillman. *A Sexual Relationship* Dublin: Poolbeg Press, 1976.

O'Brien, Edna. *The Country Girls.* London: Hutchinson, 1960.
The Lonely Girl. London: Jonathan Cape, 1962.
Girls in their Married Bliss. London: Jonathan Cape, 1964.
A Scandalous Woman. London: Weidenfeld and Nicholson, 1974.
Eckley, Grace. *Edna O'Brien.* Lewisburg, Pa.: Bucknell University Press, 1974.

O'Faolain, Julia. *Women in the Wall.* London: Faber, 1975.
No Country for Young Men. London: Allen Lane, 1980.

Plunkett, James. *The Trusting and the Maimed.* New York: Devin Adair,

1955.
Strumpet   City.   London:
Huitchinson, 1969.
Farewell   Companions.   London:
Hutchinson, 1977.

Power, Richard. *The Hungry Grass.*
London: Bodley Head, 1969.

Quinn, Niall. *Voyovic and Other Stories.*
Dublin: Wolfhound Press, 1980.
New York: George Braziller, 1981
(retitled *Brigitte: A Novella and
Stories*)

*Trevor   William.   Mrs.   Eckdorf   in
O'Neill's   Hotel.*   London: Bodley

Head, 1969.
The   Boarding   House.   London:
Bodley, 1965.
The ⸱Ballroom of Romance. London:
Bodley, 1972.
The   Love   Department: London:
Bodley, 1966.
Children   of   Dynmouth.   London:
Bodley, 1976.

Watters, Eugene. *The Weekend of Dermot
and Grace.* Dublin: Figgis, 1964.
New Passages. Dublin: Goldsmith,
1974

Index

Voltaire 61, 67

Waddell, Sam ('Rutherford Mayne') 162-3
Wadding, *Father* Luke 56
Walker, Joseph Cooper 67-9
Wall, Mervyn 264, 274
Walsh, Edward (1805-50) 114
War of Independence 201, 271
Ware, *Sir* James 65
Warren, Robert Penn 224
Watters, Eugene (Eoghan Ó Tuairisc) 321
'Wearing of the Green' (song) 145
Weaver, Harriet 244
Weldon, James ('Brinsley MacNamara') (1890-1963) 273, 290
Westmeath, Co. 59, 273
Wexford, Co. 14, 55, 56, 105
Whitbread, J. W. 146
White, Terence de Vere 312
Whitman, Walt 126, 140, 203, 213
Whitty, May 148
Whyte, Laurence 59-60
Whyte, Samuel 60
Wicklow, Co. 14, 114, 165, 215
Wilde, Oscar (1854-1900) 143, 145, 154, 296
William I (King of England) 48, 73
Wilson, Charles 71
Windisch, Ernst 123
Wordsworth, William 60, 113, 115, 139, 195
World War I 201, 208, 209, 290

World War II 217, 288, 293, 301, 303-5

Yeats, John Butler 158
Yeats, William Butler (1865-1939) 28, 33, 48, 53, 54, 57, 78, 86, 103, 117, 120, 124, 169, 170, 189, 191, 192, 195, 201, 203, 217, 227, 229, 230, 303; and drama 23, 25, 27, 142, 145-9, 150, 151-2, 154, 156, 165, 171-5, 176, 289, 294, 295, 325; (with Abbey Theatre) 142, 156-60, 163, 287, 293; influence of 138, 140, 175, 204, 210, 214, 220, 236, 313, 319; and Literary Revival 125-9, 131, 133, 136, 138, 139, 141; in London 127, 128-9; Nobel Prize 165; poetry of 46, 126, 127, 132, 134, 135, 139, 140, 141, 202, 207-10, 218, 221, 319; prose of 210-13, 285; *Cathleen Ni Houlihan* 150, 154-5, 171, 172, 176, 213; *Countess Cathleen* 145-6, 147, 148, 171-2; *Deirdre* 156, 172, 173; *The Green Helmet* 23, 160, 173; *The Hour Glass* 151, 172; *The King's Threshold* 151, 152, 172, 173; *On Baile's Strand* 149, 153, 154-5, 172, 173; *Unicorn from the Stars* 156, 158, 172, 176; *The Wanderings of Oisin* 53, 127, 142, 208
Young, Arthur 55
Young, Ella 134, 139, 286
Young Ireland movement 85-6, 108, 126, 128, 133; *Poems and Ballads of Young Ireland* 126-7
Zola, Émile 188